THE SHAAR PRESS

THE JUDAICA IMPRINT
FOR THOUGHTFUL PEOPLE

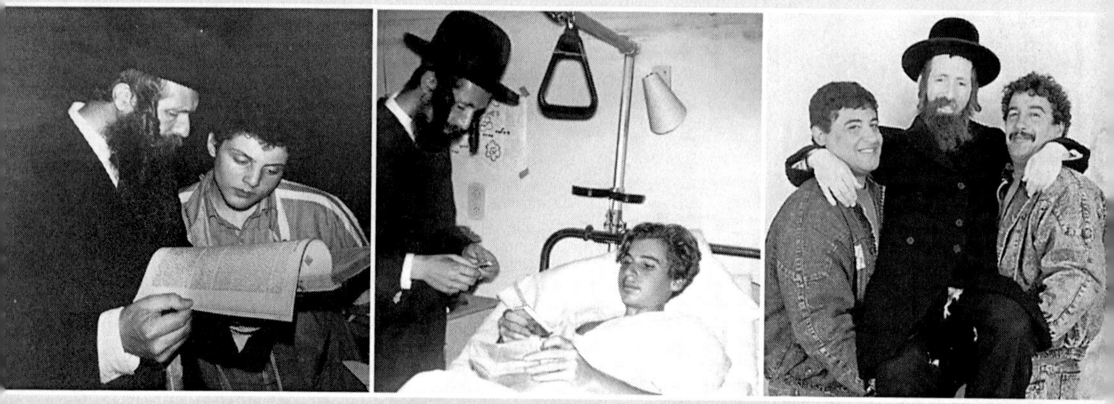

LEONIAN-ROSENBAUM EDITION

LIVING

Rabbi Grossman

THE SHAAR PRESS

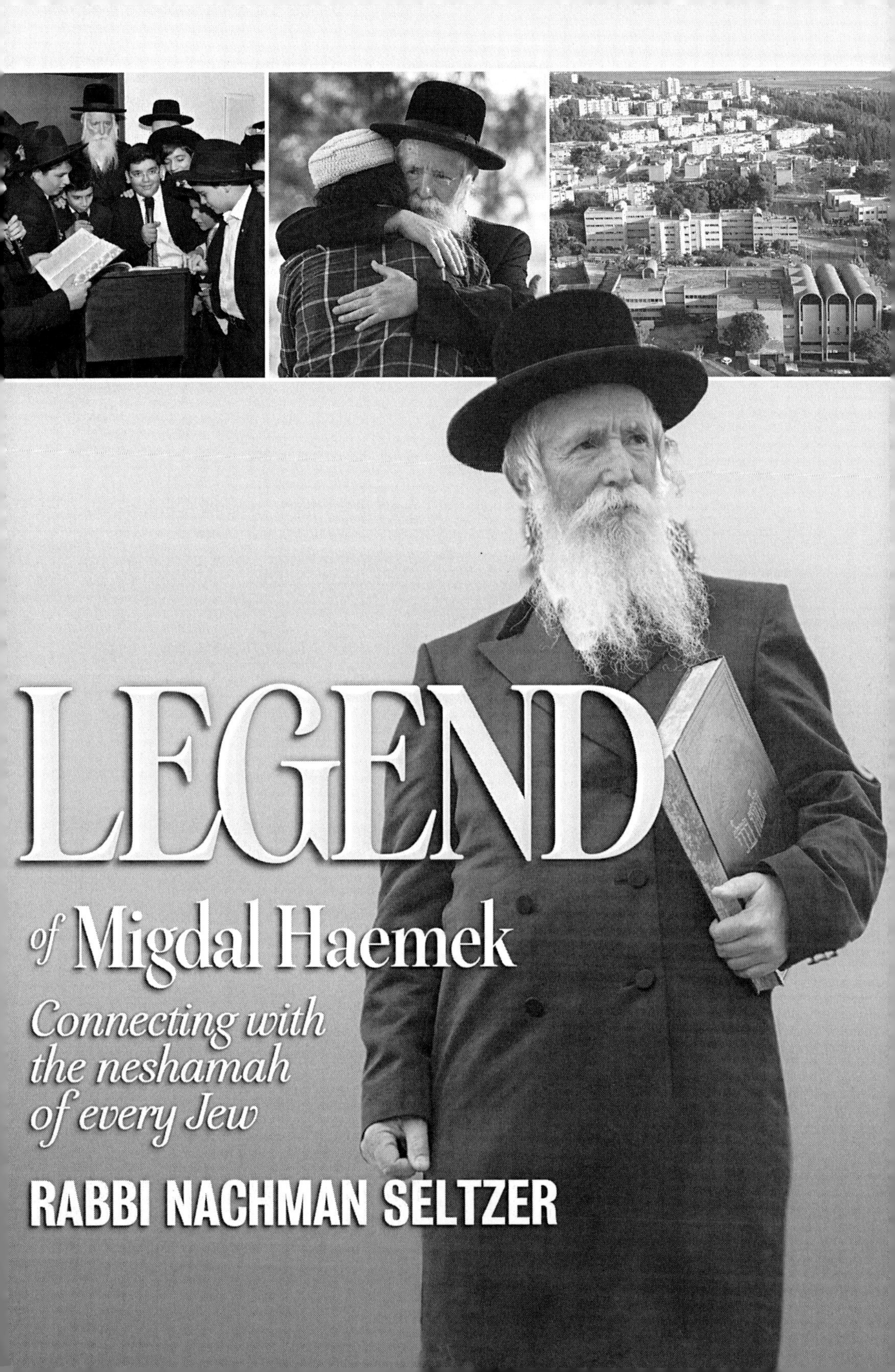
LEGEND
of Migdal Haemek
Connecting with the neshamah of every Jew
RABBI NACHMAN SELTZER

First edition – First impression / March 2021

Published by **SHAAR PRESS**
Distributed by MESORAH PUBLICATIONS, LTD.
313 Regina Avenue / Rahway, N.J. 07065 / (718) 921-9000

Distributed in Israel by SIFRIATI / A. GITLER
POB 2351 / Bnei Brak 51122

Distributed in Europe by LEHMANNS
Unit E, Viking Business Park, Rolling Mill Road
Jarrow, Tyne and Wear, NE32 3DP/ England

Distributed in Australia and New Zealand by GOLDS WORLD OF JUDAICA
3-13 William Street / Balaclava, Melbourne 3183 / Victoria Australia

Distributed in South Africa by KOLLEL BOOKSHOP
Northfield Centre / 17 Northfield Avenue / Glenhazel 2192, Johannesburg, South Africa

ISBN 10: 1-4226-2808-6 / ISBN 13: 978-1-4226-2808-9
ITEM CODE: LLEH

Printed in the United States of America
Custom bound by Sefercraft, Inc. / 313 Regina Avenue / Rahway, N.J. 07065

We were at the King David Hotel. It was late Shabbat afternoon and my wife was hungry and looking for something to eat. As Shabbat was not yet over, we couldn't go anywhere to dine.

We went into the bar where we knew they served food and drinks, but, no luck!

They were just closing down and had already sent all the food back to the kitchen. They suggested that she have a cocktail drink instead of some food. Fine.

There was just one problem — my wife didn't want to drink a cocktail on an empty stomach, and she asked the staff for some nuts to go with the drink.

Unfortunately, we were informed that they were out of nuts. Suddenly the man sitting one table over pushed his bowl of nuts toward her. Thanking him, she recognized a Montreal friend of hers — Marc Kakon.

Marc was in Israel as part of his philanthropic work for an organization called Migdal Ohr, which is located in a city up north called Migdal HaEmek. The next thing we knew, Marc started telling us about this institution and its founder and leader, Rabbi Yitzchak Dovid Grossman.

Within minutes we were "sold" and decided, through the Leonian-Rosenbaum charitable trust, to support Migdal Ohr in a meaningful way. And thus we embarked on a wonderful and joyful journey of connecting with an admirable Israeli institution whose accomplishments always leave us humbled and in awe of its staff's dedication and hard work.

To the best of my knowledge, one million dollars remains the record price ever paid for a bowl of peanuts.

Jacques Aaron Preis and Evelyne Salama Preis

In honor of our children
**Mischele Corin, Sarah Marie Preis,
Elisabeth Dana Preis, Lior-Haim Salama
and Yaniv E. A. Salama**

And in honor of our grandchildren
**Benjamin, Natalie, Isaac, Ariel,
Maya, Jackson, Scarlett, Delilah
and Dezi-Zipporah**

Table of Contents

PART FOUR: 1870–1980

PART FIVE: 1980–1987

PART SIX: 1988–1995

PART SEVEN: 1995–2006

PART EIGHT: 2003–2013

PART NINE: 2011–2021

Acknowledgments

As always, I must thank those who were part of the very special journey involved in the process of writing a book.

I want to begin by thanking the Master of the World for enabling me to meet a tzaddik like Rav (Rabbi) Yitzchak Dovid Grossman. It was a rare privilege to have been given the opportunity to develop a relationship with Rav Grossman, who is, without exaggeration, one of the most unique people in the world. Rav Grossman deserves a real thank you for going above and beyond to give me the time needed (finding the time was no simple matter) so that this book would become a reality. I am thankful for the opportunity to have spent so much time with such a great man, and for our friendship, which I hope will extend far beyond.

To Marc Kakon, whose support for Migdal Ohr is legendary, and who introduced Jacques Preis and Evelyn Salama to the Migdal Ohr family. And, of course, to Jacques Preis and Evelyn Salama, for making this book possible, and for their generous million-dollar donation.

To the staff of Migdal Ohr, those in Eretz Yisrael (the Land of Israel) and those around the world — Only Hashem knows how much *s'char* (reward) you deserve for saving the world, one child at a time.

To the donors of Migdal Ohr — It is your financial support and more importantly your friendship with Rav Grossman that keeps him going and gives him the moral support that he so needs to keep up his critical work for Klal Yisrael, the people of Israel.

Special thanks to Reb Yisrael Katzover, a long-time friend of Rav Grossman, for serving as the "shadchan" for this project and for introducing us. Reb Yisrael's own book (which I wrote) will be published in the near future. Stay tuned...

Thank you to Reb Nuchum Donner who has stood at Rav Grossman's side for many decades, assisting him and always available to help facilitate Rav Grossman's holy work and the wonders that he accomplishes on every given day. It is a testimony to Reb Nuchum and who he is that although he lives in the United States and Rav Grossman is in Eretz Yisrael, he is still the "Rebbe's" right-hand man.

A great thank you to the team at ArtScroll — Rabbi Gedaliah Zlotowitz, Reb Shmuel Blitz, and Mrs. Miriam Zakon — for believing in the project and for working tirelessly to get it out on time. Mrs. Suri Brand did a stellar job of editing. Reb Mendy Herzberg, Reb Eli Kroen, Mrs. Esther Feierstein, and Mrs. Estie Dicker, as always did a marvelous and professional job, under tight deadline pressure.

To Aliza and kinderlach — once again we embarked on another project together. We drove to Migdal HaEmek together and met Rav Grossman together. And now he has become part of our family history. Thank you for taking part in this journey with me.

Readers may notice that this book contains many Yiddish and Hebrew expressions, reflecting Rav Grossman's Yerushalmi background and his day-to-day reality in Israel. Because his world also includes many to whom these languages are completely foreign, they are defined in the text. This was done at his personal request — for, as always, Rav Grossman considers the feelings and needs of everyone around him, whatever their background.

Introduction

Writing the introduction for a book like ***Living Legend!*** on the life and accomplishments of a man like Rav Yitzchak Dovid Grossman is quite a challenge. What should the focus of the introduction be? There is so much to write about, so much to discuss — it is difficult, almost impossible, to choose.

In introducing my books, I often choose one chapter from the book and put it in as an introduction, giving my readers a taste of what lies in store. But in this case, finding such a chapter was a true challenge.

Should I use the story about Rav Grossman's trip to post-Communist Russia with Mordechai Ben David, and the amazing follow-up story in Bnei Brak decades later?

But that only showed the focus and work that he did with Russian Jewry.

What about starting the book with the story of how Rav Grossman turned a London disco into a kind of Sefardic beit knesset (synagogue), complete with the Selichot, the special prayers of Elul, on a Chanukah night, against all odds?

A great story — but again, just showing one facet of who he is and the incredible talent that he has for reaching others who seem so different from him.

Maybe I should write about the fact that Rav Grossman began his first school with eighteen students and how Migdal Ohr has grown and grown and grown, until it encompasses dozens of educational programs and tens of thousands of students and alumni…

That seemed like a great way to start. But on the other hand, I wasn't sure if that would give the reader a true understanding of his unique warmth and charisma.

Okay, here's an idea. What about beginning the book with the story of how Rav Grossman stood at the foot of Mount Hermon in the middle of the Yom Kippur War, and how the speech that he delivered that night altered the course of an upcoming tank battle with the Syrians?

Here too, a great story, but while it possesses a fascinating message, there are so many others that are just as amazing.

There was the Rosh Hashanah murder, and how it truly made him the rav of Migdal HaEmek. I also considered using the story of how he helped reunite a Bedouin young man with his Jewish family, or the story of how Rav Yitzchak Dovid made millions of dollars for Migdal Ohr on a flight due to an accident and a kiss on a man's forehead...

So many great stories, so many incredible moments, so many inspirational and even fantastic memories to share with my readers. But all of them captured one point, one side, one facet of his incredible accomplishments, and that just wouldn't do him justice.

In the end, I decided to start at the beginning of his journey — a young man journeying far, far away from his Meah Shearim home and roots, though never, ever abandoning or even compromising on those roots.

A young man who made a promise at the Kosel, the Western Wall — and kept it. A young man who dreamed big dreams — and built those dreams into a reality greater than anything he could have imagined. A young man who became a living legend, one of the most beloved Jews of his time.

A young man named Rav Yitzchak Dovid Grossman.

Prologue

I left my home early in the day for the drive to Migdal HaEmek, hoping for a glimpse into the miracle that Rav Yitzchak Dovid Grossman has built on the slopes of what had once been Israel's Wild West. For this visit, I had elected to take my family with me. After all, how often do we get a chance to meet so legendary an individual as Rav Yitzchak Dovid?

Whenever you visit Rav Yitzchak Dovid, you never know whom you will encounter there. It could be anyone — from the greatest rabbinical leader of the generation to a five-year-old *cheder* schoolboy, from the

The author, Rabbi Nachman Seltzer, with Rabbi Yitzchak Dovid Grossman

prime minister to a foreign king. This is the nature of his day-to-day existence.

The room we sat in was comfortable, with an abundance of *sefarim* (Jewish books) lining the walls. In a narrow alcove stood a wooden *aron kodesh* — a holy ark housing the rabbi's personal Torah scroll. Soon Rav Yitzchak Dovid entered and took his seat, while the rebbetzin served an array of fruit, nuts, snacks, and drinks. Rav Yitzchak Dovid took his time getting to know my family while sharing several stories about his life and the incredible *hashgachah pratis,* Divine intervention, that he witnesses on a regular basis.

Eventually we left for a guided tour of Migdal Ohr.

As my wife would later remark, "Having him in the car, I felt like we were being given a tour of the White House in Washington D.C. by the president himself."

I drove through the city streets, around traffic circles and past stores.

"There's the disco that I told you about. The place where I met all the 'tzaddikim' for the first time," he commented as we passed a mini shopping center. (Rav Grossman often refers to the youth of Migdal HaEmek that he met decades ago as the "tzaddikim," or righteous ones.)

"Is it still there?"

"No, it's long gone. It's a different world now than when I first arrived. You can't even imagine what it was like back then!"

Migdal Ohr boys campus

Migdal Ohr girls campus

A few minutes later we were driving down a sloping road. On our left we could see dozens of buildings.

"That's Migdal Ohr," Rav Yitzchak Dovid said simply.

"All those buildings?"

"Yes, Migdal Ohr is very large."

He wasn't exaggerating. During our tour we would come to see numerous educational institutions. Occupying some sixty-five acres, Migdal Ohr's campus is comparable in size to Columbia University and is the world's largest orphanage.

Since it was summertime, the hallways of the girls schools were empty, but here and there we could see girls coming and going, involved in their day camp programs. In one of the courtyards outside a school, we came across a teacher in deep conversation with a high-school girl. Rav Grossman beckoned for them to come over to the car. The exchange that followed was beautiful to see.

He asked the student to tell him her name. She did. He asked her what grade she was in.

"I'm going into 12th."

"I want you to be one of the leaders of your grade next year," he said.

You had to be there to see this, but the smile on her face was something out of the books. It had become clear to me beyond a shadow of a doubt that for the children learning and living in Migdal Ohr, Rav Yitzchak Dovid Grossman is the closest thing to a father, and they idolize him. Hearing her "father" tell her that he expected her to become one of the leaders of the class was high praise indeed, and you could see what his words meant to her.

"Please follow up with her," Rav Grossman said to the teacher, standing alongside the student, "and let me know how she's doing."

"I will."

When we got back in the car and left the girls campus, Rav Grossman remarked that eighty percent of the staff at Migdal Ohr were graduates of the educational institutions where they now taught. This meant that they had done well enough in their studies at Migdal Ohr to return as teachers and help more generations to succeed, exactly as they themselves had been helped. It was a kind of "Pay it Forward" moment.

We drove over to the boys campus, passing a swimming pool on the way. On the campus itself I saw a state-of-the-art gym. We parked outside a brand-new dormitory. Rav Grossman led the way into the building. Unlike the girls, the boys were still learning for the next few weeks and the school was operating in regular learning mode.

"The building you are about to see," Rav Grossman told me, "cost ten million dollars to build."

Every floor held two apartments — one for the "parents" of the children living there, the other for the twelve children in that particular "family." There was a kitchen for the children — a gleaming, spotless kitchen, with stainless steel appliances — with every dish and utensil washed and put away. This kitchen was built in addition to the personal kitchen used by the couple serving as parents for the twelve children living in the apartment. The kitchen opened into a dining room, with a long table surrounded by fourteen chairs. Across the hall was a rec room, just begging for a kid to come and have fun, and down the corridor were the bedrooms.

I am no expert in design, but just one glimpse into the rooms and you could see the incredible amount of work and thought that had gone into making every room a place where a child would feel comfortable — a place that a child would consider a home. The closets were beautiful, the floors were covered with a wood finish, the desk was nicely designed — and the beds were made, every blanket folded just so, every article of clothing in its place, shoes lined up like soldiers beneath the beds.

The children living in those rooms came from the kinds of families where nothing was taken for granted, not food, books, clothing, nothing. For these kids, living in such a place must have been akin to a stint in Gan Eden (Garden of Eden) after the challenges of their earlier lives.

As we walked across the square outside the main building, which housed a huge *beis medrash* (study hall), a massive dining room, and classrooms galore, we saw a small caravan at the edge of the yard containing a canteen. The window was open and one of my sons asked me for money to buy a soda.

Rav Yitzchak Dovid explained that the children in Migdal Ohr received an allowance so they could purchase whatever they wanted in the canteen — which was run by the school. The idea was to teach them financial responsibility.

Inside the building, the hallways were mostly devoid of students (they were inside the classrooms), but anyone who caught sight of Rav Yitzchak Dovid broke out into a huge smile, and some began tagging along behind him. Nearly every interaction between Rav Grossman and a student began with the student asking for a blessing from the rav. Rav Yitzchak Dovid showed us every part of the building — his love for his students obvious, his excitement for every facet of the operation at boiling point, though he had been doing this for over half a century and by rights should have long been retired.

It was obvious that retirement was not in the picture.

"I want to show something else," he said, leading us down a long hallway and into yet another large room. The room was packed with racks and cubicles filled with clothing — suits, shirts, pajamas, and sneakers.

"My rebbetzin knows the sizes of every boy and exactly what he needs at any given time," Rav Grossman explained, clearly proud of the rebbetzin and the incredible effort she invested in her part of the operation.

He opened several of the drawers. Packages and packages of brand-name undershirts and socks. More drawers, more packages.

"Only the best clothing for our boys," he said, smiling.

The "Mishpachtonim" (day care centers)

We stopped at a one-story building a few blocks away. Groups of young children were being cared for by a team of experienced teachers.

"Many times I found myself visiting homes in different places around the country. There I would see little children — three, four months old, hungry, dirty, uncared for, and I knew that we had to establish daycare centers where the children would be taken care of for the majority of the day. The children are looked after from seven in the morning until five in the afternoon. We also opened *ganim* (preschools)."

"How many *ganim* does Migdal Ohr have now?"

"Eighteen."

The street consisted of numerous apartment buildings, where the adoptive families lived — families chosen and hired by Migdal Ohr to raise foster children from around the country as if they were their own. While it was heartbreaking to see so many children being raised by people who are not their blood relatives, it was heartwarming to realize that Rav Grossman had created a world whose entire focus was to save as many children as possible, and to provide them with every opportunity in the world to lead successful lives and to grow up to become productive and contributing members of society.

We parked outside an unassuming one-story building.

"This building is one of the first two residences that my wife and I purchased for the initial eighteen children of Migdal Ohr. At first we

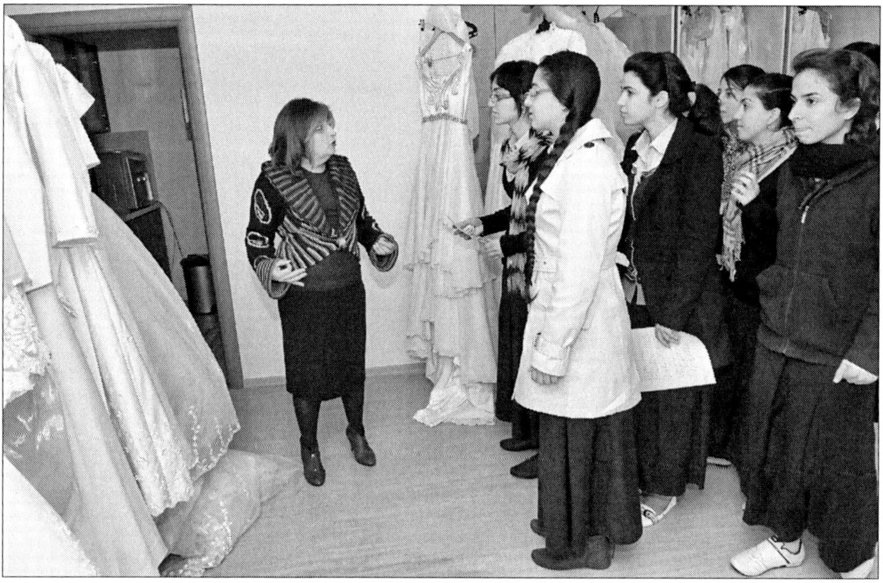

The rebbetzin showing the bridal salon to a group of girls

lived in the building across the street. Today, this building is being used for a different and very special purpose."

"What's that?"

"It's a bridal salon for *kallahs*."

"That sounds amazing!"

"It is."

We entered the garden surrounding the salon. There were grassy areas with an assortment of walkways and wood furniture that are the ideal background for great pictures. Inside, it felt like we had entered a classy business. There were rooms crammed with exquisite bridal gowns, shelves of white high-heeled shoes, glass counters showcasing an array of jewelry and makeup, and hair stations — basically everything a *kallah* (bride) needed to look her best on her big day.

"They leave from the salon directly to their weddings," Rav Grossman explained.

"Who runs this operation?"

"This is also overseen and managed by my rebbetzin, who puts her heart and soul into making sure that every *kallah* leaves the salon looking and feeling like a princess."

"How was it in the beginning?" I asked the Rebbetzin.

"My husband and I were partners in every sense of the word. We worked together, sharing the burden. This was wonderful for us as a couple because we were completely focused on the same goals and constantly working toward the same things. And because my husband traveled a lot, I was often left to run the entire operation on my own. I made sure that everyone did their jobs, and I ran the staff meetings. There were a million things to do every day — from making sure that everyone had enough to eat, to sewing buttons that had fallen off onto a child's shirt. No detail was too small.

"A while later, I traveled with the rav to New York and we went to visit the Rebbe of Lubavitch. He asked me all about my job and I broke it down for him. He then advised me to hire a staff to work under my direction.

"'Don't worry,' he said, 'there will still be plenty of work left over for you.'

"I followed his advice and hired more staff when we returned home. And he was one hundred percent correct. The more staff we hired, the more work there was.

In still another of Rav Grossman's many Torah programs, yeshivah boys from throughout Eretz Yisrael come to the Migdal Ohr campus as part of the innovative "Hemshech Hazeman" program, where yeshivah boys learn during *bein hazemanim* (the yeshivah vacation period between terms).

"When I look back at our life, there is no question that we experienced an incredible degree of *siyata d'Shmaya,* Heavenly assistance."

When we left Migdal HaEmek a short while later, Rav Yitzchak Dovid told me that I had to come back in the near future, explaining that I had only been given a tiny glimpse into Migdal Ohr and the magic that was being accomplished there, each and every day. It is not often that one gets to witness a legend in person, but that was exactly what I and my family had been fortunate to see that very day — Rav Yitzchak Dovid Grossman in his natural environment, caring for thousands of children as if they were his very own.

And I asked myself, "How did this all come to be?"

So I asked and I learned. And it wasn't long before my questions were answered.

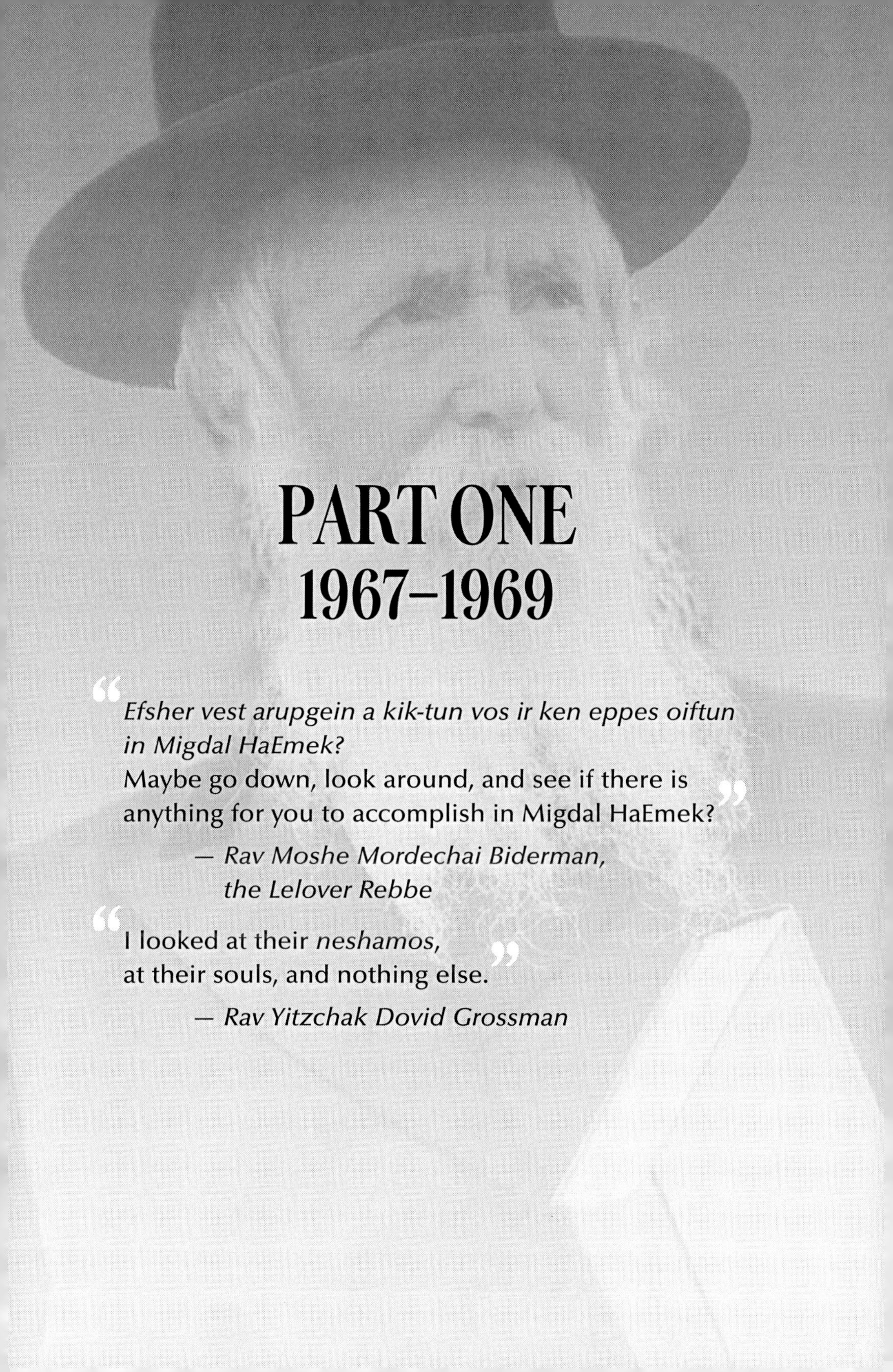

PART ONE
1967–1969

“*Efsher vest arupgein a kik-tun vos ir ken eppes oiftun in Migdal HaEmek?*
Maybe go down, look around, and see if there is anything for you to accomplish in Migdal HaEmek?”

— *Rav Moshe Mordechai Biderman, the Lelover Rebbe*

“I looked at their *neshamos*,
at their souls, and nothing else.”

— *Rav Yitzchak Dovid Grossman*

CHAPTER ONE

Cigarettes for Soldiers

He was a fine Yerushalmi boy, from a fine Yerushalmi family. His father, Rav Yisrael Grossman, was among the *gedolei hador* (rabbinical leaders) of his generation, *a* rosh yeshivah (the head of a yeshivah), and the author of many scholarly works on both Jewish law and Talmud. His mother, Guta Perel, was known as "the Rebbetzin of the Kosel" — for thirty years literally never missing a morning visit to the Wall. She was a *baalas chesed,* a person who performed great acts of kindness. This made sense considering that Guta Perel was the daughter of Leiba Gutfarb, "Leiba the Gabate" (the charity collector), who took care of the orphans, widows, and the needy.

Though there were some signs that this *yingele,* this little boy, possessed a particularly caring heart, basically his childhood was typical: Etz Chaim *cheder* (elementary school), learning in Slabodka Yeshivah, marriage at an early age, kollel (an institute for advanced Talmudic study) with other young married men.

Typical, that is, until it wasn't.

The year was 1967.

While young, recently married Yitzchak Dovid Grossman and his wife were beginning to build their lives in a quiet corner of Yerushalayim, major world events were happening in the Middle East. Though it had no interest in fighting any of its neighbors, the State of Israel was on its way to war. And while its military position was not as bad as people thought, the country perceived itself as weak and unsure.

In the weeks leading up to the Six-Day War, Israel entered a period that would go down in history as the *Hamtanah* — the Waiting Period. The Americans were urging restraint and asked the tiny country to hold back and not to attack first. Then Israel made it clear to the United States that Israel was unable to show restraint any longer, that they were going to attack. America gave Israel the green light and promised to endorse them politically. Guarantee in hand, Israel went to war, attacking Egypt on the morning of June 5, 1967, and obliterating the majority of the Egyptian air force while the planes were still on the ground.

That was miracle number one. Now Israel could operate militarily in a way it could have never done had the enemy planes been free to strike and bomb them. The string of miracles continued from the southern border to the north, and the citizens of Israel watched in wonder as they won victory after victory, vanquishing the enemy in an inexplicable series of routs.

Egypt had been dealt a decisive blow. So had Syria, who lost the Golan Heights. And while Israel had sent word to King Hussein of Jordan to stay out of the war and maintain the status quo, the king decided to join forces with the other Arab countries, forcing Israel to fight Jordan as well. This development paved the way for the capture of the Old City of Jerusalem and, most importantly, the Kosel HaMa'aravi, the Western Wall.

In the wake of Israel's miraculous victories — and in only six days — the country was filled with a sense of gratitude to the Master of the World for having delivered His people from sure disaster. It was a victory that was beyond the scope of anything anyone could have possibly imagined only a few days earlier. The streets had been shrouded with the fear of another Holocaust so soon after the Churban (destruction) of Europe. Then this, an extraordinary *yeshuah*, an incredible salvation. There were no words.

There's no question that those were incredible days. Israel would end up chasing the Egyptians across the Sinai Desert. At the same time, Israeli soldiers pursued the Syrians over the Golan Heights almost all the way to Damascus. Most importantly, the city of Yerushalayim was united once more. It was a beautiful time to be alive — a time when the Hand of Hashem was clearly visible.

Rav Yitzchak Dovid Grossman experienced this on a personal level as well, as he clearly remembers:

When the war started, my wife and I left our apartment on Rechov Chana and moved back in with my parents in Batei Warsaw near Meah Shearim. Nobody likes being alone during a time of war, and we were no exception. Since the Arabs were shelling our side of the city, most people left their apartments and spent hours on end in shelters. The shelter where we found ourselves wasn't an official bomb shelter. Rather, it was the basement of a building with sandbags piled up all around the entrance and windows that looked out onto Meah Shearim Street.

There were two shuls (synagogues) right outside the shelter. One was called Chassidim, and the other was known as Perushim. During the week my father davened in Perushim, but on Shabbos he left the neighborhood and went to daven (pray) at the Karlin shul. I knew I should stay in the shelter, but it was terribly crowded, and I found myself sneaking out and going to learn in the empty shul adjacent to the shelter.

One day I had an idea.

During the war, the army's main headquarters were located in the Histadrut building on Strauss Street, near where my parents lived. Since the Histadrut building was one of the tallest structures in the city, I knew that there were many soldiers stationed on its roof, keeping watch against the enemy. I decided to bring a large quantity of cigarettes to the soldiers to show my appreciation for their service. Back in those days everyone smoked, and I figured it was probably difficult for the boys to get hold of cigarettes at such a time. I planned on thanking the soldiers, distributing the cigarettes, and returning to my seat in the empty shul.

I left the shul and walked until I found a kiosk that was still open just outside Meah Shearim. I purchased a few cartons of Time (a brand that most people smoked back then), then made my way to the army headquarters.

I smiled at the soldiers guarding the entrance to the building and explained that I had come to give them a present. After inspecting my package to make sure it didn't contain anything dangerous, they let me enter. I climbed the steep staircase up to the roof of the Histadrut building, introduced myself to the soldiers, and distributed the packs of cigarettes I had brought.

Try to imagine the scene: Most of those soldiers had never spoken to a Yerushalmi chassid in their lives. Whatever they knew

The Perushim shul that was hit by a missile

about chassidim came from the media, which didn't portray people who looked like me in the most flattering light. Yet here I was, beard and *peyos* (sidelocks) prominently displayed, yet expressing only positive vibes. It made a huge impact.

I would later learn that while I stood on the roof of the building giving encouragement and appreciation to the soldiers, a bomb struck the roof of the Perushim shul and landed directly on the seat that I always used while learning! If I had been in my usual seat, there is no question that the story would have been over before it even began. But I wasn't there, because I had gone out of my way to make a *kiddush Hashem* (to sanctify G-d's Name) and show my appreciation to the men who were putting their lives in danger for the Jewish nation day in and day out.

This episode taught me a lesson. It was as if Hashem was telling me in the clearest way possible that He wanted me to learn from what had happened, that I should continue doing *chesed,* kindness for others, especially for those who were distant from Him.

The feeling of euphoria that abounded throughout the country following Israel's victory over its enemies lasted for days. The most wondrous part of it all was the recapture of the Kosel, a place that Jews had been forbidden to visit for nineteen years. While military people, politicians, and Torah leaders were able to visit the Kosel almost as soon as it was retaken, the vast majority of Israel's citizens were able to approach the Wall for the first time only on the Yom Tov (holiday) of Shavuos that followed the war. Chaim Herzog, the military governor of Jerusalem, gave the order to raze the Arab houses that were crowded in a jumble directly across from the Kosel, and when the bulldozers had finished their work and the dust had finally cleared, there was a plaza in front of the wall that could hold a record number of people.

Rav Yitzchak Dovid would never forget his first time at the Kosel after the Six-Day War. It was ten o'clock in the morning, and one hundred thousand Yidden stood crammed into the area in front of Jaffa Gate, anxiously awaiting the moment when the soldiers would open the gigantic gates and allow them to enter. Then the doors were thrown open, and one hundred thousand Yidden (Jews) began to pour through the narrow entrance and head for the Old City.

No one had any idea in which direction to go, but that didn't stop them as they rushed through the Arab *shuk* in search of the path that would lead them through the tangle of narrow alleyways and over to the Wall they had been dreaming about visiting since it had been forbidden to them in 1948.

It was surreal. Just a few days earlier, everyone had been afraid it was all over — that they were all going to be murdered by the Arab armies that were closing in on them. And then the exact opposite occurred. It was like living in a dream…

It's impossible to describe the emotions coursing through the people who had the good fortune to visit the Kosel so soon after the liberation. Words have been invented to describe most thoughts and feelings, but there are no words for the experience of a person's first visit to the Kosel after such a long separation. It was pure spirituality, and it sizzled through Rav Yitzchak Dovid's entire being as if he had just been touched with a live wire of spiritual transcendence. When he looks back at that moment beside the roughly hewn Kosel stones, Rav Yitzchak Dovid thinks that the next time he'll feel the same kind of spiritual intensity is when Mashiach, the Messiah, finally arrives. Until then, he's not sure he will ever experience the same incredible feelings he felt at that time.

As he stood before the wall, Rav Yitzchak Dovid asked himself, *How can I thank Hashem for the awesome miracles that happened to us? For*

Then and now: At the Kosel

reuniting Yerushalayim and for giving us back the Kosel? When you receive a present, you have to say "thank you." But how?

Then it came to him.

"Ribbono shel Olam," he prayed. "Master of the World, in thanks to You, I am offering to leave Yerushalayim for a year and move to a place where I will be able to devote myself to helping the youth and the local population."

When he concluded his prayer, a *tefillah* that had emerged unplanned and unexpected from the depths of his heart, the young man left the Kosel plaza and retraced his steps in the direction of Meah Shearim.

CHAPTER TWO

The Thank-You Promise

Rav Yitzchak Dovid had an extremely close relationship with the Lelover Rebbe, Rav Moshe Mordechai Biderman, a truly righteous man, a tzaddik, renowned for his great holiness. Rav Yitzchak Dovid trusted the Lelover Rebbe to such a degree that he never made an important move without first consulting with the Rebbe and asking his advice. Now, too, he went to tell the Rebbe about the experience he'd just had at the Kosel, the thoughts that had gone through his mind, and the thank-you promise that he'd offered up to Hashem like a *korban* (sacrifice) on a modern-day altar.

The Lelover Rebbe

"Itche Duvid," the Rebbe said affectionately in a singsong voice, using the *chassidish* version of his name, *"efsher vest arupgein a kik-tun vos ir ken eppes oiftun in Migdal HaEmek?"*

Maybe go down, look around, and see if there is anything you can accomplish in Migdal HaEmek?

Yitzchak Dovid Grossman had never even heard of Migdal HaEmek before the Rebbe mentioned it to him. The name didn't ring any bells and set off no alarms. It meant nothing to him. He didn't even know whether the city was situated in the northern part of the country or down south.

But the Rebbe had spoken, and that was all Itche Duvid Grossman needed to hear. As soon as he left the Rebbe's presence, he began asking around to see if anyone knew anything about Migdal HaEmek.

Later he would learn that Migdal HaEmek had a fearsome reputation as a city with a large criminal element. The rate of crime among the youth in the city was among the highest in the country. Statistically speaking, the number of murders that took place in the little northern city near Afula were far beyond the norm, not to mention other serious crimes. Needless to say, Migdal HaEmek featured prominently in the national papers. Nobody had anything positive to say about Migdal HaEmek.

But all he knew at that point was that the Rebbe had told him to go to Migdal HaEmek.

Rav Yitzchak Dovid Grossman went to speak with his wife.

Rebbetzin Grossman had been raised in a Chabad home. She had grown up in a home where the concept of "going out on *shelichus*" (on missions for the Rebbe) was venerated. More than that, words such as "the Rebbe said" put an end to all subsequent conversation, and this was the case whether the Rebbe in question was the Lubavitcher Rebbe or the Lelover.

The young wife met her husband's gaze and said, "If the Rebbe said go, we go."

Seeing that her husband was just a little bit overwhelmed, she said reassuringly, "We don't have to move there tomorrow. Why don't you just go to the city and take a look around, like the Rebbe said? Then you'll have a better idea of whether this is for you or not."

So the die was cast: Rav Yitzchak Dovid was going to Migdal HaEmek. Beyond that, he knew nothing. He didn't know which step to take to embark on the upcoming journey or what lay at the other end. He didn't even know which bus went to Migdal HaEmek. But he was going to learn. His Rebbe had spoken, and Itche Duvid always listened to his Rebbe.

He left Yerushalayim early in the morning on a bus to Tel Aviv. At the Central Bus Station in Tel Aviv he caught a Haifa-bound bus, and from the Central Bus Station in Haifa he caught another bus to Nazareth, where he purchased one final ticket for a ride that would drop him off at a bus stop on the highway outside Migdal HaEmek. He had no idea where in the Haifa-Nazareth-Afula triangle he was, but he gamely went along on each new stage of the journey when it was presented to him by the person manning the information counter in each place he stopped.

He found out that this part of the country is called Emek Yizre'el, or Jezreel Valley. Many kibbutzim, moshavim, and rolling fields that seem to stretch to infinity dot the landscape. For a young man who grew up within the stone-wall confines of Meah Shearim, the journey to the other side of the country was an eye-opening experience. But he soldiered on, the Rebbe's instructions ringing in his ears.

As he traveled halfway across the country, he alternately learned from the *sefer* (Torah book) he had brought with him and reminded the driver where he needed to alight. Eventually the driver looked over at the Yerushalmi Yid sitting a few seats back and said, "This is your stop."

The bus pulled up, the doors opened, and a young man with a long black beard and eyes that blazed with intelligence disembarked. As he stepped onto the pavement, he squared his shoulders and checked to make sure he had all his belongings before he thanked the driver. The bus roared off.

He had been traveling for the better part of the day, and the shadows were growing longer as he ascertained the direction he needed to go. He began walking along the highway toward the city of Migdal HaEmek.

An observer couldn't have helped but notice the tall, angular figure with the long beard and *peyos*. Though at first glance he may have looked like any other young Yerushalmi, there was a presence about him. Here was a person who caught one's attention.

It was his eyes. Eyes that radiated friendliness, intelligence, and good humor. They stood out more than anything else.

Turning off the highway, he entered the city and stopped to get his bearings. A man passed by.

"Excuse me?"

"Yes?"

"Where can I find the local yeshivah?"

"What yeshivah are you talking about?" the man said. "There are no yeshivot here."

"Then where's the Talmud Torah — the Torah school for the children of this town?"

"There is no Talmud Torah."

Slightly discomfited, the newcomer tried again.

"Well, then, if there is no yeshivah and no Talmud Torah, where can I find the youth of Migdal HaEmek?"

The stranger brightened. Finally, a question he was able to answer.

"In the disco."

In his entire life, Yitzchak Dovid Grossman had never heard the word *disco*. He didn't know that a disco was a place where teenagers went to hang out, listen to blasting music, dance, and shoot pool. He thought that maybe a disco was another name for a place where teenagers went to learn Torah.

Yeshivas HaDisco.

What did he know? He had never been in such a place before, and if this was how the locals referred to their yeshivah, who was he to question them?

"Where is the Disco Yeshivah?" he asked the passerby.

"Continue walking down the street," the man explained. "On the right side of the street you'll see a shopping center. The entrance to the disco is under one of the stores."

Migdal HaEmek 1967: The "disco" is underneath the stores

As he walked, the light of day was gradually replaced by the darkness of night. It wasn't long before he arrived at the brightly lit shopping center. Most of the stores were closed, except for a falafel stand, a kiosk where a few teens had congregated, smoking and holding bottles of beer, and the entrance to the disco where he would find the youth of Migdal HaEmek.

When he entered the disco, he was in for the shock of his life. It was like some kind of weird Purim in the middle of the year. A youthful crowd was jumping and dancing in the center of the room beneath a gigantic crystal ball that sent beams of bright, colored lights flashing in every direction. Groups of kids were clustered around video games, and others were gathered around a pool table. Loud music blared from powerful speakers, and the bartender was dispensing tall mugs of frothy beer from the tap. It was quite a scene for a sheltered lad from Meah Shearim.

Rav Grossman wasn't the only one who was in shock. Ironically, so were the kids in the room (there were at least forty-five of them) at the sight of the rabbi wearing a fur hat, long coat, and the kind of beard that made a statement. A religious stranger had just entered their world, and they couldn't wrap their minds around it. They stared at him with wide eyes, trying to figure out who he was and what he was doing there. It was as if two very different movies were being filmed at the same time, and the star of one of them had walked off his set and onto the set of another film.

Some of the brighter minds in the crowd assumed that someone had died in the neighborhood, and he was searching for a minyan (ten Jewish men) so that the mourners could recite Kaddish. When the rabbi reassured them that he wasn't in search of a minyan, they were at a loss.

"So what are you looking for, then?"

The next line was delivered with the trademark Grossman tendency to say the right line at the right moment. It would happen numerous times over the decades.

"I'm from Yerushalayim, but I want to live here."

The teenagers stared at the rabbi, the expressions on their faces growing even more incredulous, if that were possible. He knew exactly what they were thinking: *This man is crazy! Why would anyone want to live here?!*

One of the teens spoke up. "You live in Jerusalem, and you want to move here? Every one of us is dreaming of escaping this place and moving to Tel Aviv or Jerusalem, and you want to come here? Why would you want to do such a thing?"

"Our nation just experienced such incredible miracles," Rav Grossman said. "We won what some people thought was an unwinnable war. The Kosel is back in our hands. With everything going on right now, Mashiach can't be far away! All of you here are my brothers. Do you think that just because you came from Morocco and my family comes from Eastern Europe, we're a different people? That's nonsense! We are all brothers, and I have come here because I want to teach you what it means to be a Jew so that when Mashiach walks through the door and into our lives, you will be ready for him."

By that time, Rav Grossman had already been working with kids in Chinuch Atzmai, a network of religious day schools in Israel, for a year, so he knew the lingo; he knew how to talk to them and how to handle them with sensitivity. He knew all about Morocco, where their grandparents had lived, their heritage, their traditions. He knew what spoke to their hearts and souls. But they didn't know that he knew, and they couldn't believe what they were hearing.

"Even with all my newfound knowledge," Rav Grossman said many years later, "I still can't fully explain how the miracle happened. In truth, there is no explanation for the instant spiritual connection that sprang up between me and the youth of Migdal HaEmek. From our first encounter, there was a bond that couldn't be ignored. A protective wall formed itself around us, enveloping a Meah Shearim rabbi and a bunch of random teens from a poor development town into a relationship that would span decades and never fade, only growing stronger with time as it matured and went places nobody had ever dreamed."

It all began in those first few surreal moments after the rabbi walked into a disco for the first time in his life. Little did Rav Grossman dream that Israeli television would come to film a documentary about him in 1970 titled *Disco Rabbi,* that he would become famous all over Israel, and that his fame would spread even across international waters in a matter of a few short years. And the spark that set the whole chain of events into motion happened that night when he walked into a Migdal HaEmek disco.

After that, there was no turning back.

CHAPTER THREE

"I'm With You!"

The young rabbi ended up sticking around at the disco for three hours — three hours that passed in a blur. It didn't feel like three hours. It felt like he'd been there for a few minutes. Then he glanced at his watch and couldn't believe his eyes. It was too late to return to Yerushalayim that night.

After a few more minutes of conversation, he wished them all a pleasant evening and left. He walked out of the disco, up the stairs, and into the street, where still another group of teens were dancing to the

Hanging around in Migdal HaEmek

music blaring from a radio, drinking Coke, and eating *garinim* (sunflower seeds) in front of the nearby kiosk.

He blinked as if waking from a dream. *What on earth am I doing here?* he asked himself yet again, and, of course, the words of the tzaddik came back to him: "Maybe go down, look around, and see if there is anything for you to accomplish in Migdal HaEmek?"

Well, he had made the first move. Now he just needed a place to sleep for the night.

Rav Grossman headed toward the teens dawdling in front of the kiosk and asked if there were any rabbis living in the neighborhood.

There was a tzaddik, a righteous man, who was also a rav who lived not far from there, they told him.

"What's his name?"

"Rav Meir Yonah."

Later Rav Grossman would find out that Rav Yonah had become the first Sefardic chief rabbi of Migdal HaEmek shortly after moving to Israel. Originally from Tunisia, he was a Kabbalist and Torah scholar who would end up serving as a rabbi in Migdal HaEmek for thirty-one years. But Rav Grossman didn't know any of this at the time. All he knew was that "a tzaddik and rav" lived in this city that had a disco but no yeshivah.

With nowhere else to go, the young visitor from Yerushalayim found the building where Rav Yonah lived and knocked on his door.

The rav opened up, invited him into his apartment, and asked him what had brought him to Migdal HaEmek. Rav Grossman shared his story with Rav Yonah, and the rav invited him to stay the night.

Wrapped in the lambskin he had been given by his host, Rav Grossman didn't have an easy time falling asleep. It was a very cold night and the walls were thin. He could hear the winds from the Golan howling as they battled for supremacy right outside the window.

Closing his eyes, he found himself remembering the faces of the teenagers he had met that night, the questions they'd asked, and their fierce desire to become better people and better Jews that he sensed bubbling right beneath the surface. There was no question in his mind that he could help these kids and give them something else to live for.

At the same time, he didn't know if he had what it took to pick himself up from Rechov Chana in Yerushalayim and move to the middle of the spiritual desert that was Migdal HaEmek. How could he move to a town without a yeshivah or kollel (school for advanced Talmud study)? There wasn't even a Talmud Torah or Bais Yaakov school for girls. And while the couple had only one child at that point — a little girl named Chaya — he and his wife were hoping and praying for a large family. How would they succeed in raising them properly in the way of the Torah in such a place?

The thoughts and worries swirled around in his mind as he lay wrapped in the lambskin. Eventually he fell asleep, and when he awoke, the sun was out and morning had come.

It hadn't been a very restful night, and after davening (prayers) he gathered his belongings, thanked Rav Yonah, and left the simple apartment. A bright sun shone down benevolently from a cloudless sky, and the fierce winds of the night before had been replaced by a balmy breeze from the Galil. Before returning to the bus stop on the highway, Rav Grossman decided to give himself a tour of the town to see how many schools there were and to ascertain the real status of Jewish life in Migdal HaEmek.

He ended up walking the streets for hours. He found a *mikveh*, a Jewish ritual bath, but it was very small and would need a major overhaul. The biggest shul in the town davened *nusach Ashkenaz,* in the style of the Ashkenazim. It was called Beit Knesset Yotzei Europa (the Synagogue for European Jews) and catered to recent immigrants from Romania and Hungary, virtually all of whom were Holocaust survivors. He would later learn that the city's entire population was between seven and eight thousand people. About sixty percent of the residents were of Sefardic origin, the other forty percent Ashkenazic. Interestingly, though it was a relatively small city, the population was extremely varied and hailed from over thirty different countries.

He davened Minchah, the afternoon prayer, with the Ashkenazic congregation. They were simple Jews, many of them broken and shattered after living through the horrific experiences of the war and its aftermath. Between Minchah and Maariv, the second and third prayers of the day, one of the congregants asked the visitor to say a few words. The young rabbi went up to the front of the shul and turned to face the older men sitting in the rows of seats. Tired faces stared blankly in his direction. Then he opened his mouth and began speaking in Yiddish.

The response was electrifying.

Suddenly the elderly Yidden in the room were alive and smiling. They wanted to know where the rabbi was from.

"Mir hert a Yiddish vort — We hear some talk in Yiddish."

"Mamesh a mechayah, a mechayah — You are bringing us back to life."

"Mir ken eppes redden mit a Yid — What a pleasure it is to converse with a fellow Jew."

They thanked him over and over for his warm words and for gracing their humble shul with his presence.

"Ich vill kumen du voinen," he said to them. "I want to come live here."

"Halevai, Rebbe, halevai zolt ehr kumen! Halevai, der Rebbe vet unz mechayah zein! Please come, Rebbe. You have revitalized us. Please come live in our town!"

They spoke for a while, and he learned that many of the Yidden he was meeting had known the Skulener Rebbe, Rav Eliezer Zusha Portugal, back in Romania. Some of them had even been saved from prison by the Rebbe. (Later the Skulener Rebbe would come and visit Migdal HaEmek for a reunion with those precious Yidden.)

The more Rav Grossman spoke with the Yidden in that little shul, the more he understood how much there was to do in Migdal HaEmek.

It had been a whirlwind two days. Before he walked into the shul, Rav Grossman had felt exhausted and wrung out, overwhelmed and in doubt. But within the walls of that shul, seeing people who were mitzvah observant with nobody to speak to, European Holocaust survivors with an urgent thirst that was just waiting to be quenched, the young rabbi spoke from the heart.

"I am going to move here. I am coming to be with you. I'm with you!"

And when he saw the grateful smiles on their faces, he knew that he had made the right decision. This was where he needed to be.

"I have a question for you," he said before he left.

They nodded in encouragement and looked at him expectantly. "I will want to establish a kollel here in Migdal HaEmek, a place where *yungeleit*, young married men, will be able to study Torah. Could I use your premises for the kollel?"

"Avadeh! Without question," they replied. "You can use the entire building. Just come!"

When Rav Grossman parted from the men he had just met, he knew without a shadow of a doubt that he would be returning to this town in the near future.

CHAPTER FOUR

The Steipler's Psak

Upon his return to Yerushalayim, Rav Grossman went to give a detailed report to the Lelover Rebbe, who encouraged him and blessed his chassid with *siyata d'Shmaya* (Divine assistance) and success. He also visited his father and told him the story. In the decades to come, Rav Grossman would often ask his father for guidance as to how to conduct himself in the world that would become his. Now his father asked him a question, a question for which he demanded an honest response.

Rav Yisrael and Rav Yitzchak Dovid Grossman

"Itche Duvid, how were you able to stand in such a place and talk to such a group?"

Rav Grossman answered his father from the heart.

"Tatte," he replied, "I just looked at their *neshamos,* at their souls, and nothing else."

Rav Yisrael scrutinized his son and peered into the very depths of his being.

"You can go," he told him, "and you will succeed."

After taking leave of his father, Rav Grossman's next move was to arrange for a source of funding for the kollel he would be bringing with him to Migdal HaEmek. He knew that a new organization called Talat — an acronym for Tenuat L'Hafatzat Torah (the Movement for the Spreading of Torah) — had just been established in Israel. Its mission statement: "We will support any Torah scholar willing to leave Yerushalayim to teach Torah in far-flung communities of Eretz Yisrael." The head of the organization, Rabbi Eliezer Kugel, was a grandson of Rav Aryeh Levin, the famous "Father of Prisoners," and the love he had for the Jewish People was reminiscent of that of his grandfather. Rabbi Kugel was well connected and even received funding from Israel's Interior Ministry to further his goals. Goals that fit in very nicely with Rav Grossman's new objective.

Off Rav Grossman went to meet with Rabbi Kugel. He explained his decision to leave the safe, warm, and familiar confines of Meah Shearim to establish a *kollel* in the remote, crime-ridden world of Migdal HaEmek. He told Rabbi Kugel about his experience at the Western Wall and his vow to devote a year of his life working with youth from underprivileged homes and backgrounds — youth whose lives could be turned around forever if they had the opportunity to develop a relationship with a man who came from the world of Torah and Chassidus.

"I will support your kollel," Rabbi Kugel promised.

With the necessary funding in hand to take the initial steps at least, Rav Grossman began reaching out to select young men, both married and unmarried, whom he felt would be good candidates to join his group of pioneers. The stipends he offered weren't large, but they were respectable, certainly enough to live on. No one expected more.

Before long a seven-man kollel was formed, which included Rav Avraham Biderman, the future Lelover Rebbe. Once they had settled on

Rav Eliezer Kugel (sitting to the left of Rabbi Grossman) on a visit to Migdal Ohr. He was Rav Grossman's first supporter.

the prospective members of the kollel, apartments were rented for the families. It was all coming together.

Moving to a crime-filled city like Migdal HaEmek was no simple thing. On the family's way to the city for the first time, the taxi driver stopped at a gas station, where Rav Grossman got out of the car to buy a bottle of water.

The driver said to Rebbetzin Grossman, "Do you know where your husband is taking you?"

"Not really. This will be my first time seeing the city."

"Lady," the driver said, "he's taking you to Gehinnom!"

For most people, that would have been the worst possible welcome to a new home. But Rebbetzin Grossman took it in stride. After all, the Lelover Rebbe had instructed that they go, and she had grown up in a house where one did what the Rebbe said. Still, the incident left a mark.

The Grossmans arrived in Midgal HaEmek and settled into their new life. The day was divided into parts. Morning hours were devoted to the *kollel* members learning together. The second part of the day had an entirely different focus. The idea was for every member of the kollel to gather as many of the neighborhood children together as possible and teach them Torah. The children were told that if they attended classes for the entire month, they would receive the kind of prizes that would make the effort worthwhile. It took time, but eventually every single member of the kollel gathered his own group of kids, whom he taught every day after they had finished school. It wasn't long before they had over four hundred children coming to learn Torah from the kollel members every evening.

Finding places to operate the learning program was incredibly challenging. One of the programs took place at a local nonreligious school called "Shalom Aleichem." While the school itself would have been opposed to teaching the kids Torah, the school's janitor was a religious Jew named Elbaz and he was totally in favor of what was happening in his town. He allowed them to use the school's bomb shelter without the administration's knowledge, willing to jeopardize his job to give children the opportunity to learn. The shelter had only one window, which meant that the place was hot and stuffy, but without any other options, they made the best of the situation.

One evening, while Rav Grossman was giving the children a lesson in the shelter, someone stuck his hand into the window and bombarded the room with handfuls of pebbles, creating mayhem. As the children scrambled out of the way to avoid being pelted, one of the adults ran

The "Disco Rabbi" and the "tzaddikim"

outside to catch the attacker, but he was long gone from the scene of the crime. The incident was repeated the next day as well.

After a few days of being pelted with stones, Rav Grossman decided to wait near the doorway of the bomb shelter, and as soon as the stone-thrower made an appearance, he chased after the boy, begging him to stop running and reassuring him that he wouldn't be hurt or punished.

When they were finally standing face-to-face, the rabbi asked the boy, "Why are you throwing stones at everyone in the shelter?"

He didn't receive a very satisfactory answer to his question, but he did manage to find out who the boy was and where he lived. Taking matters into his own hands, Rav Grossman went to meet with his parents.

He was invited inside the apartment and offered a chair. To his surprise and dismay, he noticed that the walls were black from soot. A few questions later he learned that the child's father worked in the coal business, which explained why everything in the room was coated with a thick layer of coal dust.

When it was his turn to speak, Rav Grossman spoke from the heart, explaining to the father that his son was a ticking time bomb. If left alone to continue on the path he was on, the chances of him turning into a productive citizen were dismal.

"What can I do?" the father asked plaintively. He was a beaten man with no prospects for advancement or any hope of a better life. His focus was on surviving, and he didn't have the wherewithal to deal with his wayward son. He knew the path his son was choosing, but he had no alternative to offer him.

"I'll take him to a yeshivah," Rav Grossman offered.

The coal man waved his hand listlessly and said, "Do whatever you want."

> I took the boy with me to a yeshivah in Bnei Brak and introduced him to the staff and to the other boys, hoping that he might find his place and make a mentch out of himself. But a few weeks later he was back in Migdal HaEmek, hanging out on the corner with the tough guys. Yet a part of me felt that he wanted a chance to succeed and that I shouldn't give up on him. So I convinced him to try out another yeshivah, this one located in Be'er Yaakov.
>
> He said he didn't want to go. He wanted me to leave him alone, to let him live his life of petty crime. I didn't give up, and in the end he accompanied me to the next yeshivah. Yet this time, too, a few weeks passed and once again I saw him back in town.

The Steipler Gaon

I was investing so much time and effort into this boy, but it wasn't working. The lure of the street proved to be too much of a temptation for him to withstand. I took him to yet another yeshivah in Lod, this one Chabad. He returned home a few days later.

I was at a loss. How much time was I supposed to invest in one boy? What was my obligation? I didn't know, so I decided to travel to Bnei Brak and confer with the Steipler Gaon, Rav Yaakov Yisrael Kanievsky, one of the greatest rabbinical authorities of that time. I knew he would give me the clarity I needed.

When I was sitting in front of the Steipler, I explained the entire situation. "What is my obligation here?" I asked after I'd finished my story. "What's the *shiur*? What's the limit?"

"There is no limit," the Steipler replied. "If there is even the tiniest chance that you will save this boy's life, you have to continue doing your best."

I returned to Migdal HaEmek, determined to renew my efforts.

Today that boy holds a position of prominence in a yeshivah. He is a *talmid chacham*, a Torah scholar, who lives in Bnei Brak. Sometimes, when I'm passing through Bnei Brak, I daven Minchah at the Itzkowitz *shtieblach*. (Itzkowitz *shtieblach* is a shul with a number of rooms where numerous prayer services are held at the same time.) I see him there, standing and davening *Shemoneh Esrei* for no less than forty-five minutes, and I start to cry as I remember all those times I traveled halfway around the country, taking him from one yeshivah to the next.

Rav Grossman would remain in close contact with the Steipler Gaon, frequently asking his advice. For his part, the Gaon loved the young rav from Migdal HaEmek and treated him with warmth and affection.

The first girls' class

The level of knowledge among the children varied, as it does in every class. It was the same thing when it came to their abilities. But Rav Grossman quickly realized that there were quite a few children who had the potential to graduate from small-town life and move on to mainstream yeshivos if they were given the necessary assistance. It was the same for the girls. It wasn't long before Rav Grossman began visiting the homes of those children, asking to speak with their parents.

He would be invited into the simple apartments, where the children slept three to a mattress and it was boiling hot in the summer and freezing cold in the winter. The parents were usually welcoming, knowing how much their children were benefiting from the rabbi's after-school Torah programs. They'd offer him a cup of mint tea and some cookies, and then Rav Grossman would get down to business and explain why he had come to see them.

"You have a child who has the potential to become a truly great scholar, a genuine *talmid chacham,*" he'd say. "But that will not happen as long as he remains here in Migdal HaEmek."

Many of the parents came from traditional Sefardic backgrounds, and a reverence for the "*chacham,*" the learned sage, was in their blood. The idea of their children growing up to become Torah scholars was enticing. At the same time, they didn't feel they had the ability to provide their children with the framework to make that happen.

"You don't have to worry about finances or anything else," the young rabbi would tell the parents. "I'll take care of everything. I will be more than happy to find your son a yeshivah in Bnei Brak or Yerushalayim, where he will be able to maximize his potential."

This was no simple promise to make. He had no car of his own nor a driver who could transport the children to the center of the country where the yeshivos were located. Rav Grossman would have to take the child by bus from Migdal HaEmek to Haifa, from Haifa to Tel Aviv, and from there to Bnei Brak. Just getting them to the yeshivah meant a journey of five hours — each way! Many times he had to remain with the young men or women, making sure that the institution was actually willing to accept the prospective student and that all the paperwork was in order. He couldn't just leave them and return home.

There were times when just bringing one boy to a new yeshivah or a few of the local girls to a school like Meor HaChaim in Bnei Brak meant that he was away from home for three days at a time. But despite all the hardships and challenges, the rav and his rebbetzin wouldn't allow anything to stand in their way, and by 1970, they had sent thirty girls to Meor HaChaim alone.

Half a century later, Rav Grossman recalls the names of each of those children, his mind filled with pictures of the families those children went on to build. Many were blessed with ten or twelve children who grew up to become teachers of Torah, rabbis, Talmudic scholars or successful professionals devoted to Torah learning and observance. The difference between what could have been had he just left well enough alone and the lives they went on to build was like the difference between night and day. Without exaggeration, an entire world was created from those early trips. But back then it meant working around the clock, leaving his wife and family behind, utter exhaustion his constant companion, and the many hours spent riding intercity buses. Suffice it to say, he would become very friendly with all the drivers…

Though Rav Grossman promised the parents of the youth of Migdal HaEmek not to worry about the costs of attending his programs and sending their kids to yeshivos, that didn't mean it was all free. Somehow, somewhere, Rav Grossman had to find a way to fund his various activities. While Rabbi Kugel provided funding for Rav Grossman's original kollel in Migdal HaEmek, it was the American branch of P'eylim (an

American-based organization) that became the first sponsor for all the other programs he was building and growing in Migdal HaEmek.

The American branch of P'eylim had an Israel office on Malchei Yisrael Street in the heart of Geulah that was run by Rabbi Yudka Paley. Rav Grossman had the feeling that Reb Yudka might prove to be the right person to help him develop his programs. Without thinking too deeply into it, he walked into the P'eylim office one day and introduced himself to the person sitting behind the desk.

"My name is Rav Yitzchak Dovid Grossman," he said. "I'm originally from Meah Shearim, but my wife and I moved to Migdal HaEmek, where I established a kollel. But that was just the beginning."

He told Reb Yudka all about the programs they were running for the local youth, and how he was constantly bringing kids from Migdal HaEmek to yeshivos and girls' schools around the country, journeys that took huge chunks of his time and ate up immense financial resources — time and resources that he didn't have.

Reb Yudka was ready to help.

"Rav Grossman, bring us all the receipts from the trips you take, and we'll reimburse you for everything."

With some more funds at his disposal, Rav Grossman was able to continue his activities, but he began to see a growing problem that would require vastly more resources to solve.

There was no question that Rav Grossman and his wife had chosen a truly challenging life for themselves and that, despite this, Rav Grossman was accomplishing wonders. Yet, at the same time, he sometimes had the sense that he was treading water. He was investing so much effort to bring kids from Migdal HaEmek to Torah institutions so they would have a chance to become true *bnei Torah* (people devoted to Torah learning), but he was beginning to realize that many of the schools were not equipped to work with these kids.

No one at these institutions was taking the time to genuinely comprehend who the children were and the background they came from. These were not kids who had grown up in religious neighborhoods. They were coming from the menacing streets of Migdal HaEmek, and they were vulnerable and susceptible to being pulled right back into the vortex of their old life. It was so easy for them to fall out of the system, but the institutions weren't taking all this into account, treating them like any other student in their schools. As for the kids, perhaps they sensed that the people teaching them couldn't devote as much time and effort as was necessary, and they began falling through the cracks. Though some succeeded and went on to raise those beautiful families, too many returned home to the slums where they had been raised.

It broke Rav Grossman's heart, but it also led him to a certain recognition: Perhaps instead of sending the children away from Migdal HaEmek, it might be a good idea to establish an institution of his own where he would be able to educate the kids the way he saw fit, seeing them for who they were, relating to them in a personal manner while never forgetting where they had come from and how they had gotten to where they were.

One thing was clear: The kids who were constantly running away from every yeshivah to which he brought them wouldn't be running from a yeshivah where people went out of their way to understand and love them. The seeds of a brilliant idea were there, but he had no funding for such an endeavor. For the time being, it was merely a dream.

Rav Yitzchak Dovid moved the dream into a compartment at the back of his mind and went on saving the local youth one child at a time, never imagining that the day would come when the seeds of his idea would blossom and become a reality.

CHAPTER FIVE
The Rebbe and the "Gazlan"

When Rav Grossman first came to Migdal HaEmek, the levels of crime in the city seemed to outweigh the population. Break-ins. Theft. Murder. The city had the potential to be a peaceful place to live, surrounded by the beautiful scenery of Emek Yizre'el. Instead, the people living there knew that they could be walking down the street and be caught in a gun battle that would end their lives — just like that.

One evening, Rav Grossman was walking by the local municipal-funded swimming pool when he noticed a slew of luxury cars parked at the side of the road. Knowing that the financial status of virtually everyone living in Migdal HaEmek was nothing to write home about, he was perplexed. There were a bunch of people hanging around outside, and he asked one of them whom the cars belonged to.

"Arabs," one man replied shortly.

"From where?"

"From Nazareth and from other Arab cities in the vicinity."

"How can they afford such nice cars?"

"The young Arab men are hard workers and know how to save their money. A lot of them hang around Migdal HaEmek and date the local Jewish girls from the poorest homes — girls who are impressed by the flashy young men and the money they throw around."

Rav Grossman was shocked. Was it really possible that these Arabs were driving into Migdal HaEmek to meet Jewish girls? *Rachmana litzlan! How terrible this was!* He had never heard of such things back in Yerushalayim.

Rav Grossman stood on the sidewalk and studied the scene, his mind racing. It didn't take him long to arrive at some conclusions.

There was no way that the Arabs would be allowed free rein in an Israeli city unless someone was allowing it — and maybe even benefiting from it.

"At the end of the day," he said to himself, "Migdal HaEmek is a center of crime, which means that there's some criminal who profits financially from whatever illegal business takes place in the city."

Rav Grossman figured that the Arabs must be paying some big honcho to allow them to drive into Migdal HaEmek and hang around without anyone interfering. There was no question in his mind that protection money was being paid here. The question was, who was the one getting paid?

"So," he asked the man who had told him that the cars were owned by Arabs, "who is giving the Arabs permission to enter the city and date these girls?"

"The boss."

"And who's the boss?"

"His name is Kobi."

"How old is this Kobi?"

"He's around thirty-five."

"And where does he live?"

"Why do you want to know?"

"I'm going to visit him."

"You can't just visit Kobi!"

"Why not?"

"He's one of the toughest men in this town. You can't just walk into his house!"

"But I can go over and introduce myself, can't I? Just to say hello?"

The man was dubious. "I guess. Just watch your back."

Rav Yitzchak Dovid smiled, touched by his concern. "Don't worry. I will."

Kobi lived in an apartment building in one of the Migdal HaEmek projects — truly a man of the people. As he walked up to the apartment, Rav Grossman heard sounds coming from behind closed doors. From one apartment he heard children crying, the sound of a mother yelling about something or other from the next. He heard several other languages amid the Hebrew, obviously from recent immigrants. He wondered how they felt living in the same building as a notorious crime boss.

Kobi

Kobi's apartment was on the building's second floor, above a Jewish family who had come to Israel from Romania. If he closes his eyes and focuses for a few seconds, Rav Yitzchak Dovid can still hear the heavy European accent of the Romanian Jew saying to his wife, "*Der Rebbe geit tzu dem gazlan*. The rabbi is going to that thief."

Rav Grossman climbed the stairs and found the apartment. He knocked on the door, which was opened by Kobi himself. He was tall and powerfully built, and made an impressive, if slightly frightening, figure. The infamous Kobi was wearing a sleeveless undershirt and shorts, decidedly underdressed in comparison with the rav, who wore his full-length long jacket and hat.

"What do you want?" Kobi demanded gruffly.

Once again, Hashem put the right words into Rav Grossman's mouth.

"I came to drink a *l'chaim* with you."

Kobi stood framed by the doorway, at a loss for words. Whatever he had been expecting to hear, it wasn't that.

"What did you say?"

"I said that I came here to sit down with you and drink a *l'chaim*," his guest said with a warm smile. "I'm relatively new in town, and I thought we could get to know each another."

"Well, then," Kobi said, finding himself disarmed by the rabbi's friendly tone, "come in and sit down."

The visitor entered the cramped apartment and followed the "gazlan" into the tiny living/dining room, where Kobi motioned for the guest to take a seat.

When they were sitting across from each other, Rav Grossman said to him without preamble, "Kobi, I'm sure you know what I've been doing for the youth here in Migdal HaEmek."

Kobi nodded. "Of course I do. All the *chevrah* (the gang) talks about you and how much they love you."

"Thank you for the compliment. But the truth is I came here tonight to discuss something else — something I saw here in town. Something that disturbed me very much."

Kobi looked at his visitor expectantly.

Rav Grossman described the scene he saw by the swimming pool the other day and how he found out that Arabs from the nearby towns were coming there to date the Jewish girls of Migdal HaEmek.

"I couldn't believe such a thing could be true. Is it really possible that Arab men could just drive into a Jewish city without anyone trying to stop them?" Rav Grossman paused and looked Kobi straight in the eye. "I've come to know this city and the way it's run, and I know that if the Arabs are coming here, someone gave them permission. So I asked around, and I learned that that someone is you."

"Wait a second, Rabbi," Kobi said. "Just because they come here to date the girls doesn't mean someone is charging them an entrance fee."

"Look, I'm not stupid. I know the way things work here. And I have to tell you something else, Kobi. I couldn't sleep last night. The idea that the Jewish girls in this city are at risk of assimilating with our neighbors kept me up all night. I can't function knowing that such a terrible thing is happening in our city.

"Kobi, do you understand what you're doing by giving these Arabs permission to marry our girls? Do you understand that when a Jewish girl marries an Arab, her children will be lost to the Jewish people? This isn't just a question of the here and now. It's a decision with ramifications that change the course of history!"

"I understand you, Rabbi," Kobi said, "but this is business. It's not easy, making money here in Migdal HaEmek, and this is a good money maker. For some reason, these Arabs want to marry Jewish girls, and they're willing to pay money for the opportunity. It's nothing personal."

"If it's about making money, one of the members of my shul owns a factory. I'll speak to him about giving you a job. A desk job, one that pays well. Then you won't need to do this and endanger the lives and futures of so many Jewish girls."

Kobi laughed. "Do you really think a person like me could ever work behind a desk? I don't care how much money he'd be paying me. I can't work for other people. I've always been my own boss, and I'll always be my own boss. Do you have any idea what I do to people who try to order me around? Try again."

"All right," Rav Grossman said. "The desk job is not a good idea. Fine, but if that's not acceptable to you, then give it some thought and tell me what you'd want to do. If you could do anything in the world, what would it be? What's your dream job?"

Kobi considered the question for a few seconds and replied, "If I had my own truck, I could do deliveries around the country and get paid very well for my work. I could make my own schedule and get up when I want and come and go when I please. If you're asking me what I would want to do with my life, that's the answer: I'd be very content working as the driver of my own truck."

Rav Grossman nodded. "I hear you. You just need a truck."

Before he left, Rav Grossman drank a *l'chaim* with Kobi, just as he'd promised. Two glasses of arak, blessings on both sides, and then he told Kobi about himself, how a young rabbi from Meah Shearim had ended up in a city like Migdal HaEmek. Kobi was fascinated by the rabbi, and the evening ended with good wishes on both sides.

As mentioned earlier, Rav Grossman's father and father-in-law had purchased the young couple an apartment on Chana Street at the time of their marriage. On the following Sunday, Rav Grossman traveled to Yerushalayim, where he put his apartment up for sale. With the money received from selling the apartment, he purchased a Volkswagen truck. Not long after his conversation with Kobi, Rav Grossman returned to his home and knocked on the door. When he was sitting across the table from Kobi for the second time, the rabbi placed the keys to the truck on the table and pushed them across the wooden surface toward the speechless Kobi.

"You said that your dream is to have your own truck. Well, here it is. Now you have your own truck."

But the rabbi didn't stop there. It was one thing to have a truck, but Kobi needed someone to pay him to make deliveries. Rav Grossman made an appointment to meet with the owner of a local factory that manufactured high-end leather clothing for export to Europe and other locations around the world. This company sent a truckload of leather jackets to the airport every evening for the night flight to Europe.

"What can I do for you, Rabbi?" the businessman asked Rav Grossman, who was sitting across from his desk in his office at the factory, the pungent aroma of fresh leather permeating the air. The factory owner's name was Philip, a Holocaust survivor from Germany who had managed to build a business from scratch after the traumas of his earlier life.

Rav Grossman proceeded to tell Philip the whole story, from the moment he spied the string of luxury cars until his meeting with Kobi, who thought he could make a living driving trucks.

Philip was impressed with the rabbi's self-sacrifice. "So what do you want from me?"

"I want you to hire Kobi to take your merchandise to the airport. If Kobi has a good job where he is making enough money, he won't have to take money from the Arabs. He'll kick them out of Migdal HaEmek and make sure none of them dare show their faces in the city again."

Philip agreed to give Kobi a trial. Kobi proved to be a more than satisfactory worker, and Philip was able to rely on him completely. More importantly, Kobi kept his side of the bargain. Of course, the Arabs from Nazareth weren't happy to learn that they weren't welcome in Migdal HaEmek any longer and tried to throw their weight around and enter the city despite their orders to stay away. What followed were a series of bloody battles in the center of town. Many of the Arabs were badly beaten and ended up in the hospital. When others came to defend their brothers' honor, they too were beaten and their fancy cars trashed. Kobi himself took a *shochet's* (ritual slaughterer's) knife and slashed the tires of every car that dared enter "his" streets after being told to stay away. The police were "busy" on those nights and made themselves scarce. So successful was Kobi in teaching the Arabs to stay away that even now, some fifty years later, you'll be hard-pressed to find an Arab wandering around Migdal HaEmek for the wrong reasons.

In addition to his job delivering leather jackets to the airport, Kobi would eventually become Rav Grossman's personal driver, ferrying the rabbi around the city. The fact that Kobi had become Rav Grossman's "chassid" made a tremendous impression on all the "tzaddikim" (that's what Rav Grossman always called the kids he helped), who couldn't believe that Kobi of all people had turned a new leaf and was now a friend of the rabbi. If Kobi was now close to the rabbi, how could the rest of them stay away?

Of course, Kobi didn't just change overnight. He'd been involved in a life of crime for way too long for that to be the case. Still, he was trying, and Rav Grossman appreciated how hard he was working to become a better person.

One day the two of them were driving on the Bikah Road, part of the highway that connects Tiveria to Beit Shean. The scenery was pleasant to the eye and invigorating for the *neshamah* (soul). Long, sweeping plains, tall trees, far-off mountains. Above, clouds had formed into a series of fascinating shapes. It was a magnificent day.

Suddenly they came across a flock of sheep being led by a young Arab shepherd. Without warning, Kobi pulled the truck over to the side of the road, jumped out of the cab, grabbed a lamb, and threw the bleating animal into the truck. Then he pulled himself back into the driver's seat and prepared to flee the scene.

"Kobi," Rav Grossman said, "give the lamb back to the shepherd right now!"

"I will do no such thing!"

The old Kobi was back. The rabbi could see it from the dangerous glint in his eye.

"Kobi, give it back now!"

But Kobi refused. He pressed down on the gas pedal and began driving like a maniac, taking the hairpin curves of the road at high speed, the truck hugging the shoulder one moment and driving in the middle of both lanes a second later. Kobi knew he had let the rabbi down, had let his baser instincts take over, and it had sent him over the edge. Seeing that Kobi was in another zone and there was nobody to talk to, Rav Grossman didn't say another word. Instead, he closed his eyes and davened to Hashem that they emerge from the incident without anyone getting hurt. Eventually they reached the end of the road, and Kobi slowed down at the light. Still, there was no word from his passenger. They didn't speak again until they reached Migdal HaEmek.

A few days later, Rav Grossman needed to travel to Nazareth for a meeting with the local chief of police, and he asked Kobi to take him there. Kobi knew that the rabbi met with the police on a regular basis, usually to discuss how to further reduce the crime in Migdal HaEmek. Kobi didn't think twice and agreed to drive him. When they arrived at the station, Kobi waited downstairs in the parking lot while the rabbi went upstairs for his meeting with Chief Yosef Levi and told him the story that had occurred on the way to Beit Shean.

"You've known Kobi for years," he said to the chief. "Thank G-d he's starting to change and he works as my driver. But I had a most unpleasant incident with him a few days ago." He told the chief what had happened on the Bikah Road the other day. "What do you think is the best way to handle this situation?" he asked.

"Wait here," the chief said to his visitor. He then gave an order to five policemen, who went down to the parking lot where Kobi was sitting and waiting for the rabbi in the truck.

"Get out," one of them demanded.

Kobi got out of the truck. The second he was out the door, the policeman snapped a pair of cuffs on him and brought him upstairs to the chief's office. He entered the room, his face white, and was then treated to an intensive dressing down from the chief of police, who explained to him that the rabbi was a dear friend of his and he took it personally when anyone treated him with disrespect.

"Put your keys on the table," the chief ordered.

In handcuffs, Kobi barely managed to extract the keys from his pocket and dropped them on the desk.

"Now go."

When his meeting with the chief was over, Rav Grossman left the building, part of him thinking that someone would be waiting outside with a gun ready. After all, he had just gotten Kobi in trouble with the police.

Rav Grossman took a taxi back home, leaving the truck behind in the police station's parking lot.

A week later Kobi came to see him. He apologized for having acted with such disrespect. He even cried, promising to repent and to never act in such a way again. Once Rav Grossman made peace with his driver, Kobi was able to retrieve his truck from the police station. Of course, he found a way to return the lamb to the shepherd he had stolen it from.

From then on, Rav Grossman never again had any problems with Kobi, who became a true chassid. The former criminal had to test the rabbi, but when the rabbi didn't back down one iota and continued demanding better behavior from the ex-convict even at the risk of getting him angry, Kobi came to respect him even more. Until that point, everyone in his life had been afraid of him, and he'd been able to do whatever he wanted, without fear of repercussions. With Rav Grossman it wasn't like that, and somewhere deep inside his heart Kobi had been waiting for a person to come along who was ready to show him another way — while showing him love at the same time.

We're only human, and we don't know the reasons Hashem does what He does. But when Rav Grossman asks himself, as he sometimes does, why he merited such incredible success in life, he always comes back to the same incident. In his mind, it all boils down to the action he took that convinced Kobi to keep the Arab men out of Migdal HaEmek. Selling his apartment to buy a truck for a small-time crime boss wasn't a typical move in anyone's book, but in Rav Grossman's mind, it was without question the key that opened the gates of Heaven in his life and for which he was repaid countless times over.

CHAPTER SIX

The Kima Minchah

When he first arrived in Migdal HaEmek, Rav Yitzchak Dovid found out that many of the stores were open on Shabbos. It was painful to see Jews walking into coffee shops, bars, and restaurants when it was already Shabbos, and he resolved to do whatever he could to alter the status quo. In one of the shopping centers not far from his shul, there was a popular restaurant called Kima.

One Erev Shabbos (Friday afternoon), on his way to shul, the young rabbi stood in the restaurant's doorway, where he had a good view of the room filled with people sitting and enjoying themselves, even as the Shabbos Queen had arrived in the city and wandered around in search of those who were happy to welcome her. Even worse, the people in the restaurant playing the games — some even playing backgammon for money, each with a bottle of beer at his elbow — every so often would raise their mugs and call out, *"Bo'i kallah!"*

This stemmed from an old Sefardic tradition to welcome Shabbos into one's life by saying, *"Bo'i kallah* — Welcome, bride." But the words were most decidedly not meant to be said while sitting in a smoke-filled establishment and gambling on a Friday night!

As he stood there looking at the scene before him, Rav Grossman recalled a story from his youth, a story involving his rebbi, Rav Aryeh Levin.

Rav Aryeh had a practice of walking through the Machaneh Yehudah *shuk* on Erev Shabbos, his very presence reminding the store owners that it was time to close up shop before the holy day began. One Erev Shabbos, Rav Aryeh passed a store that was packed with customers.

Rav Aryeh Levin could have approached the owner and given him a *mussar shmuess*, telling him off and shaming him for his actions. He could have stood outside the store and made a protest. Instead, he took a seat inside the store and sat there quietly, observing the customers and everything else that comes along with the beauty of a thriving business. He didn't move for twenty minutes, and his very presence was driving the owner to distraction.

Finally, the owner couldn't help himself and approached Rav Aryeh. "*Kevod HaRav*, honored rabbi, can I help you with anything?"

"No," Rav Aryeh replied. "I just wanted to tell you one thing. I've been sitting and watching the sheer volume of business that you are doing right now, on this Erev Shabbos. I'll tell you the truth: I don't know if I would be able to withstand the *nisayon*, the test you are facing, and I understand you one hundred percent because your test is so challenging."

Having said his piece, Rav Aryeh stood up, gave the man a kiss on the forehead, and left the store.

The store owner came to see Rav Aryeh on Motza'ei Shabbos, just after Shabbos was over.

"*Kevod HaRav*, I just wanted to let you know that I closed my store this Shabbos and that I will never open my store on Shabbos again for as long as I live."

"But how were you able to do it? How were you able to withstand such a tremendous *nisayon*?"

"I'll tell you how," the man replied. "I was able to close my store because you were the first person who understood me. You didn't yell at me. You didn't threaten me or castigate me. You empathized with me and showed me that you really understand my situation. And because you understand me and the test I am facing, I was finally able to close my shop."

Now, standing outside the restaurant, Rav Yitzchak Dovid Grossman reviewed his options. He could walk into the restaurant and deliver a blistering *mussar shmuess*, a scathing attack on the patrons within the eatery. But there was a good chance that such a *shmuess* would anger one or two of the already tipsy and more heavily inebriated patrons, who might react by throwing a frosty beer bottle at his head. Besides, he had learned at the feet of his rebbi that empathy and understanding is the way to go. And he wasn't a blistering *shmuess* kind of rabbi in any case. That was left for other people.

And so Rav Yitzchak Dovid took a different tack.

He entered the restaurant and made his way to the middle of the room, where he raised his voice, as if he were the chazzan (cantor) in a Sefardic *beit knesset*, and called out, *"Va'anachnu nevarech Kah mei'atah v'ad olam hallelukah…"*

They were the final words of *Ashrei* — the opening prayer of Minchah — and Rav Grossman recited them in an authentic Sefardic style and pronunciation. Without waiting for anyone to react, he immediately began the Kaddish that comes after *Ashrei*.

"Yitgadal v'yitkadash Shemei rabbah…"

Every person in the restaurant screamed out, "Amen!"

He continued the Kaddish. Nobody said a word. They barely breathed, unsure what their unexpected visitor was doing.

"V'yatzmach purkanei v'karev Meshichei…"

"Amen!"

He carried on, moments later belting out the words, *"Ba'agalah u'vizman kariv v'imru amen!"*

And every single person in the restaurant cried out the traditional response, *"Yehei Shemei rabbah…"*

As soon as he finished Kaddish, Rav Grossman davened *Shemoneh Esrei*, the main part of the Minchah prayer, with the others looking on, astonished. He began *chazaras ha'shatz* (the repetition of the prayer) and when it was time for *Kedushah*, the special part of the prayer where the congregation joins in, every person in the establishment rose to their feet and began saying it with him word for word.

"Kadosh, kadosh, kadosh…"

Instead of the eating, joking, and gambling that normally happened at Kima on a Friday evening, suddenly there was a minyan (a gathering of at least ten men) for Minchah — a minyan in which everyone in the restaurant took part.

After finishing the last Kaddish of Minchah, Rav Grossman took a long look at the men, who were beginning to turn their attention back to their beers and backgammon tables.

"Chevrah," he began, *"Shabbat Kodesh! Shabbat Kodesh!* — Holy Shabbos, holy Shabbos!"

Nobody spoke. The silence resounded throughout the room.

"When I walked into the restaurant, I saw many of you lifting your glasses and bottles of beer and saying the words *'Bo'i kallah, bo'i kallah.'*

"My friends, I want to ask you a question. What exactly do the words *'bo'i kallah'* mean? What does *'Lecha dodi likrat kallah'* mean? What are these words, 'Come, my beloved, to greet the bride,' with which we welcome Shabbos, referring to?

"I'll explain with the help of a short story. What do you say? Do you have time for a story?"

Everyone nodded. They would have rejected the *mussar shmuess*, but a story they were ready to hear.

"Okay, then, listen well."

There was once a newly engaged *chatan* and *kallah*, groom and bride, who each lived in a different city. One day the *chatan* called his *kallah* and said, "We haven't seen each other for a few weeks, and my family misses you. Can you hop on a train and come visit? Everyone is waiting to give you the royal treatment."

Excited at the prospect of seeing her *chatan* and his family, the *kallah* bought a ticket and settled into her seat on the train. She looked out the window and imagined how much fun they were going to have during the upcoming visit. When the train pulled into the station in her *chatan's* hometown, she alighted and made her way through the station and out onto the street, confident that her *chatan* would be waiting for her outside. To her dismay, there was nobody there.

Maybe there was a misunderstanding, and I sent him the wrong time, she thought.

She found a bus stop, waited for the bus to arrive, and then endured another long ride until eventually she reached her destination and got off the bus near her *chatan's* house.

She knocked on the door, her excitement at seeing her *chatan* returning, when suddenly she found herself being pelted with pebbles! She looked up and saw her *chatan* peeking his face out from the upstairs window, ready with another bombardment of stones. Shocked and upset, the *kallah* picked up her feet and ran as fast as she could from her *chatan's* house and the nightmare she had just experienced.

It goes without saying that she called off the wedding the moment she arrived home.

No one spoke a word when Rav Grossman concluded his parable. He looked around the crowded room, letting the silence grow before he spoke again.

"My friends, you might feel bad for the *kallah* in the story, but you are treating another *kallah* in exactly the same fashion as the *chatan* who abandoned his *kallah* at the train station! You sit here in the restaurant every Friday night drinking your beer and playing your backgammon, but at the same time you lift your mug in the air and call out '*Bo'i kallah!*' What does '*bo'i kallah*' mean? It means that when Shabbos comes, you promise to treat her with love and respect. It means that you promise to take care of her and welcome her into your homes. It most certainly does not mean that you ignore her when she arrives. Otherwise, what's the difference between you and a *chatan* who throws rocks at his bride? Aren't you doing the exact same thing?"

It was a truly passionate speech, one that emanated straight from Rav Grossman's heart. Soon the restaurant was completely empty, and from that week on, Kima was closed on Shabbos.

When he saw that he had been successful at getting the Kima restaurant to close on Shabbos, Rav Grossman began paying Friday afternoon visits to other stores and culinary establishments. For the next two years of his life, Rav Grossman didn't set foot in a shul on Friday night. Instead, he made it his business to daven every single week at a different store, restaurant, kiosk, or barber shop. Sometimes he davened in the store; sometimes he just spoke to the people or sang songs with them. Always he did his best to make a positive, friendly impression. At other times, he went to see the business owners in their homes for a more private conversation.

It took time, it was a slow process, but eventually the city of Migdal HaEmek closed down on Shabbos until you couldn't find a single business still in operation once candle lighting time had arrived. Today, if you happen to visit Migdal HaEmek and you need to fill up on gas for your car, you'll see huge signs by both of the city's gas stations that read, "This gas station keeps Shabbos and Yom Tov."

"This gas station keeps Shabbos and Yom Tov"

And it all started on a Friday night when Rav Grossman stood in the middle of a crowded restaurant, raised his voice to the heavens, and began to recite the words of *Ashrei* before explaining to the patrons the meaning of "*Bo'i kallah*" and how it applied to them and their lives.

CHAPTER SEVEN

The Prisoner's Chanukah Embrace

One evening, Rav Grossman couldn't help but notice that one of his regular attendees at the *shiur* (Torah lesson) that he gave for Migdal HaEmek's youth wasn't his normal, smiling self.

"What's wrong, Alon?"* he asked the boy.

"My brother was just sentenced to prison."

Rav Grossman wasn't surprised to hear this bit of news. For many of Midgal HaEmek's youths, and their family members, spending time in prison was very much a normal part of life.

"Where did the judge send him?"

"Shata Prison near Beit Shean."

"Tell me, Alon, when are you going to visit him?"

"Friday afternoon is the time when family is allowed to visit."

"Well, then, I am coming with you the next time you go. Your brother is my brother. We're going to see 'our' brother together."

That Friday Rav Grossman made the trip along with Alon and his family. It was the first time he had ever been inside a prison, and the experience made a profound impact on him. As he was buzzed through gate after gate, he could feel the atmosphere of tension, stress, and incredible pain all around him as if it were tangible. Everything he witnessed at the prison tore at his sensitive insides like nothing he'd ever experienced. Just seeing a space that had been designed for no more than five people being used for fifteen men was a sight he would never

Shata Prison

forget. Arabs and Jews were crowded together, as were minor offenders and hardened criminals, and his heart broke. He couldn't believe that such a thing existed in Eretz Yisrael.

Unable to rest after everything he'd witnessed during his Friday visit, Rav Grossman made an appointment to meet with the prison warden, a man by the name of Moshe Koppelman.

Koppelman's office was situated in a quieter section of the prison, with walls that were thick enough to keep the sounds of a crowded prison at bay. An assistant showed him to the office, and he took a seat at the warden's desk. He stared at pictures of Israeli politicians hanging on the whitewashed walls, along with an array of plaques and awards. Eventually Koppelman entered the room and sat down across from his distinguished visitor.

The warden's expression was plainly curious. He was clearly wondering what such a religious rabbi could possibly want from him. Rav Grossman didn't beat around the bush.

"I would like to come and visit the prisoners twice a week," he said without preamble. "I'm interested in creating a learning program for them."

"Rabbi," Koppelman said, "I have to be honest with you. If you're doing this because you want to get paid, there's no room in the budget to pay you."

"That's all right," Rav Grossman said mildly. "I'm not doing this for money."

"In that case," the warden said, "you can come to my prison whenever you want and spend as much time learning with the prisoners as you want. I have nothing for the prisoners to do, and they suffer because of it. Most of the day they just end up sitting around, watching television, and getting into fights from sheer boredom. I have a feeling that your being around here will only help them."

That turned out to be an understatement.

There's a famous saying: If you want something done, give it to a busy man. Rav Grossman was already running a kollel in the morning, administering a program with hundreds of children in the afternoon, and spending his evenings providing counseling to the neighborhood teens. Now, somehow, he found the time to begin traveling to the prison in Beit Shean, where he immediately started giving the inmates a Torah class on *Pirkei Avos* (*Ethics of our Fathers,* a famous Torah work). The warden provided space in one of the dining rooms and spread the word that the very charismatic Rav Yitzchak Dovid Grossman of Migdal HaEmek had graciously elected to take time out of his very busy schedule to give a biweekly *shiur* at their prison.

In a prison "yeshivah"

At the first *shiur*, about ten prisoners gathered around the rabbi and listened as he shared lessons from *Pirkei Avos* and inspirational stories from his own fascinating life. As time went on, and the prisoners told their friends how enjoyable the *shiurim* were, more prisoners began attending the classes.

Change was almost inevitable for the prisoners who joined the *shiurim*. Suddenly they no longer felt comfortable in their cells with the televisions blaring for most of the day. Shabbos became an issue, because they wanted to keep it and the other prisoners didn't. Slowly but surely, a tightly knit group of like-minded prisoners formed and began requesting that the warden house them in their own wing, where they would be able to learn and daven without disturbing anyone and without being disturbed. Here the televisions would be turned off on Shabbos, there would be minyanim three times a day, and additional Torah classes would be available. Of course, they needed special permission from the Israeli prison authority, but the prisoners insisted on being accorded their rights, and eventually their request was granted.

All this led to the establishment of the prison yeshivos — or, as they are better known, "*midrashot*." In these prison "neighborhoods," everyone keeps Shabbos, and the food that is served comes from outside caterers with the most stringent rabbinical supervision. It may be hard

Cabinet Minister Dr. Yosef Burg and Rav Grossman at the opening of another prison "yeshivah"

for some to believe, but in those sections of the prisons, the atmosphere is one of *ruchniyus,* of spiritual growth.

One of the first people to join Rav Yitzchak Dovid in his prison venture was a Yid from Bnei Brak by the name of Rav Chaim Golombek. He would travel to the prison on Sunday and remain there the entire week, only returning home to his family on Thursday. He was assigned a room in the prison and remained there throughout the week, leading by example.

"It's not enough for me to learn with them," he explained. "I actually have to live with them if I want to inspire real change."

Rav Chaim would remain with his group of prisoners through the years. He learned and lived with them in prison, moved with them to a halfway house years later, and taught them in kollel when they completed their sentences. And he's still learning with this group to this day.

What he had accomplished at the prisons was truly amazing, but Rav Grossman, never one to sit on his laurels, had already begun thinking about the next step. Sure, the prisoners had access to Torah classes behind bars, and they were able to keep Shabbos and kashrus now, but what happened afterward, once the prisoners were released? Rav Grossman had built a strong support system for the prisoners inside the prison, but they would need one when their prison term was over as well. And so he made an appointment to meet with the minister of police, a man by the name of Chaim Bar Lev.

"Before you tell me why you're here," Bar Lev said to Rav Grossman, "I want to thank you for the incredible work you've been doing with the prisoners."

"You're very welcome. And that's exactly why I'm here."

"I'm listening."

"Here's the thing. We have people coming to the prisons. They teach the prisoners Torah, they reach their *neshamos,* and they are literally changing their lives. That's all great. The problem starts when the prisoners are released from prison."

Rav Grossman paused for a moment to let this sink in.

"Let me ask you a question," he said to Bar Lev. "Who do you think is the welcoming committee that is waiting to greet a prisoner when he is released from prison? Who arranges the *'chafla,'* the gigantic party that is traditionally thrown for someone who did his time? I'll tell you who. The same 'friends' who got him sent to prison in the first place. It's inevitable that the prisoners will fall right back into their earlier habits."

Bar Lev nodded. So far Rav Grossman wasn't telling him anything he didn't already know. "So what do you propose?" he asked.

"I need to be able to create a new *chevrah*, a new society, for them. Now there's a neighborhood in Afula called Givat HaMoreh. It's a quiet, residential neighborhood, and I think it would be the perfect place for the program I want to start. Ten months before a prisoner concludes his sentence, he will be brought to a building in Givat HaMoreh, where he will live until he serves out his time. He will, of course, be under scrutiny at all times, yet he will be surrounded by religious people who will help him make the transition to civilian life in a healthy and productive way that will actually last."

"Who will be these religious people that will serve as the prisoner's friends in Afula?"

"They will be families whom we will carefully select to live in the building. The ex-convicts will spend time with those people. They will learn with them. It will be both an education and an initiation back into normal life. The wives in the building will become friends with the prisoners' wives and teach them about the new way of life their husbands

Rav Grossman with "his" prisoners

discovered while in prison. Then, when their sentence is up, and it's time for them to be released, they will already be out in the regular world, with friends and a social circle, and they won't have any need for the old *chevrah.*"

Bar Lev liked the idea and the program was implemented, with the building in question having the same legal status as a regular prison while in reality serving as a sort of halfway house to ease the prisoners back into a healthy life.

"Who will be the warden in your program?" Bar Lev asked.

"I will be the warden," Rav Grossman replied with a smile and a twinkle in his eye.

And so it was. Rav Grossman was officially appointed warden, with the proper documentation by the Israel Prison Service, in the new "prison" in Givat HaMoreh.

When Chanukah arrived that first year that Rav Grossman began visiting the prison, he decided to make a party for the inmates in his prison yeshivah. He arranged for a band to come to the prison, latkes and sufganiyot were served, speeches were made, songs were sung, and overall it was an uplifting experience for everyone there. When it was over, Rav Grossman bid everyone goodbye, and then, without thinking too much about it, spontaneously gave one of the inmates an affectionate hug, radiating his special brand of warmth, which couldn't help but make its way into the prisoner's heart. The party officially over, Rav Grossman left the prison and was driven home.

The letter appeared in his mailbox a few days later. The rabbi opened it curiously. This is what it said:

> Dear Rav Grossman,
>
> I'm the prisoner whom you hugged just before leaving the Chanukah party at the prison. I am now sitting in my cell, crying and writing you this letter. I want you to know that tonight was the first time in my life that someone gave me a hug or put their arms around me just because they wanted to show me how much they cared.

He signed his name at the bottom of the page.

When Rav Grossman read those words, he was completely and utterly taken aback. Could it be possible that a grown man in his forties had never been given a hug or kiss by anyone in his life? Not even by a parent, grandparent, or a relative of any kind? For the first time in his life, he truly grasped how a person could fall in with the wrong crowd and end up running afoul of the law. It was clear to him that much of the crime being committed stemmed from the fact that so many people were being raised in environments where nobody cared about them and where they received no love.

At that moment, a light went on in his head, and Rav Yitzchak Dovid promised himself that he was going to establish a home for children like these — children who had never been hugged or kissed, who had grown up in troubled homes and needed a place to grow up surrounded by care and compassion.

I'll provide these kids with a home, and it will be the type of place where they will receive an abundance of love.

It all came flashing through his mind from one second to the next.

He could have ignored the idea. He could have reassured himself that there were plenty of state-run institutions already, not to mention foster homes and adoption agencies. But he knew that these places weren't the answer. The institution that he was going to establish would be as different from everything that already existed as night from day.

He was no longer just thinking about a school.

The vision had expanded.

Schools were important and vital, but suddenly he understood that he wanted to develop something that was much more than just a school. Suddenly he knew that he wanted to establish a home that would also include a school, and a school that would also be a real home.

All this passed through his mind as he read the brief note sent to him by the prisoner whom he'd embraced and kissed without even thinking about it. At that moment, Rav Yitzchak Dovid Grossman made the decision to establish an institution for children from troubled homes in the city of Migdal HaEmek. He had no idea how he was going to do it or where he would get the funding. But he had been taught by his parents and teachers that a Yid didn't need to have the entire plan ready to take action. It was enough to have a kernel of an idea, to do one's utmost to make things work, and then move aside and allow the Ribbono shel Olam, the Master of the World, to take over.

CHAPTER EIGHT

Opposition

While his mind was filled with ideas for all the programs he wanted to implement, Rav Grossman barely had the funds he needed to run the programming already in existence.

Itche Duvid, he said to himself, *here you are building castles in the sky, and you don't even have sufficient funds to manage what you already have!*

So the rabbi, still in his early twenties, threw himself into the activities he was already involved with, including the regular classes he delivered at the main Ashkenazic shul in Migdal HaEmek — Beit Knesset Yotzei Europa.

These were the people who had welcomed him with open arms when he entered their lives out of the blue, and these were the people who had graciously offered him the use of their building for his kollel when he had requested it. They were his people. He loved them and they loved him back. He gave a *shiur* every evening between Minchah and Maariv and delivered speeches on Shabbos as well, and the members of the shul connected with him heart and soul — largely due to the fact that he was able to address them in Yiddish, the language of their youth. They loved his stories, his *vertlach* (Torah thoughts), his manner of speaking, and the aura he had brought with him from Meah Shearim. It wasn't long before he had become their Rebbe.

Rebbe of the town's Holocaust survivors, and Disco Rabbi for the local youth.

Somehow nobody saw it as a contradiction.

By the time 1969 rolled around, Rav Yitzchak Dovid Grossman

had been living in Migdal HaEmek for a year, and the local population began floating the idea of his being appointed to the position of Ashkenazic chief rabbi of the city, a post that had long been left unfilled. Though in retrospect this seems like the obvious choice, back then it was anything but clear-cut.

The mayor of Migdal HaEmek was a powerful politician by the name of Tzvi Eldorati, who served the city for eighteen years. Eldorati was extremely well connected within the ruling Mapai party (which ran Migdal HaEmek) and would subsequently be bureau director of Prime Minister Rabin's office. When Rav Grossman arrived in the town, the mayor was the undisputed political boss of Migdal HaEmek and ruled his territory with an iron fist. Nothing happened without Eldorati's consent.

In the beginning, Eldorati made no secret of his dislike of the newcomer, fearing that Rav Grossman had been sent to Migdal HaEmek by Agudas Yisrael with the mission of generating support for the Ultra-Orthodox party among the local population. Of course, nothing could have been further from the truth. In his wildest dreams, Eldorati never imagined that a man like Rav Grossman would be willing to leave behind everything that was familiar and move to a wilderness like Migdal HaEmek for the sole purpose of trying to build Judaism in a place where it was so lacking. Consequently, Eldorati was extremely suspicious of the motivations of the rabbi from Yerushalayim, and he therefore went out of his way to create obstacles for Rav Grossman everywhere he turned. The fact is, the mayor was doing his best to make life miserable for the rabbi, but Rav Grossman ignored it all, hoping that the mayor would come to recognize that he wasn't a threat and leave him alone.

One day Rav Grossman took a local boy with him to a yeshivah in Yerushalayim, which meant that he was away from home when his landlord came knocking on the door. The owner of the apartment worked in the city municipality and had been given the message that he had done something very wrong by renting an apartment to the interloper from Yerushalayim. The landlord was informed that if he wanted to keep his job at the municipality, he had to evict the Grossmans from their home.

When Rebbetzin Grossman heard the knock on the door, she never dreamed that her entire world was about to be turned upside down. She answered the door and said hello to the landlord, who ignored her greeting. Getting straight to the point, he informed his tenant that the Grossman family would have to move out of the apartment by the next morning.

Rebbetzin Grossman protested that this was impossible. Her husband was not home and would only return in a few days.

"I don't care," the landlord replied, too focused on what might happen to his own future to have the mental energy to worry about someone else. "Just make sure that you and all your belongings are out of my apartment by tomorrow morning, or I'll evict you and your possessions myself!"

Back in the late sixties, no one had cell phones, and many people didn't even have phones in their homes, which meant that Rebbetzin Grossman was unable to contact her husband to inform him that they had just been evicted for no apparent reason. With no recourse, she went to the kollel the next morning, where she told the members that the Grossman family was being thrown out and that she needed their help. In no time at all, someone had hired a horse and wagon (that's the kind of place Migdal HaEmek was), and the kollel members moved the few pieces of furniture the Grossman family owned, along with their meager belongings, out of the apartment and onto the wagon, which was then driven to the shul, where everything was unloaded into the women's section.

Rav Grossman returned to Migdal HaEmek the day after the move. He stood in front of his door, turned his key, and found that it didn't work. Perplexed, he began knocking on the door, but nobody answered. Finally, a neighbor emerged from his own apartment and broke the news.

"You don't live here anymore."

Taken aback, Rav Grossman replied, "What do you mean, I don't live here anymore? If I don't live here, where do I live?"

"I don't know where you live. All I know is that it's not here."

"But where is my wife?"

"She left here yesterday."

Seeing that he wasn't getting anywhere with this line of questioning, Rav Grossman headed to the kollel to try to figure out his next move. The moment he walked through the door, he was bombarded by the kollel members, who told him the story and explained that he was now living temporarily in the women's section of the shul. Of course, the Grossmans didn't remain there long: they moved into another apartment the following day. But the trauma of what they had been forced to endure was a memory that would remain with them for a long time. Besides, there was no telling what Eldorati would do next. Rav Grossman decided that he had no choice but to make a move of his own.

Yisrael Kenig was the head of all the municipalities — sort of like a governor — in the northern part of the country. Since the budgets for all the local municipalities went through his office, he was easily the most powerful politician in the North. Rav Grossman had gone to pay his respects at Kenig's office in the Nazareth branch of the Ministry of the Interior soon after his arrival in Migdal HaEmek. Kenig, a religious Jew, was expecting him, since the funds Talat was providing the kollel were being funneled through the Ministry of the Interior. The two of them hit it off right away, and they became very close.

After moving all their belongings into another apartment and making sure that the rebbetzin was taken care of and had calmed down from the trauma of being thrown out of her home, Rav Grossman boarded

Friends, despite a rocky beginning: Tzvi Eldorati and R' Grossman in his succah

a bus to Nazareth, where he presented himself at the office of Yisrael Kenig and described all the unfortunate incidents that had been happening to them, culminating in their forced eviction while he was away in Yerushalayim.

"Clearly, important things are happening here," he told Kenig, "since the *yetzer hara,* the evil inclination, is doing his best to derail us. But I would very much appreciate it if you took the time to have a word with Tzvi Eldorati and ask him to please leave us alone."

Kenig gave Eldorati a call. During the course of the conversation, he made it clear that Rav Grossman was his man and that he would appreciate it very much if Eldorati would look after him. Since Kenig controlled Migdal HaEmek's budget, Eldorati needed him and couldn't afford to ignore his call. After that, the situation improved.

Rav Grossman would eventually learn why Tzvi Eldorati had been treating him with such antagonism. After that, it was only a matter of explaining to the former mayor that politics had played no part at all in his decision to move into the town. On the contrary, he explained, he had nothing to do with politics and never had. And as was his way with everyone he met, Rav Grossman didn't just make peace with the town's boss — the two of them went on to become extremely close friends.

CHAPTER NINE
The Youngest Chief Rabbi

Since the members of Beit Knesset Yotzei Europa were all in favor of Rav Yitzchak Dovid being appointed chief rabbi of the town, they arranged a meeting with Tzvi Eldorati to promote the appointment. The delegates were shown into his office and offered seats. After a few minutes of pleasant conversation, the committee spokesman took the floor.

"Mr. Eldorati," he began, "the members of the Ashkenazic community feel that it's high time for Migdal HaEmek to have an official chief rabbi just like every other city in the country."

Eldorati couldn't object to their request, but he told the committee he would have to check the budget to make sure there were sufficient funds to pay the rav's salary.

"Once the issue of the budget is settled," he told the committee, "the next step is to hold an election for the position."

"Why do we need to hold an election?" one of the delegates asked. "Rav Grossman is already living in Migdal HaEmek, and we want him to be appointed rav of the city. He moved here when nobody else wanted to come, and he has never stopped investing everything he has in the people's well-being. If anyone should be the rav, it's him."

"I hear what you're saying," Eldorati replied, "but legally I have no choice but to open the position to the public."

Within a short time, the city municipality, in conjunction with the Ministry of the Interior, made it known that they were seeking to fill the position of Ashkenazic chief rabbi of Migdal HaEmek, and the names of all interested candidates should be submitted. The first thing a candidate needed in order to even apply for the position was to receive the backing of both chief rabbis of Israel, Rav Isser Yehuda Unterman and Rav Yitzchak Nissim, which came in the form of a letter. The candidates who received the necessary backing would then be brought before a committee composed of members of the Municipality, the *gabbaim* (assistants) of the different shuls in the city, and representatives of the Ministry of the Interior. The committee would make the final decision, even though the local citizens had already made their feelings clear. The law was the law, and there was no choice but to go through the official proceedings.

There was no question that Rav Grossman was facing an uphill battle for the position for which he was by far the most qualified by virtue of everything he'd already done for the city.

All, however, wasn't lost.

Rav Grossman's father, Rav Yisrael, stepped into the picture. Knowing that his son had invested his entire heart and soul into the city he now called home, Rav Yisrael decided to pay a visit to his very close friend, Rav Chaim Stuchiner — or, as he was more famously known, Rav Chaim Shmuelevitz, the rosh yeshivah (dean) of the Mir Yeshivah in Yerushalayim. Once closeted with his close friend, Rav Yisrael told him the story and how he felt that his son was the best candidate for the position, having proved his dedication to the role every single day since first moving to the city.

"Yitzchak Dovid has made great contributions to Migdal HaEmek from day one. He gives *shiurim* in the shuls and opened a kollel in the city. He arranged for hundreds of children to learn Torah every day and spends much of his time with the teenagers, who consider his home their own. There's no question that the city will only benefit from his being appointed chief rabbi."

Rav Chaim Shmuelevitz had known Rav Grossman since he had been a young boy. He was more than familiar with his unusual talents and abilities. There was no question in his mind that his friend's son was the right person for the job, and he went into proactive mode. Together with Rav Yosef Shalom Elyashiv, Rav Betzalel Zolty, and Rav Leizer Goldschmidt, Rav Chaim Shmuelevitz paid a surprise visit to the

The young Rav Grossman often asked advice from Rav Elyashiv

home of Yehuda Gur, the man in charge of making the final decision of who would become the Ashkenazic chief rabbi of Migdal HaEmek. They didn't call before they came. They just showed up on his doorstep unannounced and knocked.

The man himself answered the door and, to his immense surprise, found himself face-to-face with the legendary Mir rosh yeshivah, Rav Chaim Shmuelevitz, and another three of the greatest rabbinical figures of the day. He stared at them in wonder and tried making sense of the unexpected sight: four Torah leaders standing on his doorstep.

He ushered them inside, and after they had all taken seats around the table, the host waited to hear the reason for the visit.

"We have come here," Rav Chaim said, "to ask you to support the candidacy of Rav Yitzchak Dovid Grossman for chief rabbi of Migdal HaEmek. You can ask anyone who knows anything that goes on in that place, and they will tell you that he has already achieved unprecedented advances in the relatively short time he has been in the city. It has been nothing less than a revolution! People are learning Torah, children are being kept off the streets, and teenagers are spending their evenings in the house of a rabbi.

"The truth of the matter is," Rav Chaim continued, "he is already filling the position. Over the past year, the people of the city have come to rely on Rav Grossman for anything related to religious life. He has spoken at every bar mitzvah, officiated at every wedding, and given the eulogy at every funeral. He's made the rounds and given a well-received speech at every shul, and he is known and, more importantly, loved by the people of the city. And it's not just about religion. The people know they can talk to him about any problem, and he will do anything he can to help.

"This is why we have come here to personally request that you do everything in your power to appoint Rav Yitzchak Dovid Grossman rav of Migdal HaEmek."

So it came to be that Rav Yitzchak Dovid Grossman was unanimously elected to the post of chief rabbi of Migdal HaEmek on the fourth of Sivan 1969. He was twenty-three years old, making him the youngest municipal rabbi in the State of Israel.

The main ceremony took place in the Beit Knesset L'Yotzei Europa and was attended by the chief Ashkenazic Chief Rabbi of Israel, Rav Isser Yehuda Unterman, and by Jerusalem's Chief Rabbi, Rav Betzalel Zolty.

It was the week when the Torah portion of *Parashas Nasso* was read, and Rav Betzalel Zolty addressed the gathering from the podium:

At the installation ceremony (l to r): Rav Unterman, Ashkenazic Chief Rabbi of Israel, Rav Yitzchak Dovid Grossman, Mayor Eldorati, Chacham Meir Yonah (Rav Grossman spent his first night in Migdal HaEmek in his home), Deputy Mayor Meir Avrohom, Rav Yisrael Grossman

"The Torah tells us that leaders of the shevatim (tribes) donated six covered wagons and twelve oxen. Moshe gave two of the wagons and four of the oxen to the sons of Gershon, 'in accordance with their work' — that is, to transport parts of the holy Mishkan (Tabernacle). In the next *pasuk*, the next verse, we learn that Moshe gave the other four wagons and eight oxen to the sons of Merari 'in accordance with their work,' under the direction of Isamar, the son of Aharon HaKohen. Now look at the next *pasuk*. Here there is a change: To the sons of Kehas he did not give wagons, but rather, '*bakaseif yisa'u*' — they were instructed to carry the objects they were assigned to transport on their shoulders.

"Why didn't the sons of Kehas receive any wagons?" Rav Zolty asked the assembled. "The reason is given in the *pasuk*: 'For the service involving the holy objects was incumbent upon them.'

"Who are the children of Kehas?" Rav Zolty asked rhetorically. "These are the rabbanim, the rabbis of Klal Yisrael, the Jewish nation. And while others are given wagons to help make their lives easier, where the rabbanim are concerned, '*bakaseif yisa'u*' — they have to use their shoulders.

"The Torah is coming to teach Klal Yisrael for all time that the job of a rav is not an easy one. There are no wagons and no wheels to lighten their load. On the contrary, the rav's life is filled with the demands of the job and his responsibility to his people."

It was a lesson that Rav Grossman never forgot.

There was another ceremony as well, this one in a wedding hall called Beit Gil. Here, Rav Grossman's teenage "tzaddikim" were given the opportunity to celebrate the appointment of "their" rabbi. Kobi, former crime boss, especially wanted to show the people how happy he was with the choice and went out of his way to arrange for a white Mustang convertible to be brought into town for the sole purpose of transporting Rav Grossman to Beit Gil for the main event. When Rav Grossman emerged from his shul together with Rav Meir Yonah and Chief Rabbi Unterman, they were directed to the Mustang, which drove slowly down the street while hundreds of the "tzaddikim" of Migdal HaEmek surrounded the car, singing and dancing wildly to show their joy at the appointment of the new rabbi.

For Rav Grossman, seeing Kobi so involved in the celebrations was a special cause for joy, because it meant that he had truly left his old

The new chief rabbi of Migdal HaEmek and his boisterous escort, in the Mustang

ways behind and was looking forward to a life within the framework of Torah guidance. Every time he looked at Kobi standing in the street, face shining with joy, the young rabbi couldn't help but recall that first visit to Kobi's home and the deal they had struck. And now here he was, the same man but completely different.

The Chief Rabbi of Israel and the new Chief Rabbi of Migdal HaEmek, in the white Mustang

It was a miracle. Kobi, the kids from the disco, the children he taught, the prisoners he had visited — it was all a miracle. When he thought about it, he couldn't believe that this had actually become his life.

Outside in the street, as they escorted their "rebbi" to the wedding hall, the atmosphere was very different from inside the shul. Here the crowd was young, exuberant, and extremely enthusiastic. Yet while the two parties were as different as night and day, they were in many ways incredibly similar.

Celebrating in different ways perhaps, but filled with joy for one and the same reason:

Rav Yitzchak Dovid Grossman, their rabbi from the first moment he had entered their lives, had been officially appointed to the role of chief rabbi. And both groups went out of their way to show him how they felt because they loved him with all their hearts and wished him all the success in the world.

Rav Yitzchak Dovid went on to receive lifetime tenure for the position — a position he still holds to this very day, over fifty years later.

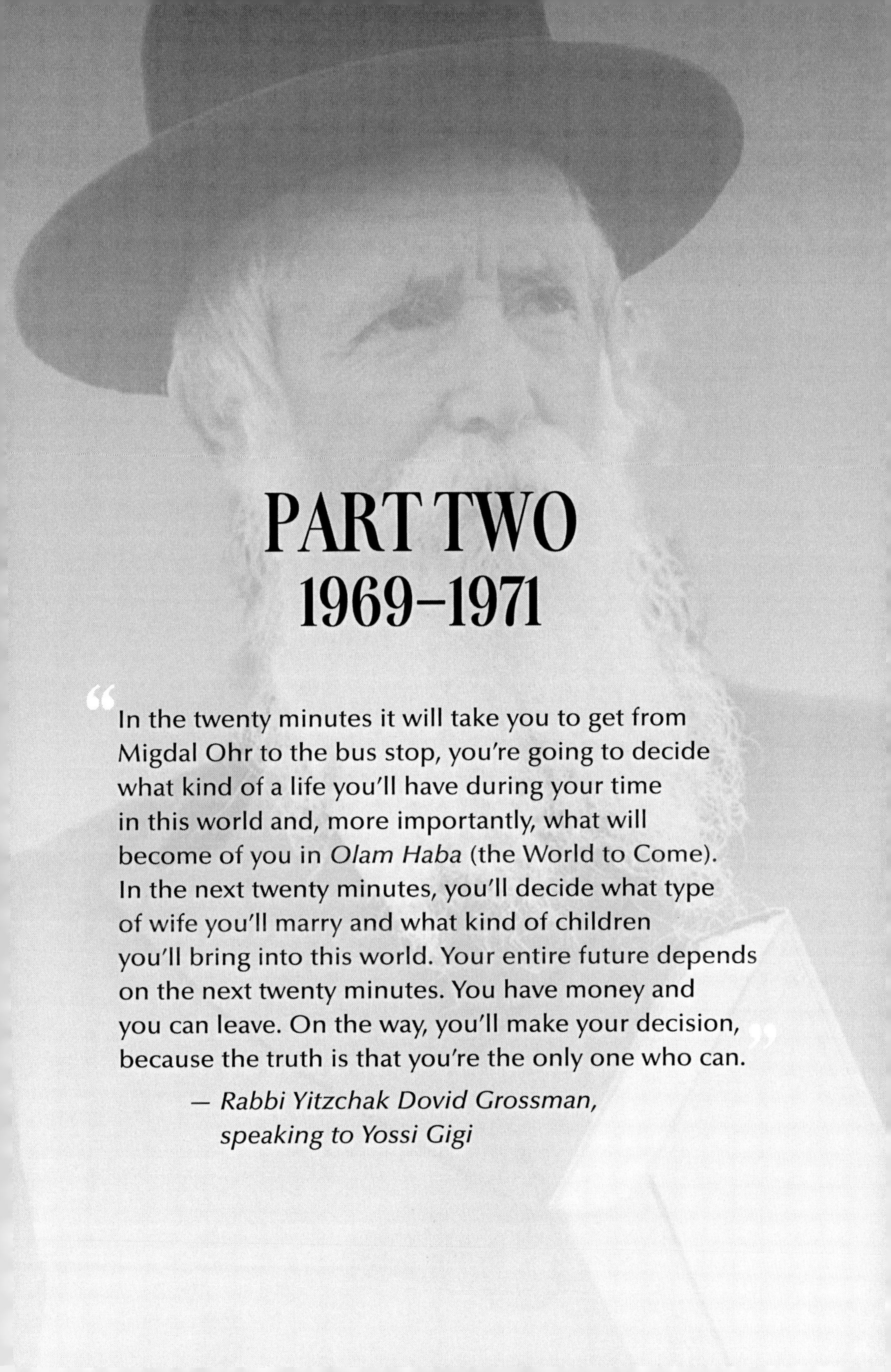

PART TWO
1969–1971

"In the twenty minutes it will take you to get from Migdal Ohr to the bus stop, you're going to decide what kind of a life you'll have during your time in this world and, more importantly, what will become of you in *Olam Haba* (the World to Come). In the next twenty minutes, you'll decide what type of wife you'll marry and what kind of children you'll bring into this world. Your entire future depends on the next twenty minutes. You have money and you can leave. On the way, you'll make your decision, because the truth is that you're the only one who can."

— *Rabbi Yitzchak Dovid Grossman, speaking to Yossi Gigi*

CHAPTER TEN
The Ribnitzer's Motza'ei Shabbos Purchase

The new chief rabbi might have been incredibly busy, but the Disco Rabbi hadn't forgotten the teenagers who frequented the local hangouts. He had the kollel, his afternoon and evening programs for children, and then, come nighttime, he was off to the disco to see the kids whom he called his "tzaddikim."

One would have thought that the owner of the local disco didn't appreciate a rabbi with a long beard showing up as a frequent guest in

With the "tzaddikim"

his establishment, but that wasn't the case. Rav Grossman had his regular corner in the disco, and the local youth would congregate around him night after night, a close relationship developing between them despite the disparity between their appearances and their life goals.

It didn't take long for the local press to begin writing articles about the rabbi from Meah Shearim who had moved to the spiritual wasteland that was Migdal HaEmek. Suddenly people were reading about a rabbi with a beard and *peyos* who was a fixture at the local disco and who was quietly and steadfastly going about the business of saving young people from a lifetime of crime and replacing their former behavior with greater ambitions.

One day the phone rang in the Grossman home, and the man on the other end introduced himself and explained that he was a reporter for Channel One of Israeli TV.

"What can I do for you?"

"I'll tell you. One of my researchers happened to come across a very fascinating article about the 'Disco Rabbi' in a local newspaper from the northern part of the country. The article whet our appetite, and we began looking into the story a little more deeply, only to realize that this isn't just another story — the story of a chassidic Jew who moved across the country to become the Disco Rabbi and was then appointed chief rabbi of Migdal HaEmek. People should know about what you are doing for the youth and how you are changing the city, person by person."

Rav Grossman always asked a *shailah* (halachic query) before embarking on anything new, and this time was no different. He consulted with his father and his Rebbe, who told him that it would create a major *kiddush Hashem,* a sanctification of G-d's Name. And so Rav Yitzchak Dovid Grossman agreed to be the subject of a documentary for Israeli TV called *The Disco Rabbi*. It was filmed by a non-religious director by the name of Michael Lev Tov, who had never been in the home of a religious Jew before meeting Rav Yitzchak Dovid Grossman.

The groundbreaking documentary succeeded in opening the eyes of Israeli society in a way that touched hearts and brought tears to the viewer's eyes. It showed the viewers a day in the young rabbi's life, following along with him as he went about his activities and showcasing the many areas in which he was involved.

The film opened with Rav Yitzchak Dovid waking up his daughter, who was two years old at the time, washing her hands with *neigel vasser* (the ritual hand washing done first thing in the morning), then having her sing the words of *Modeh Ani* (prayer said upon waking) along with her father. After dropping his daughter off at her preschool, the camera followed Rav Grossman into the local shul and showed him donning his tallis and tefillin with reverence and awe as he prepared to pray to the Ribbono shel Olam.

This was followed by a routine visit at a local poultry processing plant, which was under his kashrus supervision, and then on to the kollel where he sat and learned with the *yungeleit*. Morning over, he was seen teaching and schmoozing with the youth of Migdal HaEmek — singing, encouraging, laughing, giving this one a pat on the cheek and that one a compliment that lit up the boy's eyes and straightened the set of his shoulders. The next scene showed the rabbi marrying a couple under the *chuppah* and then accompanied him into the disco, where he sat and talked with his tzaddikim for another few hours.

The documentary ended as it had begun, with the rabbi sitting with his little girl, telling her a story about Moshe Rabbeinu while putting her to bed for the night.

"Moshe Rabbeinu was just a baby of three months old when his mother placed him in a basket and the basket was sent off to sail on the Nile River."

When he saw his daughter's eyes growing heavier, Rav Grossman said, "Okay, Chaya'le sweetheart, we'll continue the story tomorrow. Now it's time to say *Krias Shema*."

Then, together, the two of them recited the timeless words of the age-old credo that has united Klal Yisrael with HaKadosh Baruch Hu since their inception as a nation.

"*Shema,*" Rav Grossman chanted.

Chaya'le repeated the word.

"*Yisrael.*"

Chaya'le repeated the word. And so it went with the rest of the Shema.

The sight of a young father — he was only twenty-four years old at the time — reciting the prayer of Shema with his two-year-old daughter made a deep impression on the entire country.

After the documentary aired, Rav Grossman couldn't go anywhere without people commenting about the spiritual revolution that watching the clip had created in their own lives. Many times he'd be traveling on an El Al flight, and the stewardesses would approach him, shyly confessing that after having watched the documentary, and especially the part with him saying Shema with his daughter, they made sure to recite the Shema before going to sleep, wherever they were in the world.

Rav Grossman's visits to the disco eventually drew to a close. The rabbi didn't have to go and visit his tzaddikim in the disco because they began frequenting his apartment instead. Guests visiting the Grossman home in Migdal HaEmek would find themselves staring openmouthed at the pony-tailed boys and nonreligious girls who had fallen into the habit of concluding every day with a visit to the expats from Meah Shearim.

"I didn't have to go to the disco anymore," Rav Grossman would say with a twinkle in his eye. "You see, the disco had come to me."

A particularly large crowd would gather at the Grossman home every Friday night and Motza'ei Shabbos (Saturday night), and they threw a huge party on Rosh Chodesh, the first day of the Hebrew month. Everyone knew that if you wanted to have a good time, you went to the rabbi's house.

In 1970, Rav Chaim Zanvil Abramowitz, known far and wide as the Ribnitzer Rebbe, left the Soviet Union and moved to Eretz Yisrael, settling in Yerushalayim. It didn't take long for people to begin talking about the phenomenal tzaddik, and they started clamoring to see him.

One Friday, Rav Grossman received a call from someone who was close to the Rebbe, informing him that the Rebbe of Ribnitz wanted to spend the coming Shabbos in Migdal HaEmek. Naturally, Rav Grossman was honored.

The person on the phone warned that the Rebbe didn't want any fanfare and Rav Grossman shouldn't spread the word about the Rebbe's impending visit. It was supposed to be a quiet Shabbos, without *tischen* (special gatherings for followers of Chassidic rabbis) and without huge posters announcing that the tzaddik was coming to the city.

"One more thing," said the Rebbe's representative. "I need you to assign ten *bachurim* (young men) to serve as his minyan, and they should remain available and at his side throughout the entire Shabbos, ready to daven whenever he says it's time to daven."

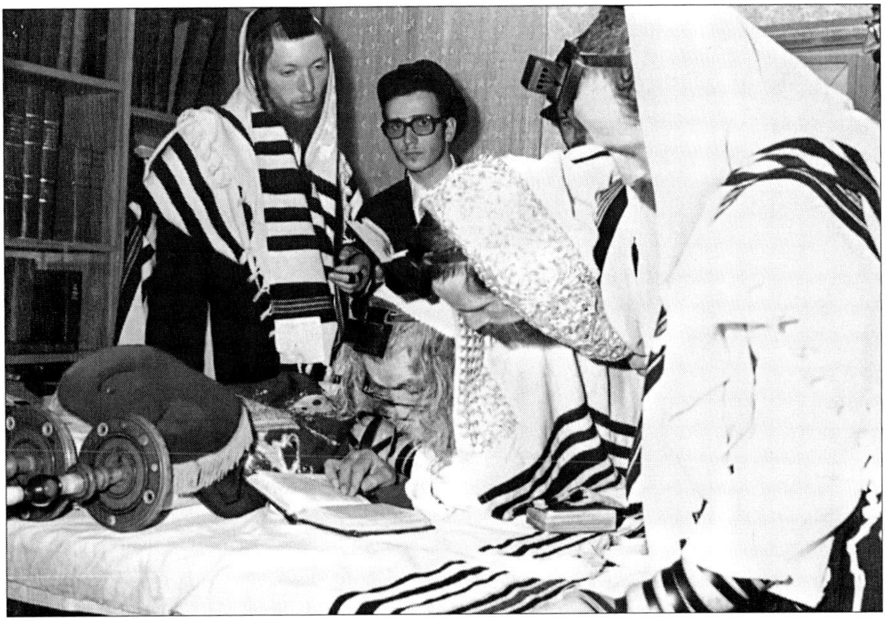

The Ribnitzer Rebbe

Of course Rav Grossman agreed to all the conditions, overjoyed that such a tzaddik would be gracing his home even for a short period of time.

The Rebbe arrived in Migdal HaEmek on Erev Shabbos, and after meeting Rav Grossman and being shown to his quarters, he closeted himself inside the room and proceeded to get ready for Shabbos. There was a *mikveh* in the house, and the Ribnitzer immersed himself several times in honor of the approaching holy day. Afterward, the *bachurim* who had been lucky enough to be chosen for the task made a minyan for Minchah. After Minchah it was soon time for Maariv, but the Ribnitzer Rebbe had retreated into his room and didn't emerge. The hands on the clock ticked away, marking the passing time, but there was no sign of the Rebbe.

When Rav Grossman peeked into the room, he saw the Rebbe standing, wrapped in his tallis. He stood unmoving for the next eight hours, only emerging at one in the morning to daven Maariv. After davening, the Rebbe began the *seudah*, the festive evening meal, only came to an end at three-thirty in the morning.

Lest you think that after his busy day the Rebbe would catch up on a little sleep, you would be wrong. He was up and getting ready to daven Shacharis at seven o'clock the next morning. The davening concluded at four in the afternoon. The third meal of the day understandably began late and continued deep into the night, after Shabbos was already long over for the rest of the country.

Motza'ei Shabbos was one of the nights when Rav Grossman's tzaddikim from the disco made a point of visiting him at his home. They would sing, schmooze, debate, and eat until the wee hours of the morning. That night the tzaddikim arrived when the Rebbe was still celebrating the final hours of Shabbos.

One of the boys who came to the house that night went by the name Uzi. Uzi had grown up in a home along with siblings who had all gone off the *derech* (ceased living a religious life), a reality that was unfortunately all too common in the homes of many immigrants with Sefardic backgrounds. Upon their arrival in Eretz Yisrael, countless parents watched in horror as their children succumbed to the lure of modern Israeli life. Such was the case in Uzi's home, where his father, a pious and observant Jew, was forced to look on as his children left the fold, one after the other.

Uzi himself had a huge *neshamah*, but it was somewhat obscured by his hair, which descended all the way down his back and slightly past his waist. It was thick, lush, and wavy, and he had left it untouched from the age of fifteen when he first made the decision to allow it to grow untamed, *nazir*-style. (A *nazir* is a person who makes a vow to G-d that he will not cut his hair for an extended period of time.)

That Motza'ei Shabbos, Uzi found an empty chair at the end of the table, across from the Rebbe who sat at the head with Rav Grossman sitting beside him. Rav Grossman told the Ribnitzer a little about the boy's background. He explained that the young man suffered from epilepsy and would collapse to the ground from seizures on a regular basis.

"*Avadeh falt ehr!* — Of course he's falling! *Ehr vet arupnemen der masa fun der kup vet ehr nisht fallen* — When he takes off the heavy burden from his head, he won't fall anymore..."

A few minutes later the Ribnitzer turned to Rav Grossman and asked, "How much would it cost me to buy his hair?"

In an instant, Rav Grossman recognized that a great opportunity had come their way. Uzi, though a young man, had been suffering from epilepsy for years. People who are afflicted with epilepsy never know when the next seizure is going to come, and their friends and family members have to be prepared to make sure that they don't bite their tongue in the middle of an episode. At the time of this story, Uzi was taking multiple pills on a daily basis — and still suffering from the illness. With the Ribnitzer's offer on the table, Rav Grossman rose from his place beside the Rebbe and circled around the table to take a seat beside Uzi.

"Uzi, I want you to listen to me," he said to the teenager. "The Ribnitzer Rebbe wants to purchase your hair. This is the opportunity of a lifetime! I want to tell the Rebbe that you are willing to sell him your hair, and that the price is a *refuah sheleimah* — a complete recovery."

Uzi grasped from the seriousness of his rabbi's tone just what an incredible offer this was. "If he can promise that I will recover completely from the epilepsy," he said, "I'll sell him my hair."

Rav Grossman returned to the head of the table and sat down beside the Rebbe, where he relayed Uzi's price for the purchase of his hair.

"If he takes the weight off his head and starts keeping Shabbos, he'll have a complete recovery," the Rebbe promised.

Uzi accepted the Rebbe's offer. The Rebbe made Havdalah, the

The Ribnitzer Rebbe at a *hachnassas Sefer Torah*

Uzi, before his "*upsherin*" (the hair goes way down further!)

Uzi, in a recent photo

prayer recited at the conclusion of Shabbos, and then it was time for the *upsherin*. (An *upsherin* can literally be translated as "the cutting." The term is normally used to describe the ceremony where a three-year-old boy's hair is cut for the first time.)

A pair of scissors was ceremoniously presented to the Ribnitzer, and the next thing they knew, Uzi's tresses lay on the table — an offering that brought a smile of unparalleled joy to the Rebbe's holy face. They continued cutting, and when Uzi's head was finally shorn of the extra burden, the Rebbe drank a *l'chaim* with him to commemorate the moment.

After that, Uzi never suffered another seizure. His epilepsy was gone — except for one isolated incident that served as a reminder of his promise.

Half a year after his "haircut," some of Uzi's old friends convinced him to go with them for a drive to the beach on Shabbos. As he lifted his foot to step into the car, Uzi fell to the ground and had a seizure there and then, his first since the night he shared a *l'chaim* with the holy Rebbe of Ribnitz. That was the end of it. He never broke his part of the deal again.

Today Uzi is a *yungerman* and a *talmid chacham* with a wife and a large family who follow in his ways.

Early one morning, as Rav Grossman exited his home, he noticed an elderly Russian Jew pacing back and forth in front of his house. Clearly the man was waiting to speak to the rabbi, but for some reason he was finding it difficult to work up the courage.

Rav Grossman approached the man. "Reb Yid," he said, "please come in and tell me what's on your mind."

The old man accepted the invitation and took a seat at the dining room table. When he was comfortable, Rav Grossman encouraged him to share the reason for his visit.

"I'll tell you," the man said, "but you won't believe me."

"Nevertheless, I'm very interested in hearing what you have to say. Please tell me what's on your mind."

So the man told Rav Grossman the story that had brought him to his house so early in the morning.

"I came to Eretz Yisrael from a town called Chernowitz," he began. "Chernowitz is a town like any other — except for one thing. There was a great tzaddik in our town. His name was Rav Chaim Zanvil Abramowitz, and he was known far and wide as the Ribnitzer Rebbe."

Rav Yitzchak Dovid looked intently at the man, but it was clear that the Russian Jew had no idea of the relationship that existed between his host and the tzaddik.

"The Ribnitzer Rebbe had the practice of immersing himself in the local river every single day, and it didn't matter to him that it was forty degrees below zero. And yet the cold would not be denied, and when the Rebbe would emerge from the water, his feet would stick to the ice and the skin would rip open, leaving bloody marks behind.

"My mother knew about the Rebbe's *mesirus nefesh*, his self-sacrifice when it came to immersing in the *mikveh*, so she started leaving towels for him to step on when he emerged from the water to protect his feet.

"Now I recently moved here from Russia, and I have no apartment or any conceivable way of obtaining a place to live."

The visitor paused, his face betraying his nervousness at telling Rav Grossman the next part of the story.

"Last night," he continued, his eyes downcast, "my mother came to see me in a dream. She informed me that the Ribnitzer Rebbe had told her to visit me and to let me know that I was to go and see Rav Grossman and tell him to help me find an apartment."

Having finished his story, the Russian Yid waited anxiously for his host's reaction.

At first, Rav Grossman didn't say anything. Then he told the man to follow him into the next room, where he pointed to a large picture on the wall — a picture of Rav Chaim Zanvil, the Ribnitzer Rebbe, holding court in the Grossman home. This was Rav Grossman's way of showing the Russian Jew that he wasn't surprised by the dream at all and he believed the Yid one hundred percent.

Rav Grossman did go out of his way to help the Yid find an apartment, but for him the lesson of the story was clear: when a person helps a tzaddik, he can expect Heaven to repay him for his actions. This man's mother had done her best to take care of the Ribnitzer Rebbe, and so the Rebbe had gone out of his way to make sure that her son was taken care of in turn.

CHAPTER ELEVEN

How the Dream Became a Reality

Yaakov (Jack) and Belle Rosenbaum lived in New York. A prominent and successful businessman, Rosenbaum possessed a heart of gold and was well known in the community for his charitable activities. But Reb Yaakov was searching for something more. One day he sought out Rav Yitzchak Hutner, the rosh yeshivah (dean) of Chaim Berlin, and poured out his heart to the world-famous *gaon* (brilliant scholar), telling him how much he wanted to learn Torah. The rosh yeshivah listened intently, and then their conversation took an unexpected turn: perhaps Reb Yaakov should take a sabbatical, where he would spend a year learning Torah in Eretz Yisrael. Rav Hutner was very supportive of the idea and encouraged the Rosenbaums to take a year off and become a kollel couple.

The Beis Yisrael

When Yaakov Rosenbaum, who came from a Gerrer family, arrived in Israel, he wanted to visit the Beis Yisrael in Yerushalayim with a *kvittel,* a

Rav Grossman and Reb Yaakov Rosenbaum, taken in Reb Yaakov's garden in Monsey

short letter containing the supplicant's request, which is written on a piece of paper and handed over to the Rebbe to read. Unsure of how to write a *kvittel*, he turned to a relative of his who lived in Meah Shearim, Rav Yisrael Grossman, and asked him to pen the *kvittel* for him.

"What do you want to request of the Beis Yisrael?" Rav Yisrael asked the prospective supplicant.

"Please ask him to daven for me that I find a good *chavrusa*, a study partner to learn with during my time here in Eretz Yisrael."

"The Gerrer Rebbe is so great," Rav Yisrael replied, "that he has already helped you even before you have gone to see him."

"What do you mean?"

"I mean that I will be your *chavrusa* while you are living here in Eretz Yisrael."

Yaakov Rosenbaum had never dreamed that the rosh yeshivah of Tomchei Temimim in Lod would agree to be his *chavrusa*, and yet his prayers had been answered before they were barely out of his mouth.

So it was. Rav Yisrael was incredibly busy, and while serving as a rosh yeshivah and *moreh tzedek* (a rabbi who gives halachic rulings), he also headed a rabbinical court and was dean of the Degel Yerushalayim kollel, located on Press Street in Geulah. Yet he was happy and willing to learn with Yaakov Rosenbaum *b'chavrusa* while he was living in Eretz Yisrael.

"You will come to the kollel every day," he told Yaakov Rosenbaum, "and the two of us will learn together."

Later during that year, the Rosenbaums took a trip to the Galil. Knowing that Rav Yisrael's son, Rav Yitzchak Dovid, was the rav of Migdal HaEmek, they decided to visit him while they were in the area.

Yaakov and Belle Rosenbaum knocked on the Grossmans' front door, expecting to meet a distinguished rav, the son of the great Rav Yisrael, of whom they were so fond. They were shown into the dining room, where they found Rav Grossman sitting at the table surrounded by a large group of teens who were doing what they normally did: shooting the breeze while eating *garinim* (sunflower seeds), cracking them open, eating the seeds, and spitting out the shells all in one practiced motion.

The crowd was large, and suffice it to say, they weren't dressed for a bar mitzvah. The guests took a look around and their mouths fell open in surprise.

Rav Grossman invited them in and pulled his visitors to the side of the room to explain what they were seeing.

"Do you see these kids?" he asked them.

"Yes."

"They all come from indigent or dysfunctional homes. Some of them are battling addiction, some are involved with criminals, and all of them are struggling with their *Yiddishkeit,* their Jewish observance. But if they would have grown up in the kind of institution I dream of opening, I would have been able to save them before it all began.

"I'm doing my best to help them and show them that their lives don't have to be this way, that there is another path they can take. But it's much harder and more challenging than it would have been had they been with me from the beginning."

Reb Yaakov Rosenbaum digested what Rav Grossman was saying, looked at the kids who wanted so badly to overcome their struggles, and started to cry, unashamed to let the tears stream down his face.

"Tell me what needs to be done," he said.

"I have a dream," Rav Grossman replied. "My dream is to establish an institution for children like these, for kids who come from broken homes and need a place where people will show them love and understand them and help them grow and guide them to a better life. A place where I can introduce them to their roots and their heritage in a meaningful way.

"Can you believe that nothing even remotely similar to what I want to build exists anywhere in northern Israel? There is nothing here for a child whose family can't look after him properly! This is what I want to do, but I don't have the funds to turn the dream into a reality."

Reb Yaakov listened closely. He understood what Rav Grossman needed. Then he uttered a line that changed the entire picture.

"I will be returning to the States in a few weeks," he said, "and when I get there, I'm going to send you a ticket and fly you to America. I'll take off from work and take you around and help you raise enough money to help make your dream come true."

Yaakov Rosenbaum was true to his word. Shortly after landing back home, a ticket earmarked for Rav Grossman was mailed to the rabbi, who set off on his first fundraising trip to the United States.

He had never flown before and arrived at the airport wide-eyed and excited, never dreaming that he would go on to become the most frequent of frequent flyers. Once settled in his seat and buckled in, he waited for take-off and did his best to pretend that he wasn't shaken by the prospect of lifting off into the sky.

As the hours passed and the plane flew through the air, the young rabbi's mind was racing.

I have no idea what awaits me in America, he thought to himself. *What am I going to do when I get there? I can't even speak English!*

He comforted himself with the thought that at least there was someone who had promised to look after him and assist him. Then he removed a few Torah books from his carry-on and learned until his eyes closed of their own accord.

Rav Grossman was indeed taken around by his host, who picked him up from the airport and devoted the next few weeks to doing everything he could for his guest, a man whose entire life revolved around doing for others and who had impressed him no end. Reb Yaakov accompanied his guest from house to house and from friend to friend, and there were times when the guest needed to comfort the host, who didn't have any firsthand experience fundraising and felt overwhelmed at the enormity of the task. Reb Yaakov had imagined that his presence alone would be sufficient to convince people to pull out their checkbooks and write hefty checks, but in those few weeks he would come to learn the way it really is for a *meshulach* (charity collector) walking the streets in the pouring rain, sleet, and hail.

Yet even taking into account all the people who didn't give, or gave only a little, or promised to send a check, the two of them still managed to raise slightly more than forty thousand dollars, which was a significant sum of money in those days. After parting warmly from his hosts, Rav Grossman was driven back to the airport and only hours later found himself back in the land he loved with all his heart.

There was no question in his mind that he had been the recipient of an incredible dose of *siyata d'Shmaya,* Heavenly assistance, and he was anxious to take the next step and begin making the desert bloom.

With the funds in place, Rav Grossman was ready to embark on his momentous endeavor. One of the decisions he faced in the process, a question that every educator faced, was which educational stream to be part of. The reason this was such a burning question was that it would establish where and how he would receive government funding. In Israel, there are four main streams: the public school stream; Mamlachti Dati, which serves the traditional religious public; Chinuch Atzmai; and a fourth stream that the Klausenberger Rebbe followed when he established his own school, a stream that is recognized by the government but is not part of any of the other systems. Though it provides freedom from politics, the institution receives less money from the government than those of the other three.

Rav Grossman wanted his school to be run according to the fourth stream. While it would have made sense for him to be part of Chinuch Atzmai, since his father was so involved with the organization, he couldn't afford to be affiliated with it because it would have reinforced the suspicions of people like Tzvi Eldorati that he had come to town for political reasons. No, it would have to be stream number four.

Before he went to meet with the minister of education to plead his case, Rav Grossman visited the Steipler Gaon to ask if there was any reason he shouldn't operate under the same guidelines as the Klausenberger Rebbe. He explained to the Steipler Gaon that his school was going to be established in a city where until a very short while before there had been no Shabbos or kashrus, and that he was doing his best to make positive changes in Migdal HaEmek.

"The moment they think I'm affiliated with Agudas Yisrael," he told the Steipler, "I'll face terrible opposition, which is why it would be better if my institution didn't operate under the auspices of Chinuch Atzmai."

"The main thing is to serve the Ribbono shel Olam, the Master of the World," the Steipler Gaon replied. "If by doing things your way, you'll be able to change the city and people will start doing mitzvos and becoming closer to Hashem, then that's the correct course of action and that's what you should do."

Knowing how challenging it would be to arrange a meeting with then Minister of Education Aharon Yadlin at his office in Yerushalayim, Rav Grossman had Kobi drive him to Yadlin's home in his kibbutz down south.

"My name is Yitzchak Dovid Grossman," he said, introducing himself to the minister. "I live in the city of Migdal HaEmek, and I am in the process of establishing an institution for underprivileged children from broken homes."

"How can I help you?"

"I would like you to please give me the necessary documents that will state that my institution is recognized under the law while not a part of any of the educational streams. I'm not a politician. I'm not connected to the Mapai, the Mafdal, or even Agudah. I belong to Klal Yisrael, to the entire Jewish nation, and that's why my school has to operate in its own system without being connected to any particular party."

The bearded rabbi had caught Yadlin's interest, and he was listening intently.

"You have two choices," his visitor told him. "Either give me a permit to run a school that stands on its own, or I will be forced to join the regular Israeli school system."

The second choice, that his school be part of the public school system, was vetoed immediately.

"Don't be a revolutionary," Yadlin cautioned his visitor. "Opening a religious school within the public school system will make a lot of people angry. But I see no reason why your school cannot operate in the category of '*mukar she'eino rishmi*' — recognized by the educational system yet officially you can make your own policies."

With the blessings of the Steipler Gaon and Rav Shach, the institution was founded along the same lines as that of the Klausenberger Rebbe's schools. Now it was time to choose a location.

While the majority of Migdal HaEmek's population lived in crowded apartment buildings, a local contractor had just finished building a row of one-family homes — or "*villot*" in the local terminology, on HaChoresh Street. The price per villa: a cool five thousand dollars.

Rav Grossman purchased two of them to be used for dorms and a dining room and asked his tzaddikim from the disco to help build another large room nearby to serve as the *beis midrash* (study hall). The tzaddikim were happy to help, and the construction was completed in record time.

With the Klausenberger Rebbe

They were so excited at being involved that they even continued building the *beis midrash* throughout Tishah B'Av, the day of fasting and mourning for the destruction of the holy Temples. At some point, Rav Grossman passed by and saw the tzaddikim taking a break from their labors and eating sandwiches to replenish their strength.

"It's Tishah B'Av!" Rav Grossman cried out, aghast at the sight.

"What's wrong?" one of the tzaddikim replied. "We're in the process of rebuilding the Beis HaMikdash, the Holy Temple, here!"

Ironically, the tzaddikim had *paskened* (ruled) that they were allowed to eat for the purpose of building a yeshivah.

Although of course he told them to stop immediately, Rav Grossman would remember the incident for years to come and the comment about building the Beis HaMikdash that had been made in all innocence.

CHAPTER TWELVE

The Twenty-Minute Walk to Life

Migdal Ohr's first eighteen residents were a motley crew, the majority of whom literally came from the street. Rav Grossman had sent a trusted messenger down to Tiveria, another to Afula, and yet another to investigate the situation in Migdal HaEmek itself. When they noticed any kids who seemed to be on their own, they would question them and ask who their parents were and where they lived. If they were forthcoming with the information, the

Then: The very first class

messengers went to meet with their parents and convinced them to send their children to the brand-new institution under the aegis of Rav Yitzchak Dovid Grossman in Migdal HaEmek.

The boys were twelve years old, mostly from traditional Sefardic homes, and were being enrolled in the new school as sixth-graders. The parents couldn't get over their good fortune when they learned that someone was opening a school where their children would receive hot, nutritious meals, new clothing, and quality schooling — in most cases, for the first time in their lives.

Of course, Rav Yitzchak Dovid and his rebbetzin would have to move. Knowing the type of children that would be attending their new school, they couldn't remain in the apartment they had been living in until that point. There was no way they could live even five minutes away. They had to be close by in case they were needed, and so they moved into an apartment across the street from the school's buildings, seeing themselves as parents of the eighteen children who, for the first time in their lives, finally had a home.

It became clear to Rav Grossman almost immediately that it was not nearly enough, and that the need for what he was doing far outstripped his current resources. When they first began, neither the rabbi nor the people he'd hired to teach had known exactly how their experiment was going to turn out, but by the time the first year had come to an end, they knew that they were good at what they were doing, and they had been contacted by many individuals, both in private and in public,

Now: Migdal Ohr Mesivta students learning in the *beis medrash*

who wanted to send them other children. After only a year, it became imperative to expand their facilities to accommodate the additional thirty-five children who would soon be joining them.

One of the original eighteen kids in Migdal Ohr went by the name of Yossi Gigi. Yossi had come to them from the city of Tiveria on beautiful Lake Kinneret, the child of a family that had strayed far from its roots and was among the lowest rung of the country's socio-economic strata. His was a hardscrabble childhood, and Yossi was a rough and tough kid when he found his way to Migdal Ohr.

Three months after joining the school, Yossi approached Rav Yitzchak Dovid and asked to speak to him.

"What is it, Yossi?"

"I can't stay here anymore!"

"What's the matter?"

"Too many rules, too much learning."

"But you're doing so well!"

"No, this isn't for me. I'm going home to Tiveria."

Rav Grossman doesn't believe in making people do what they don't want to do. Instead of trying to convince the young boy that he really loved the school, and it would be best for him to stay, Rav Grossman reached into his pocket, took out some money, and handed it to Yossi for the bus ride from Migdal Ohr back to the wilds of Tiveria. He knew that the walk from the school to the bus stop would take Yossi a good twenty minutes, and Rav Grossman hoped that the walk would prove to be the catalyst for a shift.

"Yossi," he said to the boy with as much seriousness as he could muster, "in the twenty minutes it will take you to get from Migdal Ohr to the bus stop, you're going to decide what kind of life you'll have during your time in this world and, more importantly, what will become of you in *Olam Haba* (the World to Come). In the next twenty minutes, you'll decide what type of wife you'll marry and what kind of children you'll bring into this world. Your entire future depends on the next twenty minutes. You have money and you can leave. On the way, you'll make your decision, because the truth is that you're the only one who can."

Yossi returned an hour later. Walked into the room. Handed Rav Grossman back the money.

"I thought about what you said, and I've decided to stay."

Rav Grossman was both relieved and moved that Yossi had made the right decision. On the spot, he walked the boy to the *beis midrash,* where the rest of the boys were sitting and learning, and broke into song, using a tune they were all familiar with but with words that had flown right into his mind that very second.

"Eizeh, eizehu gibbor hakoveish es yitzro... Eizeh, eizehu gibbor hakoveish es yitzro — Who is a strong man? Someone who conquers his desires!"

He sang the words to the tune of *"Tzion, Tzion, Tzion, halo tishali,"* a very popular song at that time.

The rabbi sang the song over and over, again and again, his warm voice filling the room, until every child sitting there opened his mouth and joined along.

Yossi Gigi grew up to become the head of the Migdal Ohr kollel, with over one hundred Talmud students under his care. He is a *talmid chacham* and a *dayan,* a rabbinical judge, who has raised a beautiful family. In 2020, Rav Yossi Gigi celebrated the bar mitzvah of one of his grandsons, and the entire family gathered together at the yeshivah that Shabbos.

"I walked into the dining room in the middle of the meal," Rav Grossman recalls, "and saw over one hundred and fifty family members surrounding their father, father-in-law, and grandfather with love and admiration. With his permission, I related the story of what transpired that day to the assembled crowd, which grew hushed as I

One of the first classes

described what had occurred in my office and how he had returned an hour later, determined to stay.

"'Yossi,' I called out, 'everything you see here is a result of those twenty minutes and the decision you made as you walked down the road from Migdal HaEmek to the bus station. Had you chosen differently on that fateful day, none of this would exist! But you made the right choice, and look at the magnificent world you created. All because of those twenty minutes."

There have been countless stories over the years pertaining to the children of Migdal Ohr. One that is especially memorable involves a trip to Canada, where Rav Grossman heard about a father who had abandoned his family, leaving the mother behind raising their children on her own. The situation had deteriorated to the point where one of the children, only fourteen years old, was already out of the house and working as a drug courier. Somehow the boy was convinced to meet with the rabbi from Israel, and during the course of the conversation, Rav Yitzchak Dovid asked him how he could have allowed himself to stray so far.

"I have no father!" the boy responded.

In his mind, the statement "I have no father" was unanswerable, an argument that was impossible to refute.

"You do have a father," Rav Grossman replied. "I am your father! I will not be leaving here until you agree to accompany me to Migdal Ohr."

It took a week, but in the end the boy agreed to join Rav Grossman on his flight back to Eretz Yisrael. Within a very short period of time, everyone in the school understood that this was not going to be an easy transition. The boy hadn't been in school for a very long time and hadn't opened a book in ages. More than that, he was a kid who knew what it felt like to hold a wad of money in his hand, and not just a wad, but a thick wad of drug money. This was not your average child, not in any sense of the word. How do you tell a child who is used to hanging out with wealthy businesspeople at luxury hotels that he has a curfew and can't hang out whenever or wherever he wants?

But Rav Grossman didn't give up. He arranged for the boy to learn with private tutors, who brought him up to speed and helped him catch up on the years he was missing, and for other people to talk to him and help ease him back into normal society.

It was a journey of ups and downs. Just when they thought he was finally finding his feet and starting to smile, there would be another fall and they would have to begin all over again. It was extremely challenging, but Rav Grossman had promised the boy that he would be his father, and a father doesn't give up on his son — no matter what.

Months later, Rav Grossman returned from a fundraising trip to the States, and the boy came out to greet him when he returned. To the rabbi's immense surprise and shock, he saw that his *talmid,* his student, had treated himself to a mohawk hairstyle during the time he'd been away, with the two sides of his head completely shaven and a healthy strip of hair prominently displayed right down the center. The brazenness of the haircut took Rav Grossman's breath away.

Looking at the boy, he thought to himself, *Ribbono shel Olam, I've already invested three years in this kid — three years of constant battles, three years of serving as his private therapist, three years of being at his beck and call day and night, and now he comes to see me looking like this? What am I supposed to do now?*

Rav Grossman was struggling, but then he reminded himself of his promise. At the last second, Rav Grossman said, "Benny*, I love you so much. I want to give you a hug and a kiss, but I can't embrace you looking like that. Please help me out. I want to hug you, I want to kiss you — but I can't. Not looking like that! I need you to help me. What should I do?"

The boy turned on his heel and left the room. He returned almost an hour later sporting a conventional haircut. From that moment on, there was a turnaround. He started to learn and became a *yerei Shamayim,* a person possessing genuine fear of Heaven. He went on to get married and raise a wonderful family. And Rav Grossman knew that the turnaround had come about because he had looked at the boy, and instead of telling him what he really thought, he had told him how much he loved him and wanted to hug and kiss him.

It would be this acute understanding of children and the unique world they occupy that would accompany Migdal Ohr as it grew from a modest eighteen children into a city of 130,000 square meters spread over forty-five acres of land. This was the place where thousands of children of all ages and backgrounds would receive the warmth and love they had dreamed of receiving.

The dream was finally happening. The only question was how far it would go.

The dream

The dream becomes a reality. An aerial view of Migdal Ohr. Foreground: Boys Campus. Center: Foster Home Village. Background: Girls Campus. EVERY SINGLE BUILDING IN THIS PICTURE IS PART OF MIGDAL OHR!

CHAPTER THIRTEEN

The Rosh Hashanah Murder

While Rav Yitzchak Dovid had been appointed rav of Migdal HaEmek and was widely respected and loved by the people of the city, it was during the following incident that he truly endeared himself to the residents of Migdal HaEmek. The episode took place on Rosh Hashanah, of all days, and it would prove to be a genuine test for the young rav.

That morning Rav Grossman was davening Shacharis when he felt an unexpected tap on his shoulder. Turning his head, he saw the powerful form of Mayor Tzvi Eldorati, an extremely serious look on his face.

"Rav Grossman, I need to speak to you immediately!"

Eldorati was not in the habit of wasting anyone's time. If he was at the shul on Rosh Hashanah morning, disturbing the rav's davening, there must be a very good reason. Rav Yitzchak Dovid motioned for the mayor to follow him out of the shul and into a side room, and he looked at Eldorati expectantly as he waited to hear what was on the mayor's mind.

"Did you hear what happened?"

Rav Grossman had no idea what he was talking about and told him so.

"There was a murder last night!"

Rav Grossman was shocked. Though Migdal HaEmek wasn't a stranger to crime, murder was uncommon.

"How? Where?"

"I'll tell you the whole story."

"Please."

The evening before, there had been a party held at the local Histadrut building for the Russian immigrants who had recently arrived in Israel. They were part of the wave of immigration of Soviet Jews between 1969 and 1973, when Russia opened its doors and allowed its Jews to leave the country. A large contingent of these immigrants were brought to Migdal HaEmek, where the government quickly constructed several buildings and the newcomers were assigned decent-sized apartments. The Russian Jews were also given a special tax break for the purchase of cars, which meant that many of the Russian immigrants were not only living in nice apartments but were even driving cars at a time in the country's history when that was not the norm.

If everyone living in Migdal HaEmek were Russian, life would have been fairly simple. But the majority of the city were longtime residents of Moroccan descent and poor socioeconomic status. When the Moroccans saw how the Russians were given beautiful apartments and other benefits from the start while they had been treated so poorly upon their arrival years earlier, with the government sticking ten-person families into caravans, tents, or tiny apartments, it rankled and caused no small amount of tension between the two camps.

The previous evening, the night of Rosh Hashanah, the Histadrut had thrown a party welcoming the Russians to Migdal HaEmek.

"In the middle of the party," Eldorati said, "one of the local Moroccans heard the noise and the music from outside the hall and decided that he wanted to enjoy the party, too. The Russians at the door informed him that this was a party for them and that he was not invited. Taking umbrage at being denied entry, the Moroccan forced his way into the room. This state of affairs didn't last long because the Russians surrounded him and attempted to physically eject him from the premises.

"This was a young man with a long criminal history, and he wasn't a stranger to violence. He grabbed a glass bottle from one of the tables, smashed it on the table's edge, breaking it in half, and, before anyone realized what was happening, stabbed one of the Russians in the neck, killing him on the spot.

"Then he broke free from the Russians, who stood there in shock, and ran for his life.

"The Russians are understandably up in arms," Eldorati continued, "and none of them went to sleep last night. Instead they spent the night planning their revenge. They decided that the Moroccans need to be taught a lesson and that they will be doing the teaching today, this morning, in the center of town.

"Rav Grossman," Eldorati concluded, "if someone doesn't take control of the situation, and quickly, we may very well end up with a massacre on our hands. I visited the Russian camp this morning, but I don't speak Yiddish or Russian and we were unable to communicate. I could understand enough to know that they were shouting at me to leave and threatened me with physical violence. Please come and stop them before lives are lost!"

Rav Grossman didn't waste any time. "Let's go," he said.

And so it was that Rav Yitzchak Dovid Grossman of Meah Shearim left shul on the morning of Rosh Hashanah, still clad in his tallis, and quickly headed out to the square where the Russians and Moroccans were about to face off. The words *"mi yichyeh u'mi yamus* — who will live and who will die?" had never held more meaning for him.

When Rav Grossman arrived on site, he found a large group of well-armed Russians milling around in a state of raw grief and anger. They were obviously gearing up to leave en masse to the home of the young Moroccan who had murdered their friend, and they didn't plan on leaving before they had achieved retribution. Running the show was the dead man's mother, who stood in the center of the square holding a picture of her son high in the air (he had been an only child), as if to remind all the Russians why they were there.

Seeking a place to address the crowd so that everyone would be able to see and hear him, Rav Grossman jumped on top of a low wall. There he stood, facing the crowd, enveloped in his tallis, his face framed by his long *peyos* and beard. He didn't want to give the Russians a chance to object to his presence, so he immediately began shouting in Yiddish, "Yidden! Yidden! Yidden! A terrible thing has happened here! How is it possible that such an atrocity has occurred in our city?! A young man was murdered in the prime of his days! His blood cries out from the earth! There is no question that we must protest this outrage with all our might!"

Rav Grossman was taking his cue from Kalev, the leader who addressed the Jewish people in the desert when he returned from Eretz Yisrael with the spies. The spies had spoken *lashon hara*, evil speech, about the land that Hashem had promised to Klal Yisrael. Kalev didn't agree with the spies, but after they had riled up the people into a panic, he knew that no one would listen to him. He therefore pretended to be on their side, to speak against Moshe Rabbeinu. When he finally had their attention, he turned his arguments around and spoke in Moshe's defense.

Rav Grossman did the same thing. At first, he delivered a speech that showed beyond the shadow of a doubt that he was completely on the side of the Russians. When he saw that they were beginning to quiet down and to listen to him, the young rabbi seized the opportunity to maneuver the mob away from the center of town.

"Come with me," he cried out, "and we'll continue the protest in the main shul of Migdal HaEmek! Yes, we will do this on Rosh Hashanah morning — and we will do it in the middle of davening!"

Jumping nimbly off the low wall, Rav Grossman approached the bereaved mother still holding the picture of her son and asked her to come along with him to the shul, where they would continue the protest.

She agreed.

Rav Grossman turned to the rest of the group. "Everyone, come with us!"

"יהודים הרגו אותך!"

רק מילה תגיד לי, מישקה. רק
מילה אחת. למה אתה שותק, מיש־
קה? זה לא מהגויים שאתה בתוך האד־
מה. זה לא מחבלנים. זה מהיהודים. הי־
יהודים הרגו אותך. בשביל זה עלינו ל־
ארץ מרוסיה?"

בעיניים יבשות כבר מדמעות, כשהיא
נתמכת על־ידי קרובי משפחה, הביאה ב־
יום השני דורה גרון, עולה חדשה מרוסיה
ותושבת מגדל־העמק, את בנה משה בן
ה־18 לקבורה.

בחדר־המעצר של מישטרת נצרת הד־
ביק מאיר לוי בן ה־19, בן למישפחה
מרוקאית החשוד כרוצחו של משה, את
פניו המגחכים לסורגי הצוהר הקטן, ביי־
קש מנערה שחלפה במקום: "תני לי
נשיקה, בובה. זאת הנשיקה האחרונה ב־
כל החיים שלי."

מגדל־העמק, אחרי הרצח המזעזע, נר־
אית, במבט ראשון, כמימים ימימה. ב־
פתחי הבתים משוחחות עקרות־בית. כש־
יגיע הערב שיפוג את החום, ייצאו בני־
הנוער להסתובב ברחובות. גם במעלה
רחוב קדש, שבו מרוכז חלק ניכר מעולי
רוסיה שהגיעו למקום, שוררת אווירה
של יום חול רגיל.

גם מועדון מפ"ם שומם. רק לפני יו־
מיים נפגשו שם שני עולמות — עולמו
של עולה צעיר מרוסיה, וזה של עבריין
יליד הארץ, בן למשפחה מרוקאית, שכל
ימיו עברו עליו במקום.

"לא יודע כלום"

אבל מתחת לפני השטח, מורגשות
המתיחות והעוינות בין שני המחנות:
מחנה המרוקאים מפה, ומחנה הרוסים מפה,
כשכל צד חושש מניקמתו של האחר. ב־
עיקבות הרצח של ערב ראש־השנה, ה־

בדירה המוזנחת, לא הרחק ממו־
עדון מפ"ם, גונח מכאבים שמעון אזו־
לאי, אביו של אברהם אזולאי, שנע־
צר יחד עם מאיר לוי כחשוד ברצח משה
גרון. יש לו בעיות עם חוט השדרה, ל־
אבא.

"אני לא יודע כלום ממה שהיה. אני
חולה. יש לי מחלת סוכר, ואני שוכח
הכל."

למגדל־העמק הגיע לפני כעשרים שנה,
מייד עם עלייתו לארץ. נתנו לו צריף,
ואמרו לו: זה הבית שלך. מאז הוא
עובד כטבח בצבא, ואשתו כעוזרת־בית.

החברים אשמים

על הבתים החדשים שניבנו לא הרחק
מביתו, ויועדו לעולים החדשים מרו־
סיה, הוא מסתכל עם קצת פילוסופיה:
"מה איכפת לי השיכונים היפים שלהם
שיהיה להם לבריאות. העולם הזה לא
חשוב. ואת המדינה שלנו בצריף ובשי־
כון. לכולם הכי טוב זה העולם הבא."

ערב ראש השנה היה יום הולדתו של
בנו אברהם בן ה־19. בגלל מחלתו של
האב, ערך אברהם בעצמו את הקידוש,
ויצא לשוטט עם החברים שלו.

"לא דאגתי," מספר אביו. "ידעתי ש־
אין להם לאן ללכת. אז אפילו לא שאלתי
אותו מתי יחזור. אברהם הוא בחור טוב
מאה אחוז. רק ביישן גדול. וכשהוא מס־
תובב, בגלל שלא תמיד הוא עובד, סו־
חבים אותו החברים ומקלקלים אותו."

אחד החברים האלה היה מאיר לוי,
גם הוא בן למישפחה מרוקאית ותיקה
במקום ובן גילו של אברהם.

למאיר היתה השהות בבית מאורע
יוצא־דופן. בניגוד לחברו, שהספיק להי־
גיע רק עד מוסד לעבריינים צעירים,

הקורבן
משה גרון, בן ה־18, שהתגייס לפני תשעה חודשים לצה"ל ונרצח
בזמן חופשתו על־ידי בני מגדל־העמק. בתמונה למעלה: דורה גרון

A newspaper showing the murder victim. "Jews killed you" says the headline.

With the mother and the rabbi at the head of the procession, the entire crowd left the square and began the walk to the main Ashkenazic shul of Migdal HaEmek. In true mob fashion, the group of Russians allowed themselves to be led away from the square and in the direction of the main shul.

It was Rosh Hashanah morning, and the day could still go in any number of ways. It was up to the rabbi to make sure that no one else was killed. He knew this, and the responsibility weighed heavily on his shoulders.

The city's main shul was packed when they arrived. For the most part, the *kehillah* (congregation) was composed of people from Hungary and Romania. There were also a few Russians in the mix. None of them were expecting the shul to turn into the staging ground for a major *hafganah* (demonstration) — and certainly not on Rosh Hashanah, of all days.

In an interesting turn of events, the chazzan in the shul that year was none other than Reb Yaakov Rosenbaum, who was a famous chazzan in his own right and who had agreed to come all the way from the United States to lead the prayer services in Migdal HaEmek that Rosh Hashanah. When the mob entered the shul in the middle of the davening, Reb Yaakov turned around and gestured to one of the members of the congregation to explain what was going on.

"One of the Moroccans killed a Russian last night," the man told him, "and now Rav Grossman is trying his best to make sure that nobody else gets killed."

Hearing this, Yaakov Rosenbaum, a citizen of Monsey, New York, and unaccustomed to such goings-on, promptly fainted, collapsing to the floor and contributing yet another element to an already drama-filled day. The next few minutes were spent trying to revive the chazzan, while the shul filled with angry Russians. This was eventually achieved after some water had been poured on him. Once Rav Grossman was sure that his friend was fine, he turned his attention back to the people who had crowded into the shul.

If it had been full before, now the shul was positively stuffed. Every seat was taken, and men, women, and children were crammed into the back of the room, where they stood and waited for Rav Grossman to speak.

Acutely aware of the responsibility he had undertaken, Rav Grossman made his way through the crowd and up the steps onto the *bimah* (platform). There he stood, straight and tall, his piercing eyes seeking out face after face in the crowd.

And then he began to speak.

"*Yiddelach,*" he called out in their native Yiddish, "look and see the low to which we have sunk. How can it be that such a terrible story happened on the holy day of Rosh Hashanah?!"

He didn't miss the opportunity to give *mussar,* to rebuke the Histadrut at the same time for organizing an event on Rosh Hashanah in the first place, an event with drinking and levity. Was this the only day in the year that the Histadrut found to make a party?

He spoke for a very long time. His words emanated from the depths of his heart and entered the hearts of every person in the room.

Suddenly, in the middle of his heartfelt speech, Rav Grossman descended from the platform and made his way over to the *aron kodesh.* He opened the doors of the holy ark and showcased the Torah scrolls within, to give greater impact to his words.

"My fellow Jews, you need to know that if any person standing here will seek vengeance and harm another person on this day — he will not live out this year!"

The words were delivered in a tone that made it clear to the crowd that the rabbi knew what he was talking about and that he meant every single word he was saying. A tremor rippled through the Russian camp.

Seeing how they reacted to his words, Rav Grossman knew that he had struck a chord. But he wasn't quite finished. It wasn't sufficient to warn them or scare them. It was also important, perhaps even more important, that he show them his love. He wanted them to feel that he was on their side and that he understood the enormity of their pain. In short, he needed them to recognize that he was their rabbi.

"My friends, today is the day when it is being decided what the coming year holds for every one of us. We will not surrender in silence to the murder of our dear brother. We will make sure that the murderer will be given a life sentence in prison. But under no circumstances may any of you go so far as to lift your hand toward a fellow Jew. It's not your place to seek retribution. That must be left to the police and the courts. I'm asking you all to accept upon yourselves not to harm another Jew. I'm asking you — no, I'm begging you — to make sure that no war ensues between brothers in this city!

"I'm with you and I'll fight for you. But you must do your part and promise that calm will reign and no one else loses his life."

At that moment, when the entire shul was completely silent but for the voice of their rabbi, Rav Grossman heard a strange sound coming from outside. An unexpected sound. It was the sound of a helicopter landing just outside the shul.

There is no question, he reflected as he left the shul and walked outside to meet whoever had come, *that this Rosh Hashanah is going to go down in history as a Rosh Hashanah like no other…*

As the thrumming of the rotors subsided, the helicopter door opened, and the chief of the Israel Police emerged along with several other high-ranking officials. Clearly, word had spread that war was imminent in Migdal HaEmek, and the police chief had arrived from Jerusalem to manage the crisis from up close. Luckily for him, the crisis had been averted by the time he arrived, though he still didn't know it as he walked toward the shul.

The huge crowd had followed the rabbi outside and was now watching the officials as they approached. Sensing that here was a man with the power to help their cause, the Russians bounded forward and began telling the police chief their version of the events, each one talking over the other as they vied for his attention.

"I can't speak with so many of you at once," he said. "Put together a delegation, and we'll meet in one of the side rooms of the shul."

The meeting commenced a few minutes later, with Rav Grossman serving as the translator for both sides.

Once both parties were sitting at the table, the chief of police and his people on one side and the Russians on the other, the chief invited them to state their grievances.

"We came here from Russia," one of the immigrants began, "hoping for a different kind of life than we had there. But now we realize it's not that different! Not when a young man is literally slaughtered in cold blood by a murderer. That's not what we had in mind when we left everything behind to start a new life."

The police chief proceeded to explained to the Russians why the incident had happened in the first place. He told them that the Moroccans were jealous of all the benefits that the Russians had received from the government, and this had given rise to the tension between the two camps.

Rav Grossman listened to the words emerging from the police chief's mouth, and he knew beyond the shadow of a doubt that if he translated them accurately, they wouldn't go over well. Not at all. On the spot, he decided to take some liberty with his translation.

Correction: He didn't translate a word the man said. Instead, he told them that the police chief had promised to make sure that the murderer would be sent to jail for life, and that maybe it would be possible to give him the death penalty, and that this incident would not just be ignored. Changes would be made and lessons learned.

The Russian delegation liked what the police chief said and nodded along with every word.

It was a Rosh Hashanah unlike any other. For the rest of his life, Rav Grossman knew that he would never forget that day. He never did end up davening in shul that year, nor did he have a chance to partake of the delicious meals that his wife had prepared. For those two days he barely ate or drank anything at all. He was too busy shuttling between the homes of the Russians and the Moroccans (they were feeling pretty touchy about the whole situation even though they were in the wrong), calming everyone down and making sure that no one did anything he would later come to regret. The situation would only really calm down after the Russian boy was buried.

On the day after Rosh Hashanah, the story was widely reported in the media. It was a wild story, and the papers enjoyed providing their readership with all the gory details. One paper went with the following headline on the subject of the rabbi's translation skills: "*Farteitched or Farbesert?* — Translated word for word, or improved on the original?"

It was a nod to what had really gone down in the side room of the main shul in Migdal HaEmek on the Rosh Hashanah morning when Rav Yitzchak Dovid Grossman finally took ownership of his town. The test had been a challenging one. But once passed, there was no looking back. The people had become his people once and for all. Because they knew that their rav would do anything for them, and that he belonged to them and they to him.

So it was that Migdal HaEmek acquired a rav.

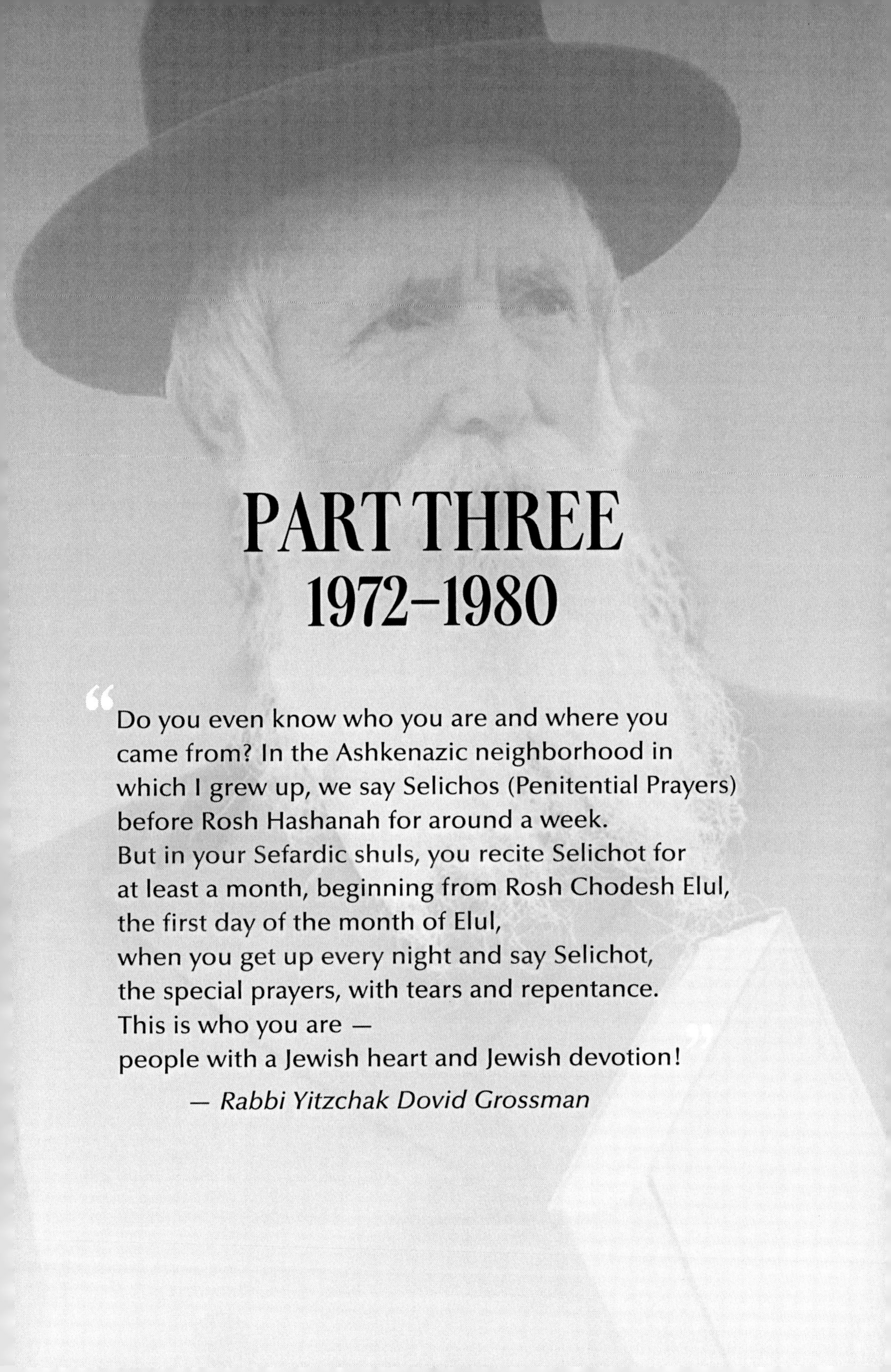

PART THREE
1972–1980

"Do you even know who you are and where you came from? In the Ashkenazic neighborhood in which I grew up, we say Selichos (Penitential Prayers) before Rosh Hashanah for around a week.
But in your Sefardic shuls, you recite Selichot for at least a month, beginning from Rosh Chodesh Elul, the first day of the month of Elul,
when you get up every night and say Selichot, the special prayers, with tears and repentance.
This is who you are —
people with a Jewish heart and Jewish devotion!"

— *Rabbi Yitzchak Dovid Grossman*

CHAPTER FOURTEEN

Shema Yisrael at the Foot of Mount Hermon

The year was 1973. The Yom Kippur War took the entire country by surprise, including the military and intelligence divisions. The failure was huge, the casualties many.

The Israel Air Force's largest base, Ramat David, was located right behind Migdal HaEmek. From the moment the war broke out, Ramat David went on high alert. One of the Syrian objectives was to obliterate the air force base with their missiles, but the missiles fell short and many of them landed in Migdal HaEmek instead. The city was under strict blackout orders. No light could be seen from any window so as not to provide assistance to the enemy, and complete darkness blanketed the city.

For the new immigrants from the USSR, the outbreak of war was incredibly traumatizing. They had just arrived in the country and now were sitting in bomb shelters and unable to understand what the people around them were saying, or anything that was being reported on the radio, because they didn't speak the language. You can imagine their panic at finding themselves shrouded in darkness, the unrelenting sound of blasting artillery their sudden companion.

Rav Grossman knew that their imaginations were working overtime and that they were afraid that the doors of the shelters were about to be thrown open by the enemy, who would kill them all. So Rav Grossman went from bomb shelter to bomb shelter in the darkness of night, conversing with the Russian Jews in Yiddish and encouraging them with words of hope. He told them the headlines, making sure to put a positive spin on the news and to convey the feeling that everything was going to be fine, even when the news was not at all cheerful and the situation seemed dire and only getting worse.

Spending so much time with the immigrants from Russia would have a major impact on their relationship that would last long after the war was over and everyone was finally able to leave the shelters.

One day a high-ranking army officer who lived in Migdal HaEmek, by the name of Avraham Zohar, came to Rav Grossman with a request.

"Rav Grossman," he said, "I don't know if you're familiar with the military situation, but the army has mounted a campaign to retake the Hermon. They've attempted it a number of times, with no success. Hundreds have been killed in the battles for the Golan. Tomorrow evening we're trying again, and our orders are to do whatever is necessary to deliver the Hermon into our hands. There's no choice but to win it back — no matter the price. Which brings me to you."

"What can I do for you?"

"I want to bring you to where the soldiers are stationed so that you can give them a talk before they go into battle. Will you do it?"

Was there even any question?

"I'd be honored to do as you ask."

The arrangements were quickly put into motion. The next day Rav Grossman was picked up from his home by an army jeep. A soldier handed him a helmet, and off they went. Upon their arrival, the rabbi found thousands of soldiers sitting and waiting for him at the foot of Mount Hermon. A makeshift stage had been erected, with a microphone on a stand. Rav Grossman was about to step onto the stage and begin his speech when another vehicle pulled up and a wildly popular Israeli band emerged.

One of the officers approached the rabbi and said, "*Kevod HaRav,* honored rabbi, as you can see, a group of singers just arrived. According to the schedule, you're supposed to go on the stage before them, but they're in a rush to do their show and head on to the next base so they

At the edge of a battleground

can perform for as many soldiers as possible. Would you mind if they went on first?"

"Tadir v'she'eino tadir, tadir kodem," replied the rabbi. He was referring to the famous Talmudic law that states that something that is done on a frequent basis has precedence over something that is done infrequently.

Rav Grossman was telling the officer that the band was in the category of *"tadir,"* since they performed all the time, while he, not being a performer, fell under the category of *"eino tadir."* The officer didn't catch the reference, so Rav Grossman said that he was more than happy for the band to "open up" for him.

Permission granted, the pop music band got up on stage along with their leader, Ido,* while Rav Grossman went to sit among the soldiers.

Ido was a popular singer and a comedian who had performed countless times, but with the rabbi sitting in the audience, Ido was clearly uncomfortable about beginning his comedic routine. His material was geared toward a nonreligious audience and was definitely not fit for rabbinic ears. He removed a small *sefer Tehillim,* a book of Psalms, from his pocket (probably distributed by the IDF) and said to Rav Grossman,

"*Kevod HaRav*, please take this *Tehillim* and wait on the side until we are finished. There you can recite *Tehillim* undisturbed, and we will be able to do our show."

At that moment, Rav Grossman had a flash of inspiration. "Ido," Rav Grossman said, "what do you say about the two of us doing a show together?"

Ido was taken aback. He had offered the rabbi the use of a *Tehillim,* fully expecting the man with the long beard to take him up on the offer. He had not expected the rabbi to request that he join him on the stage. But he didn't feel he could refuse.

"By all means," he replied, "come on up."

Nothing about the moment had been planned. Rav Grossman had been more than happy to wait for the band to finish their set. But an opportunity to make a truly memorable *kiddush Hashem* had come his way, and he seized it with both hands.

As he made his way up onto the stage, Rav Grossman suddenly heard a tune begin playing in his head, and he instinctively knew exactly which words to fit with the tune. The tune was a famous Israeli song, "*B'Shanah HaBa'ah,*" and one that every single soldier knew and loved. But the words were brand new, put together on the spot:

"*B'Yom HaKippur nichnesu hasonim v'hifriu, hifriu, latefillah...* On the day of Yom Kippur, the enemy entered our country and disturbed the prayers..."

He then raised his voice to its maximum capacity and sang out, "*Sheyiheyu, sheyiheyu, kapparah, kapparah, kapparah l'chol Am Yisrael...* — May it be an atonement for the entire nation of Israel..."

Turning to the soldiers, he urged them to point their hands in the direction of the Syrian army, who were perched on the nearby mountain, and to sing, "*Sheyiheyu, sheyiheyu, kapparah, kapparah, kapparah l'chol Am Yisrael...*"

Within seconds, the entire brigade — thousands of soldiers — were drawn into the moment and to the tune they knew so well. And every one of them was singing with all their hearts, "*Sheyiheyu, sheyiheyu, kapparah, kapparah, kapparah l'chol Am Yisrael...,*" while pointing at their enemy at the top of the mountain.

The moment the song was over, Rav Grossman said, "*Rabbotai,* it is written in the Torah that the *Kohen Gadol,* the High Priest, would address the Jewish army before they went out to war. This is what he used to say:

"'*Shema Yisrael atem kereivim hayom lamilchamah al oiveichem* — Hear, Israel, today you are approaching the war against your enemy.' Rashi comments, '*Shema Yisrael* — in the merit of your reciting *Shema Yisrael*, you will succeed in battle.'"

By now the audience was completely still and silent, as was Ido — he had never been part of such a show in his life — all waiting for the young rabbi to continue.

"*Chevrah*," he called out, raising his voice, "the entire country is looking to you right now. Every single person in the country is hoping for your success and your victory. No one here knows who will come out of this alive and who will not. With what do you want to occupy your final hour before going into battle? With the message of *Shema Yisrael* or with a comedy show, incredible as it may be?"

Thousands of soldiers, along with Ido, who had become as emotional as the rest, shouted as one, "*Shema Yisrael!*"

There and then, standing on that temporary stage set up in the foothills of the Hermon, Rav Yitzchak Dovid Grossman entered Yom Kippur mode, and in a voice filled with emotion and sincerity, he uttered the line Jewish people everywhere recite during the final moments of *Ne'ilah*, the prayer said as the Yom Kippur prayers are coming to an end.

"*Shema Yisrael Hashem Elokeinu Hashem echad!* — Here, O Israel, Hashem is our G-d, Hashem is One!"

Every single one of the soldiers belted out the words of *Shema Yisrael* from the depths of his soul, sending them up to the very heart of Heaven.

"*Hashem Hu haElokim!* — Hashem is G-d!"

Thousands roared the words with every fiber of their being.

"*Hashem melech Hashem malach Hashem yimloch l'olam va'ed!* — Hashem is our king, Hashem was our king, and Hashem will be our king for all eternity!"

Tears streaming down their faces, the soldiers uttered the final words of *Ne'ilah*, the sound of their voices reverberating through the night air and up, up, up…

And then the rabbi broke into the famous song, "*Yisrael, Yisrael, betach baShem…*," and the band began to play and Ido joined in, the sound of their voices blending together, a mixture of Yom Kippur and

Simchas Torah all in one. They sang the song again and again, over and over. *"Yisrael, Yisrael, Yisrael, betach baShem* — Israel, trust in G-d; *ezram u'maginum Hu!* — He is their savior and shield."

Gone were all thoughts of merriment and joking banter. Ido was serious now, the two of them, the rabbi and the comedian, leading the crowd in a moment of sheer spirituality.

And then, suddenly, with no warning, the order was heard.

"L'krav! To battle!"

The band jumped back into their car, while Rav Grossman was bundled into the army jeep, which sped away from the scene as quickly as possible. In his mind's eye, he could still see the sight of all those earnest faces as the soldiers recited the Shema in the moments leading up to the fateful battle that was so vital, so crucial, for the safety of their land. He could still see Ido, his eyes closed as he recited the concluding words of the Yom Kippur prayers, as if he had been religious his entire life.

"Shema Yisrael!..."

"Hashem Hu haElokim!"

"Yisrael, betach baShem!..."

As the jeep carrying the rabbi made its way down the hairpin turns

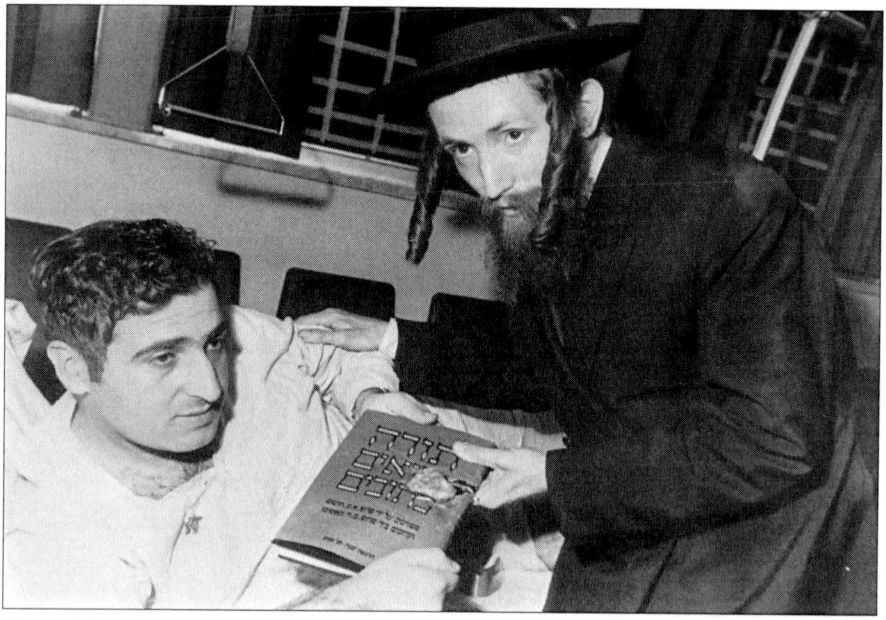

This soldier, one of those who was with Rav Grossman at the foot of Mount Hermon, was so inspired that he took this Tanach (Bible) with him in battle, where he was wounded. Here, recovering, he shows it to Rav Grossman — complete with a bullet hole. The sefer saved his life!

of the steep mountain roads, the soldiers boarded their vehicles for the battlefield, and Israeli jets streaked overhead, determined to rout the enemy. And in their minds reverberated the words that would give them the strength and courage they would need in battle: "*Yisrael, Yisrael, betach baShem!* Nation of Israel, trust in G-d!"

In the aftermath of the war, Rav Grossman received a letter from one of the officers who had been there during his visit:

> *Kevod HaRav,*
>
> Many of the *chevrah* cried in their hearts after you left us, asking themselves why it was that they had never believed until that point. Asking themselves why it was that they had never possessed the feeling of what it means to be a genuine Jew.
>
> During the time you were with us, every single soldier lifted his eyes up to the heavens and begged Hashem for forgiveness.
>
> Rav Grossman, you need to come speak to the soldiers not only before they go out to battle but even during the normal times, when all is well. Because they need to hear what you have to say!

Decades later, Rav Grossman was visiting London when he happened to run into Shimon Sheves, the chief of staff and director general of the prime minister's office during Rabin's tenure.

"Rav Grossman," he said, "I don't know if you heard, but I'm in the process of writing a book, and there's even a chapter about you."

"About me? What does it say?"

"Do you remember visiting the Chermon in '73, just before we reconquered the mountain?"

"Of course."

"I was one of the officers there that night, and I want to tell you something that I don't think you know. The army had already planned the route of their attack and decided from where the tanks were going to begin their climb to the top. To our dismay, the Syrians, perhaps in anticipation of our plans, moved their tanks to the front of the mountain, cutting us off and forcing us to choose another route, one we knew would be considerably more challenging for the tanks and the soldiers. But we didn't have a choice. The Syrian tanks were blocking our path, poised to blow up anything that approached.

"Then you stepped onto that stage and began your speech. And during

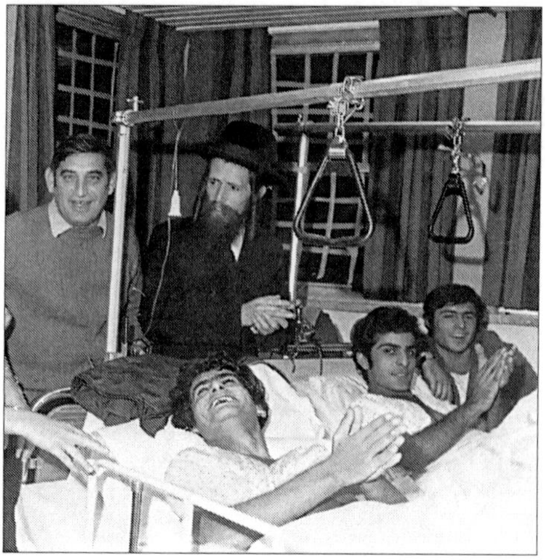

Visiting the wounded

the forty-five minutes that you spoke, sang, and prayed with our soldiers, the Syrians began moving their tanks from the edge of the mountain, seemingly without any reason. Their decision enabled the army to return to the original plan and saved countless lives."

Rav Grossman recalled the brave soldiers and the expressions on their faces, their earnestness and sincerity, the way they sang and said *Shema Yisrael* with the utmost concentration. And he was not at all surprised that they had been able to maneuver the Syrian army away from the edge of the mountain. Not after a *Ne'ilah* davening like the one they'd experienced.

Nearly fifty years have passed since the Yom Kippur War, but the impact of that pivotal time still remains. Last year the office of Migdal Ohr received a call from someone who wanted to speak to Rav Grossman about something that had happened during the Yom Kippur War.

"Did you get his name and number?" Rav Grossman asked the secretary.

"Yes. His name is Uri Sasson."

Rav Grossman dialed the number and seconds later found himself drawn back into the events that occurred fifty years earlier, in 1973.

> Uri related: During the war, I was part of a tank brigade that was supposed to fight on the southern front, but we were sent to the north by mistake. The war had thrown the entire country into a turmoil, and numerous mistakes were being made due to the vagaries of battle. One hand had no idea what the other hand was doing.
>
> Sending a brigade to the wrong part of the country would have been bad enough, but sending a tank brigade was infinitely worse, since it took us so long to transport the tanks up north. And then, when we finally arrived at the Golan, we were informed that we

were at the wrong battlefield and had to make another seemingly endless trip to the other side of the country.

As I said, it was an epic mess. With no choice, we turned around and began the long trek down south, where we were ordered to follow Arik Sharon across the Suez Canal and into Egypt. By the time we arrived down south, we were exhausted and needed some time to recharge our batteries before being sent into combat. We were directed to a forest and instructed to get some sleep in preparation for the battle to come.

And so we spread out our sleeping bags, climbed inside, and tried to drift off — a thousand soldiers all trying to rest. But it was too hard to sleep. Our hearts were pounding with fear because we knew that in a few hours we would be climbing into our tanks and heading off into battle, and who knew if we would make it out alive?

And then, in the middle of the night, we heard the sound of a song being sung — the kind of song that is determined to put joy into a person's heart and lift his spirits. Someone was singing *'V'Samachta B'Chagecha'* — a joyous holiday tune — and the sound of the song shook me out of the half slumber I'd been in. I sat up groggily, trying to figure out if I was still in this world or had been transferred to the next.

Rav Grossman listened intently as Uri Sasson told his story, and then it all came rushing back.

Rav Grossman's father-in-law, Rav Dov Berish Rosenberg, lived in the city of Lod. Since the Syrians were shelling the area around Migdal HaEmek, knocking down buildings and homes as they attempted to strike the nearby Ramat David army base, the Grossmans left Migdal HaEmek and went to stay in Lod for a few weeks, while the students returned to their homes. On Chol HaMo'ed Succos, the days between the first and last days of the Succos holiday, someone showed up at the local Chabad shul and informed the congregants that an entire brigade had been sent up north and then down south and were lying exhausted and broken in a forest somewhere near the battlefield.

"These soldiers need *chizuk,* encouragement," they were told. "Are there any volunteers?"

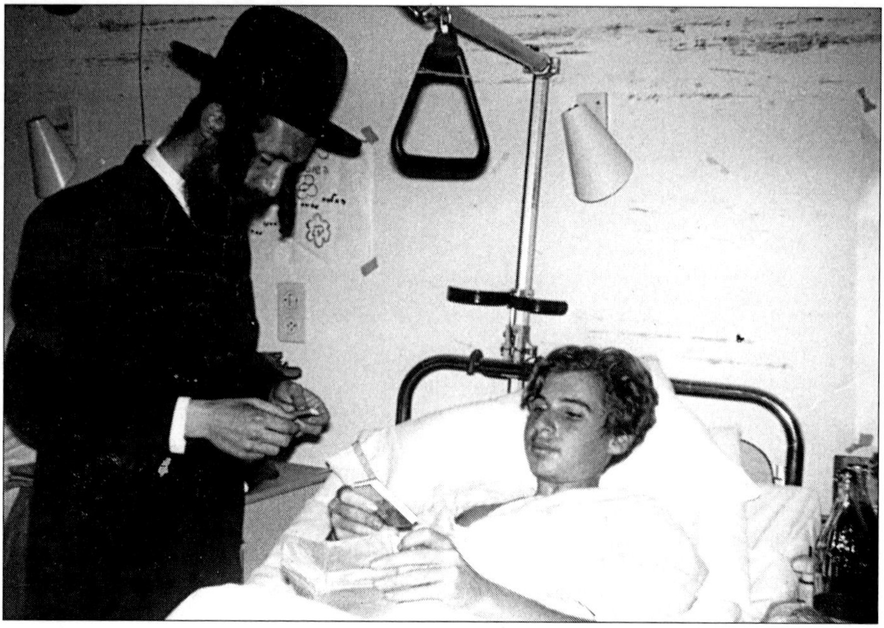

Visiting a wounded soldier

A few of the local Chabadnikim joined Rav Grossman for the trip to bring some *simchah* (joy) to the soldiers who were so weary and beaten. Rav Grossman packed boxes of fruit and cases of soda to take to the soldiers, and they set off for the drive, arriving in the darkest hours of the night.

On the way into the forest, they passed a long line of buses waiting on the side of the road to transport the soldiers to the front line. The trees towered over them, obscuring the star-strewn sky above. It was three in the morning, and the soldiers were leaving for battle within a couple of hours. Rav Grossman felt bad disturbing their rest, but he knew they had to get up soon anyway, and they might as well leave from a position of hope and confidence.

But how to rouse them?

Then the idea of singing them awake came into his mind, and together with the seven other chassidim who had accompanied him, he began to sing *"V'Samachta B'Chagecha"* with joy and fervor. Gradually the rows of soldiers came to life, the looks of groggy puzzlement on their faces gradually replaced by smiles of greeting for the visitors who had gone out of their way to travel so far to come and sing for them, to share some fruit, and enjoy a soft drink in honor of the holiday. It wasn't long before some of the soldiers joined them in song and others in dance, and the mood transformed from hopeless despair to cautious optimism in some and unbridled exultation in others.

Dawn wasn't far off as the soldiers stood at attention before boarding the buses and Rav Grossman gave them a little *chizuk*.

"My friends," he said, "I want you to remember one thing as you head off into battle: The happier you are, the more successful you will be. The more *simchah* you feel, the better you will fight on the battlefield!"

It was a short speech, but it packed the right punch, and then the seven Chabadnikim and Rav Grossman watched as the soldiers stepped onto the buses and drove off just as the day was beginning to dawn.

"The story might have had a very different ending," Uri continued, "but as bombs exploded all around us, with the sounds of shelling assaulting our ears and the ever-present fear of death or capture in our hearts, those of us who had heard the Rav's words before we boarded the buses yelled to one another, 'Remember what Rav Grossman said: *The happier you are, the more successful you will be. The more simchah you feel, the better you will fight on the battlefield!*'

"We held tightly onto those words through the coming hours and kept them in our minds when we returned from fighting for our people and country."

Forty-five years after the event, Uri Sasson was still carrying those words with him, along with the impact they had made on him and his fellow soldiers. It was an emotional moment for both of them.

The two men spoke for a few more minutes before hanging up.

"Rav Grossman," Uri said, before the conversation came to a close.

"Yes, my friend?"

"I've been waiting to tell you how much your words had an effect on us for forty-five years. That's how powerful they were."

And Rav Grossman thanked Hashem yet again for allowing His people to win a fight for their lives and for being able to have had some small part in it.

CHAPTER FIFTEEN

Night on the Kinneret

Rav Grossman had a very close relationship with the Kaliver Rebbe. They first came to know one another when the Rebbe arrived in Eretz Yisrael and traveled from one small village to another, telling his story and getting to know the people of Israel. In addition to the numerous incredible facets of his character, the Kaliver Rebbe possessed a magnificent singing voice, which he used to draw his brethren closer to the Master of the World.

One of the places in which the Rebbe spent Shabbos was Migdal HaEmek, and the two of them became extremely close. During that visit, the Rebbe invited Rav Grossman to accompany him on his trips to army bases around the country, where he spoke with the soldiers and gave them *chizuk* and encouragement.

One evening, during a visit Rav Grossman had made to the Rebbe, the two of them sat together on the porch of the Rebbe's apartment in the older part of the city of Tiveria, overlooking the Kinneret. It was dark outside, and while the lake itself was not visible, they were able to see the lights from the moshavim and kibbutzim on the other side of the lake twinkling like so many fireflies in the nighttime air.

"Tell me," the Rebbe said to Rav Grossman, "what are those lights? What's the name of the *yishuv* (settlement) that I'm seeing?"

"It's a famous kibbutz called Ein Gev."

"Who lives there?"

"*Chilonim*, Jews who are not Torah-observant."

"Only *chilonim*?"

"That's correct."

Rav Grossman and the Kaliver Rebbe, surrounded by Migdal Ohr boys

"What's a kibbutz?" came the Rebbe's next question. He hadn't been in Israel that long yet and was still unfamiliar with the local terminology.

"If the Rebbe wants," Rav Grossman suggested, "I can take him on a tour of the kibbutz and show it to him firsthand."

"I would like that," the Rebbe replied, accepting his younger friend's offer.

Since this story took place during vacation time, it was possible to hire a boat to take them across the lake even at that time of night. The walk from the Rebbe's apartment to the Kinneret was very short, and it wasn't long before they found themselves at one of the rental stands on the shores of the harp-shaped lake.

Five minutes later they were off, the two of them sitting in the stern of a motorboat as it shot across the Kinneret, skimming the waves and sending a fine spray of mist into the air. The night sky was filled with a million shining stars, and it felt like the world was alive with possibility. The journey didn't take long, and soon they were docking at Kibbutz Ein Gev. They asked the boat captain to wait for their return, and they disembarked.

Many chassidic Rebbes have the custom of wearing colorful *bekeshes*, or caftans, but the Kaliver Rebbe outshone virtually all of them with his caftans of purple and gold. He was a splendidly impressive sight, drawing the eye of anyone who met him. As they headed into the kibbutz from the dock, Rav Grossman was sure that anyone who passed them on the streets of the kibbutz couldn't fail to take note of the regal rabbinic figure, clad in wide-brimmed felt hat, opulent caftan, and shining countenance.

Soon the two rabbanim came upon a child walking down the street. At that time, the Rebbe's Ivrit wasn't yet fluent, and he said to the child, *"Yeled, eifoh habeis knesses?* Young man, where is the local synagogue?" delivering the line with a chassidic inflection.

"Habeis knesses?" the boy repeated, trying to understand the Rebbe's question.

The Rebbe nodded eagerly.

Eventually the boy grasped that the Rebbe meant to say *"beit knesset."*

"Ein po beit knesset," he replied. "There is no shul here."

The Rebbe was extremely taken aback. In fact, he was shocked to the core of his being.

"There's no shul here?! This is a Jewish town and there's no shul? How could that be?! *Mi haba'al habayis po?* Who is in charge here?"

Rav Grossman interjected and explained to the Rebbe that in kibbutz hierarchy, the person who was appointed secretary of the kibbutz was the leader.

"I need to meet with him immediately!"

The Kaliver Rebbe was adamant, and there was no swaying him. Seeing that the Rebbe wouldn't take no for an answer, Rav Grossman led him to the kibbutz administrative offices, where they found the secretary, Muki Tzur, still sitting at his desk and hard at work. Tzur would later go on to serve as an MK for the Labor Party, but at that time he was a mere kibbutz secretary with dreams of moving up in the political arena. There is no question that the last thing Tzur expected to see that night was two distinguished rabbis with long coats and black hats — one clearly of the chassidic rabbi genre. He recognized Rav Grossman from the television documentary about the Disco Rabbi, but he had never heard of the Kaliver Rebbe and was completely unprepared for the assault that was about to be launched against him.

"Eich yachol liheyos? How could such a thing possibly be true?" the

Rebbe demanded in his broken Hebrew. "I asked a Jewish child where the *beis knesses* is, and he told me that you don't have one! I was in thirty different camps in the Holocaust, I went through the horrors of Auschwitz and Majdanek, and I can't understand how Jews who have the privilege of living in Eretz Yisrael could possibly live in a place without a *beis knesses*!"

Tzur tried his best to explain to the distraught Kaliver Rebbe how life worked in a kibbutz, but the visitor would not be mollified. If anything, he only grew more agitated at the attempted justification.

"Muki," Rav Grossman interjected at last, "I have an idea."

"What's that?" Tzur asked, at a loss.

"The Kaliver Rebbe has a treasure trove of stories about his personal experiences during the Holocaust. Above and beyond his storytelling abilities, the Rebbe has a voice that is reminiscent of a violin. I suggest that you organize a 'chassidic evening in the kibbutz' featuring the Kaliver Rebbe, who will tell his stories and sing his songs. I will also attend and share some of my life experiences with the members of the kibbutz. You'll hang up posters advertising the event, which we will hold this coming Motza'ei Shabbos. What do you say?"

Not knowing what else to do and wanting to calm down his illustrious visitor, Muki Tzur agreed to host a chassidic evening in Kibbutz Ein Gev.

The next Motza'ei Shabbos, Rav Grossman and the Kaliver Rebbe did a reprise of their boat ride across the Kinneret. The sky was as star-studded as it had been on the previous Monday, but now they knew what had drawn them across the lake and to the kibbutz. They had a mission to fulfill, and they intended to do their best. The Rebbe carried a large mezuzah with him, planning on using it to make a point.

The boat docked at the kibbutz, and they retraced their steps into the village and over to the dining room, which was packed, every seat taken. Clearly, the members of the kibbutz considered the evening's entertainment the kind of attraction they didn't want to miss.

Having arrived armed with a hammer to put up the mezuzah, the Kaliver Rebbe paused in the threshold to the dining room as every person sitting rose to his feet.

"I've brought you a gift that will watch over you," he told them and proceeded to knock the mezuzah into the doorpost and recite the *berachah* (blessing) out loud, his voice trembling with emotion, which was followed by a thunderous "Amen!"

The people of Ein Gev were a little shocked by the sight of the Rebbe who had swept into their lives in a *shtreimel* and magnificent *bekeshe,* the hat and robe worn by some chassidim, along with his charismatic friend with the piercing eyes and long *peyos* and beard.

After the mezuzah-installation ceremony had reached its natural conclusion, everyone sat down, and Rav Grossman introduced the Kaliver Rebbe, giving the kibbutzniks a thumbnail sketch of who the Rebbe was and the trials he'd experienced during the war.

The Kaliver Rebbe stood at the front of the kibbutz dining room, and rather than start the evening with words, he raised his magnificent voice and began to sing. The name of the song was "*Atah Chonein L'Adam Da'as,*" a song he had composed, and from the first moment the notes of the melody began to cascade over the people sitting in the simple room, they became his. They watched him sing, and it was as if they were seeing their grandfathers from the shtetls of Europe come alive.

When he finished singing, the Rebbe began to speak, telling the audience about his time in the camps and about the *mesirus nefesh,* the self-sacrifice he'd witnessed firsthand, of how his fellow Jews refused to give in to their tormentors and remained adamantly attached to their faith. He described the many times he had been one step away from the fire and the pit, and Hashem saved him at the last instant through yet another miracle. Then it was Rav Grossman's turn, and he related how he had come to trade his life in Yerushalayim for an entirely different kind of life in Migdal HaEmek.

Eventually the Kaliver Rebbe brought the night around to the real reason they were there. He explained that he had never imagined that there could be such a place as a Jewish village without a shul and that he wanted to make a request.

"I want you to set aside a place in the kibbutz — it can be anywhere you want, even a small room — and that place will be called the *beit knesset* of the kibbutz. If the Master of the World saved so many Jewish people from the gas chambers of Europe, and we were fortunate enough to return to the shores of Eretz Yisrael, then we must have a shul wherever we live!"

Amazingly enough, his words were accepted without any opposition. Somehow the Rebbe had succeeded in getting through to the people of Ein Gev.

"I'm handing out a sheet of paper," Rav Grossman said to the crowd as the hour grew late. "Anyone who wants a mezuzah for his house should write down his name, and I'll send him a mezuzah."

Seventeen people signed their names.

A man named Baruch Zeira had attended the Kaliver Rebbe's evening. Originally from Satmar, he began to cry during the Rebbe's speech. It was the words of the Kaliver Rebbe reminding him of his past life back in Europe and the way he had grown up that had prompted the tears.

"If you do return here with mezuzos," he told Rav Grossman afterward, "please bring them to me because I want to be the one to hand them out and help to place them on their doorposts if they want."

The next day, Rav Grossman's brother, Rav Bentzion, traveled to Ein Gev with seventeen mezuzos, which he delivered to Baruch Zeira, who thanked him profusely and made sure to distribute them to everyone on the list.

Sometime afterward, Zeira sent Rav Grossman a letter:

> Dear Rav Grossman,
>
> I just wanted to tell you what happened. I took the mezuzos from your brother and distributed them to the people on the list. Some of them wanted me to put it up for them, while others asked me to tell them what *berachah* to say and then put it up themselves.
>
> These are the people of the kibbutzim, who didn't know and never heard anything about what it means to be a Jew. And yet they are so incredibly thirsty for everything you have to say!

With Baruch Zeira

But the story wasn't over yet. In fact, it circled back on itself and returned to where it began. You see, the boy whom Rav Grossman and the Kaliver Rebbe met on their way up from the dock to the kibbutz was called Effy Eitam,

Effy Eitam, visiting with Rav Grossman in Midreshet HaGalil.
To his right is the head of Midreshet HaGalil, Rav Borenstein

and he was a child of the kibbutz. Later he told Rav Grossman that from the night he and the Kaliver Rebbe came to speak to the kibbutzniks, his life was never the same again. Effy eventually became religious and grew up to make a name for himself both in the IDF and later in politics. In 2020, he was even put on the shortlist to head Yad Vashem. And it all began on a quiet Monday night in a narrow street in Kibbutz Ein Gev.

CHAPTER SIXTEEN

The Wolfson Doctrine

In the early 1970s, with his dream of a youth village beginning to turn into a reality, Rav Grossman for the second time flew to the States to raise funds. This time he contacted the heads of American P'eylim, Rabbi Avraham Hirsch and Rabbi Yaakov Weisberg, who promised they would introduce him to key players around the country and organize speaking engagements for him at various yeshivos and other institutions. He also arranged to stay with Rabbi Paysach Krohn and his rebbetzin in Kew Gardens. (For decades after he'd been there, the

Rabbi Paysach Krohn at a Migdal Ohr dinner

bedroom door in the Krohn home where Rav Yitzchak Dovid had stayed prominently displayed a plaque with the words "Migdal Ohr.") "We were Migdal Ohr's first 'office' in America," Rabbi Krohn remembers. "We became like brothers. The bookkeeping, the checks, the appointments, my wife and I took care of all of it right there in our home."

P'eylim brought Rav Grossman to Cleveland, where he gave a speech in Telz, and to Yeshivas Chaim Berlin, where he was not only given the opportunity to address the students of the yeshivah but also came to develop a relationship with its legendary rosh yeshivah, Rav Yitzchak Hutner. P'eylim made sure to introduce Rav Grossman to the rosh yeshivah of Beth Medrash Govoha in Lakewood, Rav Shneur Kotler, and they, too, formed a close bond. (At a Migdal Ohr dinner at the Waldorf Astoria in Manhattan four years after their initial meeting, Rav Shneur honored his friend by giving a speech there.) Rav Grossman was also driven to Baltimore, where he was introduced to Rav Yaakov Yitzchak Ruderman and Rabbi Naftali Neuberger of Ner Yisrael.

P'eylim was endorsed in no uncertain terms by Rav Moshe Feinstein and Rav Yaakov Kamenetsky, who were always available to help them in any way possible. The *gedolim* (great Torah leaders) treated the young rabbi from Migdal HaEmek with love and kindness, making him feel very much at home, though he was far from his family and familiar surroundings. So close were they that when Rav Yaakov Kamenetsky visited Eretz Yisrael, he traveled up north to visit with Rav Grossman at Migdal Ohr, where he spent considerable time getting to know the students, receiving immense *nachas* (pleasure) from the miracles taking place there on a daily basis.

Of course, it wasn't only American *gedolim* who appreciated what was being accomplished at Migdal Ohr. Over the years, Rav Grossman would be given the opportunity to welcome to his youth village three of the Gerrer Rebbes — the Beis Yisrael, the Lev Simchah, and the Pnei Menachem — each of whom went out of his way to make the trip to Migdal HaEmek so that he could witness what was going on there with his own eyes.

Rav Grossman also had the pleasure of hosting the Skulener Rebbe, Rav Eliezer Zusha Portugal, for Shabbos. For the Skulener Rebbe, who had survived a Romanian prison, visiting Migdal Ohr was especially poignant, since he had personally rescued many of the children learning there from incarceration in Romanian prisons. Upon catching sight of the Rebbe who had saved their lives, the children surrounded him, crying out, "Abba!" and "Tatte!" as they turned their faces up to him and begged him to bless them.

As Rav Grossman made the rounds of American Orthodox communities around the country, more and more people found out about Rav Yitzchak Dovid Grossman and the holy work he was doing in Migdal HaEmek. On his part, he felt that he was laying the foundation for the future growth of Migdal Ohr, the many buildings that were yet to be built and the many students who would benefit. Yet it wasn't only about the future, because many of those he met introduced him to generous people who became "chassidim" of Migdal Ohr after a short visit and happily contributed to the cause.

Rav Grossman had a knack for connecting with everyone he met. There was something magical about him, an intangible element that drew people to the young rabbi and made them want to learn more about his institution and his dreams for the future. Maybe it was his smile or the gleam in his eyes when he spoke. Maybe it was his authenticity or the fact that he had traded everything he had always known for a new life in one of the most crime-filled cities in the country. It was hard to put a finger on what made people respond to him as they did, but the reality couldn't be denied.

One Shabbos during that visit to the United States, Rabbi Krohn arranged for his guest to speak at a local shul in Queens. Rav Grossman stood at the *bimah* (podium) before Mussaf (the second prayer recited on Shabbos morning) and, looking around the packed room, the rabbi from Migdal HaEmek began to speak.

"There was a town where a gigantic fire broke out. The fire department arrived quickly at the scene to put out the fire, but after a while they ran out of water. The people of the town had to run to the river and bring buckets of water so that the fire department could continue putting out the fire.

"*Rabbosai*, my friends, when I arrived in Migdal HaEmek, I found a city on fire. A fire that was burning the people's very souls. I immediately began working to put out the fire, doing whatever I could to douse the flames. But I have run out of water, and I need help in getting more.

"If we want there to be Torah in Migdal HaEmek, then I need many more buckets of water to continue putting out the flames, and that is why I am turning to you for help in my mission."

A gallery of greatness — Rav Grossman

With Rav Gershon Edelstein

With Rav Chaim Kanievsky

With the Admor of Erloi

With Rav Chaim Pinchas Scheinberg and Rav Meir Bransdorfer on a visit to Migdal Ohr

Rav Yaakov Perlow, the Novominsker Rebbe, and Rav Shneur Kotler, at the first Migdal Ohr dinner in the Waldorf-Astoria Hotel

With the Sadigurer Rebbe (left) and the Lelover Rebbe (right)

With the Vizhnitzer Rebbe

With the Tosher Rebbe

meets with many gedolei Yisrael

With Rav Yitzchak Tuvia Weiss on a visit to Migdal Ohr

With Rav Yitzchak Yosef

With Rav Mordechai Eliyahu, testing the students of Migdal Ohr

With Rav Yaakov Kamenetsky, visiting Migdal Ohr

With Rav Shlomo Zalman Auerbach

With Rav Nissim Karelitz testing the students of Migdal Ohr

With Rav Shmuel Wosner

When the young rabbi finished his speech, there was a feeling of electricity coursing through the shul. He sat down, sensing that he had managed to reach the hearts of the people he had addressed. He didn't realize that the speech he had just delivered would go down in history as one of the most important speeches he would ever give, because one of the people sitting in the shul that Shabbos morning was a man by the name of Zev Wolfson.

Zev Wolfson would become renowned as one of the most prominent dispensers of *tzedakah* (charity) in the United States. Zev Wolfson was a true visionary, and he recognized a kindred spirit in Rav Yitzchak Dovid Grossman. Not a man to waste time, Mr. Wolfson approached Rav Grossman, introduced himself, and requested that the Israeli rabbi join his family for the Shabbos meal.

Rav Grossman accepted the invitation, and after the *seudah* (meal) the two of them sat immersed in conversation until the Minchah prayer later that day. It soon became clear that Zev Wolfson saw himself as a natural partner for the rabbi's endeavors in Midgal HaEmek.

While Rav Yitzchak Dovid had been dreaming of accepting more children into his youth village, Zev Wolfson introduced his newfound friend to the concept of thinking on a grander scale. If a person thought

Rav Grossman with Zev Wolfson

small, he wouldn't be able to work with Zev Wolfson. He explained to Rav Grossman that he needed to stop thinking about helping dozens or even hundreds of children and should instead begin imagining a youth village that had the resources to help thousands of children maximize their potential.

Zev Wolfson's message to his guest felt like ice water sliding down a parched throat on a boiling-hot summer's day. As he spoke, Rav Grossman began to actually envision such a place. It wasn't just a dream, but would become a reality.

"You're going to build state-of-the-art schools," Zev Wolfson pronounced, "and I'm going to introduce you to my contacts at the highest levels of government."

By the time the conversation wound to a close, Rav Grossman would never relate to his mission the same way again. His horizons had been expanded, and from that moment onward he would never cease being a firm supporter of the Wolfson Doctrine.

Over the next two years, Rav Grossman formulated a plan for what he hoped to accomplish. It was a truly grand mission, composed of multiple buildings, homes for the staff, and all sorts of other facilities. He was now thinking in terms of an entire complex, and his initial plans for one building evolved into seven, which included a beautiful study hall, dining rooms, dormitories, and classrooms. With this new vision in mind, he hired a team of architects to design the buildings and construct models of the future campus. Zev Wolfson had taught him to think big, and Rav Grossman took his vision and ran with it.

"What was amazing about Zev," Rav Grossman says, "was not that he sat down and wrote me a check. That wasn't his thing. Yes, he gave money to Migdal Ohr, but his focus was on the long-term game, on helping me develop connections within the Israeli government, with people who would understand what we were trying to achieve and would help us receive government funding to get it."

There is no question that Zev Wolfson had taught Rav Yitzchak Dovid Grossman a whole new way of thinking.

By 1975 Migdal Ohr was ready to lay the cornerstone for the campus's first building, and the plan was to hold a ceremony that would put the institution on the map.

Jewish music was still in its infancy, and one of the big names of the

Laying the cornerstone for the Migdal Ohr campus (l to r): Rav Ovadia Yosef, Rav Yitzchak Abuchatzeira, Rav Grossman, Rabbi Paysach Krohn

day was the London School of Jewish Song, run by a man named Yigal Calek from Golders Green. Besides flying in the choir from London, Rav Grossman invited numerous rabbis and political figures to the event, where the model of the future campus of Migdal Ohr would be on display for all to see.

When the emcee invited one of the rabbanim who also happened to be a relative of Rav Grossman to come up on the stage to speak, the rav turned down the invitation and remained seated. It didn't really make a difference because there were many others who were scheduled to address the crowd, all in addition to the full orchestra and musical entertainment (the choir from London was a huge hit with a new song called "*Samcheinu*" that they introduced to the audience), but still, it bothered Rav Grossman that this particular rav declined to speak.

When the festivities came to an end, and he was alone with his relative, Rav Grossman turned to him and asked, "Can you tell me why you refused to give a speech?"

"I don't give blessings to fantasies," the other replied.

Knowing that his relative was a man of *emes*, a man of truth, Rav Grossman wasn't surprised by his answer, but he couldn't deny that it stung. If this man who knew him so well didn't believe that he would succeed, who knew what everyone else was thinking?

But the next words out of his relative's mouth saved the day.

"If you succeed in fulfilling your dream and creating your youth village," the rav said, "and the day arrives when I can actually see the buildings of your village with my own eyes, I will return here for the ceremony, and then I will speak!"

Rav Grossman helps lay the cornerstone. His father-in-law, Rav Dov Berish, is behind him.

And so it was that this close relative, a man whom the rav respected immensely — a man who had given Rav Yitzchak Dovid the challenge of proving him wrong — returned to Migdal HaEmek a few years later, and he stood on the stage and delivered a rousing speech that shook the crowd and brought them to tears. And when he finished, he turned to Rav Grossman and smiled at him, and in that smile Rav Grossman understood that the other's refusal to speak at the groundbreaking ceremony had all been part of a plan to make sure that the young rabbi would carry out his "fantasy," turning it from a dream into seven very real buildings, which stood tall and proud and heralded the many others that would be added to their number over the coming years.

Rav Grossman's relationship with Zev Wolfson only intensified and became stronger through the years. The two traveled together to the Soviet Union, South America, and France, establishing an educational Torah network in those places whose goal was to teach as many Jewish children about *Yiddishkeit* and authentic Torah Judaism as possible. Wolfson liked to quote the verse "*Ki ner mitzvah v'Torah ohr* — For a mitzvah is a candle and the Torah is light," explaining that Torah is like a fire because just as fire gains power and gets stronger as it spreads, so does Torah grow the more it is spread.

In addition to Zev Wolfson's firm belief that every dollar he invested in Torah and mitzvos was the best kind of investment a person could make, there was another incredible facet to his personality, and that was that he went out of his way to run away from honor. He didn't want anyone to put his name on the buildings he built or the projects he developed. He didn't seek recognition. If Rav Grossman wanted to honor him at a dinner, he didn't allow it, and he did his utmost to keep his picture out of the limelight.

But Rav Grossman wanted to do something for his dear friend, and he thought long and hard about what kind of gift a man like Zev Wolfson would appreciate.

Finally, it came to him.

He would give to his dear friend, who had been personally responsible for the phenomenal growth of Torah among those who had merited to benefit from his endeavors, a Sefer Torah, a Torah scroll. And not just any Sefer Torah. Rav Grossman was thinking of a particular Sefer Torah, one that had survived the concentration camps. This was a perfect gift because Zev Wolfson was a person who single-handedly helped save so many Jews from a spiritual Holocaust. And while he had donated so many *sifrei Torah*, he himself didn't own one.

At first, he didn't agree to accept the gift, but Rav Grossman convinced him to take it, explaining why he felt it was so fitting. At the *hachnassas Sefer Torah*, the ceremony where the Torah scroll is brought to its new home, Mr. Wolfson took the Sefer Torah in hand, hugged it, and began dancing with fervor as he burst into tears. It was an unforgettable moment for all who had the good fortune to be present.

"As for me," Rav Grossman says, "I was filled with *hakaras hatov*, with gratitude to Hashem for having given me the opportunity to repay just a little to a man like Zev Wolfson, who did so much for Klal Yisrael and for Migdal Ohr."

Rabbi Leizer Rosner was handpicked by Mr. Wolfson to be his representative in Israel for the Wolfson Foundation. Mr. Wolfson discovered Rabbi Rosner, who was then working as a rabbi in Canada, and convinced him to chart a new course in life and relocate to the other side of the world, where he would work tirelessly day and night to establish more and more Torah institutions. Having set the wheels into motion, Mr. Wolfson then called Rav Yitzchak Dovid Grossman and asked him to please meet Rabbi Rosner at Ben Gurion Airport and to welcome him to Israel.

Rav Grossman agreed.

In retrospect, Rav Yitzchak Dovid admits that at the time he couldn't comprehend Wolfson's decision to take a rabbi from Canada, send him into the rough and tumble Israeli society, and hope that he would succeed in such a challenging environment. He couldn't imagine that such a person could possibly be equipped to fill the role that Zev Wolfson had in mind for him. But Zev Wolfson turned out to have made the perfect choice, because Rabbi Rosner went on to help establish around one hundred institutions during his tenure as Wolfson's man in Israel.

Rabbi Rosner and Rav Yitzchak Dovid were close friends almost from the first moment of meeting, with Rav Grossman always available to do whatever he could for Rabbi Rosner and vice versa.

In the late 80s, Migdal Ohr was in dire need of new classrooms for the students. Reb Leizer used his connections within the Israeli government to arrange a meeting between a top-level official at the Ministry of Education and Rav Yitzchak Dovid.

The meeting that Reb Leizer arranged for Rav Grossman was scheduled for a specific time at the Sheraton Plaza in downtown Jerusalem. Rav Yitzchak Dovid was supposed to come and plead his case for the classrooms that he needed so desperately. He was not far from the hotel when he passed a woman in the street — who upon recognizing the rabbi, called out his name. The rabbi stopped in his tracks and turned to the woman, who was clearly distraught. Though he was on his way to a crucial meeting, Rav Yitzchak Dovid didn't have the heart to ignore her, and he stopped and asked her what the problem was.

She explained to the rabbi that she was an *almanah,* a widow, who was experiencing many difficult challenges. Chief among her issues were her two daughters and the fact that she had no idea how to get along with them.

"I traveled today to Yerushalayim, because I had a meeting with one of the institutions that are geared to accept children like mine."

"What happened?"

"I explained the situation and was turned down. They told me that they would not be accepting my daughters. I begged them. I told them how terrible it is at home, but they didn't listen. I was on the way back to the central bus station to catch a bus to take me home," she said, "when I saw Rav Grossman passing by and I told myself, 'if there is one person in the world who might be able to help me get my daughters into the right environment for them, it's him.' That's when I called out your name," she concluded, wiping the tears from her eyes.

Rav Yitzchak Dovid didn't hesitate. Whereas many people would have told the woman that while they sympathized with her, they had no time to deal with her situation just then because they were on the way to an important meeting, he did no such thing.

"I'm coming with you," he told her. "Let's go back to the school where you want to send your daughters."

Together, the two of them made their way over to the institution in question — with Rav Grossman ignoring the fact that he had to be at the hotel to meet with an official who possessed the capability to funnel large quantities of money to Migdal Ohr so that they would be able to build many additional classrooms. He wanted to be at the meeting — he needed to be at the meeting — but there were two Jewish children in need of salvation, and that had to come first. He had always lived his life with that principle and he would continue to do so, come what may. Children came first, money second.

At the school, Rav Yitzchak Dovid made it very clear that he was there as the personal representative of the two girls and that it was very important to him that they be accepted as students. He let nothing get in his way and was not deterred by any excuses. In the end, the girls were accepted.

While all this was going on, Rabbi Rosner was sitting in the hotel with the representative of the Ministry of Education. He couldn't understand where Rav Grossman was. These were pre-cellphone days and he had no way of reaching the rabbi. In the end he reassured the official that if Rav Grossman wasn't there, no doubt there was a good reason for his absence.

Rav Grossman knew that he had to let Rabbi Rosner know that something had come up and he would be late. While the mother of the girls was pleading her case, he asked to use the phone, dialed the hotel, and had them page his friend.

"Where are you?"

"I'm sorry, something came up."

"What do you mean?"

"I mean that I am now in the process of helping two girls get into a school and I will not be able to attend our meeting."

Rabbi Leizer Rosner knew Rav Yitzchak Dovid. He knew that when his friend was on a mission there was no use talking to him. The education of Jewish children came before everything else. Wishing Rav Grossman *hatzlachah* (success) in his self-imposed mission he hung up the phone, and turning to the rep from the Ministry of Education, explained that Rav Grossman would in fact not be attending the meeting and that he would be standing in for him.

"What happened?"

Rabbi Rosner told him the truth. "Rav Grossman met a mother who begged him to help get her two daughters into a school that is right for them here in Yerushalayim."

"So?"

"So he agreed to help her and he is at the school right now, doing his utmost to persuade the principal to accept the girls."

Once it was established that Rav Grossman would not be attending the meeting that day, the two men got down to business, with Reb Leizer explaining the classroom needs of Migdal Ohr and the government man listening carefully. The end result was fantastic, with Migdal Ohr receiving a truly generous budget for a large number of new classrooms.

Many times when Rabbi Leizer Rosner would speak in public, he would tell the crowd that in his opinion, the fact that Rav Yitzchak Dovid Grossman chose to miss a meeting that could possibly net millions for Migdal Ohr because of his devotion to the children of Klal Yisrael was the reason he was so successful and saw so much *siyata d'Shmaya* (Heavenly assistance).

"Because he didn't come to the meeting, Hashem rewarded him, and the results were better than we could have ever imagined..."

CHAPTER SEVENTEEN

An Eye-Opening Encounter

During that second visit to America, Rav Grossman merited meeting the Lubavitcher Rebbe at 770 Eastern Parkway in Crown Heights. The introduction was made through another relative, Rav Yehudah Leib Groner, one of the Rebbe's secretaries and a member of his inner circle.

The Rebbe knew Rav Grossman's father, Rav Yisrael, who was the rosh yeshivah of Tomchei Temimim in Lod, a Chabad yeshivah. During

Receiving one of the Lubavitcher Rebbe's famous "dollars." Rabbi Groner, who is Rav Grossman's cousin, is on the left.

the course of that two-and-a-half-hour conversation, it became clear that the Rebbe was well versed in what was going on everywhere in the Jewish world. He knew that his visitor was known throughout Israel as the "Disco Rabbi," that he was changing the religious landscape in Migdal HaEmek, and that he had established a program in the prisons. More than that, the Rebbe seemed to know everything there was to know about Jewish life in Migdal HaEmek, down to the last detail. His visitor was astonished by the Rebbe talking to him about the state of the various *mikva'os* (ritual baths) in the area and discussing what was needed to be done to improve them. They also talked about the state of kashrus supervision in Eretz Yisrael. Then the conversation turned to educational issues, as the Rebbe told Rav Grossman that it bothered him immensely that in Israeli schools, boys and girls learned together in one classroom.

In response to the Rebbe's request that he do his best to separate the girls and boys in the Migdal HaEmek school system, Rav Grossman promised to try. He would bring the top politician in the town — Tzvi Eldorati — to a meeting with the Rebbe in the hope that the Rebbe would succeed in persuading him to make changes.

Rav Grossman returned a year later with Mayor Eldorati and his wife, who was in charge of the local schools. The Rebbe spent close to an hour with them, but it was to no avail and the schools remained as they were.

Years later, when Rav Grossman's oldest daughter was in high school, she developed a severe eye infection. Her eye swelled up, and the entire area changed color and became filled with pus and blood. For eight months straight, she was taken from doctor to doctor and from specialist to specialist, but no one was able to give an accurate diagnosis. They suggested all kinds of treatments, but none were effective. One doctor claimed it was a problem with the eye, another said it was a skin ailment, and yet another claimed it was an allergic reaction. None of them were proven correct.

During that critical period, Rav Grossman wrote a letter to the Lubavitcher Rebbe asking him to daven for his daughter. The next time Rav Grossman was in the United States on a fundraising trip, someone who heard Rav Grossman talking about his daughter's eye ailment mentioned the name of an eye specialist who lived in New Jersey.

Rabbi Grossman with Israeli President Chaim Herzog (left) and Rabbi Leizer Rosner (right)

"He's a top professor and eyes are his specialty," Rav Grossman was told. "In my opinion, it couldn't hurt for you to consult with him."

Rav Grossman made an appointment to meet with the specialist, bringing his daughter's medical records for the doctor to review.

"Rabbi," the doctor said, "I can't make an accurate diagnosis from reading medical records alone. I need to examine your daughter here in my office. Otherwise, we're wasting our time."

Rav Grossman immediately called home and instructed his wife to send their daughter on the next flight to America.

"But who will travel with her?" the rebbetzin asked.

Rav Grossman had already made the arrangements. "Rabbi Leizer Rosner, Zev Wolfson's man in Israel, is flying to America on the next El Al flight. He'll make sure she gets here safely."

So it was that Chaya Grossman boarded a flight to America a few hours later. It was a dreadful flight, since the air pressure made the inflamed eye even worse and Chaya was in horrific pain throughout the plane ride. When the plane landed, it was six in the morning — fortunately there had been no delays — and her appointment with the specialist was scheduled for two hours later, at eight o'clock sharp.

The doctor performed a scan on the eye and informed the patient and her father that he would give them his diagnosis in three days' time. As they left the doctor's office, Chaya Grossman, all of seventeen at the time, told her father that since she had suddenly found herself in America of all places, there was something she really wanted to do.

"What's that?"

"I want to see the Lubavitcher Rebbe."

Her request came as no great surprise considering the Grossman family's strong connection to Chabad. Chaya herself was a student at a Chabad high school in Tzefas. Rav Grossman wanted to oblige his daughter and take her to the Rebbe. The question was how to make that happen. Knowing that the Rebbe arrived at 770 every morning at ten o'clock, Rav Grossman decided that the best thing to do was to just bring his daughter straight there.

Since many people knew the Rebbe's schedule, they would line up outside 770 waiting to catch a glimpse of the legendary tzaddik as he entered the iconic Crown Heights address on his way to yet another day of taking care of Jews all over the world. The Rebbe would get out of the car and pass between the lines of people, greeting them as he walked up to the doors of 770, where a child waited with a *tzedakah* (charity) box. He would put *tzedakah* in the box and then enter the building.

That morning, Rav Grossman was one of those waiting to greet the Rebbe as he arrived at 770. Rav Grossman waited on one side of the Rebbe's path, while his daughter waited on the other.

When the Rebbe began making his way through the lines of people, Rav Grossman detached himself from his spot in the line and stood directly in the Rebbe's path, effectively blocking the Rebbe from continuing to his destination. (What a father doesn't do for his daughter…) When he saw Rav Grossman standing in his path, the Rebbe understood that there must be an emergency situation that needed his attention. The Rebbe gestured with his hand, as if to say, "What's wrong?"

Pointing with his finger in Chaya's direction, Rav Grossman said, "This is my daughter — the one I wrote to the Rebbe about, the one who has a problem with her eye."

The Rebbe glanced toward her for a second, then turned back to Rav Grossman and said, "You need to check the mezuzos immediately. She will have a *refuah sheleimah* (a complete recovery) right away, and you should raise her to Torah, *chuppah,* and *ma'asim tovim* (Torah, marriage and good deeds)."

After this very quick but surprising encounter with the Rebbe, Rav Grossman found a public telephone inside 770 and called Israel, telling his wife that they needed to check the mezuzos on the door of Chaya's room at home and of her dorm room in Tzefas right away. A *sofer* (scribe) was quickly dispatched to check the mezuzos, and he found that in the mezuzah that was on the doorpost of her dorm room, the word *einecha,* "your eyes," was erased. The problem was resolved without delay, and Rav Grossman felt a huge weight roll off his shoulders.

Best of all, Chaya's medical issue all but disappeared within the next twelve hours. Three days later, they returned to the specialist in New Jersey for his professional diagnosis. The moment Chaya walked through the door, the doctor's jaw fell open, and he could not get over what he was seeing. It didn't seem possible that the girl he had examined a few days earlier was the same person he was seeing now, especially considering the fact that the scan he had taken three days earlier was lying on his desk and indicated a serious condition that needed to be treated urgently.

Rav Grossman told him the entire story. And that was it. There was nothing more to say.

Seventeen years later, Rav Grossman was attending a Shabbaton in Teaneck when a Yid standing in the corner of the shul, his siddur opened to the beginning of davening, noticed Rav Grossman enter the room. The man rose from his seat and ran over to hug the rabbi, tears rolling down his cheeks.

Rav Grossman felt bad because he didn't recognize him. But after a few words of conversation, the mystery was solved. It was none other than the doctor who had examined his daughter so many years before.

"After meeting you and your daughter," the doctor said, "I saw the Ribbono shel Olam with my own two eyes! The miracle you shared with me just a few short days after I had examined your daughter and knew the danger facing her made a huge impression on me and set me on a different path in life. Here I am today, *shomer Torah u'mitzvos,* a person who is completely religious, and I have to thank you for entering my life and sharing your story with me because it spurred me to change my life in a dramatic way."

On yet another trip to the States, Rav Grossman was contacted by one of the Rebbe's secretaries, Rabbi Binyamin Klein.

"At this moment," he told Rav Grossman, "I am accompanying the Rebbe. He is davening at the *kever* (grave) of his father-in-law, the Rayatz."

Rav Grossman was surprised that he was being called at such a time, since it was widely known that the Lubavitcher Rebbe could not be disturbed when he was at the Ohel, the world-famous location of the previous Lubavitcher Rebbe's final resting place There were instances when the Rebbe would stand at the *kever* for ten hours straight without budging and nobody could contact him.

"Fifteen minutes ago," Rabbi Klein said, "the Rebbe motioned to me to enter the Ohel. He told me that Rav Grossman from Migdal HaEmek is currently here in the States, and I should please ask him in his name to travel to the Sing Sing Correctional Facility. There he will find a Jewish inmate who needs *chizuk* (encouragement)." Here Rabbi Klein supplied Rav Grossman with the name of the prisoner.

Sing Sing is located about thirty miles north of New York City, in the town of Ossining, on the east bank of the Hudson River. It's a

Rav Grossman with Rabbi Moshe Sherer (left) and NY Mayor Abe Beame

maximum-security prison, and it was not easy for Rav Grossman to be given permission to go there. But the Rebbe had made a request, and Rav Grossman made every effort to comply — and he succeeded, primarily through the intervention of Rabbi Moshe Sherer of Agudas Yisrael.

As Rav Grossman relates, it was certainly a unique experience:

> When I was finally seated across from the prisoner that the Rebbe had asked me to see, I was in for a surprise. I had originally imagined that I was going to see a Lubavitcher chassid. But the man sitting in front of me wasn't even slightly religious. I asked him what he had been before he landed in prison.
>
> "I was a doctor," he told me. He explained that he'd prescribed a certain medicine to a patient. As a result of the medication the patient died and he was jailed.
>
> "I want you to know something," Rav Grossman told him. "I'm here on behalf of the Rebbe of Lubavitch. It was the Rebbe who told me about you, and he is the one who asked me to come here and visit you."
>
> When he heard that, the ex-doctor began to cry. Under Rav Grossman's skillful questioning, he explained that he had become extremely depressed over the last few days.
>
> "I used to be a respected doctor, and now I'm just a prisoner with no hope for a better life and nothing to look forward to. My depression kept growing worse until finally I decided that I didn't want to live any longer and was going to kill myself.
>
> "I planned on carrying out the act today.
>
> "But now you showed up completely out of the blue, offering words of kindness and hope, words that arrived just in time to pull me back from the brink of despair."

After that visit, Rav Grossman remained in contact with the doctor in Sing Sing. They exchanged letters, and their friendship gave the doctor the will to carry on. They stayed in touch until the prisoner's passing years later. But Rav Grossman could never get over the Lubavitcher Rebbe's incredible ability to know what was happening in the lives of countless individuals even when he couldn't see them — and how he was constantly thinking about Klal Yisrael and willing to interrupt whatever he was doing for the sake of a Jew who needed *chizuk*.

CHAPTER EIGHTEEN

The Rabbi and the Guru

One evening Rav Grossman found himself in a Flatbush living room showing a slide show about Migdal Ohr to an appreciative audience. When the last slide had been shown, the host told his visitor how impressed he was with everything he'd seen and asked him if he could share something personal with the rabbi from Migdal HaEmek.

"By all means," Rav Grossman replied encouragingly. "What's on your mind?"

"My son has fallen into the wrong crowd."

"What kind of wrong crowd?"

"Not what you're thinking. Much worse."

Rav Grossman braced himself. "Tell me."

"I don't know how it happened, but he was in the mountains last summer, and he met some people who call themselves followers of an Indian guru. He spent time with the group, and I really don't understand how this happened, but my intelligent, Torah-observant son became convinced that the truth lies with this Indian cult and its leader, whom he now venerates beyond all measure."

"Where is your son at the moment?"

"The cult rents a compound in the Catskills, and he's there right now. Even worse, the guru is coming to the States to spend time with his followers at the compound, and I'm afraid that after my son spends some time with the big boss, I'll never see him again.

"I just watched your slide show. I saw how you interact with the kids in the discos, how you know how to talk to everyone you meet… Do you think you can help my son?"

"Tell me something," Rav Grossman said to his host. "Are you still in contact with him?"

The man shook his head. "No, we're not speaking."

"That's a mistake. One should never break off contact with a child."

"What's done is done."

"True, but now you need to fix it."

"What should I do?"

"First, you need to invite your son back home. Don't tell him that you met me. Just ask him to come home for a short visit. If he agrees to come, then we'll arrange for me to show up at the house. When I knock on the door, welcome me inside as if we've never met before."

"Then what?"

"Then I'll put on my slide show from Migdal Ohr, and we'll see what happens."

They shook hands on the deal.

Rav Grossman returned two nights later at the agreed-upon time. Standing on the porch looking for all the world like any fundraiser who had just flown in from Eretz Yisrael, he knocked on the door and the boy's father answered it and invited him into the living room. Rav Grossman introduced himself to all the family members in attendance, explaining that he had established an institution in Migdal HaEmek for children who had nowhere else to live.

"I happen to have a slide show with me," he told them, "and I would be glad to show it to you so that you can understand what we do and learn about the many programs that we provide."

Everyone gathered around the table, including the son who had just returned from the Catskills, to watch the slide show. Within moments they were drawn into the world of Migdal Ohr (or, as the narrator Steven Hill called it, the "Tower of Light") — a world where children from underprivileged backgrounds were given every opportunity to succeed in life.

When the show was over and the lights in the living room had been turned back on, the wayward son turned to Rav Grossman and said, "You know something? I've also found myself a tower of light!"

"Really? Where is your tower?"

It wasn't long before the two of them were deeply immersed in conversation, while Rav Grossman utilized every bit of ingenuity at his disposal to question the boy and get a real picture of how deeply he was ensnared. He found out about the guru from India and how "amazing" he was and about the place in the Catskills where the guru would be staying on his upcoming visit to the States.

"That sounds fascinating," Rav Grossman said to his new friend. "Do you think it would be possible for me to go there for a visit?"

"Why not? I'll be more than happy to show you around and introduce you to everyone I know."

They exchanged phone numbers and promised to be in touch with each other so they could arrange a visit.

A few days later, Rav Grossman pulled up to the now-defunct Homowack Hotel, which was a half-hour's drive from the compound. It so happened to be that the rabbi's arrival coincided with a speech that the guru from India was to deliver in the compound's amphitheater. When Rav Grossman got there, everyone was lining up in two rows to give their leader an appropriate welcome. It wasn't long before a black Cadillac drove onto the hotel grounds and came to a stop in front of the crowd.

Rav Grossman happened to be standing close to the spot where the car had pulled up, and he attracted the guru's attention as the Indian cult leader passed him on his way into the hall. He looked at the rabbi curiously, no doubt wondering what someone like him was doing there.

Rav Grossman spoke up. "I'm visiting from Israel."

The guru nodded in acknowledgment.

"I'm the chief rabbi of the Galilee," Rav Grossman added for good measure.

Duly impressed by his visitor, the guru took Rav Grossman by the hand, and together the two of them walked into the building leading to the amphitheater where the speech was to take place. Seeing the guru treat the rabbi with such respect made a major impression on the people who observed the scene, and they immediately started regarding Rav Grossman as someone to be taken seriously. If the guru was treating him with such deference, clearly this was a person who deserved their attention.

As they entered the building, Rav Grossman realized that he was supposed to take off his shoes, and he was concerned that the act of removing his shoes could be construed as idol worship.

"I can't remove my shoes," he told the guru.

"Why not?"

Rav Grossman made up a reason on the spot.

"I have a tradition from my grandfather that the members of our family do not take off their shoes."

This meant that he was unable to enter the amphitheater. He waited until the ceremony had finished and then sought out the young man he had first met in Flatbush. Their conversation was interrupted by two girls who approached them to speak to the rabbi.

It turned out that he knew these girls from Migdal HaEmek. "Rav Grossman," they said, "what are you doing here?"

"I have a better question," he replied. "What are both of *you* doing here?"

They explained that the cult had a branch in Haifa where people were trained in meditation and similar practices. The training culminated with a trip to meet the guru.

The newcomers joined the conversation, which continued unabated well into the night. By the time the conversation finally wound its way to its natural conclusion, Rav Grossman had become friends with the young man.

He invited the boy to visit him in Eretz Yisrael, and the boy took the rabbi up on his offer. The young man remained in Eretz Yisrael for a while, long enough to grow stronger in his Jewish observance, and cut off all ties to the guru and the cult. Eventually he returned to the States, where he learned in a yeshivah while he attended college to earn a degree. He went on to get married, had children, and left the foolish behavior of his youth far behind.

When Rav Grossman returned to Eretz Yisrael, he set up a meeting with the Haifa municipality and told them what was really going on at the "meditation center" situated in their city. The municipality promptly shut it down, putting an end to yet another danger to the Jews of the north.

CHAPTER NINETEEN
Shimon Fachima

Rav Grossman met Shimon Fachima in Migdal HaEmek in the mid-1970s. Shimon was blind, and, in addition to that truly challenging infirmity, suffered from a disfigured face. People found it uncomfortable to look at him, to the point that some even crossed the street to avoid passing him. Suffice it to say, there was nothing easy about Shimon's life.

Yet Shimon never let anything get him down.

Shimon was no simple man. He knew the prayers of Shacharis, Minchah, and Maariv by heart. He also knew the entire Rosh Hashanah and Yom Kippur machzor by heart, as well as the prayers of all the holidays. He knew the entire *Tehillim* (Book of Psalms) by heart. He knew the entire *Tanach* (the Bible) by heart. He knew an immense number of *Mishnayos* by heart. (The Mishnah is the first major compilation of the Jewish nation's oral traditions, and Shimon had managed to master a large amount of it.) Rav Grossman never figured out how he came to learn so much Torah by heart, but there was no question that Shimon utilized his brain to the utmost.

In addition to all his learning, Shimon devoted a lot of attention to his *avodas Hashem* (service of G-d), rising every morning before dawn and making his way to shul with the aid of his cane.

One day he sought out Rav Grossman with a special request.

"I need the Rav's help," he said.

"What kind of help do you need?"

"I want to travel to America."

Rav Grossman was taken aback. "Why do you want to go to America?"

"I'm in my thirties, and I don't see any opportunities for me to get married here. I've tried, but my hopes have been dashed time and again. It seems to me that it might be a good idea to switch directions and move to a different place. Maybe in America my *mazal* (luck) will change, and I'll find a girl who is willing to marry me.

"Besides, I'm having a hard time finding any work here. I thought that once I'm in the States, I could look for a job and finally receive a decent paycheck. Maybe then the girls will start taking me seriously..."

Rav Grossman tried his best to dissuade Shimon of his grand idea, explaining that despite what he might think, the streets of America were not and have never been paved with gold, and that it was much more difficult to get hired for a good job in the States than he might think.

Then Rav Grossman tried a different tack.

"Tell me something."

"What?"

"Where exactly are you going to stay once you get there? Do you have relatives in America who will provide room and board?"

"That's no problem at all," Shimon told the Rav. "I'm going to do what so many others do."

"What's that?"

"I'll go to Chabad in Crown Heights. They'll take care of me. I'm sure that my future is waiting for me in New York."

Seeing that Shimon refused to change his mind, Rav Grossman conceded defeat and agreed that Shimon could go to the United States. Shimon was overjoyed. A short time later, he booked a flight to the airport and took off for New York.

The Lubavitcher Rebbe davened Minchah every day at three o'clock. While davening, the Rebbe would place his hand on his forehead, covering his eyes. There are many pictures of the Rebbe in this pose. But on the day Shimon Fachima walked into 770 for the first time, the Rebbe put his hand down and didn't block his eyes. He wanted to ensure that nobody would erroneously imagine that he didn't want to look at Shimon due to his physical appearance.

"I'd warned Shimon against going to America many times," Rav Grossman says. "I told him it would be difficult for him to find work, and I asked him where he was going to stay. But Shimon had been right all along, because once in the States, he was introduced to a very, very

Rav Grossman with Reb Nuchum Donner

dear friend of mine, Reb Nuchum Donner, and Reb Nuchum helped Shimon find an apartment where he lived for the next five years. Though he lived by himself during the week, on Shabbos and Yom Tov Shimon liked to spend time with many of the friends that he met in the States." (Reb Nuchum, who lives in the United States, has been working with Rav Grossman and Migdal Ohr for decades.)

Reb Nuchum didn't stop there. His care for Shimon was legendary. Whereas most people who met Shimon heard that he was searching desperately for a suitable life partner and moved on, Reb Nuchum never gave up trying to help him find a wife. But although many girls were introduced to Shimon, none of the *shidduchim* worked out.

So it went for five years, with Shimon going out on many *shidduch* dates but never succeeding in achieving the goal he longed for with his entire being.

Then one day Shimon heard about the *segulah* (a kabbalistic ritual) of going to daven for a specific *yeshuah* (salvation) at the Kosel for forty days in a row, and he became very excited. Shimon knew that it was time to return to Eretz Yisrael.

When Shimon arrived in Yerushalayim, he staked out a corner for himself in Yeshivas Porat Yosef, and then, for the next forty days,

Shimon Fachima went to the Kosel every morning and davened to Hashem to send him a wife. Not long after his forty days of visits, Shimon was reunited with an old friend of his, a very fine Jew by the name of Shabtai Wishky.

Shabtai was also blind, and as young boys the two of them had been students together at a school for the blind located in Haifa. Now they were meeting one another for the first time in twenty years, and they had a lot of catching up to do.

"Where do you live?" Shimon asked Shabtai.

"In Ohr Yehudah, in a neighborhood called Yismach Moshe."

"Do you work?"

"Yes, I work for the municipality of Ohr Yehudah."

"Very nice. And what about a wife? Are you married?"

"I married a very nice girl named Tzippora, who is also blind like I am."

But all was not rosy in Shabtai's life. During the course of their conversation, Shabtai revealed that he hadn't been well for quite some time and that his kidney had been failing. He had recently undergone a kidney transplant.

"I didn't hold out much hope for getting one." This was many years ago, when kidney donors were few and far between. "Then an American girl named Shoshana, a friend of my wife, decided to donate one of her kidneys to me."

When Shimon heard about Shoshana, he grew excited. Here was a girl who had just donated a kidney to someone who wasn't even a relative, for no reason other than that she wanted to help another person. Maybe this girl would consider going out with him. Maybe she would be willing to marry him.

Shimon asked his old friend to introduce him to his kidney donor. Shabtai couldn't refuse and agreed to set them up.

One date led to another, and it wasn't long before Shoshana let it be known that she was very interested in marrying Shimon Fachima, even though he was blind and she was not. In truth, his *chein* (charm) made a big impression on her from their very first meeting.

By now you may have figured out that Shoshana was no simple person. But aside from her huge penchant for *chesed* (kindness), she also held seven university degrees, spoke multiple languages, and was a gifted artist. Clearly, Shoshana was a very intelligent person — and she knew that Shimon was the right one for her.

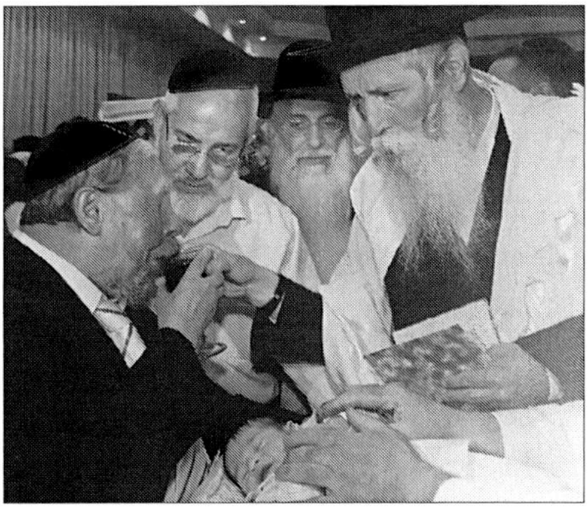
Shimon Fachima at the bris of his son

Shoshana's mother met Shimon two days before the wedding, and after speaking with him for two hours, she said, "Now I understand why my daughter is so happy!"

The couple married and eventually were blessed with a son. Rav Grossman attended both the wedding and the bris. The two had remained in touch all those years, and few were happier than Rav Grossman to see his old friend Shimon finally achieve his heart's desire. Shimon's son Yochanan Yaakov grew up into an exceptional person who gave his parents a lot of *nachas*, while also providing them with beautiful grandchildren.

Shimon and Shoshana ended up moving across the street from Shabtai and Tzippora Wishky, and the two of them learned together in the neighborhood shul for the next couple of decades, best friends for life.

Years later, Shimon was visiting family in Los Angeles when he fell into an open hole in the street that he hadn't been able to see. He passed away that Shabbos. On Motza'ei Shabbos, Rav Grossman received a call from a tearful Shoshana, who wanted to let him know that Shimon had passed away and that they were bringing his remains to Eretz Yisrael. As they spoke, Shoshana revealed that there was a problem.

"What can I do to help?"

According to Israeli law, a citizen is supposed to be buried in the location stated on his or her *teudat zehut* (ID card). If he or she chooses to be buried somewhere else, they have to pay for the gravesite, and graves do not come cheap. Shimon's *teudat zehut* stated that he was from the Tel Aviv region, which meant that legally he was supposed to be buried in the Tel Aviv cemetery. This was a problem for Shoshana, who was

Shabtai Wishky, *kvatter* at his friend Shimon's son's bris

not well and confined to a wheelchair. She would have a very difficult time navigating Tel Aviv's massive cemetery.

"If they bury Shimon there, I'll barely ever manage to visit his grave!"

"So where do you want him buried?"

"In the city of Yehud. It's a small city with a small cemetery, and it will be very easy for me to visit his grave. Yehud is a much better option for me."

As soon as he got off the phone with Shoshana, Rav Grossman called the mayor of Yehud. He knew that the mayor was under no legal obligation whatsoever to help this family, but he was asking him for a personal favor on behalf a tzaddik whose life had been filled with challenges from beginning to end, who had overcome formidable adversity and gotten married, raised a family, and become a genuine Torah scholar along the way.

"I would consider this a real favor," he concluded.

The mayor promised to see what he could do. "I'll get back to you in a few hours," he told Rav Grossman.

The mayor kept his word. He called back three hours later and informed Rav Grossman that while he really wanted to help, there was simply no extra room for anyone not legally entitled to a plot.

As Rav Grossman sat in his car pondering the situation, the phone began to ring. The person who had been hired to print the posters announcing the funeral was on the phone.

"The Fachima family told me that all the details regarding the funeral are being decided by Rav Yitzchak Dovid Grossman from Migdal HaEmek. So I'm calling for the details. Where are the funeral and burial?"

"I don't know what to do. I need some time to try and find an appropriate place."

"Call me back when you know the answer," the printer said.

"Before we hang up," Rav Grossman said, "maybe you have an idea for a suitable grave site for a man like Shimon Fachima? A tzaddik, a man of great *yiras Shamayim* (fear of Heaven). Any ideas?"

"Listen, I have absolutely nothing to do with graves. My line of work is posters." He was quiet for a moment, then said slowly, "Except for one time. Then I did help someone with a grave."

"What are you talking about?"

"I had a neighbor named Shabtai. He was a genuine tzaddik and I helped find a gravesite for him. But that was the only time I had anything to do with graves."

Rav Grossman heard the name Shabtai, and his head began to spin. Could this be the very same Shabtai who was Shimon's old friend, the man who had introduced Shimon to his wife, the man to whom Shimon's wife had donated her kidney?

Amazingly, it was.

"Tell me something," Rav Grossman said when he had caught his breath. "Where is Shabtai buried?"

"In Petach Tikva."

"Which section?"

"The section of the rabbinical leaders of the Spinka dynasty."

"Do you think there is any space there for one more person?"

"Not a chance in the world. It's a very old cemetery. I can't imagine that there is anything available."

"Who helped you find the grave for Shabtai?"

"A member of the local *chevrah kaddisha*, the society tasked with dealing with funerals and burial. His name is Shmuel."

"Can I have his number, please?"

"Absolutely."

Rav Grossman called Shmuel from the Petach Tikva *chevrah kaddisha* and told him the entire story. He didn't get the reaction he was hoping for.

"There is no way," Shmuel told him. "We've stopped burying people in that section for a while. It's all full."

"Do me a favor," Rav Grossman said to Shmuel, "and go down to the cemetery. Maybe you'll find that there is something available. Maybe you'll find one last grave. Do me a favor and go now. Time is of the essence!"

Shmuel agreed. He called back an hour later.

"Rav Grossman, you'll never guess what I found!"

"What did you find?"

"There is one available grave."

"Where is it?"

"Right next to a man named Shabtai Wishky."

So it was that Reb Shimon Fachima was laid to his eternal rest right beside his close friend Shabtai — friends in this world and friends in the next.

CHAPTER TWENTY

Chanukah "Selichos" at the Disco

Chanukah in London, 1979. Rav Grossman was visiting England on a fundraising trip to raise money for Migdal Ohr and was staying at the home of Reb Shlomo Tagger in Stamford Hill. One afternoon he was in Golders Green, knocking on the doors of a number of wealthy supporters. He was passing Rav Chuna's *shtiebel* (small synagogue) on Golders Green Road when he ran into a boisterous group of young men speaking to each other in Hebrew.

"Shalom!" he called out to the passing boys. "Are you from Israel?"

The group turned to look at the man who had interrupted their chatter. One of them recognized him and called out, "Aren't you the Disco Rabbi? I've seen you on television."

They were clearly excited about being in the presence of a "TV star," and one of the boys said, "Rabbi, can I ask you a question?"

"By all means."

"I'm currently dating a non-Jewish girl from London, and we want to get married. My parents are unhappy that I want to marry a non-Jewish girl, and they've told me that the only way they'll agree to the match is if she converts to Judaism. Would the Rav help me convert her?"

"I'm going to answer your question," Rav Grossman replied, "but before I do, I have to tell you that I would have expected you to feel a little shame when telling me that you're dating a non-Jewish girl. But you're clearly at peace with the idea of dating a non-Jew. How can that be?! Where's your shame? Where's your embarrassment? It's almost as if you're waiting for me to give you a kiss on the forehead and wish you mazel tov on your upcoming wedding!"

"It's not only me," the boy retorted. "There are plenty of Israelis here in London right now who are dating non-Jewish girls." The boy was obviously stung by the rabbi's harsh words, and his only recourse was to become defensive.

"I don't understand," Rav Grossman said. "Have you established a brand-new intermarriage movement in London? What's going on here?"

"It's not like that. None of us comes to London with the intention of marrying a non-Jew. We just happen to meet them at a disco on Finchley Road."

"Why there?"

"It's an Israeli disco. It's the place everyone goes to hang out."

"What's this disco called?"

"Hanegev."

"Hanegev," the rabbi repeated slowly.

"Yes, that's our place. It's not our fault that so many non-Jews like hanging out there, too."

"Hanegev on Finchley Road?" Rav Grossman repeated again.

"Yes."

"Maybe I'll see you there later…"

Before they parted ways, Rav Grossman gave the number of the Tagger home to the young man who had started the conversation and promised to be in touch with him.

As soon as Rav Grossman heard about what was taking place at the Hanegev disco, he knew that he couldn't possibly stay away. After lighting the menorah that night with his host, Rav Grossman turned to Reb Shlomo and asked him if he had an extra menorah that he might use for the evening.

"Why do you need another menorah?"

"I want to go light Chanukah *licht* (candles) at the Hanegev disco on Finchley Road."

Reb Shlomo gave his guest a dubious look. While they went back a long way and Reb Shlomo knew all about his friend's activities, as well as the adventures that somehow seemed to fall in his path, it was still difficult for him to imagine a man who looked like Rav Grossman kindling the Chanukah lights in such a place.

A local *askan* (community activist) named Rabbi Abba Dunner happened to have been visiting Reb Shlomo at that time, and he graciously offered to drive the Israeli rabbi to the disco on Finchley Road. It wasn't far, and minutes later Rav Grossman stepped out of the car, menorah under his arm and resolve in his heart.

The door was wide open, and he entered the cavernous room, which seemed to be filled with hundreds of people. To the left was a stage where a DJ stood and worked his machines, making "music" for the crowd. Red and yellow strobe lights shot their beams in every direction, and the sound was deafening. Under the blinding lights, no one noticed the rabbi with the long black beard walking over to the stairs leading up to the DJ's platform.

Suddenly the DJ noticed that he wasn't alone, and his mouth fell open in surprise when he saw that his companion was a rabbi in a long black coat, a fur hat, and sidelocks.

"May I?" the rabbi asked the DJ (who was also an Israeli), gesturing at the microphone. The DJ, too stunned to offer even token resistance, allowed Rav Grossman to take hold of the mike. He even lowered the volume of the music so that the crowd would be able to hear what the surprise visitor wanted to say.

"*Rabbotai*," Rav Grossman called out, "*Chanukah samei'ach! Happy Chanukah!*"

He waited a beat as all the youths on the dance floor came to the realization that some rabbi straight out of Meah Shearim had just fallen into their lives with no warning at all.

"I came here," Rav Grossman announced, "to light the Chanukah menorah with you. Are you ready?"

One may have thought that the crowd would have been angry at the visitor for disturbing their fun, but somehow they weren't upset at all. On the contrary, they seemed pleased that he was there, prepared to conduct a menorah-lighting ceremony for them.

"*Anachnu muchanim!* We are ready!" the crowd roared back.

Without further ado, Rav Grossman set up the menorah right beside the DJ's equipment and poured the oil into every cup.

"Since you don't have *kippot* (yarmulkes/skullcaps) on you," he said to them when the menorah was all set up and ready, "all of the men should cover their heads with their hands. Who among you knows how to say the *berachos* over lighting the menorah? Who knows how to recite the blessings?"

One boy raised his hand and called out, "I know how to say them."

Rav Grossman always wears two yarmulkes on his head. If you ask him why, he'll explain that he likes to be prepared in case he needs to give a *kippah* to someone who doesn't have one.

"Come up here with me," he told the boy, and when the volunteer had climbed the stairs to the stage and was standing beside the rabbi, Rav Grossman handed him the extra kippah.

"You can start now," the rabbi prompted.

"I don't remember how it begins."

"No problem. I'll help you."

Rav Grossman provided the first few words, and the boy remembered the rest. When they began reciting, the entire room spontaneously joined the two of them in saying the blessing, word for word. After a spirited round of *"Ma'oz Tzur"* (a traditional Chanukah song), Rav Grossman explained to his audience that he had come to London from Eretz Yisrael, and that he wanted to speak with the boys privately.

"Please apologize to your friends who've come here with you," he told the Israeli boys, "and then come and join me."

The rabbi was directed down a flight of stairs to a hall, and he told the boys to meet him there. The rabbi's announcement was followed by a mass stampede down the stairs as the crowd of young Israelis rushed to hear what he wanted to tell them.

They couldn't help it — they were curious. It wasn't every day that some rabbi with a long beard joins you in the disco and stops the music so he can light the menorah. No, this was someone who made you stand up and pay attention.

After everyone had gathered, Rav Grossman addressed his attentive audience. He told the crowd how he had come to hear of the Hanegev disco in the first place and why he had made it his business to seek them out on a Chanukah night.

"Today I met one of you on Golders Green Road. He told me that he was going out with a non-Jewish girl and that his parents wanted her to convert before they gave the marriage their blessing. When I asked this young man why he wasn't even slightly ashamed of his behavior, he explained to me that many of his friends were involved in exactly the same type of behavior. Hearing this has given me no peace, that so many Israeli boys — young men who have risked their lives to protect their nation — are dating non-Jewish girls and seriously thinking about marrying them."

One of the boys stood up and said, "In all honesty, I don't see any difference between Jews and non-Jews."

"Please introduce yourself," Rav Grossman said, "and tell me where you're from."

The boy introduced himself and told the rabbi that he came from the city of Ohr Akiva. Then he removed a small picture from his wallet, and Rav Grossman saw that it was a photo of the boy's father — an authentically religious Jew replete with beard and *peyos* (sidelocks).

Upon seeing the photo, Rav Grossman couldn't hold back his tears, and he began to weep. Then he spoke in the universal singsong voice that Jews use when learning Gemara.

"It would be one thing if you were from an Ashkenazic family, because I've heard statements like the one you just uttered from people who come from Hungary and Germany. People whose family had long assimilated. But you come from Morocco, where every Jew was traditionally religious and retained their heritage.

"Do you even know who you are and where you came from?

"In the Ashkenazic neighborhood in which I grew up, we say Selichos (Penitential prayers) before Rosh Hashanah for around a week. But in your shuls, you recite Selichot for at least a month, beginning from Rosh Chodesh Elul, when you get up every night and say Selichot with tears and repentance. This is who you are — people with a Jewish heart and Jewish devotion!"

As soon as Rav Grossman uttered the word Selichot, he triggered a memory of the famous song that Sefardic congregations sing when they gather together and daven, and, motivated solely by his emotions, Rav Grossman began to sing the age-old words, with the melody and accent that should have been so familiar to these youths: "*Adon haselichot bocher levavot gollel amukot doresh tzedakot chatanu lefanecha racheim aleinu...*"

The moment he began to sing, the words and the tune rippled through the room like fire in a field of dry wheat. The young men sitting in front of him were instantly transported to the synagogues of their youth, where they stood beside their fathers in the middle of the night, reciting these very words. Powerless to resist, they all began to sing together with the rabbi. "*Chatanu lefanecha racheim aleinu...* We have sinned before You, have mercy on us..."

Rav Grossman had seen many amazing sights in his life, and this one was no less miraculous. Here was a group of young disenfranchised Jews sitting in a disco in the middle of London singing the song of Selichot. *I wonder what impression this is making up in Heaven*, he said to himself.

And then, while the mood was one of *teshuvah* and *hisorerus*, of repentance and inspiration, the rabbi from Migdal HaEmek began to give the boys a serious *mussar shmuess* (stern lecture). That night he told it like it was, and gave it to them for having allowed themselves to stoop so low. He knew that his words would be taken in the spirit he intended them, and he was correct. They started asking questions and he answered them, and the night wore on and on, and nobody there wanted it to end since they had suddenly realized just how thirsty they were for a taste of authentic Judaism.

So it went until three in the morning.

Rav Grossman was utterly exhausted. His clothing was soaking wet from exertion, and he could barely move. He asked one of the boys to find him a taxi to take him back to Stamford Hill.

As Rav Grossman was about to leave, two young men approached him.

"Rabbi, we need to talk to you."

"*Chevrah*," he replied, "it will have to wait. I'm exhausted!"

But they wouldn't take no for an answer and insisted that he had to hear their story and give them advice. It couldn't wait.

In the end, they accompanied him back to Stamford Hill, where he sat down with them to listen to their story. They opened their mouths to speak, but they weren't able to get two words out before bursting into bitter tears.

"What's the matter?" Rav Grossman asked.

They confided in the rabbi that they had fallen prey to the crime scene in London and had become immersed in a life of complete impurity.

"When we heard you speak to us tonight," they said, "we decided that we no longer want to live that life. We need you to help us do *teshuvah* (repent)."

"I'll be more than happy to help you," Rav Grossman said.

"You don't understand," one of the boys said emphatically. "You can't just leave us and return to Eretz Yisrael because there is no way in the world that we'll be able to do this on our own."

"I have an idea," the rabbi said, so tired by then that he was beginning to have double vision. "I'll take you back to Eretz Yisrael with me. I was supposed to have flown from London to New York. But I'll change my ticket and take you boys back to Eretz Yisrael. I'll make sure that you're settled in a new religious environment before flying to New York. This way you won't have to do this on your own."

"If only we would be able to do that."

"What do you mean?"

"There is no way we can go with you to Eretz Yisrael."

"Why not?"

"Because we were involved with the underworld when we lived there. Who knows what's waiting for us if we return. We're afraid, Rav Grossman. Afraid."

"If that's the case," Rav Grossman said, "I have an idea for you. I have a friend named Rav Gershon Leibman. Rav Gershon runs a yeshivah outside Paris, which I think will be perfect for the two of you." [Rav Yitzchak Dovid was introduced to Rav Gershon by his uncle, the *gaon hatzaddik* (brilliant and righteous) Rav Yisrael Dovid Neivoner, who was a student of Rav Gershon. After many years of noteworthy work in Jewish education, Rav Neivoner came to Eretz Yisrael with his rebbetzin Rochel, who herself was an accomplished *mechaneches* (educator), and they became partners with Rav Grossman in building Migdal Ohr.]

Rav Grossman with Rav Neivoner

Rav Gershon had been a student at the Novardok yeshivah in Bialystok before the war. After the horrors of the Holocaust were behind him, Rav Gershon decided to start over and opened his own branch of Novardok in France, and one yeshivah led to an entire network of institutions.

It was to one of these yeshivos that Rav Grossman proposed to send these boys.

"Rav Gershon's yeshivah is called Beis Yosef, and it is part of the Novardok network. I've already sent quite a few Israelis to Rav Gershon's yeshivos, with wonderful results. It's more than a yeshivah. It's an entire community of *baalei teshuvah* — people who have returned to Torah and Judaism — and I think there's a good chance that the two of you will find your place there."

Rav Gershon Leibman and
Rav Yitzchak Dovid

The two men agreed to accompany the rabbi to Paris. And so, instead of traveling on to the States, Rav Grossman flew to Paris together with the two young men who were eager to change their lives and find their way back to the Ribbono shel Olam.

Rav Gershon Leibman welcomed them with open arms, assuring them of a place to learn and good study partners who would help them transition into genuine Torah scholars. The two remained at the yeshivah outside Paris for quite a while. After several years of serious learning, they married and established beautiful Jewish homes.

For years, Rav Grossman made it a point of traveling to the States via France. This gave him the opportunity to visit the boys he had sent to Rav Gershon before continuing on the next leg of his journey, wherever that might be. During one such visit, Rav Gershon decided to accompany his friend to the airport and see him off. Upon entering Departures, they happened to meet the legendary Rav Mordechai Elefant, the rosh yeshivah of Itri in Yerushalayim.

A conversation ensued and then suddenly Rav Elefant turned to Rav Gershon and said, "I don't understand something."

"What's that?" Rav Gershon replied.

"I don't understand how the world allows a person like Reb Yitzchak Dovid to travel the world fundraising when he should be back in Migdal Ohr taking care of his children!"

"I agree with you completely," Rav Gershon responded. "Let's make a calculation," he continued. "Right now he's traveling to America to raise funds for the institution. What is the maximum amount he could raise according to the natural order of things? Probably in the region of a hundred thousand dollars?"

Rav Mordechai nodded.

"Well, then," Rav Gershon said with a twinkle in his eye, "let's make a deal. If you agree to raise fifty thousand for Migdal Ohr, I will do the same — on condition that Reb Yitzchak Dovid agrees to board the next flight back to Eretz Yisrael and spends the three weeks that he would have been running around America with the precious *neshamos* who are waiting for him back home."

The two of them shook hands on the deal, and Rav Grossman purchased a ticket for the next flight back to Tel Aviv.

As for the boy who had initiated the entire sequence of events that led Rav Grossman to a disco in Golders Green and to saving the lives of two Jewish souls, Rav Grossman was unable to bring him back to a life of Torah and mitzvos. But he did break up with the non-Jewish girl. And for that alone, the entire endeavor was worthwhile.

CHAPTER TWENTY-ONE
A Sleepless Night in Manhattan

As his name spread across the globe, the Disco Rabbi received numerous invitations from shuls worldwide, inviting him to come and address their congregants or to spend a Shabbos with the *kehillah* (congregation). Since this was a productive way for him to meet new supporters, Rav Grossman often spent Shabbos in various far-flung locations. One such Shabbos took place at a prestigious synagogue in New York City, where he was advertised to speak after *Krias HaTorah,* the reading of the weekly Torah portion, to the very large crowd that was regularly in attendance.

It was arranged that Rav Grossman would stay at the hotel suite that the shul normally reserved for visiting scholars-in-residence. He would daven there Friday night and give his speech in the morning, before the Mussaf prayers.

That Shabbos began uneventfully. Rav Grossman checked into the hotel, unpacked, then made his way to the shul for the Friday night davening, which was very well attended. After davening was over, he joined the shul's rabbi, and the two of them walked home for the Shabbos meal, which was spent in a very convivial atmosphere, with much inspired singing and many words of Torah. It was close to midnight when the meal finally came to an end, and Rav Grossman headed to the hotel.

Rav Grossman's suite was on the third floor of the hotel. Not a bad climb, even at three in the morning. But when he entered his room he noticed, to his shock and dismay, that there was someone sleeping in his bed! In the dim light emanating from the bathroom, Rav Grossman was able to make out a gigantic head of hair and a face in repose peeking out from under the blanket.

Later he would figure out what had happened. He had asked the hotel staff to leave the door to his room slightly ajar so that he would be able to get in even without a key. It appeared that a homeless person who knew that this particular hotel room was often used for shul guests who would not carry a key on Shabbos had come that night to try his luck.

Rav Grossman turned on his heels and returned to the lobby, unsure of his next move. Not knowing what else to do, he took a seat on one of the couches in the lobby and remained there until morning. He could have asked hotel security to remove the person who had snuck into his room, but he was loathe to make such a move without knowing the background of the person sleeping in his bed.

He remained on the couch the rest of the night, until the sky gradually began to lighten and the first rays of dawn slowly spread across the Manhattan skyline. It was Shabbos morning, and he needed to go to the *mikveh* as he did every Shabbos morning. He'd asked for the address of a *mikveh* in the area, and he decided to set aside his room problem for now and walk the twenty blocks, though the morning cold was biting and the winds were blowing without letup.

It was six o'clock by the time he arrived at the *mikveh*, and instead of being able to go straight inside to warm up from the long walk, he faced another challenge: the building was locked.

Now what? He couldn't ring the bell and ask to be let in, but he didn't want to leave without immersing in the *mikveh* in preparation for davening and the upcoming speech he was scheduled to deliver to at least a thousand Jews.

In desperation, Rav Grossman looked up at the heavens and implored, "Ribbono shel Olam, You know what kind of night I just had. Now I want to immerse in the *mikveh* before davening so I can purify myself before I pray to You! Please help me succeed in finding a way inside so that I can serve You to the best of my abilities!"

The words were barely out of his mouth when Rav Grossman heard someone calling down to him from a window on the fifth floor.

"What are you looking for?"

"*Mikveh!*" Rav Grossman answered, projecting his voice so the man would hear him.

"Wait there!"

The man who had noticed him from the fifth floor came running downstairs to open the door to the building.

"Tell me something," Rav Grossman said to his benefactor. "How did you come to look out of your window at six o'clock in the morning?"

"The head of my bed is beneath the window," the man explained. "I can't explain why, but a few minutes ago I woke up suddenly, for no reason at all. Without knowing why, I opened the window shade and looked down at the front of the building. I've never done this before, and I can't explain why I did it today. That's the whole story."

As Rav Grossman immersed in the welcoming waters of the holy ritual bath, the rabbi from Migdal HaEmek felt remarkably close to the Master of the World, Who was clearly looking after his every need.

Rav Grossman would return to that Manhattan shul a number of times over the years. But the next time he went, he made sure to instruct the hotel staff to keep the door of his room locked — and to open it for him when he returned.

Just in case.

"One Shabbos that I spent together with Rav Grossman in Manhattan," Reb Nuchum Donner recalls, "we experienced a beautiful and uplifting davening and *seudah*, and when the meal was over, some thirty people decided to escort the rav back to his hotel. Along the way, we ran into a young Israeli couple. The boy recognized the rav from back home and explained that he and his fiancée were planning on getting married soon."

Rav Grossman congratulated the couple with all the warmth in the world.

Then the boy took advantage of the chance meeting and asked, "Would the Rav be willing to serve as our *mesader kiddushin* and officiate at our wedding?"

Rav Grossman told him to be in touch when they returned to Israel, and he would check his calendar.

They weren't far away from the hotel when Rav Grossman asked the group if anyone knew of a *mikveh* in the nearby vicinity.

"I do," one of them offered. "I'll make sure to bring the Rav a key."

Since Rav Grossman did not use the *eiruv* (the ritual halachic enclosure built so that people are able to carry outside their homes on Shabbos), he thanked the boy for his generous offer but told him that he shouldn't bother to bring him the key. This meant that he didn't have a way to get into the *mikveh* on Shabbos morning. Knowing Rav Grossman, Reb Nuchum wasn't that worried. Rav Grossman would find a way.

Rav Grossman woke Reb Nuchum at seven o'clock that Shabbos morning. It didn't matter that Shacharis began at nine. Rav Grossman wanted to go to the *mikveh*.

"But it's closed," Reb Nuchum protested, "and we don't have a key."

"We're going to the *mikveh*," Rav Grossman said emphatically.

That was it. Once Rav Grossman repeated himself, Reb Nuchum never made him say it a third time.

They left the hotel ten minutes later and made the short walk to the *mikveh*, where they found that someone had left the door open and thoughtfully positioned a brick there to serve as a doorstop.

Rav Grossman was concerned that the boy whom he had specifically instructed not to bring the key had disobeyed him and done it anyway, making sure to leave the door open for him should he choose to arrive. Later that day, Rav Grossman met the boy in shul, and he asked him if he'd had anything to do with the open *mikveh* door.

"Not at all," the boy said. "I wasn't even near that area today."

"So you didn't open the door for us?"

"Of course not."

"So who did?"

It would forever remain a mystery. But Reb Nuchum Donner wasn't surprised. Not even slightly. Things just had a way of working out when Rav Grossman was involved.

"On a different occasion," Reb Nuchum says, "we were visiting Florida, and I was driving us back from Palm Beach on the 95 at two o'clock in the morning. We had been visiting a donor, and the meeting had stretched on. By now you've probably realized how important *mikveh* is to Rav Yitzchak Dovid. When it comes to *mikveh*, Rav Yitzchak Dovid reminds me of the Ribnitzer Rebbe, who was *moser nefesh* (acted with great self-sacrifice) in order to immerse in the *mikveh* even in below-freezing weather."

For no reason in particular, Reb Nuchum happened to mention that the exit for North Miami Beach was coming up momentarily. He just wanted the rabbi to know that they'd be back at their lodgings soon, but it just so happened to be that there was a shul in North Miami Beach that was named for the Ribnitzer Rebbe — and, of course, it boasted a *mikveh*.

Rav Grossman and Reb Nuchum Donner share a quiet conversation

"Not that I considered that to be of any relevance in the middle of the night," Reb Nuchum relates. "So I was more than a little surprised when Rav Yitzchak Dovid suddenly called out, 'Nuchum, get off the highway and drive to the *mikveh*!'"

Actually, though, even a *mikveh* situated in a shul named after the Ribnitzer doesn't stay open all night. Even in Boro Park you would be hard-pressed to find an open *mikveh* at such a late hour, let alone in North Miami Beach.

"There is no way in the world that the *mikveh* is open now," Reb Nuchum protested. "It's almost three o'clock in the morning!"

But Rav Grossman brooked no refusal, and Reb Nuchum knew there was no point in debating further. Taking the upcoming exit, he drove in the direction of the shul, and when they arrived, they saw that the lights were on. An interesting development, considering the time.

"Stay in the car," Reb Nuchum told Rav Grossman. "I'll go and check it out."

He made his way to the *mikveh* and found that it was open and that there was someone inside. There was a man standing inside on one of the steps, his pant legs rolled up, and he was doing a thorough job of cleaning every inch of the *mikveh's* walls.

"*Shalom aleichem*," Nuchum Donner said to the man. "Listen, there's a Yid outside in the car who wants to come in and use the *mikveh*. Would you be willing to shut the hose for a few minutes and let him in?"

"Sorry," the man replied. "I don't have any time right now. It's Thursday night, the night when I clean the *mikveh*, and I really have to finish up right now."

Seeing that he wasn't making any headway, Reb Nuchum returned to the car and informed Rav Grossman that he wouldn't be allowed in.

That might have been that, but then the *mikveh* cleaner stepped outside for a moment, and he spied who exactly the person was sitting there in the car.

"Rav Grossman," he called out, "you're here! Why didn't your man tell me that Rav Grossman is here instead of saying that 'someone' wants to use the *mikveh*? He should have said who that someone is!"

With that, he turned around, ran back inside to turn off the hose, and told Rav Grossman to make himself at home and use the *mikveh* for as long as he wanted. Meanwhile, Nuchum Donner conversed with the cleaner, who explained that he had served as the shul's president for many years, but even though he'd retired from the job, he still insisted on retaining the role of *mikveh* cleaner.

"While we're waiting for Rav Grossman to finish up," he said to Reb Nuchum, "I want to tell you a story that just happened in this shul. It's about the Ribnitzer Rebbe."

Reb Nuchum was more than happy to hear it.

A few weeks ago, a man wearing chassidic garb walked into our shul. We started schmoozing, and I asked the visitor if he had ever heard of the Ribnitzer Rebbe, whom our shul was named after.

"Did I ever hear of the Ribnitzer?" the visitor replied. "Let me tell you about the Ribnitzer Rebbe!"

I was very curious to hear what the chassid knew about the Ribnitzer Rebbe, and the story he told me was incredible.

"My father served as the Ribnitzer Rebbe's *gabbai* (assistant) back in Russia," the chassid related. "My parents didn't have any children and would ask the Ribnitzer for a blessing on a regular basis. The Rebbe reassured them each time that they were going to have a child.

"Thirty years passed this way with no progress and my parents only getting older. One day my father went into the Rebbe to ask him for a *berachah* (blessing). He told the Rebbe that he wasn't going to leave his presence until he promised him that he was going to be a father.

"The Rebbe gave the requested promise, and a short while later my parents learned that they were expecting a child. But when my mother went to the doctor for a checkup, the doctor gave her the bad news: it seemed the baby she was carrying was no longer alive. My parents rushed to the Ribnitzer, relaying what the doctor had said, but the Rebbe wasn't impressed and reassured my parents that the baby was fine.

"Three months later, my mother returned to the doctor again, and again the doctor examined her and repeated his earlier diagnosis, reiterating that the baby she was carrying was no longer alive. Of course, my parents rushed back to the Rebbe, who repeated his earlier pronouncement: '*B'ezras Hashem*, with the help of G-d, the baby will be fine.'

"When the time came, my mother went to the hospital to have her baby, but when the baby emerged, it wasn't alive. My father immediately left the hospital and went running to the Rebbe's house, where the rebbetzin told him that her husband wasn't there.

"'Where is he?'

"'*Der Rebbe is in vasser* — The Rebbe is in the *mikveh*.'

"This was very common behavior for the Ribnitzer, who immersed in the *mikveh* multiple times every day.

"My father raced back to the hospital, where he found the baby covered with a white sheet and the doctor in the process of preparing his death certificate. My father was going out of his mind with worry and distress, when another doctor appeared on the scene, a female physician in a white coat and a stethoscope around her neck.

"'What happened?' she asked.

"'A woman gave birth to a child that was not alive,' she was told.

"'Where's the baby?'

"The doctor who had delivered the baby pointed at the little form lying under the sheet. The doctor who had just walked into the room uncovered the baby and poured a bottle of water over the motionless child, who immediately started to cry.

"So it was that the words of the Ribnitzer Rebbe came true, and the baby" — here he pointed at himself — "was healthy and well. Clearly, the Ribnitzer had sent water from the *mikveh* in which he was immersing to bring me back to life."

This was the story that the *mikveh* cleaner heard from a chassid who walked into his shul one day. And if it sounds a little strange, a bit unbelievable, just remember: This was the Ribnitzer!

Rav Grossman emerged a few minutes later, beard and *peyos* still damp from the holy water of the *mikveh*, and he and Reb Nuchum got back into the car. It was almost four in the morning, and Shabbos was on its way.

Though Rav Grossman is dedicated to the practice of immersing in the *mikveh*, there was one time when he was so sick he couldn't immerse. Not that he didn't try. But when he arrived at the *mikveh* that Shabbos and tried to go inside, he found that the water was frigid, and that, combined with the fact that he was feeling so sick, compelled him to withdraw his feet and to forego his normal custom with vast regret. It was the first time such a thing had happened to him, and it disturbed him greatly.

When Shabbos was over, Rav Grossman, feeling much better, traveled to the Lelover Rebbe for his *melaveh malkah tisch* (post-Shabbos assembly). In the middle of the Rebbe's *derashah* (Torah speech), the Lelover suddenly uttered a line that seemed to be completely tangential to the rest of his speech.

"There was once a time when *der Zeide*, my grandfather, Reb Duvid Lelover, didn't feel well," he said. "When he stuck his feet in the *mikveh* that day, he found that the water was cold."

The Rebbe pounded on the table and said, "And he still went into the *mikveh*!"

Then he carried on with his previous remarks as if he hadn't made any detour at all. No one in the room had any idea what the Rebbe was referring to or why he decided to suddenly include that anecdote in his *derashah*. But Rav Yitzchak Dovid Grossman knew why. And that was enough.

CHAPTER TWENTY-TWO

Kiryat Nachliel

In the seventies, the Migdal HaEmek municipality received government funding to build additional apartment buildings in the city to attract people to settle there. Nitzanim Street would be graced with one hundred new apartments, and Solel Boneh, one of the oldest construction companies in Israel, was awarded the contract.

As everyone knows, sometimes the best-laid plans go awry, and here too, though the apartments were built and ready for people to purchase, there were no buyers, and the buildings stood empty and forlorn. One day Rav Grossman saw an advertisement informing the public that the buildings were going up for sale at a vastly reduced price. Recognizing a major opportunity when he saw one, Rav Grossman traveled to the office of the company handling the sale in Tel Aviv and informed the executive in charge that he wanted to purchase all one hundred apartments. The people in the office stared at the prospective client as if he had lost his mind.

"Which bank would be willing to give you one hundred mortgages?" the executive demanded. Rav Grossman would have to come up with the funds before the company would agree to the deal.

But Rav Grossman wasn't prepared to give up, and he arranged to meet with the minister of construction and housing and somehow convinced the government official to give him a good deal on the hundred apartments, which were being sold for around five thousand dollars apiece. It took time, but the deal eventually came together, and he did receive mortgages for as many apartments as were necessary.

But why was Rav Grossman in the market for one hundred apartments in the first place?

In the religious communities in Eretz Yisrael, parents do their best to assist their children in purchasing a place to live when they get married. But it had never been that way in the nonreligious world, and Rav Grossman knew too many young and idealistic *baal teshuvah* (returnees to Judaism) couples who were struggling to find the money to pay their rent every month. He envisioned a beautiful neighborhood of families devoted to Torah, growing and developing together.

It was around this time that the Lev Simchah of Gur embarked on a campaign to help young Gerrer couples find places to live outside Yerushalayim, where the prices were prohibitive. Housing initiatives like this would lead to the establishment of Gerrer communities in cities like Arad down south and Chatzor HaGlilit up north.

The Lev Simchah heard about Rav Grossman's initiative and offered to purchase all one hundred apartments for his chassidim for a very nice price. Rav Grossman turned down the offer, explaining that the reason he had worked so hard to acquire the apartments in the first place was to provide housing for *baalei teshuvah* who didn't have anyone to help them purchase apartments. The only question now was who would end up being the recipients of those brand-new homes.

Little did Rav Grossman know that the apartments he had bought

The Lev Simchah on a visit to Migdal Ohr

would end up being the catalyst for his partnership with one of the great thinkers of the past fifty years, the illustrious *talmid chacham* (Torah scholar) Rav Nachman Bulman.

Rav Mendel Weinbach, rosh yeshivah (dean) of Ohr Somayach in Yerushalayim, was also heavily immersed, together with Rav Yudka Paley, in the work of the American P'eylim organization. That is how he came to know Rav Grossman, and the two of them forged a close relationship. One day Rav Mendel reached out to Rav Grossman to tell him about a very special Yid by the name of Rav Nachman Bulman who had left his prestigious rabbinical position in Far Rockaway, New York, and was now serving as a member of the faculty at Ohr Somayach.

"Rav Nachman makes a profound impact on the people he meets," Rav Mendel told his friend. "He's a phenomenal speaker and a master communicator. His influence on *baalei teshuvah* is phenomenal."

Rav Grossman was intrigued.

"I happen to know that Rav Nachman Bulman is actively searching for a place to build a community. It could very well be that he is the perfect person to move to Migdal HaEmek and create something incredible for *baalei teshuvah*. I know that you had those buildings designated for Israeli *baalei teshuvah*, but I'm sure you won't mind if they end up being occupied by American *baalei teshuvah*, am I right?"

He was.

The next time Rav Grossman was in Yerushalayim, he dropped in at Ohr Somayach for an unscheduled meeting with Rav Bulman. He walked right into the *beis midrash* and introduced himself to the rav from America.

"Rav Mendel Weinbach has told me so much about you," Rav Grossman said, "and from what I understand it's very possible that we might be able to create a wonderful thing together while helping you build your dream *kehillah* (community)."

Rav Bulman immediately dropped what he was doing and went to have a conversation with Rav Mendel. Rav Mendel must have said all the right things, because Rav Bulman agreed to travel up north to Migdal HaEmek to see what Rav Grossman was talking about.

Rav Grossman and Rav Bulman

Rav Grossman gave him a tour of the city and Migdal Ohr. It wasn't long before they had connected on a very deep level, and Rav Grossman decided to offer him the use of the hundred apartments so that Rav Bulman would be able to build his dream *kehillah,* which he called Kiryat Nachliel.

Rav Bulman would remain in Migdal HaEmek for the next fourteen years, giving everything he had to building his community, a *kehillah* that revolved around its rav and the classes he gave, the leadership he so richly dispensed, and his brilliant guidance and outlook on life.

Though Kiryat Nachliel would eventually disband, with the different members of the *kehillah* moving away in many different directions, those who had the good fortune to be part of Rav Bulman's community would remember those years as some of the best times of their lives.

CHAPTER TWENTY-THREE

The Mysterious Hand

In the wake of the Camp David Accords between Israel and Egypt in 1978, a formal peace treaty was signed by the two countries in Washington, D.C., on March 26, 1979, and became effective in January of 1980. It wasn't long before El Al initiated flights from Tel Aviv to Cairo, although that particular route pretty much worked in one direction. A record number of Israeli tourists traveled to Egypt, but very few Egyptians took advantage of the flights to come and visit Israel. The peace between Israel and Egypt would remain a cold peace, and that never changed. But at the time that the treaty was being signed, many people had high hopes for ties between the two countries, and the new El Al route was given prominent space in the Israeli news.

Rav Yitzchak Dovid Grossman and his wife were guests on that maiden flight. Rav Grossman had been interested in visiting Egypt ever since he heard that the illustrious ancestor of the Baba Sali was buried there. The Baba Sali was a legendary giant in the study of Kabbalah and a truly righteous man, and Rav Grossman had developed a close relationship with him from a young age. The Baba Sali's ancestor, Rav Yaakov Abuchatzeira, otherwise known as the Abir Yaakov, was buried in an Egyptian city called Damanhur.

Rav Grossman figured that it was a short flight, and there was no reason one couldn't fly into Egypt, visit Damanhur, and return on the next flight back to Tel Aviv.

When the plane landed in Cairo, Rav Grossman and his rebbetzin disembarked, only to find themselves on the receiving end of stares from every person they encountered. The Egyptians had never before seen anyone who looked quite like Rav Yitzchak Dovid Grossman, with his long beard and *peyos* and his chassidic dress, and they couldn't contain their fascination.

There must have been hundreds of Arab taxi drivers standing outside the arrivals gate at the airport, and as soon as the Grossmans walked outside, they were surrounded by drivers yelling, "Abuchatzeira! Abuchatzeira!" and begging for the four-hour fare to Damanhur.

Needless to say, the Grossmans were overwhelmed. Here there were what seemed like two hundred drivers all clamoring to convince Rav Grossman and his wife to ride with them. Many even grabbed on to his clothing and attempted to pull him toward their cabs.

Removing his chassidic hat from his head, Rav Grossman tossed it high up in the air. All eyes followed the hat's trajectory and watched as it landed on the head of one of the taxi drivers.

"You are the driver," Rav Grossman said. "Let's go."

That was it. The crowd dispersed, and Rav Grossman and his wife got into the cab, which sped away from the Cairo airport. Destination: Damanhur.

The drive to Damanhur was uneventful, and when they were finally standing before the grave of the holy Abir Yaakov, Rav Grossman and his rebbetzin were overcome with emotion at having being granted the opportunity to daven at the *tziyun* (grave) of this famous tzaddik. When they finished davening, it was still early in the afternoon, and since the return flight was scheduled to leave late that night, they had just enough time to visit another site.

There was a local resident standing by the *tziyun* of the Abir Yaakov, a Jew, and Rav Grossman asked him if there were any other graves of tzaddikim that would be worthwhile for him to visit while he was in the country. The man thought for a few seconds, then replied, "Yes, there is a grave you should go and see. The grave of Rav Chaim Kapusi."

"Who was Rav Chaim Kapusi?"

"He was a *dayan* (rabbinical judge) in Cairo and a student of the famous Kabbalist, the Arizal. He was also known by another name: Rabbi Chaim Baal HaNes (Rabbi Chaim, Master of the Miracle)."

"Where is his grave located?"

"In the old section of Cairo. Once you're in Cairo, ask a cab driver to take you to *kabra el-Yahud*. That is the Jewish cemetery in Cairo."

Their flight was scheduled to take off from Cairo, which meant that they needed to return there in any case. They would be heading back in the direction they needed to go while combining the journey with a visit to yet another tzaddik's grave.

The journey back to Cairo took them four long hours, and by the time they pulled up outside the Jewish cemetery of old Cairo, it was pitch black outside — literally "*choshech Mitzrayim*" ("Egyptian darkness" — a reference to the ninth plague to strike the Egyptians, the plague of darkness). It was wintertime, and the sun had long since set.

Rav Grossman and his wife began to walk through the cemetery. When they reached the first row of graves, he took a box of matches from his pocket and, striking one against the side of the box, used the flame to read the inscription on the grave. He could make out the letters *pei* and *nun*, Hebrew letters one will find on every Jewish grave, which stand for "*po nikbar* — here lies." It was a bona-fide Jewish grave, which confirmed that they were in the right place. Now the question became how to find the *kever* (grave) of Rav Chaim Kapusi. There was no map, and the darkness was complete.

Rav Grossman was able to discern that the grounds sloped upward like a hill, and he thought he could just barely make out a grand building at the top of the hill, with a roof supported by pillars, and in his mind he was fairly sure that it must house the grave of Rabbi Chaim Baal HaNes. The tzaddik had surely been honored by the community after his passing with a grand structure for his final resting place.

We'll let Rav Grossman tell the rest of the remarkable tale:

> Having come to this conclusion, I began to run up the hill in the direction of the building. Meanwhile, my wife was making her own unhurried way up the hill behind me, knowing that she would get there in plenty of time even without running.
>
> As I approached the building, I realized that there were no doors. The structure was nothing more than a roof held up by pillars, leaving it completely open to the elements.
>
> I had almost reached the wall-less building when I felt as if someone was grabbing my shoulder from behind and pulling me backward. I thought I was going to pass out from the shock. There I was, in the middle of a cemetery, and "someone" was grabbing

me and forcibly holding me back from entering the *kever* of Rabbi Chaim Baal HaNes.

I stopped in my tracks to get my bearings and tried to take stock of the situation, looking around me in vain for the person who had grabbed me.

There was no one there.

When I calmed down from the shock, I approached the building again, this time much slower, and when I was almost there, I used another match to illuminate my surroundings. By the dim light of the tiny flame, I was able to see that there was no building. There was no floor. The roof was situated over a deep pit filled with water and had been placed there for no discernible reason that I could see. Had I continued running into what I had imagined was a structure, I would have fallen a good sixty feet into a huge cistern filled with water!

I stared at that pit, my heart beating like a giant drum, and realized just how close I had come to never returning home again. Had I not been tackled by the mysterious hand that held me back from rushing forward, I would have continued straight over the edge and would have been unable to pull myself out of the water.

There was no question in my mind that my life had just been saved. I don't know how to swim, and even if I did, I wouldn't have been able to keep treading water until my wife found someone to rescue me. There was no question that I had just experienced a miracle in the proximity of Rabbi Chaim Baal HaNes.

Just then Rav Grossman's wife caught up to him, and he related to her what had happened. As they absorbed the enormity of the miracle, Rav Yitzchak Dovid Grossman began to weep, and he thanked the Ribbono shel Olam for His incredible kindness. When he was a little calmer, Rav Grossman stood at the edge of that deep pit and raised his voice as he called out, "Rav Chaim Kapusi, Rabbi Chaim Baal HaNes — even after their passing, tzaddikim are called living. Rav Chaim, I'm sure that you can hear me. If you want me to daven at your *kever*, then please show me a sign so I can find my way. If no sign comes, then I will daven right where I am, and I know that you will hear me from here."

Rav Grossman was thinking about a statement from the *Zohar* that says, "After leaving this world, the tzaddik can be found in the entire universe." It was with this statement from the *Zohar* that Rav Grossman asked Rabbi Chaim Baal HaNes for a sign.

He had barely finished speaking when he noticed two lights in the distance. As they approached, he realized that the two lights belonged to the headlights of an Egyptian army jeep. The soldiers inside had noticed the taxi idling by the cemetery and had pulled up, gotten out of their jeep, and, pointing a military flashlight at the driver, asked him what he was doing there.

"There's a sheikh from Israel who is wandering through the cemetery in search of the grave of a famous righteous man."

Moments later, Rav Grossman heard the soldiers calling out in English, "Come here!"

Rav Grossman and his wife made their way down the hill, where they found the soldiers and were able to communicate with them a little bit since they knew a smidgen of English.

"I'm looking for a holy place," Rav Grossman explained.

They gestured with their hands for the two to get into the taxi and follow the jeep. They drove for ten minutes until they arrived in a little Arab village that had been built in the middle of the cemetery. There the jeep stopped, and the soldiers informed the Grossmans that they had arrived at the place they'd been seeking.

Rav Grossman entered the courtyard, and to his great joy, he saw a large *matzeivah* (tombstone) with the words, in Hebrew, "Here is interred HaRav HaKadosh Rav Chaim Kapusi, Rabbi Chaim Baal HaNes, who served his people as a *dayan* in Egypt." A chain separated the grave from the rest of the courtyard, and it was clear that the area was well-tended.

There and then Rav Grossman raised his voice once again, and, still feeling the emotion from the earlier miracle that he had experienced, he began to daven out loud. When they finished davening, the Grossmans got back into the taxi and flew down the roads of Old Cairo, pulling up outside the airport only minutes before the flight was due to depart. By the time they got out of the taxi and found the right gate for the departure, it was very late. Rav Grossman was sure that they had missed their flight.

El Al didn't yet have an office in the Cairo terminal, temporarily making due with a window in some corridor. But the window was closed, and there was no one to talk to. Rav Grossman opened the door to a nearby office, where he found an Arab sitting at one of the desks. Rav Grossman explained that he was a "sheikh" from Israel and seemed to have missed his El Al flight. The Arab took out his walkie-talkie and began describing the situation to someone on the other end. Moments later, two El Al security men showed up.

"Rav Grossman," one of them said, recognizing the Disco Rabbi, "so now you're a sheikh?"

"Please, you need to get me out of Mitzrayim," Rav Grossman replied, "like Moshe Rabbeinu led the Jewish people out of here thousands of years ago!"

They immediately contacted the pilot of the plane and ordered it to wait for a few more minutes. The Grossmans were then taken through the airport, their passports were stamped, and soon they were walking up the stairs to the plane for their return flight to Eretz Yisrael.

So ended Rav Grossman's trip to the *kever* of the saintly Abir Yaakov and the very holy Rav Chaim Kapusi, otherwise known as Rabbi Chaim Baal HaNes. It was a day he would never forget. Not only had he merited praying at the grave of the Abir Yaakov, but he had been the recipient of a clear miracle. It seemed to him that this was yet another indication that the Master of the world had a plan for him — a mission that he needed to fulfill.

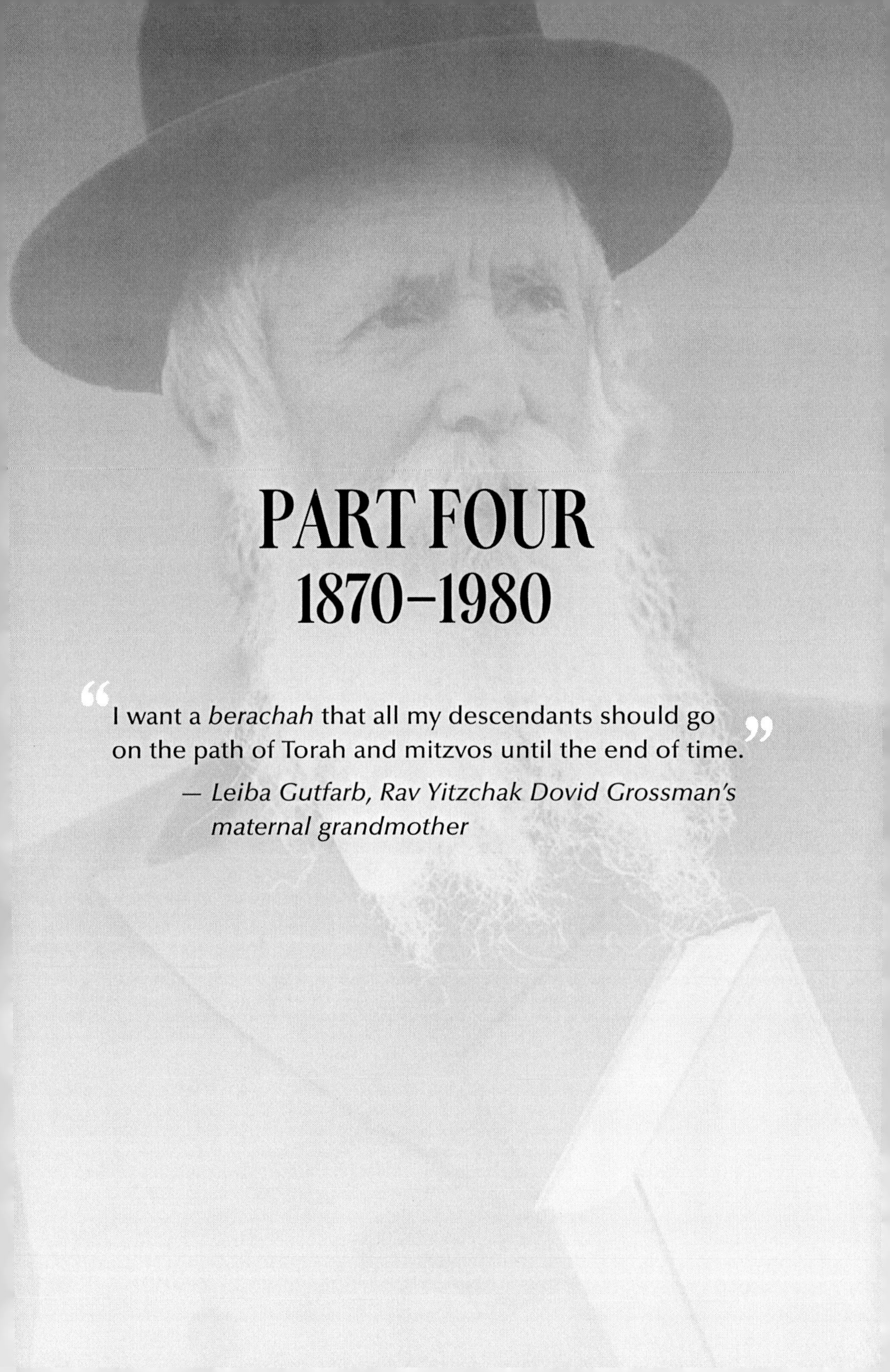

PART FOUR
1870–1980

"I want a *berachah* that all my descendants should go on the path of Torah and mitzvos until the end of time."

— *Leiba Gutfarb, Rav Yitzchak Dovid Grossman's maternal grandmother*

CHAPTER TWENTY-FOUR
Yitzchak, Refael, and Yitzchak

People aren't simply born great. Greatness has to be cultivated and developed. So it was with Rav Yitzchak Dovid Grossman.

If you were to ask the rav of Migdal HaEmek how he, who had barely ventured out of Meah Shearim until he was a young man, came to do the things he has done, he'll say that he was blessed with an inordinate degree of *siyata d'Shmaya*. He'll also tell you stories about his father, the indomitable Rav Yisrael Grossman, and his Rebbe, Rav Moshe Mordechai Biderman, the Lelover Rebbe. He'll explain that these two great tzaddikim molded him and gave him the tools he needed for his incredible journey through life.

The Grossman family had long-standing ties to the holy city of Yerushalayim. The Grossman side of the family had been living in the city for quite a few generations, but they couldn't compare to the Gutfarbs, the family of Yitzchak Dovid Grossman's mother, who could trace its lineage in Yerushalayim all the way back ten generations.

His grandmother Leiba Gutfarb was well known in a city renowned for its *baalei chesed,* for those who helped care for their fellow Jews. She had standing accounts in many of the butcher shops, grocery stores, and fruit-and-vegetable enterprises, and when a person walked in and couldn't afford to pay for what they bought, the owner would give them a "discount" and put the actual amount on her bill.

Leiba made the rounds of the city's hospitals every day, visiting Shaare Zedek and Bikur Cholim to bring cheer and happiness to the patients. If she passed a bed where the patient was alone, without visitors, Leiba

Rav Grossman's grandmother Leiba (at far right of the Kosel)

would appoint herself their family, discussing their care with the doctors and hospital staff and making sure they were being looked after properly. Her entire life was devoted to *chesed* (kindness), and significant sums of money passed through her hands as she went about her day, dispensing love and kindness to many. Yet, despite the fact that she handled so much cash on a regular basis, she herself lived in a tiny home in Batei Wittenberg with neither running water nor electricity.

There was greatness on both sides: His father's mother, Fradel Grossman, would take in people who had no place to stay, and they lived in her home for years.

Their legacy of kindness would live on in their grandson, clearly evident in the life he would grow up to lead. But *chesed* doesn't usually skip a generation. Rav Yitzchak Dovid Grossman's parents were well-known *baalei chesed* in their own right.

Yitzchak Dovid Grossman entered the world in 1946. When the War of Independence broke out two years later, the Grossman family took refuge in the nearby shelter, which happened to be a wine cellar belonging to the Teperberg Winery. It was only large enough to accommodate fifty people, yet somehow three hundred people managed to squeeze into the space, Yitzchak Dovid, his parents, and brother and sister among them. There his father, Rav Yisrael, sat beside the window and learned nonstop, using whatever tiny bit of light entered the dark room.

His father would have been content to sit out the war learning in his little corner in the shelter, but he was forced to venture outside to obtain kerosene to heat water for his small children. This was no simple matter since the Jordanian Legionnaires had the high ground on the Old City walls and spent much of their time shooting bullets and bombing the streets of Beis Yisrael and Meah Shearim. Numerous innocent people

(l to r): Bentzion, Rochel, and Yitzchak Dovid (far right) and their mother, Guta Perel Grossman

Decades — and so many accomplishments — later: Rebbetzin Guta Perel Grossman with her son, Rav Yitzchak Dovid

were killed during those trying times, but with no recourse, Rav Yisrael headed in the direction of Pinsk-Karlin near the Mir Yeshivah to purchase the kerosene.

On his way back to the Teperberg wine cellar, a bottle of kerosene in hand, Rav Yisrael ran into Rav Gershon Lapidos, known as the "*masmid* of Yerushalayim" (the diligent student of Jerusalem). Seeing the bottle of kerosene, Rav Gershon ran to Rav Yisrael Grossman and begged him for a little bit of the precious liquid, explaining that he had been learning outside for the past few nights, using the light of the moon to see the words on the pages of his *sefer*.

"Please, I need some kerosene for my lamp. My eyes have become too swollen to continue learning this way."

Rav Yisrael couldn't say no and donated a cup of kerosene to the cause — one *masmid* to another.

In the morning, Rav Yisrael was informed that Rav Gershon was outside the shelter asking for him. He emerged onto the street to find the *masmid* of Yerushalayim waiting. "What's the matter?" he asked. "What can I do for you?"

"Rav Yisrael, can you perhaps spare a little more kerosene for me?"

"But I just gave you a cup of kerosene yesterday!"

"Yes, but I learned the entire night and now it's all gone."

Such was life in Yerushalayim back then.

(l to r): Yitzchak Dovid's great-uncle, Rav Shimon Grossman, his great-grandfather, Rav Yaakov Groner, and Yitzchak Dovid himself

As a child, Yitzchak Dovid lived with his family in Batei Warsaw and attended a branch of the famous Etz Chaim Talmud Torah. This was in the early fifties, when a large group of Yemenite Jews left their native land and immigrated to Eretz Yisrael. Many of them were sent to live in a city called Rosh HaAyin. Since this took place shortly after the establishment of the State, there was little money to be had, and the Israeli government erected rows of tents for the new immigrants and their many children and newborn babies. This is where they lived during the harsh and bitter winter, doing their best to avoid the ubiquitous thick mud that made their lives miserable.

Hearing about the newcomers' dire situation, Rav Yisrael and his wife traveled to Rosh HaAyin, where they walked from tent to tent, introducing themselves to every family and offering to take care of their children if the families didn't feel capable of looking after them at that time.

"Your children will live with us in Yerushalayim for as long as you need," they told the immigrants. "The moment you get on your feet, you can come and take them back. Meanwhile, they won't be forced to live in a freezing cold tent with mud everywhere."

Lest you think the Grossman family had but one or two children and plenty of room, that was not the case. They had been blessed with ten boisterous children who filled the small apartment with joyful commotion. Yet along came the Grossmans to offer the hapless arrivals a place to house their children for as long as they needed.

Fifteen children accompanied Yitzchak Dovid's parents back to Yerushalayim from Rosh HaAyin. Two were given beds in his house, and the rest were divided among the neighbors.

"For the next few years," Rav Yitzchak Dovid recalled, "I slept in the same bed as two Yemenite boys. One was Refael, the other Yitzchak."

Years later, Rav Yitzchak Dovid was sitting shivah for his father in his parents' home, and one morning a contingent of government officials, including the prime minister, came over to pay a condolence call. This wasn't a surprise: though Rav Yisrael had been a *masmid* and huge *talmid chacham*, not to mention a rosh yeshivah, he also somehow managed to be involved in many of the primary developments of Torah observance in Eretz Yisrael in the years following the formation of the State. Among other things, he cofounded the legendary P'eylim *kiruv* (Torah outreach) organization alongside Rav Sholom Schwadron, was involved in the establishment of Chinuch Atzmai, and was even appointed secretary of the Moetzes Gedolei HaTorah (the Council of Torah Sages), a role he served with distinction.

Upon entering the apartment, the dignitaries couldn't help marveling at how tiny it was. Rav Yitzchak Dovid explained that they were mistaken. The apartment wasn't tiny at all.

"Not only is this not a tiny apartment," he told the group of politicians, "it was even big enough to host several Yemenite children who had just arrived in the country and were suffering terribly since they were forced to sleep in tents surrounded by muddy rivers.

"The iron bed we three slept on is still here," he told his government visitors, pointing at the bed, which was still in position, as if waiting to

A poignant reunion: Rafael and Yitzchak Dovid sitting on the bed they'd shared so many years earlier

be used. "During the day it folded up against the wall, and we pulled it down at night."

It so happened that at that very moment one of the Yemenite boys who had lived with the Grossmans during those years arrived to pay a shivah call. Refael entered the apartment, and upon seeing Rav Grossman, he promptly burst into tears.

"That's my bed!" he cried, pointing at the iron bed still folded up against the wall after so many decades.

Chazal (the Sages) tell us there is no comparison between hearing something and seeing it with your own eyes. The people in the room had been listening to Rav Grossman's stories, but there was no comparison between hearing a story about a man from Meah Shearim who had adopted two Yemenite children and invited them to live with him for as long as they wanted and actually meeting one of the children in question. It brought the entire story alive and changed everything, because here was tangible proof of the Grossman family's care and compassion for Klal Yisrael.

"He was part of the group," Rabbi Dovid Levin, a schoolmate from Etz Chaim days, recalls, "but at the same time he gravitated toward our rebbeim (Torah teachers) and role models. He wanted to spend time in the presence of the people who impressed him. One time he told me, 'One day I'm going to be like your grandfather.'"

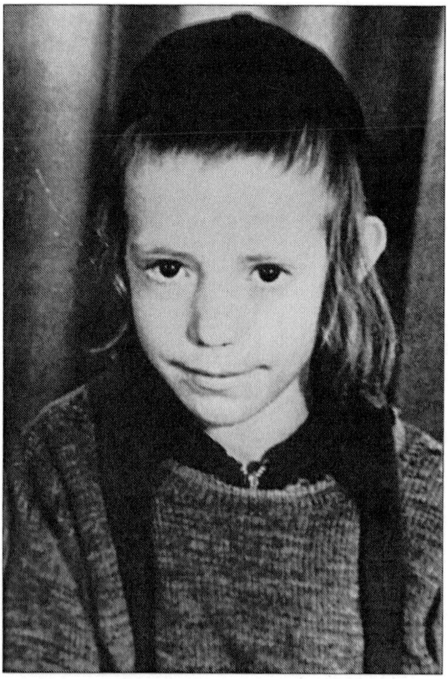

Young Yitzchak Dovid

Who was Rav Dovid Levin's grandfather, whom young Yitzchak Dovid hoped to emulate? None other than Rav Aryeh Levin, a legend in Eretz Yisrael, famously known as the "father of prisoners." Rav Aryeh was also the *mashgiach* (dean of students) of the Etz Chaim Yeshivah, which the boys who graduated from the Etz Chaim Talmud Torah went on to attend.

"The fact that Yitzchak Dovid Grossman already viewed himself as following in the footsteps of such a person even at so tender an age was a very telling sign about his personality and the type of life he would end up leading."

There is no question that Yitzchak Dovid Grossman possessed an internal drive to help others from a very young age. In fact, his father used to enjoy relating a story that took place when his son was a young boy.

"We weren't the kind of family that purchased new shoes or clothing for our children on a regular basis," he'd say. "But there came a time when my son's shoes were all ripped, and we couldn't postpone buying him new ones any longer."

Two days later, he saw Yitzchak Dovid walking into the house. He happened to glance at his son's feet, expecting to see the new shoes. But the shoes Yitzchak Dovid was wearing were terribly ripped and coming apart at every seam.

"Yitzchak Dovid," his father said to him, "what happened to the shoes I bought you? Where did they go?"

"There was a boy in my class who needed new shoes. He is a *yasom*, an orphan, and I knew that he doesn't have anyone to help him. I decided to give him my shoes and to wear his..."

"But those were your new shoes!"

"Yes, but he is a *yasom* and doesn't have a father to help him..."

It was at that point that Rav Yisrael Grossman understood beyond a shadow of a doubt that his young son's life was going to be one of constant giving.

CHAPTER TWENTY-FIVE

The Horse Thief of Lodz

After graduating from Etz Chaim Yeshivah, Yitzchak Dovid Grossman went on to learn at the Slabodka Yeshivah, located on a hilly road in Bnei Brak, where he learned Torah under the guidance of Rav Isaac Sher and Rav Yechezkel Abramsky.

When his brother Bentzion got engaged, Yitzchak Dovid knew that he had some time before he would get married, because the custom in their circles was for one child to get engaged and then married before

Rav Abramsky, surrounded by students. Young Yitzchak Dovid is directly behind him.

the parents even began listening to suggestions for the child who was next in line. Happily *shteiging* (learning seriously) away in Slabodka, Yitzchak Dovid, who was only nineteen at the time, was fine with having a little more time in which to prepare himself for life.

Two months after his brother's engagement, a *shadchan* (matchmaker) named Reb Dovid Hurwitz arrived at the Grossman home and suggested a *shidduch* (match) for Yitzchak Dovid.

"Which family do you have in mind?" his mother asked the *shadchan*, despite herself.

"I'm talking about the daughter of Rav Dov Berish Rosenberg from Lod."

Rav Dov Berish Rosenberg was a leading member of the Chabad community in the city of Lod and a good friend of Rav Yisrael Grossman, who served as rosh yeshivah of Chabad's Tomchei Temimim Yeshivah in Lod at the time.

"I'll tell you the truth," his mother said to the *shadchan*. "My older son Bentzion got engaged two months ago, which means that it will probably be at least another year before Yitzchak Dovid can get married."

Rav Yisrael Grossman was out of the country when the *shidduch* came up, fundraising on behalf of Chinuch Atzmai in South Africa. In those days, there was no such thing as making an international phone call between two countries like Israel and South Africa. But Yitzchak Dovid's mother wanted to tell her husband about the *shidduch* suggestion for their son, so she sat down and wrote down all the information in a letter.

Rav Dov Berish

"A *shadchan* named Reb Dovid Hurwitz came to suggest the daughter of Rav Dov Berish Rosenberg for Yitzchak Dovid," she wrote, including all the pertinent information.

As soon as the letter reached Rav Yisrael Grossman in South Africa, and he'd had the chance to read it, he sent a telegram — not a letter — back to his wife in Yerushalayim.

"If he is suggesting the daughter of Rav Berish Rosenberg, close the *shidduch* immediately!"

Rav Grossman visiting the Baba Sali

The series of events leading to his engagement went back to a chance encounter that Yitzchak Dovid and his brother Bentzion had with Rav Yisrael Abuchatzeira, the Baba Sali, when Yitzchak Dovid was sixteen years old and his brother only a little older. The Baba Sali had recently moved to Eretz Yisrael from Morocco and was already well known throughout the country. When he arrived in the Holy Land, he first settled in Yavneh, and the two brothers happened to have traveled there to visit the grave of Rabban Gamliel HaNasi. Upon hearing that the famed Kabbalist was living there, they decided to walk over to his humble home to request a *berachah.*

They knocked on the door, and the Baba Sali himself answered.

"What can I do for you?"

"We want a *berachah,*" Bentzion replied.

"What type of *berachah* do you want?"

Bentzion, aware of the Gemara that instructs a boy to marry before the age of twenty, said, "I want a *berachah* that I will merit to get married before turning twenty."

The Baba Sali gave him the desired *berachah*. Then, turning to Yitzchak Dovid, the younger brother, he placed his palm on the young man's palm and said, "And you will follow immediately after him!"

So it was that when a *shidduch* was suggested for Yitzchak Dovid two months after his brother

Yitzchak Dovid and his bride at their wedding

Bentzion had gotten engaged, his parents took the idea seriously and responded with alacrity.

And so the Baba Sali's words came to fruition, and the two brothers from Meah Shearim got married during the same year. In the end, Yitzchak Dovid married at the age of nineteen, with Rav Chatzkel Abramsky serving as the *mesader kiddushin*.

Unlike the Grossman family, who had resided in Yerushalayim for generations, Rav Berish Rosenberg, who was to become Rav Yitzchak Dovid's father-in-law, was born in Europe, where he suffered through the Holocaust. When he arrived at Auschwitz and descended from the train to the accompaniment of barking dogs and shouting Germans, he was ordered to throw anything holy he had on his person into a nearby pit — a pit that was already filled with *tashmishei kedushah* (holy objects), particularly many pairs of tefillin. Needless to say, the pair of tefillin he arrived with was quickly confiscated and thrown into the pit, where it lay on top of numerous other velvet bags.

The moment his tefillin were thrown into the pit, Rav Dov Berish reacted instinctively and literally threw himself into the pit, intent on retrieving his most precious possession. The Nazi officers standing nearby had no patience for such behavior, and he was pulled out of the pit and given a beating he would long remember.

Standing nearby and witnessing the entire sequence of events was a man known throughout the camp as the "Horse Thief of Lodz." The Horse Thief was a powerfully built individual who knew how to get around the system. He was not a sensitive person; some would even call him a boor. Yet even so, when he saw the obviously religious Jew jumping into the pit to save his tefillin, the sight of such *mesirus nefesh* (self-sacrifice) ignited a spark within his soul, and he decided to do something for the hapless prisoner. He waited until the group of Jews had been sent on their way, some to the gas chambers and others to the barracks. The Horse Thief jumped into the pit himself, and removed a velvet bag of tefillin from the pile. He tracked down the Jew and went to visit him in his new abode.

"*Tzaddik'l*," he said to Rav Dov Berish, "here is a pair of tefillin for you."

While the Horse Thief had gone out of his way to make things right, little did he dream of what he really accomplished that day in the barracks in Auschwitz.

Having just been given the gift of a lifetime by no less a personage than the Horse Thief of Lodz, Rav Dov Berish began smiling again. But as he sat down on his bed, he couldn't help noticing that a few beds over sat an elderly Yid with a long white beard who was crying as if his heart had been broken into a million pieces with no hope of putting it back together. He made his way over to the distinguished-looking Jew and asked, "Why are you crying?"

"I am a son of the great tzaddik, the Divrei Chaim of Sanz," the other replied, "and I was extremely fortunate because I was given my holy father's tefillin, which I had the privilege to use — until today."

"They took away your tefillin?"

"Yes, and they threw them into the pit! The holy tefillin of my saintly father, the Divrei Chaim of Sanz. His most precious possession thrown away for all eternity! Do you even wonder why I'm crying?"

The Divrei Chaim's son couldn't control himself and began weeping again, and Rav Dov Berish wept with him.

"Don't worry," he said at last. "At least you will have a pair of tefillin to put on every day."

"How?"

Rav Dov Berish told him how he had lost his tefillin and how the Horse Thief had come to see him, a velvet pouch containing tefillin in his hands.

"Look, I will show you."

A moment later Rav Dov Berish handed the velvet pouch containing the tefillin to the son of the Divrei Chaim, who almost passed out when he saw it.

"What is it?" Rav Dov Berish asked the chassid. "What's wrong?"

"It's them! This pouch contains the tefillin that belonged to my father, the Divrei Chaim!" the tzaddik's son replied, and sure enough, he showed Rav Dov Berish his father's name, which was embroidered on the pouch.

The next day, the Horse Thief of Lodz returned to the barracks.

"*Nu, tzaddik'l,* are you happy with your tefillin?"

One of those who overheard the exchange spoke up. "You can't imagine what a tzaddik that young man is. You brought him a pair of tefillin, and he promptly gave it away to an old man in the same barracks."

The Horse Thief was so moved by the story that he returned to the pit, jumped inside, and returned with another two pairs of tefillin — one *Rashi*, the other *Rabbeinu Tam*. (To fulfill the commandment according to all the different halachic opinions.) The two pairs of tefillin were promptly hidden in the head of a broom, which was secretly hollowed out in order to contain the precious treasure.

There would be a million stories throughout the war involving those two pairs of tefillin. Suffice it to say, both pairs survived the Holocaust and made it out of Europe to Eretz Yisrael.

The inauguration of the Yerushalayim branch of Chinuch Atzmai's high school took place just after Rav Yitzchak Dovid married in 1966. He was not yet twenty years old. Knowing the type of children who learned in the Chinuch Atzmai educational system — kids from traditional homes on the lower socioeconomic range of the spectrum — and knowing the unusual abilities of his son, Rav Yisrael informed his son that he wanted him to begin teaching in the school.

Actually, this wouldn't be Rav Yitzchak Dovid's first teaching experience. Just a few years before, when Yitzchak Dovid was sixteen years old, a few students in the Etz Chaim Yeshivah heard about a Yid named Reb Isaac Levi who was a patient at Hadassah Ein Kerem. He had no family, and they decided to take turns visiting and spending time with him. One Shabbos, Yitzchak Dovid left his home in Batei Warsaw for the lengthy walk to the hospital. He passed through Kiryat Menachem on the way, where he decided to stop and daven Minchah.

At the time, the neighborhood was new, populated by immigrants from many different countries. People lived in caravans, and children wandered the muddy streets, unsupervised and free to get into trouble. It was obvious to the sixteen-year-old *yeshivah bachur* that nothing was being offered in the way of *Yiddishkeit* to these kids and that none of them had any chance of remaining religious unless something drastic was done.

Having grown up watching his parents in action, Yitzchak Dovid understood that the situation rested on his shoulders. It was up to him to do something and make a difference in the lives of these people who were newly arrived in Eretz Yisrael. When Minchah was finished, he stepped up to the front of the shul.

"*Rabbosai* (Gentlemen)."

They looked at him in surprise. No doubt they were asking themselves what a Yerushalmi kid was doing there and what possessed him to stand up and address them.

"*Rabbosai,*" he said again, "I have a proposal for you."

They stared at him, curiosity written on their faces.

"I see you have children, and I understand that none of them are being given the opportunity to learn Torah. I would therefore like to offer my services to teach your children. I will come to Kiryat Menachem twice a week in the evening and give classes. But I need you to help me by sending your children. Tell them that whoever attends the classes will receive prizes, and it will be worth their while. Are you interested in my offer?"

They were. They promised to send their children to learn Torah from the sixteen-year-old boy who just happened to enter their lives one Shabbos afternoon.

So it began, and so it continued a few years later when a Chinuch Atzmai institution opened in Yerushalayim.

Near Yeshivas Mir in the Beis Yisrael neighborhood of Yerushalayim was the building that housed the Zhviller institutions, and it was in this building that Chinuch Atzmai set up its first school in the capital city. When Rav Yisrael Grossman asked his son to get involved, there could be only one answer. And so, for the first year following their marriage, the young Grossman family lived in the apartment that had been purchased for them by their parents, and Rav Yitzchak Dovid devoted much of his time to help build the fledgling school. Their apartment was centrally located on Chana Street, across from the Tchebiner Yeshivah, and the Grossmans were very happy there. Not that Rav Yitzchak Dovid was home very much...

Whereas most young couples enjoy a somewhat leisurely *shanah rishonah* (first year of marriage), with the husband staying at home in the evenings, Rav Yitzchak Dovid was busy day and night with the new school.

"I invested my *neshamah,* my heart and soul, into that school," he remembers. "I was there from morning until night, doing everything I could to instill Torah values into the children we were trying to reach."

The brand-new Rebbetzin Grossman would quickly learn whom she had married. It didn't take her long to comprehend that her husband's heart would always be open wide and that he would never be the type of person who sat quietly at home when he could be changing the world, one person at a time. To her credit, the young wife not only embraced what she recognized as a wonderful character trait, but also did her best to help and support him.

This would become the pattern of their marriage: two people who were aware of the challenges people around them were facing and were determined to take an active role in helping them overcome those challenges. If that meant her husband wouldn't be around at night to have coffee and cake with her, Rav Yitzchak Dovid's wife was fine with that.

As long as he was helping Klal Yisrael.

CHAPTER TWENTY-SIX

The Karlin Connection

There is no question that his family background played a pivotal role in who Rav Grossman became. Rav Yitzchak Dovid came from a long line of truly phenomenal individuals, all with stories of their own, and he was undoubtedly influenced by every one of them.

Because that's the way it works. We transmit our values to our children, and they hand them over to our grandchildren, and so the *mesorah,* the traditions of Torah and mitzvos, are bequeathed to the next generation. In Rav Grossman's case, the legacy that he inherited was greater than most.

Rav Grossman's paternal grandfather was Rav Moshe Shneur Zalman and his great-grandfather was Rav Yitzchak Dovid — the man for whom Rav Grossman was named. Rav Yitzchak Dovid's father, Rav Mordechai, was an esteemed *talmid chacham* and the rav of Kimpolung, a large European city on the border of Romania and Austria-Hungary. This was around the time that the holy Rav Yisrael of Ruzhin had to escape from his own city due to allegations made by the government that he behaved as if he were king. If convicted of such a crime, the Ruzhiner could be sentenced to death for treason.

Part of the Rebbe's troubles came about when a student wrote him a letter and referred to his master as "king of Israel." That, along with the fact that the Ruzhiner Rebbe rode in a royal coach and wore boots of the finest leather, made for probable cause in the government's eyes. But the government didn't know that the boots had no soles and that the Ruzhiner walked with no protection from the hard and rocky ground. Now they wanted to arrest him. It was an emergency, and the Ruzhiner managed to escape from Ruzhin and eventually reached the city of Kimpolung, where he was brought to the home of the rav, Rav Mordechai.

Back in Europe, the Grossman family were Karliner chassidim for generations. So much so that Rav Mordechai's father was buried beside Rav Shlomo of Karlin, and on his gravestone it states, "*Talmid-chaver* of Rav Shlomo Karliner." (The term "*talmid-chaver*" refers to the fact that the person was both a student and a friend.) And yet, despite the family's extremely close connection to Karlin, Rav Mordechai was so overwhelmed by the holiness of the Ruzhiner that he decided to become his chassid.

At that time, there was a powerful *machlokes,* a terrible disagreement, between Ruzhin and another prominent Chassidus, and the *shochet* (ritual slaughterer) in the city came out against the Ruzhiner. When Rav Mordechai heard what the *shochet* said, he forbade the people of Kimpolung from purchasing his meat, and suddenly the city of Kimpolung found itself embroiled in a mini-war, with the majority of the community siding with the man who slaughtered their meat. This led to a community meeting, where it was decided that the community would cease paying the rav his salary, which led Rav Mordechai to fall into debt. Though on the surface, all his challenges came about because he had taken the Ruzhiner's side, Rav Mordechai never told the Rebbe what was happening.

One day the Ruzhiner Rebbe sent Rav Mordechai on a mission to the illustrious Rav Meir Apter. After fulfilling his mission, Rav Mordechai unburdened his heart to Rav Meir. He explained that he hadn't received a salary for many months now, he was in great debt, and he had no way to support his family, just because he was an outspoken chassid of the Ruzhiner. He then requested a *berachah* from the Apter Rav.

"Bend down toward me," said Rav Meir, who was already very elderly and found it difficult to stand.

Rav Mordechai bent down before the venerable tzaddik, who lifted his visitor's rabbinical hat off his head and took a good look at his forehead.

"Meir sees that the rav from Kimpolung will not be stranded in the street in *Olam Haba* (the World to Come). And if he's not stranded in the street in *Olam Haba*, then he won't be stranded in the street in this world either."

When Rav Mordechai returned to Kimpolung, the entire community came out to greet him, reminiscent of the way matters had been before everything fell apart. They expressed remorse for having chosen the other side, and suddenly all was right in Kimpolung once again. There was no real reason for the people's change of heart, but it happened nevertheless. Rav Mordechai had no doubt that it had everything to do with his encounter with Rav Meir of Apt.

Yet Rav Mordechai didn't want to live in a place where such *machlokes* could rage, and he decided to leave Europe and move to Eretz Yisrael, where he settled in the city of Tzefas. He passed away not long after his arrival and is buried in the city's cemetery, not far from the grave of the Arizal.

Rav Mordechai's son, Rav Yitzchak Dovid, moved the family out of Tzefas and they settled in Yerushalayim in about 1890. There he joined the community of the Perushim, a group of people who spent their days in sincere and devoted service of Hashem. There he became renowned as a truly uplifted Jew, especially since he began studying Kabbalah with some of the greatest Kabbalists in the city. He also made a practice of visiting the Kosel every night for *Tikkun Chatzos* — a prayer mourning the destruction of the Temple and designated to be recited at midnight — which he read with tears and a broken heart. Prior to standing before the Kosel, he would descend to the Arab neighborhood of Silwan, where he would immerse in the Shiloach Pool.

One of the Arab neighbors noticed that a Jew was going to the spring by himself every night, alone and unprotected. One night, when Rav Yitzchak Dovid went under the water, the Arab placed his hand on the Jew's head and wouldn't allow him to come up for air. Rav Yitzchak Dovid tried his hardest to fight back, but every time he managed to get out from beneath the Arab's hand, his enemy overpowered him and thrust him beneath the water again. It wasn't long before he felt that his strength was waning, and he knew that he wouldn't be able to fight back any longer.

A few seconds before it was too late, the Arab was surprised by the

Lelover Rebbe, Rav Dovid'l Biderman, who learned Kabbalah with Rav Yitzchak Dovid *b'chavrusa* (as a partner in learning). The Lelover had suddenly felt the need to immerse in the mikveh, and when he arrived he saw the Arab trying to drown his friend. He removed one of the wooden slippers he wore on his feet, raised it in the air, and slammed it on the Arab's head with all his strength, saving Rav Yitzchak Dovid from certain death while ensuring that the Arab would never attack a Jew again.

When he had gotten his breath back after nearly drowning, Rav Yitzchak Dovid turned to his friend and asked, "What made you come down to the Shiloach to save my life?"

"A good friend feels," the Admor of Lelov replied.

Rav Yitzchak Dovid was a loyal member of Karlin in the Old City of Jerusalem. Those were dangerous times, and one afternoon the Arabs began to attack the Jews of the Old City without warning. Many of the local women came running to the shul and called out to their husbands to come and save them. Within seconds, the entire shul emptied out as the congregation ran home to protect their families. Meanwhile, Rav Yitzchak Dovid continued standing in his place near the wall, immersed in his davening, oblivious of everything happening around him.

The tradition in Karlin was for the chazzan (prayer leader) to wait until Rav Yitzchak Dovid finished davening the silent *Shemoneh Esrei,* at which point the chazzan would begin the repetition of the prayer. But on that day Rav Yitzchak Dovid took three steps back, and instead of hearing the voice of the chazzan, there was only silence. Turning around, he was shocked to see that not only had the chazzan disappeared, but virtually everyone else was gone as well! There was only one other person still in the room: a yeshivah student who had gone into shock from the fear and the screaming and was hiding beneath one of the benches.

Rav Yitzchak Dovid asked the young man to explain what on earth had occurred to have emptied out the shul.

The boy was incredulous. "You didn't hear? Everyone was screaming at the top of their lungs. How could you not have heard?!"

"I was immersed in my prayers," he replied.

Though he lived in Eretz Yisrael, there came a time when Rav Yitzchak Dovid decided that he needed to travel back to Europe to visit his Rebbe, the Beis Aharon of Karlin. Rav Yitzchak Dovid would remain in Karlin for two years. At the time, Rav Aharon was known as the "old Rebbe," and his son, Rav Asher, as the "young Rebbe." Rav Yitzchak Dovid was extremely beloved in the court of Karlin, and the Beis Aharon promised the visiting chassid that he would never forget him — not in *Olam Hazeh* (this world) and not in *Olam Haba*.

Rav Yitzchak Dovid booked passage on a small boat to take him back to Eretz Yisrael. Unfortunately, it suffered an accident on a Friday afternoon when their craft collided with another, larger ship on the open sea. The small boat became partially stuck beneath the larger boat, and the sailors from the craft that hit them were willing to save only the non-Jewish passengers on the smaller boat, while leaving the Jewish passengers below to drown in the rough sea.

The sailors on the ship's deck above planned on separating the two boats on Shabbos morning, with everyone on both boats understanding that the bigger ship would survive, while the smaller boat would capsize immediately, along with all the Jewish passengers. That Friday night they cried for hours, certain that this was their final night on this earth. Along with the tears, many of the passengers spent the night praying and repenting their sins in preparation for what was to come on the morrow.

Only Rav Yitzchak Dovid didn't react in the same fashion as the rest of the passengers. Instead of sitting on the floor with a *Sefer Tehillim*, he sat himself down on a chair and began chanting the Friday evening prayers of *Kabbalas Shabbos*, seemingly at peace with himself and the world. It was Friday night, and he was greeting the Shabbos Queen as he did every week.

While he sat and swayed over his siddur, completely at ease with his situation, everyone else on the boat stared at him, thinking that he had lost his mind. Rav Yitzchak Dovid paid them no attention. He davened with his usual *kavannah* (concentration), saying every word as if he were counting gems. In the middle of the davening, he rose from his chair and began to dance with joy, as he did every Friday night. But unlike every week, he danced for even longer than usual, his heart filled with gratitude to the Ribbono shel Olam for all the incredible things He had done for him until now.

He took his time, and his davening that week was something

other-worldly. As far as he was concerned, the merit of Shabbos was going to come to their rescue and there was nothing to worry about.

With the advent of morning, the sailors on the bigger ship began the process of disengagement, and the two boats were forced apart, the maneuver accompanied by the sounds of much creaking and groaning. And then, as the smaller craft was finally released from the hold of the bigger boat, it shook back and forth, and then, instead of collapsing on the spot and capsizing, it righted itself and began to sail away, while the bigger ship showed signs of distress.

The sloop's passengers watched as the big ship took on water, capsizing in such a short amount of time that they weren't able to save any of the passengers or crew. Meanwhile, the Jews on the smaller boat, who had been so sure of their approaching death, sailed off into a glorious Shabbos morning on the tranquil sea.

A few days later, the little boat docked at Haifa, and Rav Yitzchak Dovid stepped off the boat and onto the shores of Eretz Yisrael, incredibly glad to be home again after all his adventures.

When Rav Yitzchak Dovid was approaching the end of his life, his daughter Malka and son Rav Shneur Zalman took turns staying with him in the hospital. On the final night of his life — it was the first night of Chol HaMo'ed Succos — Malka stayed with her father until midnight, when her brother arrived. When Rav Shneur Zalman found that his sister was waiting outside the room instead of sitting by their father's bed, he was surprised and asked her why she had left the room.

"Half an hour ago," she explained, "Tatte opened his eyes and said to me, 'Malka, *derech eretz* (polite behavior), how can you behave this way! Didn't you see that the Beis Aharon and his son have arrived?' I quickly left the room, making sure to give the two Rebbes time alone with their chassid."

Half an hour later, Rav Yitzchak Dovid passed away.

CHAPTER TWENTY-SEVEN

Rav Zalman Shomer Shabbos

Rav Yitzchak Dovid's son Rav Moshe Shneur Zalman, known as Rav Zalman, made a very important decision upon learning what had happened to his father on his voyage to Eretz Yisrael. From that time on, Rav Zalman would stay awake throughout Shabbos, explaining his reasoning by saying that he was a "*shomer Shabbos*," a person who "guarded" Shabbos, and in the army someone who is tasked with guard duty isn't permitted to sleep. It wasn't long before everyone in Yerushalayim knew that Rav Zalman stayed up every Friday night learning and serving his Creator with *simchah* (joy) and a song on his lips.

Rav Zalman Shomer Shabbos

"If you want to stay up on Friday night," they would say in Meah Shearim, "go to the Karliner *beis midrash* where you'll find Rav Zalman Grossman, and you'll be able to spend the night *farbrenging* (*farbreng* is a unique word meaning to spend time engaged in enjoyable yet spiritual pursuits) with him, listening to Torah and words of Chassidus and singing songs to bring you closer to our Creator — all wrapped up in the zeal and fervor of the authentic chassid."

In a city like Yerushalayim, where people were given affectionate titles in accordance with their behavior, it wasn't long before Rav Zalman became known as Rav Zalman Shomer Shabbos.

Rav Zalman, the guardian of Shabbos.

In those days, there were many Jews living in poverty around the world, but the poverty level in Yerushalayim was in a class all its own. We can't even imagine what life was like then. One of the ramifications of not having any money was that people couldn't afford to visit the doctor when they were sick, and even if they could manage to see a doctor and get a diagnosis and prescription, they couldn't afford to purchase the medicine. There was no such thing as insurance. Everyone was on his own. This meant that the poor suffered, and it seemed as if few people cared. Even if they did, what could they do about it when they themselves had their own problems?

But someone did care and did decide to do something about it, and his name was Rav Zalman Shomer Shabbos. And because he cared so much, he formed an organization, calling it Ezras Cholim — Help for the Sick. The way it worked was simple. Any poor person in the city who was sick and needed to visit a doctor presented himself at the Ezras Cholim office, was given a paper — a chit, as it were — to visit a doctor, and the organization would pay the bills at the end of the month. The same procedure was used for the medicine that was needed. They would purchase the medicine from the pharmacy, which would forward the bill to Rav Zalman's organization at the end of every month.

In short order Rav Zalman had racked up huge debts. There was no way he would be able to pay everything he owed by remaining in Eretz Yisrael, so he decided to go to America and do some fundraising.

Once the idea entered his mind, it wasn't very long before Rav Zalman was taking leave of his family and traveling halfway across the world to the Brooklyn neighborhood of Brownsville (the prominent religious neighborhood of its day), where he rented a small apartment.

There was a certain Karliner chassid living in Brooklyn who woke up one Friday night with a terrible migraine headache that wouldn't allow him to go back to sleep. Hoping that a little fresh air would drive away the throbbing pain, he got dressed and began walking through the streets. Without even realizing it, the chassid ended up quite a distance away from his home, almost as if he were walking in a trance and completely unaware of what he was doing. Suddenly he realized that he had been walking for more than an hour without paying attention to where he was.

"It's the middle of the night," he said to himself, "and if I turn around and go home now, it's going to take me a long time to get there. I doubt I'll be sleeping much more tonight. Instead of returning home, I'll head over to the apartment of Rav Zalman Shomer Shabbos in Brownsville. He never sleeps on Shabbos, and there's no question he'll be up learning and singing. I can't think of a better way to spend a Friday night."

Without further ado, the chassid carried on walking until he reached the building where Rav Zalman was renting his tiny apartment. He climbed the flights of stairs until he was standing in front of the door. Before he knocked, he listened for the sounds of his friend learning and singing, but he was surprised to hear...silence.

That wasn't right.

He raised his hand and knocked.

No answer.

He knocked again.

Again nothing.

Now he began to worry.

Pressing his ear against the door, he was able to make out faint cries from within, as if someone was in terrible pain. The sound was growing steadily weaker. There was no question that Rav Zalman was suffering and that it was an emergency, and the chassid began pounding on the neighbor's door until someone opened up, disheveled and sleepy-eyed.

"What is it?"

"There's a problem with the rabbi next door. You need to send someone for help immediately!"

The neighbor's son raced to the nearest police station. The police arrived, broke down the door, and found Rav Zalman Grossman on the floor of the apartment in excruciating agony from a burst appendix. He had tried to get to the door but had collapsed on the floor from the intense pain. All he could do was lie there moaning and hope that someone would hear him.

This had continued for several hours — the pain had started early that evening. His friend had arrived just in time to save his life. It was a miracle.

The police summoned an ambulance, which brought Rav Zalman to the hospital. There they operated and managed to save his life. It was an extremely close call, and the only reason he was still alive was that everyone knew Rav Zalman never went to sleep on Friday night because, as he always said, "If you're the guardian of Shabbos, you can't go to sleep."

After that, he adopted another saying: "*Ki eshmerah Shabbos Keil yishmereini* — If I watch over Shabbos, Hashem will watch over me!"

Rav Zalman remained in the United States for five years before he decided that he'd raised enough money and could finally return to Eretz Yisrael. Because he'd lived an extremely frugal existence during his time in the States, he would be returning home with quite a lot of money. He hadn't consumed any meat products all the time he was there because of kashrus concerns, and he hadn't eaten dairy products because they weren't *chalav Yisrael* (milk that had been supervised by a Jew). He didn't even eat bread because it was *pas akum* (bread baked by a non-Jew). Which meant that for the most part he'd subsisted on vegetables. From time to time, one of his relatives baked him some challos, and he managed to stretch them to last for a couple of weeks. Now he was returning with all the money he'd saved, which he'd stashed in one of his suitcases.

He was supposed to have docked in Haifa well before Rosh Hashanah, but the journey coincided with the outbreak of World War II, and the skies began to fill with planes that had no qualms bombing the ship. The captain had no choice but to take a longer, more circuitous route, and the ship pulled into port on the morning of the first day of Rosh Hashanah, which was on a Thursday that year.

After docking, the captain and crew informed the passengers that they needed to remove all their belongings immediately, since the ship was needed for the war effort and would not be remaining at the pier more than was strictly necessary. This presented a problem for Rav Zalman, who was unable to move his suitcases because they were filled with *muktzeh* (items that one is not allowed to move on Shabbos). But how could he leave behind his suitcases and the money he had worked for the last five years to collect?

After struggling with his decision, he finally decided to disembark, leaving his suitcases behind while accepting the fact that this would mean losing everything for which he had worked so terribly hard. He found that even after having made the decision, he was still standing there on the dock, unable to leave. Eventually everyone got off the ship, and he watched as the Arab workers manhandled his suitcases onto the pier.

The suitcases were there, right in front of him. He could stand beside them for the next three days, and then, when Rosh Hashanah and Shabbos were over, he could pick them up and go home. But how could he remain on the pier all through Rosh Hashanah? Was he prepared to miss all the davening or hear the blowing of the shofar? How could he possibly give up partaking of the holiest days of the year because of something as mundane as mere money?!

In the end, he realized that he couldn't remain where he was. Leaving the pier, he walked to a neighborhood called Hadar HaKarmel, where he knew there was a Karliner *shtiebel* (small synagogue). He arrived at the shul in the early hours of the morning, and as the chassidim arrived at the *shtiebel* that Rosh Hashanah morning, they were astounded to find that Rav Zalman Grossman had arrived in Eretz Yisrael and was planning on spending the rest of Yom Tov in their midst.

The shul members couldn't get over their good fortune. Rav Zalman had the reputation of being an exceptional *baal tefillah* (prayer leader), someone who had served as the chazzan on Rosh Hashanah in his shul in Yerushalayim for many years. And now he was here with them!

For the next three days — Thursday, Friday, and then Shabbos — Rav Zalman Grossman stood before the congregation davening his heart out, and it was impossible to detect that there was anything in his life causing him distress or making it harder for him to concentrate.

When Shabbos was over, after three days in which he'd steadfastly ignored the fact that he had abandoned all his money and belongings on the pier, his host, Reb Berel Friedman, suggested that they go over there to see if any of his things were still there. Rav Zalman Grossman didn't think there was any reason to go, but his friend convinced him that he had nothing to lose.

And so they went — and there they discovered Rav Zalman's luggage nonchalantly sitting exactly where he had seen it last, untouched and in perfect condition. And all the money was there, too. Clearly the Ribbono shel Olam had sent His messengers to watch over the suitcases and protect them from all harm.

Rav Zalman's brother, Rav Shlomo Levi, lived in the Galil.

He was part of a group of people who established a number of settlements in the Galil. He himself resided in a community of chassidim called Mishmar HaYarden. The lives of those living in the settlements in the north were extremely challenging. Malaria was rampant, aided in its spread by the gigantic mosquitoes that frequented the swampland where many of the villages were established. There were few doctors to care for the sick, and even if there had been, most of the inhabitants couldn't afford medicine. Besides disease, these settlers faced backbreaking poverty and a lack of food. They were building Eretz Yisrael from the ground up, but the land wasn't making it easy for them.

While his brother was struggling in his northern settlement, Rav Zalman decided to make a trip to Karlin to spend time with the new Rebbe of Karlin-Stolin known as the "Yanuka" (literally, the "infant"). The Yanuka, Rav Yisrael Perlow, was the four-year-old son of Rav Asher, the son of the Beis Aharon of Karlin. Rav Asher had been designated Rebbe after his father's passing, but he passed away only one year later. That was when his son, the Yanuka, was crowned Rebbe of Karlin-Stolin even though he was still a child.

Since the Yanuka was now Rebbe, Rav Zalman decided to go and spend time in his presence. In those days, travel was not a regular occurrence, and when someone was making a trip to another country, everyone talked about it. It was big news. So it made sense that before he left the shores of Eretz Yisrael, his brother Rav Shlomo Levi came to see Rav Zalman, together with a group of chassidim from the Galil.

"I'm giving you a list of the names of everyone living in the northern settlements," he told his brother. "Their names and the names of their mothers. Please give this list to the Rebbe as a *kvittel* (a petition asking for a blessing), so that it may serve as a merit for us to emerge from the hardships we've been facing on a daily basis."

The next Friday night Rav Zalman was aboard a Turkish ship ferrying him across the Mediterranean Sea. Since it was Shabbos he didn't sleep, but instead of singing and dancing in his tiny cabin, Rav Zalman headed up to the deck where there was more room for him to maneuver. As the ship made its way through the ocean waves, Rav Zalman ascended the steep staircase with a pile of *sefarim* cradled in his arms, almost losing his footing a number of times but always catching himself. He found a chair on the deck and settled in for a night of serious learning and other spiritual pursuits, illuminated by the light of the moon in the cloudless sky.

Suddenly he noticed a modern-looking Jew, in the garb of a prosperous businessman, standing on the deck and staring at him in wordless wonder. Rav Zalman didn't let the man distract him from his learning. For the next several hours, Rav Zalman immersed himself in his studies, with some breaks for singing songs of *deveikus*, of longing for closeness with the Creator of the world. All that time the onlooker never took his eyes off him. Eventually the man approached Rav Zalman and said, "I see that you are a holy man. I want to give you a gift. Please tell me what it is that you need, and I will do my best to provide it."

The promise was made without any introduction, and Rav Zalman had no idea who the man was. All he knew was that the person appeared to be a man of means — the kind of individual who actually had the ability to keep such a promise.

Rav Zalman made it clear to the man that he didn't want to discuss mundane matters on Shabbos, and the stranger told him that he would return to continue their conversation when Shabbos came to an end.

The man turned out to be Baron Benjamin Edmond James de Rothschild. A man of means, indeed.

"The truth is," Rav Zalman told the baron, "I am in debt because of the expense of running an organization I established in Yerushalayim. But I want nothing for myself, only that you direct your offer to the community where my brother lives, a small settlement in the northern part of Eretz Yisrael called Mishmar HaYarden. They have also helped establish a number of other settlements, and all of them are suffering."

Baron de Rothschild made a notation in his notebook, and the two parted.

Rav Zalman Grossman ended up staying with his Rebbe for two years. He had been there for eight months when the letter arrived from his brother.

> Dear Zalman,
>
> I am writing on behalf of my *kehillah*. We want to thank you from the depths of our hearts for mentioning our troubles before the Rebbe, for our trials have suddenly been addressed. Out of nowhere, a group of doctors and nurses have arrived in our midst from France and have opened clinics to heal the sick.

The visitors have also brought eucalyptus trees with them, which they have planted. These trees help drain the swampy land, which has proven effective at getting rid of the mosquitoes, too. From one week to the next everything has changed, and there is no question that this is all in the *zechus* (merit) of the Rebbe.

I have also heard some claim that Baron Rothschild had a hand in everything that has occurred here.

In conclusion, I want to thank you again for your help in raising the matter of our situation to the Rebbe's attention.

Shlomo Levi

None of them would ever know of the role that Rav Zalman played in saving their lives. He never told them and they never learned the truth. Besides, in Rav Zalman's mind, everything that happened had been in the merit of his traveling so far to spend time with the Rebbe. So, in essence, his brother was right.

As mentioned earlier, Rav Grossman's maternal grandmother, Leiba Gutfarb, was known throughout Yerushalayim as "*Leiba di gabate*" — Leiba, the *gabbai tzedakah* (the one who dispenses charity) — a name that showed that caring and charity were just as much part of the lives of the women of Rav Yitzchak Dovid's clan as that of the men. For many years she supported Rav Yosef Shalom Elyashiv financially (without his knowledge), allowing him to learn without worry. She did the same for Rav Gershon Lapidos, the "Masmid of Yerushalayim."

In the year 1929, the Rebbe Rayatz of Chabad, Rav Yosef Yitzchak Schneerson, visited Eretz Yisrael. While in the holy land, the Rebbe did his best to visit all the different camps of Yidden, from that of Rav Kook to the chassidim, *litvaks*, and the Neturei Karta. When the Rebbe was concluding his visit to the yeshivah of Meah Shearim, he saw a large group of people standing still.

"Why did everyone stop walking?" the Rebbe wanted to know.

"There's a woman standing in the way and stopping everyone from passing."

"What does she want?"

"She is demanding a *berachah* from the Rebbe, and she stated in the most emphatic and decisive terms that she will not move unless she receives what she came for."

When he heard this, the Rayatz agreed to bless her. When she was standing before him, the Rebbe asked Rav Yitzchak Dovid's grandmother what *berachah* she wanted.

"I want a *berachah* that all my descendants should go on the path of Torah and mitzvos until the end of time."

The Rebbe did as Leiba requested. And until today (many great-grandchildren later) the *berachah* is still holding strong.

These were the stories that Rav Grossman grew up hearing about his grandparents. They are the kind of stories that mold a person and show him in the clearest way possible that he, too, could and should strive for greatness of his own.

And so he did.

CHAPTER TWENTY-EIGHT

The Tatte to the Rescue

When Rav Grossman first established Migdal Ohr in the early seventies, he started with sixth-graders, who were with him for three years, until they completed the eighth grade. This was followed by the establishment of a high school program, which in Israel spans three years, which means that by the time the eighteen boys graduated from the program, they had been learning together for six years straight.

When it was time to find yeshivos for the boys, Rav Grossman found to his chagrin that the yeshivos he approached were not in a rush to accept them. He took the boys from yeshivah to yeshivah to be tested, explaining to the roshei yeshivah that they were excellent boys, but time and again the response was negative.

For the boys, the idea of being separated and sent to different yeshivos was not simple at all. They had been raised like brothers, had been living under the same roof with Rav Grossman and his wife as their parents. It would have been challenging enough for them to handle the separation had their entrance into new yeshivos gone smoothly. But faced with being turned down by every yeshivah they approached, the eighteen "brothers" were suddenly not looking forward to the years to come in yeshivos that didn't want them.

Rav Grossman needed to find an entirely different solution. He met with two educators who claimed that they were up to the task. One was a brilliant Talmud scholar, the other known for his genius at bringing out the best in students. One would serve as rosh yeshivah, the other would oversee the students' spiritual development.

"Rav Grossman," they said, "you provide the facilities and the resources. Meanwhile, we'll bring a group of top *bachurim* (students) from Slabodka and Ponevezh to join your eighteen *bachurim* and give it the prestige that every new yeshivah needs."

Rav Grossman traveled to Kfar Yona, a city located near Netanya, where he rented a large campus, complete with dormitory and dining hall. There was a shul nearby, and he persuaded those in charge to allow the *bachurim* to learn there. Rav Grossman then outfitted the entire operation from start to finish, bringing beds, desks, and *sefarim*, as well as everything that was needed to run a real yeshivah kitchen. It was a major undertaking, but he was happy to do it. Anything for his boys.

On Rosh Chodesh Elul the eighteen boys from Migdal HaEmek were brought to the yeshivah to begin the new term. Rav Grossman had kept his part of the bargain, but he had yet to see even one *bachur* from a prestigious yeshivah sitting down in the *beis midrash* at Kfar Yona.

"Where are the *bachurim*?" he asked his newly appointed rosh yeshivah.

"Don't worry. They'll be here in another week or two."

But more than two weeks went by, and not one *bachur* showed up at Kfar Yona — not from Ponevezh and not from Slabodka. Meanwhile, the eighteen boys were having a truly challenging time settling into their new yeshivah. They had been removed from their natural environment, from the home of their "parents" in Migdal HaEmek. What was worse was the fact that they were all by themselves with two Bnei Brak–style roshei yeshivah on their heads. If the new *bachurim* would have arrived, it would have made the situation more palatable. But no one came, and they didn't see any reason for their banishment from Migdal HaEmek.

This explains why the eighteen *bachurim* all burst into tears when they caught sight of their "father" during his first visit to the new yeshivah. They pleaded with Rav Grossman to save them from their prison at Kfar Yona. Rav Grossman didn't know what to do. So he traveled to Lod to see his father, who was serving as rosh yeshivah in the local yeshivah, Tomchei Temimim.

"I came here straight from the yeshivah at Kfar Yona," Rav Grossman told his father, "and in all honesty, I don't know what to do for my *bachurim*!"

"The first thing you have to do," Rav Yisrael told his son, "is to take them back to Migdal HaEmek immediately. Rent a new building for them — this way there will be a freshness in the learning — and I will send ten of my best *bachurim* to join them in Migdal HaEmek."

The administration of Tomchei Temimim wasn't very pleased with Rav Yisrael's decision, telling him that they never made major changes without express permission from the Lubavitcher Rebbe in Crown Heights.

"I'm a *posek*, a halachic authority," Rav Yisrael replied, "and I have no doubt that the Rebbe will agree with my decision to send the boys to Migdal HaEmek. Obviously, if the Rebbe doesn't agree with me, they will return to Lod. But right now, I need them to go immediately."

Rav Yisrael recognized that this was an emergency situation that required a quick response.

So just like that, he sent his *bachurim* from Lod to Migdal HaEmek, and the yeshivah's attendance went from eighteen to twenty-eight overnight.

That was just the beginning. Rav Yisrael called a meeting of several roshei yeshivah and asked them if they would be willing to start traveling to Migdal HaEmek on a regular basis to serve as rosh yeshivah in the fledgling institution. No one agreed to go.

Then and there, Rav Yisrael made a decision. "If no one is willing to serve as rosh yeshivah in Migdal HaEmek, I'm resigning my position at

Rav Yisrael Grossman teaching "his boys" in Migdal HaEmek

the yeshivah in Lod and will begin serving as rosh yeshivah in Migdal HaEmek myself. I will leave tomorrow."

For the next year, Rav Yisrael Grossman left his home in Yerushalayim early every Sunday morning and remained in Migdal HaEmek until Friday. Eschewing the offer to live at his son's home, he chose to sleep in a room in the dorm, remaining in the *beis midrash* until close to midnight, learning with the *bachurim* from morning till night. The results were incredible: Every single one of those boys grew up to become a true *talmid chacham*.

"The greatest miracle I witnessed in relation to my father," Rav Grossman says, "was this story. Because this was where I learned what genuine *mesirus nefesh* is."

A postscript: From those first 18 boys came a yeshivah that has literally hundreds of *talmidim* learning with diligence and with *ahavas Torah,* love for Torah.

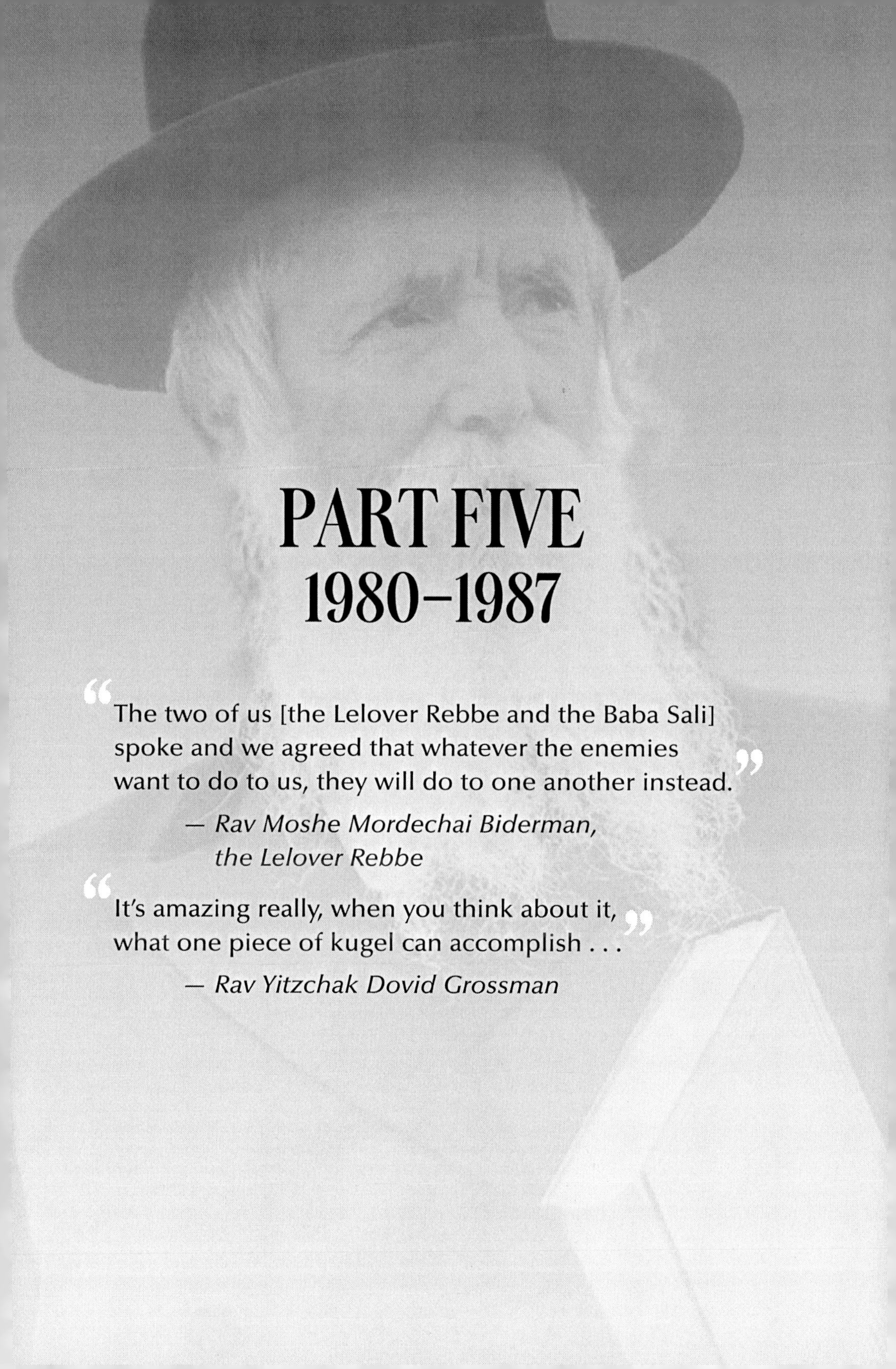

PART FIVE
1980–1987

"The two of us [the Lelover Rebbe and the Baba Sali] spoke and we agreed that whatever the enemies want to do to us, they will do to one another instead."

— *Rav Moshe Mordechai Biderman,*
the Lelover Rebbe

"It's amazing really, when you think about it, what one piece of kugel can accomplish . . ."

— *Rav Yitzchak Dovid Grossman*

CHAPTER TWENTY-NINE
A Visit to Sedom

When Rav Yitzchak Dovid was sixteen years old, the sixth Lelover Rebbe, Rav Moshe Mordechai Biderman, left Tel Aviv and came to live in the city of Bnei Brak, at 65 Rabbi Akiva Street. In the basement of the building was a *miklat*, a bomb shelter, which the Rebbe used to provide a place to sleep for those in need. It also served as a *hachnassas orchim* (hospitality) room, with facilities for guests to use for making a cup of hot coffee or tea.

At the time, there was a holy Yid in Bnei Brak named Rav Bentzion Apter. He was a Holocaust survivor and a Breslover chassid, and he would spend his nights sleeping on a bench in the Lelover *beis midrash*, not far from the Rebbe's home. This tzaddik of a Yid would then rise very early in the morning, go to the building where the Rebbe lived, and make himself a cup of tea in the *hachnassas orchim* room in the basement. He would then return to daven Shacharis.

One Thursday night, after Yitzchak Dovid had finished his day of learning in Slabodka Yeshivah, which was in Bnei Brak not far from the Rebbe's home, he decided to go and visit the Lelover Rebbe. He stepped into the *beis midrash*, where he found Rav Bentzion holding court, sharing words of Torah, telling stories, and singing songs. The *farbrengen* continued until the middle of the night, and when it was over, Yitzchak Dovid was too tired to return to Slabodka. He decided to spend the rest of the night in the basement apartment. The room had no windows and was furnished sparingly, with two beds and nothing more. Yitzchak Dovid took one bed, and one of the Rebbe's sons, who had decided it was too late for him to walk to his own home, went to sleep in the other.

Early the next morning Rav Bentzion came as usual to make himself a cup of tea. When he finished preparing his daily glass of steaming liquid, he blew out the fire but forgot to turn off the gas. He closed the door to the bomb shelter and off he went to daven, leaving Yitzchak Dovid and the Rebbe's son sleeping in an unventilated room that was steadily filling with gas.

The Lelover Rebbe never went down to the *hachnassas orchim* room before davening, but that day, for some reason, he made his way down there. The smell of gas was everywhere, and he began shaking Yitzchak Dovid and his son awake. Yitzchak Dovid woke up and saw the Lelover Rebbe standing at his bedside, telling him urgently to get up and leave the room.

It was a very close call. Close enough that Yitzchak Dovid could literally taste the gas as he stumbled out of the room. If the Rebbe hadn't come at that moment to wake them up, there is no question that Yitzchak Dovid and the Rebbe's son would have passed away in their sleep.

It was the first time the Rebbe saved his life, but not the last.

The Lelover Rebbe suffered from skin ailments and was advised by his doctors to travel to the sulfur pools at the Dead Sea in the Sedom region. This was many years ago, when visitors to the sulfur baths were housed in caravans. There were no buildings yet, and the entire area was more or less undeveloped. Tourists were able to go down there for day trips, but there was no hotel.

Since the Rebbe would be staying in the Sedom region for an extended period of time, he rented a caravan to stay in. Though he and his *gabbai* were alone during the week, at the week's end a minyan of *bachurim* would drive down to the Dead Sea and spend Shabbos in one of the most ruggedly beautiful sites in the world.

Most of these *bachurim* seldom left the city, and the novelty of spending a Shabbos with the Lelover Rebbe by the Dead Sea was something they would never forget.

The *bachurim* were housed in a caravan adjacent to the Rebbe's caravan, and the Rebbe insisted that they leave as soon as Shabbos was over. Most of the people who worked in the area were not religious, and the Rebbe didn't want the *bachurim* exposed to things they didn't need to see or hear.

One week, Itche Duvid Grossman was part of the minyan that came for Shabbos, davening, eating, and sleeping in the caravan assigned to them. For some reason, one of the nonreligious workers showed up without warning to take part in the minyan. When the davening was over and the Rebbe had left the caravan, the *bachurim* broke out in an uplifting Shabbos dance, singing a Shabbos song called "*Sabeinu MiTuvecha*" in full voice as they joined hands and whirled around the caravan.

"*V'taher libeinu, v'taher libeinu, v'taher libeinu l'avdecha be'emes!. . .*" The atmosphere was festive and joyful. It was Shabbos Kodesh, and they were staying with the Rebbe at the Dead Sea. They had been chosen to spend time in the Rebbe's presence. How lucky they were!

On the spur of the moment, Itche Duvid Grossman grabbed the hands of the young man who had joined them, the worker with long hair and a deep tan from spending hours and hours beneath the blazing sun of the Negev, and pulled him into the circle, the two of them dancing together as if they had known one another forever. At that moment, the Rebbe opened the door to the caravan for a second and then closed it again.

When Yitzchak Dovid presented himself to the Rebbe that evening to say farewell before returning home to Yerushalayim, the Lelover Rebbe caught him by surprise.

"You will remain here," he instructed.

Minutes later, the van carrying the *bachurim* left Sedom for the return journey, while one *bachur*, Itche Duvid Grossman, remained behind to share a room with the Rebbe's personal *gabbai* until further notice.

The night passed uneventfully, until three in the morning, when Yitzchak Dovid heard the Rebbe talking to himself.

"*Chacham, chacham*, wise one, wise one," he chastised himself, "when are you going to get up already?! You've slept enough. Get up and start serving the Ribbono shel Olam!"

The Lelover Rebbe always spoke gently to the people around him. Even when someone made a mistake, the harshest word you might hear from the Rebbe was "*chacham*" — wise one. There was something extra special in being given the opportunity to sleep in such close proximity to the Rebbe that you were even able to overhear him dispensing *mussar*, rebuke, to himself!

The next morning was beautiful, like every morning in that part of the world. Itche Duvid took pleasure in the turquoise hue of the water, the sounds of the chirping birds, and even the harsh aroma of the sulfur. Looking down at him from the other side of the road was a majestic mountain range, and across the sea he could discern the land of Jordan.

The Rebbe took his time davening, and it was only later in the day that Yitzchak Dovid went in to see the Rebbe and wish him a good afternoon. Upon seeing his chassid, the Admor of Lelov sat him down to have a little talk.

"There's a young man working here," he said, "who is the son of one of the managers. Please go see him and ask him if he has a chess set."

"If he says yes?"

"Tell him that the Rebbe wants to play against him."

Only someone who knew the Rebbe can comprehend how foreign was the idea of the Lelover Rebbe playing a game of chess with anyone, let alone a nonreligious boy working at the sulfur pools. If he hadn't heard the words directly from the Rebbe's mouth, Itche Duvid would have never believed it. But the Rebbe had told him to find the boy and invite him for a game of chess, so Itche Duvid went off to find the manager's son.

The Rebbe prepared himself for the game as seriously as someone preparing himself to listen to the sound of the shofar on Rosh Hashanah. He donned his caftan and wide Yerushalmi *gartel* (the special belt mainly used by chassidic Jews while praying) and was in full rabbinical garb when the boy arrived, chess set in hand.

Yitzchak Dovid had a job to do throughout the game. He was told to stand by the door, and every time the Rebbe lifted his eyes in Yitzchak Dovid's direction, he was supposed to give the mezuzah a kiss. It was almost as if he were serving in the role of messenger for the Lelover Rebbe, kissing the mezuzah for him whenever he wanted to do it himself. It was clear to him that the Rebbe was constantly focused on the maxim, "*Shivisi Hashem l'negdi tamid* — I have set Hashem before me all the time."

The game lasted for about an hour, and when it was over, the Rebbe said good night to his visitor. Other than that, they didn't speak at all. (The Rebbe let the young man win that first game; afterward, the Rebbe was the victor every time!) Itche Duvid accompanied the boy back to his caravan, the two of them walking quietly side by side in the stillness of the night.

Suddenly, and without any warning at all, the boy began to weep. Clearly, just being in the presence of the Rebbe had managed to touch a chord in his soul, even without their making any conversation.

They reached his caravan, and being of a sensitive nature, Itche Duvid felt that he couldn't just leave the boy there crying. He murmured words of comfort to the young man, and the two ended up deep in conversation, which went on until close to one o'clock in the morning.

Suddenly they heard a pounding on the door.

"Who's there?" the boy asked.

It was the Rebbe.

Itche Duvid left the caravan with the Rebbe, who looked at him and said, "Who gave you permission to be here?!"

The Rebbe didn't utter another word during the walk back to their caravans. He wanted Itche Duvid to know that he wasn't happy that he had spent so much time with the young man in a part of the compound that was outside his supervision, but after one line of remonstration, he said nothing more.

But that was sufficient. Nothing more needed to be said.

It was very difficult for Itche Duvid to fall asleep that night, and the next day followed the same pattern of the day before. Once again, the Rebbe instructed Itche Duvid to ask the young man if he was interested in playing a game of chess with him. The worker agreed, and the story repeated itself, with the two of them playing the game while Itche Duvid stood beside the mezuzah to kiss it whenever the Rebbe cast him a glance.

But then the Rebbe deviated from his behavior of the day before: He began talking to the boy, explaining to him what life was like when the ancient people of Sedom had lived in the area. From there the Rebbe brought the conversation around to Avraham Avinu, the three angels who came to visit him, and his dealings with the people of Sedom. The discussion continued for a long time, with the Rebbe telling the boy stories from the Chumash, and the young man listening to the "Bible stories" with every fiber of his being.

The Rebbe left for home the next day. The young man came to see him off, and when the Rebbe entered the vehicle, the boy with the long hair threw himself on the ground in front of the wheels, trying to stop the Rebbe from leaving him.

Itche Duvid wasn't surprised when the young man became a complete *baal teshuvah* a short while later, exchanging his life at the sulfur pools of the Dead Sea for a completely different existence filled with Torah and the service of Hashem.

In the years to come, he would often wonder if it had been that story, along with his dance and deep conversation with the boy, that served as a catalyst for the Rebbe sending him away from Yerushalayim and into the wilds of Migdal HaEmek. But he never asked, and the Rebbe never said.

CHAPTER THIRTY

The Sports Center Kaddish

There was a certain period when the Lelover Rebbe was spending considerable time in Tiveria. One Shabbos Rav Grossman decided to leave his family and join him there, wanting to bask in the Rebbe's presence.

On Shabbos morning, Rav Grossman left the apartment where he was staying and headed to the nearby *mikveh*. Along the way, he encountered a lively group of seventeen-year-old boys all dressed in sports jerseys and shorts, clearly preparing for a ballgame.

"*Shabbat shalom*," Rav Grossman greeted them.

"*Shabbat shalom, haRav*," they greeted him in return.

"Can I ask you boys a question?"

"Certainly."

"I want to understand what I'm seeing. It's only six-thirty in the morning, and I can't help asking myself why you're starting your day so early. I know why I'm out and about this early in the day. I got up at this hour because I wanted to go to the *mikveh* before I go to shul. But I see that you boys are dressed for a day of sports. Why are you starting your day so early in the morning? Why don't you go and play at eleven or twelve? What's the rush?"

"Usually we don't begin playing ball until the afternoon," one of the boys confirmed. "But today is a special day. This Shabbat all the games are being played in memory of the athletes who lost their lives in the Yom Kippur War. There's a whole day of sports activities planned — basketball, soccer, volleyball. The games are starting early and will take up the morning, while the second part of the day will be attended by the families of the athletes who lost their lives in the war."

Ribbono shel Olam, Rav Grossman said to himself, *how can this be happening? Here is a group of sweet Jewish kinderlach* (children), *and they're telling me that they will be spending an entire Shabbos playing ball in memory of soldiers who fell in battle! What kind of tribute is that?*

Of course, he didn't betray his thoughts. "Tell me, boys," Rav Grossman said, "where are the games going to be held?"

They pointed at a nearby athletic center called Moadon HaTzofim. HaTzofim is the Israeli version of the Boy Scouts, and this was their premises there in Tiveria. Adjacent to the building were playing fields for soccer and track. The complex wasn't far from the *mikveh*, and after taking leave of the group, Rav Grossman continued on to his destination.

But he couldn't get the conversation out of his mind. Those boys had such good intentions — they thought they were paying a tribute to the heroes of Israel — but in the meantime they were desecrating Shabbos in public! He decided that he was just going to have to go to the event himself.

Rav Grossman found out that the games were being played on the grounds until four o'clock, and from four and on, the bereaved families were arriving to take part in the day's program. Later that day, Rav Yitzchak Dovid presented himself at the entrance to the sports center, clad in his Shabbos best, a fur *shtreimel* (special hat worn by some chassidim) worn proudly on his head.

"Can I help you?" asked the person at the door.

"Yes, I would like to take part in today's program."

The man looked at Rav Grossman dubiously. "I'll have to ask the person in charge of the center if that's possible."

"I'll wait."

When the boss arrived, he took one look at the rabbi waiting at the door and exclaimed, *"HaRav Grossman, Shabbat shalom!"*

This warm welcome was followed by a powerful embrace, while the man at the door tried to figure out what on earth was going on. How was he to know that the two of them had met during the Yom Kippur War when Rav Grossman had been invited to give a speech at the foot of Mount Hermon? The man running the center had been one of the soldiers in the audience that day, and he remembered the experience as if it had occurred the week before.

"Please come in," he told the rabbi, ushering him into the hall while repeatedly mentioning what an honor and *zechus* it was to be able to host him on such a momentous day. As soon as they were inside, the head of the sports center introduced Rav Grossman to the crowd, explaining that he had been fortunate enough to meet the rabbi on the evening the IDF engaged the Syrians and regained the Hermon during the Yom Kippur War. He then invited Rav Grossman to say a few words to the families in the audience.

And so it was that against all odds Rav Grossman had been given the opportunity to share whatever message he felt the people needed to hear.

With a prayer that Hashem grant him the right words, he began to speak.

> When I was chosen to serve as the rav of Migdal HaEmek, a number of ceremonies took place to celebrate the occasion. It so happened to be that the prime minister of Israel, Mrs. Golda Meir, attended one of the ceremonies. During the course of that meeting, Golda Meir turned to me and said, "I've heard that you have a nickname, that they call you the 'Disco Rabbi.' Is that true?"
>
> "Yes, it is, Madame Prime Minister," I replied.
>
> The prime minister looked at me for a long moment and said, "I don't understand. I'm looking at you, and I see the way you dress. Everything about you screams Meah Shearim. So I have to ask you: How on earth did you manage to develop such a connection with people who are so unlike you?"
>
> "Madame Prime Minister," I answered, "we learn in *Tanach* about a war that occurred between King David and the Philistines. The verse states that 'David didn't have water to drink.' Three powerful men put their lives in danger, crossing the border into the Philistine camp, in order to find water for David. But the verses go on to inform us that David didn't want to drink the water, explaining, 'G-d forbid that I should drink this water! Should I drink the blood of these people? This water was brought to me by people who endangered themselves for this purpose. I cannot drink it!'
>
> "King David considered the water that had been brought to him

to be too holy for him to drink. He therefore went and poured it out as a *korban,* an offering before Hashem.

"Madame Prime Minister," I continued, "so much blood has been spilled fighting over the Land of Israel. There are so many bereaved families, so many people who have lost their children and husbands. But besides all the loss and sorrow, so many people are living lives of horrendous poverty and crime! How could I possibly ignore all that 'blood' and not do my best to make things right? How could I not help the people of Israel make a better life for themselves?"

"That's what I said to the prime minister," the rabbi said to the families sitting before him, "but now I have a message for you, my dear friends.

"You have lost your sons, your star athletes, in whom you invested so much love and hope. Your sons died to sanctify the Name of G-d, they died *al kiddush Hashem* for Eretz Yisrael, the land they loved so much."

Now he raised his voice.

"My friends, we are here today to commemorate the memories of all these fine young men. Is it fitting to commemorate them through sport on Shabbos? Is this the best way to preserve their memories? Don't we

The Lelover Rebbe, Rav Shimon, at a bris of a "Migdal Ohr baby." At Rav Grossman's right is Migdal HaEmek mayor Eli Bardah.

have an obligation to commemorate their memories in a spiritual way?

"My friends, just as King David said that he couldn't drink that water because it was too holy, and that he had to consecrate it before Hashem, I too would like to remember your sons, not through sports on Shabbos, but by saying a chapter of *Tehillim* and by reciting a chapter of *Mishnayos*, as well as establishing a regular Torah class in this very place every single week. This is what we should do to commemorate the soldiers and elevate their holy souls!"

The response to the proposal was electrifying. Rav Grossman followed his speech with the recital of *Tehillim*, Kaddish, and the prayer *Keil Malei Rachamim*, with everyone covering their heads. The next day, Sunday, he returned to Tiveria with kosher mezuzos, which he put up on the doorposts at the entrances to the sports center. And true to his word, a weekly Torah class was established — one that was widely attended by many of the local youth, with whom he became very close. Many of them began keeping mitzvos.

Interesting postscript: The sports club that used to be run by HaTzofim is now a Sefardic *beit knesset* — dedicated in the memory of the Lelover Rebbe.

CHAPTER THIRTY-ONE
A Piece of Kugel

The Lelover Rebbe had the annual tradition of spending every Shabbos *Parashas Beha'aloscha* in Meron, at the site of Rabbi Shimon bar Yochai's grave. There he hosted an enormous *tisch* for the many chassidim who made it their priority to travel up north to join him for the annual Shabbos. Bleachers were set up in the courtyard outside the entrance to Rabbi Shimon's place of burial, and while the younger chassidim stood on both sides of the bleachers looking down at the Rebbe's saintly visage, the older chassidim were accorded seats at the table with the Rebbe.

One of the traditions of the yearly Shabbos was the gigantic Yerushalmi kugel that was delivered from a top caterer and served at the Friday night *tisch*, steaming hot, fragrant, and peppery. A kugel of that size, when prepared right, is a culinary work of art and a monument to the willpower and stomachs of the Jewish people. The Rebbe would partake of a mere morsel, while the remainder, the *shirayim*, were divided between the *tisch* participants.

Rav Grossman, too, made it his business to travel to Meron for the Shabbos of the Torah portion of *Beha'aloscha* every year, and he was one of those accorded the honor of sitting at the Rebbe's table. One year, in 1980, as Rav Grossman observed the *gabbai* balancing the magnificent kugel on a large platter, about to dispense slices to the chassidim, a stranger dressed in an army uniform who was standing on the bleachers caught sight of the enormous kugel. He clambered down to the table and stuck out his hand to take a piece from the tray.

The *gabbai* who was handling the kugel let the man know in no uncertain terms that he'd better remove his hand from the tray. There are rules in how a kugel is given out — rules that are sacrosanct — and this man was not going to just grab a slice whenever he wanted.

Having witnessed the entire sequence of events, Rav Grossman watched as the chastised soldier left the area, clearly wounded by the *gabbai's* reaction to his simple mistake. Not wanting the soldier to leave feeling so badly about himself, Rav Grossman stood up from his seat at the table and went off in search of the man in uniform.

He found the soldier sitting on the staircase leading up to the roof of the *kever*, mortified by his faux pas. Now that he knew where the soldier had gone, Rav Grossman returned to the table, where he removed a serious slice of kugel from the tray (he knew that the *gabbai* wouldn't yell at him), placed it on a plate, and brought it over to where the soldier was sitting on the stairs.

"This is for you," he said, handing him the kugel.

The soldier stared at the man holding out the plate, clearly not knowing what to make of this new and unexpected turn of events.

"You wanted kugel," Rav Grossman said, "and now you have some. Enjoy it while it's hot."

Leaving the kugel with the soldier, Rav Grossman returned to his place at the table. Under normal circumstances, he would have spent a few minutes with the young man getting to know him, but they were in the midst of a *tisch* and his place was at the table. Ten minutes later, someone tapped him on the shoulder. Turning, he saw that it was the soldier who had wanted a slice of kugel.

"Are you Rav Grossman?"

"Yes."

"I need to talk to you."

"I'll be more than happy to talk to you when the *tisch* is over."

They had a conversation later that night. The soldier told Rav Grossman that he had been raised on a moshav in the north.

"My father is a religious Jew, and that's the way I was raised. But I fell in with the wrong people. I ended up making friends with two guys from Tel Aviv."

"I'm going to assume they weren't a good influence on you?"

"You would assume correctly. They were a very bad influence. We went around holding up stores at gunpoint, robbing the owners of their hard-earned money. This continued for a while, until we realized that the police were breathing down our necks. The other members of the gang went to hide out in the Yarkon Park in Tel Aviv, sleeping beneath the trees and trying to evade the cops. I fled north to Meron. And," he continued, "I'm not really a soldier. I just wear this uniform so no one will bother me. Recently the police caught my partners in crime, and they haven't given up on finding me either, which is why I walk around with the constant feeling of a noose tightening around my neck."

"How long have you been in Meron?"

"Two very long months."

Rav Grossman was astonished. "But where have you been living all this time?"

"I found a cave in the hills near the graves of Beis Hillel and Beis Shammai. I've been sleeping on a mattress in the cave and waiting for a miracle."

"What do you do for food?"

"There's always something happening here in Meron. People are constantly coming here to celebrate different milestones, and inevitably they bring food along. I live off the leftovers. But I can't keep living this way. I've heard of you. You've helped so many people. I'm begging you to help me, too!"

Rav Yitzchak Dovid told the man that he would see what he could do.

On Motza'ei Shabbos Rav Grossman went to see the Lelover Rebbe and relayed the story of the kugel snatcher who was on the run from the Tel Aviv police. After considering the situation, the Rebbe advised Rav Grossman to outfit the young man in the distinct garb of a Reb Ahrele chassid and bring him to Yerushalayim, where he would be given a place to live at the home of a family in Meah Shearim, while they figured out how to deal with him. Here was a young man who had made mistakes, but he wasn't a bad person and had no intention of returning to a life of crime. All he wanted was to be rehabilitated and become an upstanding member of society.

After the young man was safely lodged in Meah Shearim, Rav Grossman paid a visit to the police station where he pleaded the kugel snatcher's case to the detective in charge.

"The only way we would be willing to drop the charges against him," the detective told his esteemed visitor, "is if you take full responsibility for him."

This led to another meeting, this time with a judge, who gave the erstwhile robber a suspended sentence dependent on good behavior. Recognizing how lucky he was, the reformed man threw himself into his new life, completely turning himself around until he was no longer recognizable as the person he'd been before.

The young man that Rav Grossman had met on a Friday night in Meron went on to become a religious Jew in every sense of the word. And whenever he relates this story, Rav Grossman smiles at his audience and comments with a playful smile, "It's amazing really, when you think about it, what one piece of kugel can accomplish..."

Rav Grossman first met the Baba Sali at the tender age of sixteen. Years later, he would witness an incident involving both the Baba Sali and the Lelover Rebbe, a story that also took place, interestingly enough, in Meron.

One year the Rebbe was joined on *Parashas Beha'aloscha* by none other than the *gabbai,* the personal assistant of the Baba Sali, a man named Rav Eliyahu Elfasi, who had traveled to Meron to be with the Rebbe. When he returned to Netivot, the Baba Sali asked his *gabbai* where he had been for Shabbos.

"I went to Meron."

"It's not Lag BaOmer now," the Baba Sali said. "Why did you travel to Meron specifically for this Shabbos?"

"I went to spend Shabbos with the Lelover Rebbe."

"The Rebbe of Lelov is in Meron?"

"Yes."

"I want you to take me to him right now."

At the time of this story, the Baba Sali weighed very little. His health had deteriorated dramatically, and traveling was no doubt a dangerous proposition, but there was no changing his mind about making the trip up north to Meron.

The Lelover Rebbe was partially paralyzed for the last six years of his life, until his passing in 1987, so when he visited Meron, he was given a small hut belonging to the Ministry of Religion to use while he

The Lelover Rebbe and the Baba Sali

was there. The hut was adjacent to the tomb of Rabbi Shimon, so it was very convenient for the Rebbe to stay there. When the Baba Sali arrived at Meron, he was driven up the hill and shown into the hut where the Rebbe was resting.

The Baba Sali greeted the Lelover Rebbe with a respectful kiss on the hand, and the Rebbe replied in kind, kissing the hand of the Baba Sali. The Baba Sali then took a seat near the Rebbe, neither of them speaking at all. This was extremely interesting behavior considering that the Baba Sali had just traveled all the way from Netivot to come and see the Rebbe! One would have expected a conversation, at least. And yet, nothing.

Eventually the Baba Sali rose and bade the Rebbe farewell. Then Rav Grossman, who always made sure to spend *Parashas Beha'aloscha* with the Rebbe in Meron, accompanied him into the actual building housing the tomb of Rabbi Shimon bar Yochai. The Baba Sali spent a few minutes davening there, and then he returned to his car and went home.

After the Baba Sali left, the Lelover Rebbe said to his *gabbaim*, Reb Simcha Krakovski and Reb Mordechai Gelbstein, "The two of us spoke, and we agreed that whatever the enemies want to do to us, they will do to one another instead."

No one understood what the Rebbe was talking about — the two tzaddikim hadn't even exchanged a word. But three weeks later everything became clear when war broke out between Iran and Iraq. It was a war that would cost both countries an astronomical sum of money in weapons and end up killing over a million soldiers. What's fascinating is that it's still unclear what Iran wanted from Iraq and vice versa.

The picture becomes clearer when one understands that the two tzaddikim sitting in a small hut in a little village in the Galil knew about the weaponry and large-scale armies being prepared by our enemies to fight Israel and proceeded to hold a spiritual conversation (a conversation without one spoken word), in which they succeeded in making sure that what the enemies wanted to do to Israel was done to one another instead.

In general, Rav Grossman would remain in Meron on Motza'ei Shabbos *Parashas Beha'aloscha* and part from the Rebbe early Sunday morning. One year when he came to say goodbye, the Rebbe altered course and told him not to leave, reminiscent of the Rebbe's request all those years earlier on a Motza'ei Shabbos at the Dead Sea. A little taken aback, Rav Grossman asked no questions. Instead, he returned to the tomb for a few more hours of learning and davening in the presence of Rabbi Shimon bar Yochai. He returned to the Rebbe in the early afternoon, explaining that he had come to say goodbye.

"Stay," the Rebbe said, repeating his earlier command.

It was only at seven in the evening that the Rebbe finally gave Rav Grossman permission to return home. The moment he walked into his house, he heard a huge explosion. It was so loud it sounded as if the entire city had been blown up.

It turned out that one of Rav Grossman's neighbors was making a bar mitzvah celebration for his grandson in his home. The bar mitzvah boy's parents had gotten divorced a while back, but the grandfather invited his ex-son-in-law to take part in the happy celebration, not wanting him to feel excluded from his child's milestone. The father did decide to attend. Unfortunately, he didn't come with peaceful intentions. He entered the room carrying three grenades in his pocket, which he set off in the middle of the party, killing five people and wounding many others.

"I carried many of the wounded children into my home," Rav Yitzchak Dovid says. "They left trails of blood behind them. It was one of the worst sights I've ever seen. The next day the newspaper headline read, *'Leil HaRimonim'* (Night of the Grenades), and all this took place a mere two-minute walk from my home."

What's truly incredible was that Rav Grossman had been invited to the bar mitzvah. Not only was he a neighbor but he was also the rav of the city, and he would have attended the party — and very possibly become a casualty when the grenades exploded. The only reason he wasn't there was because the Lelover Rebbe asked him to remain behind in Meron and didn't allow him to leave. Listening to the Rebbe had saved his life. Yet again.

מגדל העמק נתונה
בסיוט ליל הרימונים
החשוד ברצח, שהודה במעשיו. שיחזור את פעולותיו
שהביאו למותם של חמישה אנשים ולפציעתם של 13
מאת עמנואל אלנקווה

5 נהרגו, 13 נפצעו בהתקפת־רימונים
למשפחה בעת בר־מצוה במגדל־העמק
כחשוד בהתקפה נעצר צעיר שהיה נשוי לבת המשפחה והתגרש ממנה; הנער שחגג
את בר־המצווה קפץ מן המרפסת וניצל; בני החשוד היו בתוך הדירה אך ניצלו

Tragic Headlines: "Nightmare in Migdal HaEmek: Leil HaRimonim"; "Five killed, thirteen wounded, in grenade attack… during a bar mitzvah in Migdal HaEmek"

CHAPTER THIRTY-TWO

The Rebbe's Coin

The court of each tzaddik operates in its own unique fashion, and that of the Lelover Rebbe was no exception. A tradition that stood out was his insistence on never asking anyone for money, not for him and not for his institutions. Yet there was one time when the Lelover Rebbe raised money, not on his own behalf, but for another cause dear to his heart. The Lelover Rebbe had a strong connection with Rav Avraham Elimelech Perlow, the Karliner Rebbe, a tzaddik who was murdered *al kiddush Hashem* during the Holocaust. The Karliner chassidim commemorated his memory by establishing a Talmud Torah in Eretz Yisrael called Ohel Avraham Elimelech. To honor his Rebbe's memory, the Lelover Rebbe organized a fundraising campaign for the Talmud Torah and asked Rav Grossman to serve as the campaign organizer.

After the campaign reached its successful conclusion, the Lelover Rebbe gave out a few commemorative coins that had been designed for the occasion to those few who had been particularly active in running the campaign. The coins were made of silver and had flowers engraved on the surface, with the words *"B'ezras Hashem Yisbarach, hatzlachah* — With the help of the blessed G-d, success" inscribed in the middle of the coin.

The coin

When he handed the coin to Rav Grossman, the Rebbe held on to his hand for a very long time before

The Lelover on a visit to Migdal Ohr

blessing him. That coin became one of Rav Grossman's most prized possessions, and he guarded it closely. He kept the coin in his pocket throughout the week, only removing it before Shabbos and returning it to his pocket on Motza'ei Shabbos. The coin was a token of the Rebbe's gratitude, but the Rebbe made it clear that it was meant to be kept as a token of protection and success. To Rav Grossman, the coin was akin to a *kemeya*, an amulet, and he treasured it with all his heart.

One Erev Shabbos, years after that campaign, Rav Grossman stuck his hand into his pocket to remove the coin and realized to his intense horror that it wasn't there. He became extremely agitated and searched the room, but it was nowhere to be found. He ran into the kitchen and found the rebbetzin going about her last-minute Shabbos preparations. He told her that they had an emergency and that she should drop everything and help him search for the Lelover Rebbe's coin. Together, the two of them searched everywhere they could think to search, to no avail.

Suddenly Rav Grossman remembered that on the previous Tuesday he had been at a bar mitzvah celebration for the only son of Shaul Amur, one of the politicians in Migdal HaEmek. The party had been held at a hall on the shore at Atlit, not far from Haifa, and since Amur was a well-connected member of the Likud Party, he had invited the prime minister, the president, and numerous other important personages to the affair. And because there were so many important people, the security team in charge of the event had set up a metal detector at the top of the path leading down to the water. Everyone had to pass through the metal detector, and all weapons were temporarily confiscated and returned to the guests when they left.

"When I passed through the metal detector," Rav Grossman told his wife, "it started to ring, and I was compelled to remove the Rebbe's coin from my pocket. I left it there in the sand next to the guard, planning on returning it to my pocket just as soon as I passed through. But before I had the chance to reach down and retrieve the coin, I was approached by the mayor of Karmiel, Avi Eldar, who greeted me warmly and embraced me. A conversation ensued, and I forgot about the coin that was still lying in the sand. The fact is, I never ended up picking up the coin from the sand, and I left the bar mitzvah without returning it to my pocket."

When Rav Grossman realized that he had lost his coin on the edge of the ocean, a frantic sense of anxiety took hold of him and he began to literally drip with nervous perspiration. From one moment to the next, his clothing became soaking wet. It was now fifteen minutes before candle lighting, but Rav Grossman picked up the phone and dialed the number for the home of Shaul Amur, famed politician and father of the bar mitzvah boy.

"Shaul," Rav Grossman said when Amur answered the phone.

The politician detected the note of urgency in the rabbi's tone. "Rav Grossman, what happened?"

"A terrible catastrophe!"

"What are you talking about?"

"At the bar mitzvah, I misplaced a coin given to me by the Lelover Rebbe many years ago, a coin that is one of my most precious possessions."

"Where did you lose it?"

"At the entrance to the beach, right near the metal detector."

"I am so sorry. Is there anything I can do right now?"

"Yes. I would appreciate if you could call the officer in charge of security at the event and ask him if anyone reported finding a special coin near the metal detector."

"All the security arrangements were organized by my assistant, Gabi Buskila. The best thing would be for you to call Gabi right now.

If anyone would know anything about the coin, it would be him."

Thanking Shaul Amur for his time, Rav Grossman dialed Buskila's number, whereupon the same conversation was replayed. Buskila was understandably shaken to receive a call from the rabbi ten minutes before Shabbos. Rav Grossman told him about the missing coin and asked if there was any way for him to contact the officer in charge of security at the event and find out if he knew anything about the missing coin.

Gabi Buskila

"Does the Rav want me to drive to the Kiryah in Tel Aviv to talk to the security people?"

"*Chas v'shalom,* heaven forbid. I don't want you to break Shabbos over this, but I do want you to launch an investigation as soon as Shabbos is over. Speak to everyone who took part in the security of the event and ask them if they saw the coin."

"I'll do it," he promised Rav Grossman, "but can I just ask what's so special about this coin?"

"It's not a regular coin. It's a silver medallion, and it was given to me by the Lelover Rebbe."

"What does it look like?"

"There are flowers engraved on the surface of the coin, and the words *'B'ezras Hashem Yisbarach, hatzlachah* are inscribed in the middle."

They were still speaking when Rav Yitzchak Dovid heard a shout from the other side of the phone line.

"I don't believe this!"

It turned out that as the organizers of the bar mitzvah event, Buskila and his wife had remained on the beach until the end of the party. When all the guests had left and the festivities were over, Mrs. Buskila had taken some of the leftover food and desserts home with them. She also took a very nice bottle of whiskey, which Shaul Amur had graciously given to them as a gift for all their help. While her husband was on the phone talking to Rav Grossman, Mrs. Buskila was setting the table for the Friday night Shabbos meal they enjoyed every week (a tradition that many Jews in Eretz Yisrael follow even if they are not observant). She was almost finished setting the table when she remembered the bottle of whiskey that Shaul Amur had given to them and decided to go and get it so they could enjoy a *l'chaim* or two at the Shabbos table.

As she removed the bottle of whiskey from its bag, she noticed that the bag wasn't empty. There was something shiny sitting at the bottom of it. Reaching inside, she pulled out a silver coin.

Coin in hand, she ran over to her husband, who was still on the phone with Rav Grossman, and held up the coin that the rabbi was in the process of describing at that very moment. "Look at what I just found!" she exclaimed. "What do you think this is?"

That was when Gabi Buskila cried, "I don't believe this!" He realized that his wife had somehow come to be holding the very coin that Rav Grossman was describing.

"Gabi," Rav Grossman said, "please bring me the coin right away."

Five minutes later the coin had returned to the Grossman home, and Rav Grossman was holding it in his hand, staring at the Lelover Rebbe's precious gift to him, still unable to comprehend how the coin had miraculously made its way back to him from the beach at Atlit.

A week later Gabi and his wife held a party for two hundred people in honor of the fact that the Lelover Rebbe had "visited their home" to return the coin to its rightful owner. Then they danced with the Rebbe's coin, as people dance with a Sefer Torah (Torah scroll) on Simchas Torah.

And though many tried to unravel the chain of events, no one was able to explain how the coin ended up making its way from the sand to the bag holding the whiskey. And while no doubt there is a logical explanation of how the whole thing came to be, Gabi Buskila and his wife believed with complete faith that the Lelover Rebbe (from his spot in Gan Eden) had placed the coin in the bag just when Rav Grossman was desperately looking for it.

PART SIX
1988–1995

"I'm not looking for checks.
I'm looking for *neshamos.*"

— *Rav Yitzchak Dovid Grossman*

CHAPTER THIRTY-THREE

A Dance With the Baal HaTanya

For over 70 years, the Jewish population of Eastern Europe had been under the harsh rule of the Soviet Communist regimes. Hashem works His wonders in mysterious ways and in 1989, the Iron Curtain came down, allowing millions of Jews who had been trapped in the USSR to leave the country. Life would also never be the same for the Jews who remained behind: they were now free to learn Torah and live a Jewish life if they so desired.

All these developments in the political arena gave Rav Grossman an idea. *What if I organize a concert for the Jews in the USSR?*

He couldn't get the idea out of his mind. He decided to reach out to Mordechai Ben David, whom he had gotten to know through their mutual connection with the Ribnitzer Rebbe. It would be the first time ever that a religious Jewish performer would hold a concert in Russia.

They decided that they would give two concerts — one in Moscow and one in Leningrad. Soon huge posters were plastered in the streets of Moscow and Leningrad announcing the coming events. They looked like the kind of signs you'd find in Meah Shearim (except that they were in Russian!), with huge block lettering that said:

DISCO RABBI FROM ISRAEL

CHASSIDIC POP STAR FROM NEW YORK

Coming to Russia to bring joy to Jewish lives!

Am Yisrael Chai!!!

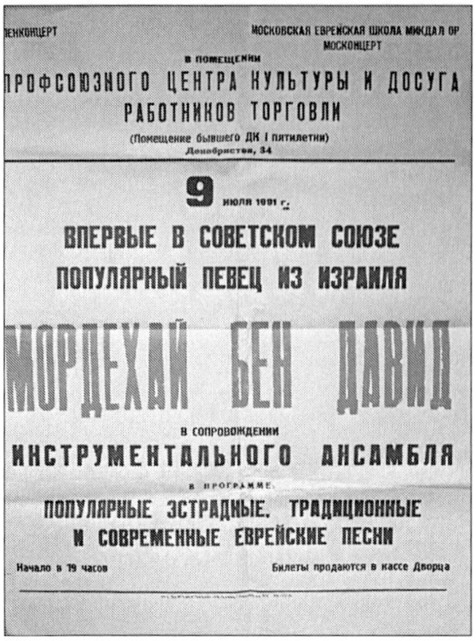

The concert poster

At the bottom of the posters was the usual fine print providing the information where the events were going to be held, the dates, and the times.

Two massive concert halls were booked for the events — one in Moscow, one in Leningrad — each capable of holding thousands of people. Each was filled to capacity on the night of the event. After all, who wouldn't want to come and hear the "Disco Rabbi" from Israel, and the "Chassidic Pop Star" from New York? But the Russian Jews who had the good fortune to be at those events were in the dark about what to expect. Cut off from the outside world for so long, there was no way they could have possibly imagined a performance like the one given by Mordechai Ben David, backed up by an orchestra conducted by the one and only Moshe Mona Rosenblum.

Organizing that concert and finding musicians to perform in the orchestra was not an easy undertaking. Rav Grossman and Reb Mona Rosenblum had taken a flight from Ben Gurion to Moscow, where they met MBD, who had flown in from New York. Mona arrived holding a bag filled with the sheet music he planned on using at the concert. He was ready to go. There was just one tiny issue: they needed to find an orchestra, and fast.

That night Rav Grossman and Mona Rosenblum left their rooms and went downstairs to their hotel's gigantic ballroom, where the guests were busily gorging themselves, all to the strains of a large orchestra that was sawing away at a famous classical piece.

"Take a good look at the orchestra," Rav Grossman told Maestro Rosenblum. "Tell me which musicians you want, and I'll make sure we have them for the shows."

Mona stood before the orchestra listening carefully and assessing each musician's particular level of professionalism. Then he told Rav Grossman which musicians he wanted. When the orchestra took a break, Rav Grossman summoned the musicians who had been selected with the help of a Russian Jew who was serving as their interpreter.

The American dollar was king of the world at that time, and no Russian musician was able to withstand an offer to come and play for greenbacks, especially since they would be able to make more money playing at those two shows than they made in half a year.

The American dollar went far in the Russia of 1989. It didn't even cost that much to charter a private plane, which they flew from Moscow to Leningrad for the grand price of five hundred dollars. At one point during the trip Rav Grossman had a picture taken of him standing on the wing of the chartered plane in the middle of the Russian night, blowing the shofar with fervor like a beacon for Eliyahu HaNavi.

It was an unforgettable trip, one that showed Rav Grossman that the *pintele Yid* (spark of Judaism) was still alive and kicking in the hearts of Russian Jews. On the Shabbos morning prior to the first show, he found himself standing outside the Great Synagogue of Moscow, which was situated on top of a hill on Arkhipova Street. There he saw an elderly Jew fighting his way up the steep road, clearly determined to make it to shul in time for davening. The aged Yid was barely able to make it up the road, huffing and puffing and trying to catch his breath.

Blowing a shofar on the wing of their chartered plane, as the Iron Curtain finally comes down

Rav Grossman approached the man and said, "Reb Yid, I see that you are unwell and that walking is very difficult for you. Why are you working so hard to climb up the hill? Surely you could be excused if you were late to shul or even if you davened at home."

The Yid began to cry. "For seventy years," he replied, "I wasn't able to come here. Now that they are finally allowing us to come and daven, shouldn't I come? I would do anything, go through any hardship, for the privilege of being able to go to shul!"

Rav Grossman gave the elderly Jew a hug and wiped away a few tears of his own.

The night of the first show arrived. Rav Grossman stood backstage in the Moscow concert hall listening to a few thousand Russian Jews chattering excitedly among themselves to the background of the orchestra tuning their instruments. Suddenly the emcee appeared.

"Show starting in five minutes!"

When it was time, Rav Grossman walked out from behind the thick velvet curtain to the center of the stage — the "Disco Rabbi from Israel" — and addressed the assembled crowd in Yiddish, a language many of his audience understood.

"Yidden," he said, his voice throbbing with excitement, "*mir zennen gekumen* — we came here to celebrate your newfound freedom together with you! We came here to remind you that you are Yidden! We came here to sing and dance with you. We also came here to establish a brand-new school where your children will be able to receive a first-class education. We're going to call the school Migdal Ohr."

Every Jew in the hall listened intently to the words spoken by the Israeli rabbi with the long beard. They sensed his strength and were riveted by his charisma.

"In this school, your children will learn many things," he continued, "but at the same time, they will not forget that they are Jews! Here your children will be able to become lawyers — but Jewish lawyers! They will study to become architects — but Jewish architects! Most importantly, after learning at this school, your children will go on to marry other Jews!"

The moment he uttered that line, the entire hall burst into thunderous applause.

He then took a risk when he belted out, "The KGB is finished!"

This time they didn't clap. They were sure that the doors of the hall were about to fly open and fifty armed members of the KGB would come storming inside to arrest Rav Grossman. But the doors remained closed and nothing happened.

Rav Grossman grabbed the moment to break into song. It was a Yiddish song exhorting the crowd to return to what they once were, and it was sung in the classic *grammen* style. He sang the song over and over, and the people in the audience sang along, sensing the import of the words, knowing that they were part of a major historic event. It was at that point in the evening that Rav Grossman brought Mordechai Ben David out onto the stage.

After introducing MBD to the audience, Mona Rosenblum began conducting the orchestra, which played the intro to one of the most popular songs of the seventies, "*Shema Yisrael*." MBD sang the song slowly and with tremendous emotion. Within seconds, the entire hall was swept up in the music and the meaning. It's virtually impossible to describe the fervor that resonated within every heart that night.

Only a short while earlier, every single Jew in that Moscow hall had been afraid to identify himself or herself as Jewish. And now? Now they were sitting in a huge hall surrounded by thousands of Jews all singing "*Shema Yisrael*" in unison. It was an incredible feeling.

Reb Moshe Mona Rosenblum was flying. The orchestra was flying. Most importantly, the audience was flying, every person there caught up in the awesome atmosphere.

Music has the power to accomplish things nothing else can do, and everyone was deeply touched by the magic. The singing went on for a long time, and the people sang and danced and celebrated the fact that they were Jewish and hadn't given up while still praying for the day when they would step off the plane onto the ground of Eretz Yisrael.

The group left Moscow on a high and took the private jet to Leningrad for concert number two, where the same thing occurred. Both shows turned out exactly as Rav Grossman had hoped.

At the end of the first concert, seventy parents signed up their children to enroll at the brand-new Migdal Ohr institution in the former Soviet Union. The school would garner a stellar reputation, not only for its excellence in academic studies, but also for providing its students with seventeen hours of Jewish studies a week, from the history of the Jewish people to Gemara and *Tanach*. The teachers were a mix of local Jews and professionals flown in from Israel to teach the Torah studies part of the curriculum. When the first graduating class celebrated their important milestone, sixty percent of them went on to continue their Jewish and academic studies at educational institutions in Israel while making aliyah.

That, however, was all in years to come.

When the little group left the USSR, it was with incredible memories and the knowledge that the real work lay ahead.

Many decades went by. One evening, the phone rang in the Grossman home in Migdal HaEmek. Rav Grossman answered.

"Hello?"

"*Shalom aleichem*, Rav Grossman."

"*Aleichem shalom*, who is this?"

It was the mayor of Bnei Brak. After the requisite small talk, the mayor got to the point.

"Rav Grossman, we are organizing a special *simchas beis hasho'eivah* (a celebration made on the nights of Chol HaMo'ed Succos to mark a certain Temple service) at a local hall, and we would like to extend a personal invitation to you to come and join us as our guest of honor."

"What type of program are we talking about?"

"There will be a few speeches and a lot of singing. We'll be featuring some of today's top performers, and Reb Moshe Mona Rosenblum will be leading the orchestra. It promises to be a great night! But it will be that much more enjoyable if you can make it as well."

Rav Grossman demurred. "I'm a man of teaching, not music. If you don't mind, I'd rather be home in my succah."

But the mayor didn't relent, and he pressed Rav Grossman to attend — not even to speak but just to come and be a part of the evening.

"You know what kind of life I lead, how things come up on a minute-to-minute basis," Rav Grossman told the mayor. "I don't have time to spend a few hours just sitting and listening to music, as much as I would love to do so. I just can't commit."

But the mayor of Bnei Brak wouldn't take no for an answer. Rav Grossman didn't understand why it was so important to the mayor that he attend this event. They barely knew one another. But for some reason his presence was extremely important to the mayor, and he decided to do him a favor and attend the show. So in the end, he gave in and told the mayor he would be there.

The fact is, Rav Grossman has a giant heart, and if it would take driving all the way to Bnei Brak from Migdal HaEmek to make another Jew happy, then that's what he would do.

"Rav Grossman," the mayor said before they hung up, "do me a favor and give me a call when you're five minutes away. This way we'll be able to welcome you in the proper fashion."

Rav Grossman agreed to do that, too. At the same time, he couldn't help wondering what all the fuss was about.

On the night of the Chol HaMo'ed event, Rav Grossman and his driver left Migdal HaEmek and made the relatively long drive to Bnei Brak. With the advent of Highway 6, travel time had been cut drastically, but it was still quite an outing for the pleasure of hearing some music, even if the night did feature his old friend Reb Moshe Mona Rosenblum. When they were five minutes away from the hall, Rav Grossman dialed the mayor's number and waited as it rang a couple of times.

"It's so wonderful to hear your voice, Rav Grossman," the mayor said. "How was the ride?"

"We just turned onto the bridge leading into Bnei Brak. We'll be there in a few minutes."

"I'm very sorry to trouble you," the mayor said, "but would you mind waiting just a few more minutes before entering the hall?"

This was really strange. After all, it wasn't as if Rav Grossman had wanted to attend this gathering. If anything, it had been forced on him. But he was here, and if he needed to wait a little longer, then that's what he would do.

They passed the Coca-Cola factory and inched along in the heavy Bnei Brak traffic, eventually making a right onto one of the side streets leading toward the hall. They found a parking spot — a miracle in itself — and then they waited in the car until the mayor called back and told him that they were ready for him.

When he walked into the auditorium, Rav Grossman's eyes were drawn to the huge screens serving as the backdrop on the stage. To his shock and surprise, he saw himself on the screen. It was a much younger version of himself: his beard was still black, and he was walking the streets of Moscow together with Mordechai Ben David and Mona Rosenblum. The scene suddenly switched and he saw himself dancing with a young Russian boy, the two of them whirling around and around, immersed in a world of their own. And as he watched, the decades fell away and he recalled the series of events that had led to that unforgettable dance.

After their incredible success at the concert in Moscow, Rav Grossman, Mordechai Ben David, and Mona Rosenblum boarded the chartered plane and flew to Leningrad to reprise the excitement and fervor for another crowd of Russian Jews who also couldn't wait to see the "Disco Rabbi from Israel" and the "Chassidic Pop Star from New York."

In Leningrad (today called St. Petersburg), they visited one of the most beautiful shuls they had ever seen. It was the morning of the Leningrad performance, and they had plenty of time before they had to be at the hall for the sound check and preconcert rehearsal.

At the side of the building, Rav Grossman found a little *shtiebel*, which had clearly been around for a very long time. Entering the old-fashioned shul, he saw a group of elderly Jews sitting on the benches, which was pretty much the scene one would see in any Russian shul in those days. But then his eyes lit on what was clearly an anomaly, because there was a young boy sitting on one of the benches among the old men. Rav Grossman couldn't help wondering how this boy had come to find his place among them.

It turned out that there was a story here. The boy, though Jewish, had been raised with no knowledge of Judaism at all. Somehow, he had come across a book that stated that Jews are not supposed to eat pork. He turned to his father and asked him to explain.

His father didn't know the answer. "If you really want to know why Jews aren't allowed to eat pork," he told his son, "go to the shul and ask the old men. They'll know."

Curious by nature, the boy made his way to the shul, where the old men did their best to explain the reason to him. They opened *Chumashim* and showed him what the Torah wrote about eating

Rabbi Grossman and the young Russian boy

non-kosher and what it meant, and they realized that here was a child who possessed a lofty soul. After that, they began drawing him closer to the spiritual side of life.

From that moment on, the young boy stopped eating at home because he wanted to make sure that he didn't eat food that wasn't kosher anymore. Instead, he ate his meals in shul with the old people, who were happy to share whatever meager provisions they had with a child who only wanted to eat kosher. Soon the shul became his new home and the old Yidden his family.

Rav Grossman became extremely emotional when he heard the story of the young boy who had been adopted by the old Yidden of Leningrad. Feeling a kinship with the boy, he told him that he planned on visiting the prison where the Baal HaTanya, the first Lubavitcher Rebbe, had been incarcerated many years earlier, and he invited the boy to join him. Chabad history is full of stories about that period of time and the Baal HaTanya's stay in prison. Now, Rav Grossman had the opportunity to step into that hallowed place.

I'll let Rav Grossman tell the rest of the story.

> I took the young Russian boy with me to the prison. We were an interesting group — Mordechai Ben David, Moshe Mona Rosenblum, me — and a young Russian boychik.
>
> There was a sense of spiritual exhilaration and devotion in the prison cell as the four of us tapped into the events that had taken place within that dismal room. I was so inspired that I pulled the tzitzis I was wearing from under my long jacket and slipped it over the boy's neck, enveloping him in the tzitzis while I was still wearing it. Then, with both of us enclosed in the

Many years later:
MBD and Rav Grossman

An unusual foursome: Moshe Mona, Rav Grossman, the Russian boy with the "lofty soul," and MBD

same pair of tzitzis, I began dancing around the cell with the boy, dancing and crying.

"Do you want to know why the Alter Rebbe was locked in this cell?" I asked the others. "It's because the Russians were punishing him for teaching Torah to Klal Yisrael. Do you think the Rebbe ever dreamed that so many years later, a young boy would willingly choose to abandon his home because he wants to be a religious Jew and to eat only kosher?"

Then I addressed the Baal HaTanya himself and said, "It says in the holy *Zohar* that after they pass away, tzaddikim can be found all over the world. This means that you, the holy tzaddik, are here now with us. I want you to look at this Jewish child, a child who despite having grown up under Communist rule, is willing to give up everything in order to keep kosher!"

After the short speech that emerged from the depths of his heart, the two of them, Rav Grossman and the boy, continued their dance around the cell until it was time to leave for the concert hall.

For the rest of their time in Leningrad, the boy remained by Rav Grossman's side, accompanying him everywhere he went. When he returned to Israel, Rav Grossman used all his contacts to bring the boy to Israel, where he entered a yeshivah.

At first, Rav Grossman kept in touch with the boy — he even spent a Shabbos at the Grossman home in Migdal HaEmek — but as the years went by, they lost contact with one another.

Though it hadn't taken Rav Grossman long to figure out where the footage was from when he entered the hall in Bnei Brak, he was still trying to figure out why they were showing that particular footage.

He was led to a seat in the audience beside the mayor, where he waited patiently to see where this was all going. The wait wasn't long. A few minutes later, Reb Moshe Mona Rosenblum approached the microphone, and after a few words of introduction, he welcomed his old friend Rav Yitzchak Dovid Grossman. He told the crowd the story of their trip to Russia so many years before and then went on to explain the series of events that had led them all to the hall in Bnei Brak on a Chol HaMo'ed evening.

"Not long ago," he said, "I received a phone call from a *kollel yungerman* (Talmudic student) living in Ofakim.

"'Is this Reb Moshe Mona Rosenblum, the composer and arranger?'

"'It is,' I replied, 'how can I help you?'

"'I composed a song, and I would like your help in arranging it so that others will hear it, too.'

"'Tell me something,' I said to the man on the other end of the line. 'What's your connection to the world of songs and music?'

"His next words almost knocked me out.

"'What's my connection to the world of songs and music?' he repeated. 'I'll tell you my connection. My connection began when I sang with you, Moshe Mona Rosenblum, and Mordechai Ben David on stage!'

"I was taken aback by his claim and said, 'What are you talking about? When did you sing with me and MBD?'

"'When I was a boy back in Leningrad.'

"Suddenly it all came rushing back to me, and I was stunned by the enormity of what he was saying. 'Are you telling me that you are the little boy we met at the shul — the one who was with all the old men?'

"'Yes, that's me. Today I live in Ofakim, and I composed a song that I have a feeling you'll like and appreciate.'

"I invited my old friend over to my home," Reb Moshe Mona said.

"There he taught me the song, which I have arranged for this evening's performance."

Then he turned to Rav Grossman and said, "Tonight is the first time the song is going to be performed for the public, and I wanted you to be here so that we could all be reunited with the little boy from Leningrad — a little boy who is now all grown up."

Reb Moshe Mona Rosenblum is completely at home on the stage. He has, after all, been performing for decades. Even so, you could tell that he was excited as he walked up to the mike.

"I would now like to invite the little boy from Leningrad to get up on this stage and teach his song to everyone sitting here, and I want to ask Rav Grossman to please come on up here and stand beside him."

The *yungerman* rose from his seat in the audience and walked up the short flight of stairs onto the stage on one side of the hall, while Rav Grossman walked up the flight of stairs on the other side. They met in the middle, in front of the microphone, where they both burst into tears as memories of their first meeting and the dance they had shared in the Baal HaTanya's prison cell flashed through their minds.

Moshe Mona Rosenblum, Rav Grossman,
and the "little boy from Leningrad, all grown up"

"Jamming" after the concert

After the song had been sung and the music quieted down, Rav Grossman took hold of the microphone and waited until the room was completely and utterly silent. He removed his *shtreimel* from his head and reached down inside his *kapote* as if searching for something. Then, lifting up his tzitzis, he slipped it over the head of the *yungerman* from Russia, just as he had done many years before, and said, "Come, let us dance again, just as we did when you were a little boy back in Leningrad."

And so they danced and the room went wild.

So it went on a Chol HaMo'ed night in Bnei Brak.

CHAPTER THIRTY-FOUR

The Baal Shem Tov's Promise

Today everyone knows how important it is to Breslover chassidim to travel to the grave of Rabbi Nachman of Breslov in the Ukrainian city of Uman for Rosh Hashanah. Over the years, more and more chassidim (and many non-chassidim as well) have begun making the trip to Uman for Rosh Hashanah, and today thousands of people come together every year from all over the world. But back in 1989, the Iron Curtain had just come down, and a small group of extremely dedicated Breslover chassidim led by the tzaddik Rav Shmuel Shapiro decided to try to make the trip to Uman for Rosh Hashanah. They had been dreaming of this their entire lives, and now it had finally entered the realm of possibility.

In an interesting turn of events, there was an official Communist Party in Israel at that time called Rakach. Many of the party members were Arabs, and their headquarters was located in Nazareth, not far from Migdal HaEmek. Knowing of Rav Grossman's influence in the northern part of the country, the Breslover chassidim asked him to speak to the Arab MKs from the Communist Party and ask them to please intercede with their bosses in Moscow and convince them to issue visas for the chassidim for a brief trip to Uman. While today Uman is under Ukrainian rule, in those days it was still ruled by Russia and the visas would be issued in Moscow.

Rav Grossman contacted the MKs, and they in turn reached out to their connections in Moscow. The chassidim waited on pins and needles until the response came back from Moscow that the visas had been approved for one hundred and eighty people.

It's impossible to describe the joy the chassidim felt when they learned that they would be able to make the trip for the first time in their lives that Rosh Hashanah. Having played a part in helping to turn their dream into a reality, Rav Grossman was given one of the precious visas and was invited to join that momentous pilgrimage to Uman.

Imagine how those chassidim felt when they reached the *tziyun* (grave) of Rabbi Nachman for the first time. Every person there had been waiting for this moment for years. Now it was finally here, and they were grateful beyond measure. There were a lot of tears at the *tziyun* of Rabbi Nachman of Breslov that Friday afternoon.

After the initial visit to the *tziyun*, they were taken to the hotel. It was rundown, shabby, and lacking proper bathroom facilities. Running water was available for a grand two hours a day. And though officially the Iron Curtain had come down, there was still Communist influence at all levels, and no one could feel absolutely certain they wouldn't be deported or worse in the environment of semi-anarchy that prevailed.

All went well the first day of Rosh Hashanah, until after the holiday meal, when the group headed over to the Uman reservoir to recite *Tashlich* (a prayer normally said near a body of water). Since chassidim often dance after saying the prayer (when *don't* chassidim dance?), the group did so — all the way back to the hotel. This proved to be one move too much for the local police, who viewed the dancing as some form of protest and were not inclined to look the other way. It was time, they felt, to show some muscle.

When the group returned to the hotel, they found that it had been turned into what amounted to an army base, with dozens of soldiers and military equipment strategically placed throughout the hotel. It seemed as if an entire platoon of the Red Army had arrived to quash the insurgency.

And then came the order — on Rosh Hashanah — from the top-ranking officer on the scene.

"You have an hour to get all your gear together. We will then be leaving for the airport. *Desvidanya*."

With no recourse, a delegation left the hotel for a meeting with Uman's mayor, where they explained that it was Yom Tov and they were not allowed to drive anywhere. Aside from that (so the rumor went), they promised him a hefty sum — in dollars! — if he succeeded in convincing the army to turn a blind eye and leave them alone.

The mayor got to work (American dollars went a long way in the Ukraine back then), and the army agreed to back off. But first thing the next morning, everyone was expected to clear out of the hotel and head back to the airport, where they would sit and wait until it was time for their flight.

There was no denying that the army's decision was a huge disappointment. The original plan had been to spend the next day — a fast day known as Tzom Gedaliah — traveling around the Ukraine and visiting an assortment of *kivrei tzaddikim*, the graves of great men like Rav Nosson of Breslov (Rabbi Nachman's primary disciple) and the Baal Shem Tov, founder of Chassidism. On the bright side, at least they were allowing the chassidim to remain in Uman until Yom Tov was over.

Most of the chassidim accepted the army's order, instinctively feeling that there was nothing to be done. But Rav Grossman found that he couldn't make peace with the change of plans. He had been looking forward to visiting the *kever* of the Baal Shem Tov, and it bothered him very much that it was suddenly off the table. He came to the conclusion that he was going to have to try his best to get to the Baal Shem's *kever* no matter what. In retrospect, Rav Grossman still can't believe what he did next.

On Motza'ei Yom Tov, at midnight, he left the hotel and began walking in the direction of Rabbi Nachman's grave, intent on davening there for the privilege of being able to visit the Baal Shem Tov. At the same time, he kept his eyes peeled for a driver who would be willing to take him to Medzhibozh.

When he arrived at the *tziyun*, the entire area was shrouded in darkness. He entered the gate and stood beside the house near the *kever*, davening to Hashem that he be granted the merit of a visit to the *kever* of the holy Baal Shem Tov. When he finished davening, he left the *tziyun*, and as he began walking down the street, he was just able to make out three shapes — or were they apparitions? — in the utter darkness of the night.

Who were they? Uman is located in the Ukraine, and they could have been three drunken peasants out of a chassidic tale. But as it turned out, they weren't peasants. They were two Breslover chassidim from America and their local driver.

"Tell me," he said, "how were you able to come here for Rosh Hashanah?"

"We've been coming for the past few years," they replied. "We land in Kiev, and a driver who lives there takes us to Uman. He's Jewish and speaks a fluent Yiddish."

"So you don't have a visa for Uman, just for Kiev?"

"That's right. But our driver hides us in his van and gets us here every year."

"But where do you stay while you're in Uman?"

"We found a cave near the cemetery."

Rav Grossman was astonished. "You stay in a cave over Rosh Hashanah?"

"Yes, every year."

"So when are you returning home?"

"Our driver is here to take us back. Our flight leaves tomorrow from Kiev."

Suddenly Rav Grossman had a brainstorm. Turning to the driver, he said in Yiddish, "Tell me, would you be willing to drive me to Medzhibozh?"

"How can I take you to Medzhibozh? I have to drive them back to Kiev now, which is a journey of four hours. Then I'd have to drive back here. That's another four hours!"

"I'll give you fifty dollars to take me to Medzhibozh. Does that change your mind?"

It did.

"Be in front of Rabbi Nachman's *tziyun* tomorrow morning at eleven," the driver said, "and I'll come to pick you up."

Promise in hand, Rav Grossman walked down the street, crossed the bridge into the outdoor market, which was long deserted, and returned to the hotel, excited that he had managed to secure a driver for the morrow. Then another thought occurred to him. There was no way he could do this on his own. Going off by himself into the middle of the USSR was not a very smart thing to do. He needed to have at least one additional person with him. And he knew just the man to take along.

The second he got back to the hotel, he found the room he was looking for and knocked on the door. It was one in the morning, but he didn't have to wait long for the person he was seeking to answer.

"Yes?"

"I've come here to offer you the opportunity of a lifetime."

"What are you talking about?"
And Rav Grossman told him.

The reason Rav Grossman chose this man for his mission was because of something he had noticed during the course of that Rosh Hashanah. He had witnessed a chassid from America approaching Rav Shmuel Shapiro, a well-known Breslover tzaddik, and some of the other great rabbis who were there, and beg them to daven for him and to give him a *berachah* to have children. It was obvious that this man desperately wanted a son or daughter, and Rav Grossman hoped that he could help.

"I'm traveling to the *tziyun* of the Baal Shem Tov," he told the man, "and I'm offering you and only you the opportunity to come along with me for the trip."

The man considered the offer, then shook his head regretfully.

"I can't."

"Why not?"

"Many of my family members are not fans of Breslov. They don't even know I'm here. They think I traveled to Eretz Yisrael for Rosh Hashanah. They have no idea that I joined this trip and flew to the Ukraine. If we are caught by the police and I'm arrested, my family will find out and I'll be in real trouble back home. I'm very sorry to turn you down, but I'm afraid that you're going to have to do this on your own."

"I have to tell you something," Rav Grossman said. "I couldn't help but overhear you approaching various *gedolim* over Yom Tov to ask them for *berachos* for children. From the time we were little children, we were raised on the miraculous stories that happened in the Baal Shem Tov's court. I promise that if you are *moser nefesh,* and show true self-sacrifice by coming with me to visit the *kever* of the Baal Shem, you will be blessed with a child this year!"

With tears in his eyes, the chassid from America said, "All right. I will remain with you and we'll go together."

Rav Grossman's next conversation was with the trip organizer.

"Tomorrow morning, when you leave the hotel, don't look for me." He also told the man not to look for the American chassid, because instead of going straight for the airport, they were leaving for Medzhibozh.

At seven o'clock the next morning, every chassid left the hotel and boarded the buses that would take them to the airport in Kiev — all except for two. Instead, those two headed over to the *tziyun* of Rabbi Nachman, where they davened and learned until eleven o'clock when the driver showed up at the agreed-upon time. They bade the Rebbe goodbye, got into the van, and off they went to the village of Medzhibozh, home to the burial place of the legendary Baal Shem Tov.

Over the next few hours, they passed through five different checkpoints, giving the police five opportunities to arrest them or at least send them straight to the airport. At each of the checkpoints, the police emerged from their little booth, spoke with the driver, glanced into the back of the van, and gave him permission to proceed. It was as if Hashem had taken away the guards' ability to see the van's passengers, who were sitting right there.

They might have been helped by the fact that every time they came to a stop, Rav Grossman turned to his fellow traveler and said, "Now let's say together, 'Ribbono shel Olam, Master of the World, in the *zechus* (merit) of Rabbeinu, Rabbi Yisrael ben Sarah Baal Shem Tov, please have mercy on us and help us escape the notice of the police. Let it be that they won't be able to see us!' "

And that was exactly what happened.

Hours later they arrived at the *tziyun* of the Baal Shem Tov. They stumbled out of the van and made their way over to the grave, which lay exposed to the elements. On the grave were written the words, "*Poh nitman Yisrael Baal Shem Tov* — Here is interred Yisrael Baal Shem Tov."

That was it. There was nothing else. No building, no monument, just a few words on a simple, unadorned stone.

> I began to cry. This was it, the reason I had come all the way here, the reason I had stayed behind in Uman when everyone else left for the airport. This was the reason I had stowed away in the van and passed through five police checkpoints. The feeling of inspiration was incredible — more than incredible. It was wondrous. I said *Tehillim*, I davened, I begged Hashem, I asked and beseeched and implored.
>
> Meanwhile, the chassid from America was davening with all

At the *tziyun* of the Baal Shem Tov

his heart to be blessed with a child, and I joined his prayers, asking the Ribbono shel Olam to send him his heart's desire and turn a childless couple into the happiest people on earth. Then I told the Baal Shem Tov that it had taken immense effort and genuine *mesirus nefesh* to be able to come and stand at his *kever,* and I asked him to please show us an example of the incredible power that Hashem had granted him and intercede with the Master of the Universe to grant a child to this man and his wife.

When their mission was completed, the van left the Baal Shem Tov's *kever,* carrying Rav Grossman and the Yid from America, and drove through the night, arriving at the Kiev airport with plenty of time to catch their flight. They entered the terminal and found one hundred and seventy-eight chassidim waiting for them. The Russians had forced them to wait in the airport all day, and they were exhausted and hungry and waiting to board the plane and return home.

Later that year, the chassid from America held his baby daughter in his arms.

Decades later, Rav Grossman happened to be visiting New York and walked into one of the local shuls looking for a minyan for Shacharis.

There he learned that someone was about to celebrate his newborn child's bris. Rav Grossman entered the room where the bris was taking place and recognized the grandfather of the infant. It was none other than the American chassid who had come along for a trip that had led them through five police checkpoints and on to the grave of the Baal Shem Tov. He had been rewarded with a daughter and many grandchildren.

So ended the story of Rav Grossman's first trip to Uman for a Rosh Hashanah that he will never forget.

CHAPTER THIRTY-FIVE

Misha's Letter

When the Jews from the former Soviet Union first began arriving in Israel in large numbers, many of them settled in the north. While it seemed like a dream come true that so many Yidden had finally been given permission to leave what had been the world's largest prison, very few religious institutions were equipped to accept their children, especially since they knew nothing at all about their Jewish heritage. The teenagers at sixteen and seventeen years old were the most challenging. They were at an age when they should be entering high-level yeshivos, yet they didn't know the *alef-beis* and had never even heard of our forefathers, Avraham, Yitzchak,

Rav Grossman speaking to the students of Midreshet HaGalil

and Yaakov, which meant that even if they were interested in finding out more about what it meant to be a Jew, they were stymied.

Rav Grossman had an idea. The idea involved a friend of his named Rav Sholom Burstein, who was serving as a rosh yeshivah in the city of Hadera and whose wife hailed from the former Soviet Union. Rav Grossman and Rav Burstein also shared a mutual connection with the Ribnitzer Rebbe. Rav Burstein was a stellar educator, and Rav Grossman decided that he was the perfect person to establish the new institution for boys from the former Soviet Union. He would call it Midreshet HaGalil.

The Bursteins agreed to relocate, and so began a brand-new adventure in Jewish education. Midreshet HaGalil was so successful that at its heyday it had a student body of 1,700 students, many of whom grew up to become *talmidei chachamim*. Rav Elyashiv once commented to Rav Grossman that "one just doesn't see *bachurim* of such caliber in the regular yeshivos..." A number of them finished the entire Talmud in their younger years, and Rav Grossman had the *zechus* to watch them develop into devoted Torah Jews.

And just as they created Midreshet HaGalil for the boys, so was established Ulpanat HaGalil for girls so that they, too, would have a place to study and an opportunity to see if they were inclined to live a

Rav Elyashiv and Rav Grossman

Torah life. It goes without saying that many *shidduchim* were arranged between the students of both academies.

One of the students of the Russian program eventually joined the Belzer Yeshivah for *baalei teshuvah* and learned there until he married, which was quite a few years after he'd left the Migdal Ohr family.

One day Rav Grossman received a call. It was the *baal teshuvah*-turned-Belzer chassid, who informed Rav Grossman that his wedding day was approaching, and he wished the rav to serve as the *mesader kiddushin,* to officiate at his wedding.

"What is the date of the *chasunah*?" Rav Grossman asked.

"The middle of Sivan." It was taking place at the Sha'ar Ha'Ir hall on Jaffa Road in Yerushalayim.

Rav Grossman agreed to attend the wedding, and on the designated day, he traveled to Yerushalayim to serve as *mesader kiddushin* at his former student's wedding. As he approached the hall, he saw that the street outside the hall was filled with Belzer chassidim in *shtreimlach, bekeshes,* and white socks (traditional chassidic garb). At the sight of all the chassidim, Rav Grossman wondered if he had come to the right place. Then he saw the *chassan,* the groom, who had the appearance of an authentic Belzer chassid. Rav Grossman couldn't believe that this was the same person he had known back in Migdal HaEmek, looking for all the world as if he had been born into one of the most prestigious of Belzer homes.

There was another group of people also walking to the *chuppah* and also happy to be at the wedding. They were the *chassan's* relatives, who couldn't have looked more different from the people the *chassan* had chosen to be a part of on his path in life.

Soon it was time for the *kallah,* the bride, to join her future husband under the *chuppah.* She, too, was accompanied by a group of refined and gentle Belzer women as well as nonreligious family members as far removed from the chassidim around them as could be.

Feeling extremely emotional, Rav Grossman decided to say a few words, just prior to starting the proceedings.

"Respected guests," he said, "I have no doubt that the upper worlds are incredibly moved by what is taking place down here on earth. I'm sure that all the angels are happy to observe the marriage of such a couple, who have come from a place where no one was allowed to even mention Hashem for seventy years. Yet, despite the adversity they faced, here they stand today, ready to establish a *bayis ne'eman b'Yisrael* — a genuine Jewish home.

"As we all know, if a man and a woman merit it, the *Shechinah*, the Holy Presence, dwells between them, and I have no doubt that there is a frenzy occurring up in heaven right now!"

What happened next was something out of the storybooks. As if to underscore Rav Grossman's words, the weather changed from one second to the next. Though it had been a beautiful Sivan day when the *chuppah* began, suddenly the sky filled with thick dark rain clouds. Winds began buffeting the *chuppah* (in Eretz Yisrael, *chuppahs* are set up outside, beneath the sky), and moments later the rain started to fall — harsh and slashing, coming at the people gathered outside the hall from every direction. It was such heavy rain that Rav Burstein, who had been honored with the reading of the *kesubah*, the marriage contract traditionally read under the *chuppah*, secreted it under his jacket so that it wouldn't get soaked.

The storm lasted for a few minutes, and when it was over, the sun emerged again, the sidewalk dried up, and it was impossible to imagine that there had ever been a storm, but anyone who was there can tell you that they will never forget the sudden and brief torrential rain they witnessed on that wedding day. It was a storm that seemed to confirm the words of the *mesader kiddushin* about the spiritual storm that had been unleashed in heaven upon the advent of such a momentous occasion.

One family who came from Russia arrived in Migdal HaEmek when their son was already old enough to enroll in university. The parents were both professionals and they had high hopes for their boy — his name was Misha* — to learn a respected profession and make them proud. For his part, Misha had every intention of following in his parents' footsteps, and he attended his classes, did his homework, and took school seriously.

Following in the tradition of the family, Rav Grossman's son-in-law, Rav Shmuel Henig, lives in Migdal HaEmek, where he's been successfully delivering Torah classes for the neighborhood youngsters for many years. One young man often brought another, and so it was that Rav Henig ended up teaching Misha's group of friends on a regular basis and watching as they gradually incorporated Torah and mitzvos into their lives. A while after he had begun teaching them, a few of the boys, Misha included, finished high school and prepared to leave the north and transfer to Tel Aviv University in the center of the country.

In the nonreligious world, many Israeli parents, especially from the lower-income brackets, expect their children to put themselves through school. Most of them do this by getting jobs as waiters or waitresses in local restaurants.

Actually, Misha didn't have to work as hard as his fellow students. Misha's parents, who were hardworking and successful, had bought him an apartment and a car. He could have rented out the place and used the rent money to pay for his share of an apartment in Tel Aviv, but since his friends didn't have that option and would definitely have to find work in the local culinary establishments, he was planning on joining them just for the experience.

The group hadn't counted on Rav Grossman, who met with them before they left for university and made them a very enticing offer.

"I'll pay the rent on your apartment," he said.

"That's great," they replied. "What's our contribution to the deal?"

"Very simple. In order for you to be eligible for my offer of free rent, you need to make sure that you don't take jobs for yourselves as waiters."

"What should we do instead?"

"I want you to leave your evenings open so that you'll be free to study with the *chavrusas* that I will send you through Arachim. If you agree to learn Torah with a study partner at least a few nights a week, you have my word that I'll take care of your rent. Aside from that, I'd expect you to keep Shabbos in the apartment. How does that sound? Do we have a deal?"

The boys from Migdal HaEmek discussed the offer among themselves and agreed that it was a good deal. Rav Grossman kept his word and paid their rent, and they began learning with the private teacher Arachim sent their way. It wasn't long before they were drawn to spirituality and a genuine Torah way of life.

Misha in particular had a close relationship with Rav Grossman. They grew close enough that Misha felt comfortable asking the rabbi for a special favor.

"Rabbi, would you deliver a letter to my parents from me?"

Intrigued, Rav Grossman agreed. When Misha handed him the envelope, he saw that there was nothing typical about the letter. For one thing, it was quite large. For another, there were items lying at the bottom of the envelope. Rav Grossman asked Misha if he could take a look inside.

"You can look inside and read the letter. Just wait until I leave."

When he was by himself, Rav Grossman opened the envelope and removed the pages from within. This is what he read:

> Abba,
>
> There once was a king who had a son. One day the king called his son to his bedside. "My dear son," he said, "my time in this world is swiftly coming to an end. I am therefore leaving you with a letter containing my last will and testament to be opened when I pass away. I hope with all my heart that you will be successful in the mission I have given you."
>
> After his father passed on, the prince opened the letter in the privacy of his chambers. With trembling fingers, he held the sheets of paper in his hands and began to read.
>
> "My son," the king wrote, "you know that I have a treasure house filled with beautiful and expensive items — gold, silver, diamonds, precious stones, and jewelry. I want you to have the treasures in my storehouses. But in order for you to do so, you must first find the key that is hidden somewhere in the palace. I leave you with all my love and best wishes for success in your mission."
>
> The prince didn't waste any time. Immediately after reading the letter, he began to search for the keys. It took him time, but he had methodically gone through almost the entire palace. It was only when he started searching the cellar, amid all the unwanted possessions that had been discarded by other members of the royal family who were long gone, that he finally found what he was looking for.
>
> Filled with incredible joy at his good fortune, the prince made his way over to the treasury and, fingers shaking in anticipation, inserted the key into the lock. To his immense excitement, the key turned and the door opened. He stepped across the threshold and saw the gigantic hallways and high-ceilinged rooms filled with the most precious items known to mankind.
>
> The prince sat down on a jewel-encrusted chair and surveyed

all the priceless items, knowing in his heart that he was going to do his best to safeguard the treasures he'd been entrusted with for the rest of his life.

Abba, the One Above created the world, and He also gave us a treasure. The treasure is the Torah. And in order to find the treasure, He made us look for it in the basement of the palace, which is the materialistic world that we live in, a place filled with base desires and enticements that pull us away from what we know is important.

I found the key to the treasure house, and now that I'm here, I never want to leave. I have therefore made the decision to leave university and to begin studying at a yeshivah instead. I know that this decision will make you angry, and that it will be difficult for you to understand it, but I'm choosing the path that I feel is right.

I also know that you might be upset because you purchased an apartment for me (with tremendous love), and yet here I am taking a different path from the one you had always planned for me. I am therefore returning the apartment to you. I have included the key in this letter. I am also enclosing the key to the car that you purchased for me. I will also repay the money that you gave me to use on college-related expenses. This way there will be no misunderstandings.

You have graciously supported me all my life, and I don't want you to feel that I accepted your gifts under false pretenses. I'm sorry if my decision upsets you, but I honestly feel that I'm making the right choice, and that going to learn Torah is the best way I can possibly live my life.

Your son, Misha

True to his word, Misha transferred out of university and entered a yeshivah where he began to learn full speed ahead. Meanwhile, Rav Grossman had no choice but to deliver the letter to Misha's father. This was no simple matter, because Misha's father was certain that his son's surprising decision to abandon everything he'd been working toward and replacing it with Torah was all due to Rav Yitzchak Dovid Grossman, who had somehow managed to ensnare his son in the rabbi's cult. Misha ignored all the accusations and acrimony swirling around him and continued delving into the sea of Torah. Eventually he decided that he was ready to get married, and he was introduced to a very special girl who had been educated at Migdal Ohr.

Yet while everyone who knew Misha and his *kallah* was very happy for them and were looking forward to taking part in the upcoming celebration, the big question was whether Rav Grossman would be able to convince his parents to attend their son's wedding. And even though they ended up coming, it was with half a heart and much bitterness.

But those feelings didn't last forever.

When the grandchildren were born, Misha's parents took one look at them and realized that perhaps, just maybe, they had misjudged the situation and their son and daughter-in-law weren't so bad, after all.

Misha eventually became a chassid, and the family moved to a *chareidi* (Orthodox) city. He continued learning for a while before he returned to university (as a religious Jew), completed his degree, and went into business.

Years later, Rav Grossman had a conversation with Misha's father.

"I want to tell you something," he said to Rav Grossman. "You know that we were very angry at you when Misha left university for yeshivah. But the truth is, our real *nachas* in life comes from him and not from our other children. He is the one with the beautiful family. His children all know what it means to have *derech eretz,* and that stems from the fact that he is a person who learned Torah. And for that we owe you a debt of gratitude.

"I know that this is coming many years after the fact, but I feel that it's high time that I look you in the eye and say, 'Thank you for everything.'"

CHAPTER THIRTY-SIX

Torah Learning for All

When the Ethiopians first began arriving in Israel with the help of the Israeli government, Rav Ovadia Yosef asked Rav Grossman to come and see him.

"I am of the opinion," he said, "that it is a big mitzvah to accept the Ethiopian Jews into our community. If we don't, the government will place all their children into nonreligious schools, and they will lose all connection to Torah and mitzvos."

At Rav Ovadia's request, Rav Grossman himself brought one

Rav Grossman with his students at the Kosel

hundred Ethiopian children to Migdal Ohr. The more he came to know the Ethiopian community, the more he realized that there was an inherent problem that needed to be addressed: the Ethiopians had no actual rabbinical leadership. Of course, they had elders whom they looked up to, but these rabbis (they were called *"kessim"*) had never had the opportunity to study in a yeshivah and were not halachically qualified to answer halachic queries or to give authentic Torah guidance. A new generation of halachic leadership was needed — young men who would grow up to take their places as the future rabbanim of the community.

The first group of Ethiopian students at Migdal Ohr received intense guidance, particularly in the laws discussed in the *Shulchan Aruch,* the Code of Jewish Law. They were taught the laws of kashrus, Shabbos, and everything in between. Rav Grossman wanted these young men to become the equals of anyone else their age in knowledge of Torah and halachah.

Though the Ethiopians came to Israel many years ago, many of them never found their place in the larger Israeli society and have long felt that they were being discriminated against by the establishment. One of the ways that the Ethiopians expressed their disapproval and unhappiness with the way they were treated was by organizing protest rallies.

One such rally was planned to make a major statement throughout the country. The idea was a simple one: thousands of people — men, women, and children — would walk the 130-mile distance from Tzefas to Yerushalayim. This was no simple matter and entailed a huge mob of people walking alongside some very narrow and dangerous roads.

When he heard what they were planning, Rav Grossman made a decision. Accompanied by a large group of his Ethiopian *talmidim,* he met the huge throng of protestors in the middle of the route. There and then, Rav Grossman addressed the crowd.

"You see all these boys who are with me?" he cried. "They are your children! Listen to me. The road to Yerushalayim is very long. Instead of your making this trip, I promise to work with your leaders and connect them with the government officials who would be in the best position to assist you in securing your objectives. But please, I beg of you, don't do this to yourselves! There are better and more effective ways to achieve your goals."

At the demonstration that was called off — Rav Grossman being interviewed by a journalist from the New York Times

Words that emanate from one heart will always enter the heart of the person on the other side of the conversation. The crowd listened and heard what Rav Grossman was telling them. They disbanded and returned home.

It's now thirty years later, and many of the Ethiopian alumni of Migdal Ohr have gone on to become the rabbanim and spiritual leaders of their communities around the country. Today the Ethiopian community has authentic Torah leadership and sufficient rabbanim to serve their needs.

There was an MK from the Shas party by the name of Rabbi Gamliel, who was of Yemenite descent. One day he approached Rav Grossman and informed him about a number of Yemenite children who had been brought to America by a certain Chassidus but didn't manage to find their place there.

"They weren't able to connect with the whole Yiddish thing, and they didn't like having to trade in their own traditional clothing with the chassidic garb. Would you be willing to establish a special division at Migdal Ohr dedicated solely to the Yemenite children?"

Baking matzos with the Yemenite children

Rav Grossman responded to the request by putting together a team of Yemenites who were already living in Eretz Yisrael to teach these children. Conveniently, they didn't need to learn how to read Hebrew because they had been taught the language from a very young age back

Rav Wosner visits with the Yemenite children

in Yemen. Not only were they completely fluent in Hebrew, but five of them were capable of reading from one *sefer* at the same time, which is how they had been taught back home. Some were proficient in reading upside down and others were experts in reading sideways.

Much effort was invested in bringing the children up to par in their learning, and it paid off, because Rav Grossman saw them grow up to become *bnei Torah* in every way.

The number of different institutions that Rav Grossman has worked to create under the Migdal Ohr banner is truly astounding. Among them is an elementary school geared to the Russian community. The school is called Machshavah: Beit Sefer L'Tikshoret V'Umanut — "Thought Academy for Communication and the Arts."

People from Russian backgrounds generally appreciate art and they want their children to get a foot in the door to that world from a young age. Girls who are enrolled in this school come from families who live all over the Galil — Nazareth, Migdal HaEmek, Afula — with the goal of instilling *Yiddishkeit* into their children while still providing them with the type of education their families value so much. Rav Grossman couldn't have described the school as a place for learning Torah. Nobody would have come. But call it "Communication and the Arts," and it's a whole different story.

The children in this school begin learning English already in the first grade. Among the four hundred students, every one of them plays a musical instrument. The music program in the school is on such a high level that the Israeli Philharmonic Orchestra performs with the student body.

Young musicians in "Machshavah"

Everything about the school is state-of-the-art, using the most advanced technology. This is done on purpose. By giving these families what they want, Rav Grossman is able to teach their children what it means to be a Jew at the same time. This is a priceless opportunity that makes the entire investment of operating such a school completely worthwhile. Because it is a means to an end. And that end is being achieved.

In addition to that school, there is another school with an additional four hundred students — this one meant for girls from religious homes — called Pninat HaEmek, named after Rav Grossman's mother, Penina.

The next project was yet another girls school, this one aimed at girls from traditional Sefardic homes — not religious but not opposed either.

Three schools, each with its own direction and style, teaching parents by way of their children, which has long proven to be extremely effective, in line with the *pasuk, "V'heishiv lev avos al banim…* — The hearts of the fathers will return through their sons."

One of the most effective keys to a person's heart is through his children. If the children want to become more religious, there's a good chance that the parents will come along for the ride and grow themselves. For Rav Grossman, these weren't just schools, mere educational institutions — he viewed them as *kiruv* operations.

CHAPTER THIRTY-SEVEN

Taking the Fun Out of Fundraising

Even for a man of Rav Grossman's formidable abilities, raising funds for his lengthy list of institutions was a never-ending and often thankless job. Of course, there were always key supporters through the years who helped out often and with generosity, and frequently their support meant the difference between success and failure. At the same time, he sometimes ended up in interesting situations.

On one trip to the States, Rav Grossman emerged from the plane and had barely entered the terminal when he ran into one of his donors, who was waiting for him just inside the building. Upon greeting the rabbi and expressing how happy he was to see him again, the donor — we'll call him Jimmy* — accompanied Rav Grossman through passport control. Rav Grossman would describe Jimmy as a big man with a big heart —"not a religious Jew, but a man with a huge *neshamah*."

Outside the terminal, he showed Rav Grossman into a waiting Rolls Royce, which had been idling at the curb. (This particular donor happened to have been the proud owner of two Rolls Royce vehicles — one red, the other white.)

"Jimmy," he said to the donor as they merged with the traffic, "I wasn't expecting you at the airport."

"I know, Rabbi. But I heard that you were coming in, and I decided to pick you up myself."

"That's fine, Jimmy. Just remember that it's Friday morning, and I need to get to Monsey before Shabbos."

"About that, Rabbi…"

"Yes?"

"I was wondering if you would be willing to do me a favor."

"What kind of favor?"

"I need you to come with me to visit a friend of mine in New Jersey. After that, I'll drive you to Monsey."

"Can I have some background about this visit?" Rav Grossman asked his driver.

"Certainly, Rabbi. I'm taking you over to someone I know so you can give him a *berachah*."

That sounded fairly reasonable, and the two of them headed for New Jersey.

They drove for a very long time. On a normal day, Rav Grossman wouldn't have minded that this visit was taking up so much of his time. But it was Erev Shabbos, and he didn't have endless hours for riding around. Just when he was about to tell Jimmy that they were going to have to do this a different time, Jimmy pulled into a neighborhood with the kind of houses Rav Grossman had never seen in his life.

"Rabbi, you see that house over there?"

"Yes."

"That's where a former President of the United States lives."

They rolled on through the wide, tree-lined streets, with Jimmy acting as tour guide, pointing out specific houses to Rav Grossman, until they finally arrived at the driveway leading up to a home that looked like a castle. Jimmy parked the Rolls in the driveway just outside the house, and they ascended the short staircase to the stately front door. Jimmy knocked and his friend answered.

It didn't take Rav Grossman long to comprehend that this man was clearly a multi-millionaire. Understandably, Rav Grossman was a little surprised that he had been brought to meet such an individual for the purpose of dispensing a *berachah*. Moreover, it appeared the man wasn't even Jewish!

Jimmy noticed Rav Grossman's puzzlement and explained.

It seemed that his friend owned a dog. Unfortunately, the dog was elderly and had suffered a stroke.

"I told my friend that he shouldn't worry about his dog," Jimmy said, "because I know a holy rabbi from Israel who can bless the dog to have a full recovery."

Rav Grossman was a little nonplussed by the turn of events. More than twelve hours on a plane, followed by a long drive, and now he was being told that the only reason Jimmy had brought him there was to give a *berachah* to a dog! Not to mention that it was Erev Shabbos, and time was of the essence. The ironic part of the whole scenario was that Jimmy himself seemed to think that he was asking the rabbi a perfectly normal request.

"I want you to know something, Rabbi," Jimmy's friend said. "This dog means everything to me. I love him with all my heart. One time he got lost — this happened a number of years ago — and you know what I did? I took out a full-page ad in the *New York Times*, with the dog's picture and everything. It cost me tens of thousands of dollars, because I ran the ad for a while, but it was worth it, because in the end, I got my dog back!"

Rav Grossman was speechless. What to say? How do you give a blessing to a dog?

"Ribbono shel Olam," he finally said, "You have so many dogs. Please let this one live as well!"

Rav Grossman uttered the "*berachah*" in Ivrit, and the man didn't understand what had been said. Neither did Jimmy, but he was extremely pleased that he had been able to be of service to his millionaire friend and had been able to acquire a blessing from the rabbi for him.

The blessing was followed by the shocking sight of the elderly and unwell dog rising to his feet and taking a few steps. It was a "miracle" against all the odds.

They left shortly afterward, and Jimmy drove Rav Grossman over to Monsey, arriving in plenty of time for Shabbos. Jimmy thanked his rabbi over and over and told him that he was sure the dog's recovery was directly connected with his blessing.

Then he sent Migdal Ohr a check for fifty thousand dollars.

In the years to come, Rav Yitzchak Dovid would experience numerous eventful situations as he crisscrossed the globe raising money for Migdal Ohr. On one trip to Florida, he was introduced to a wealthy man who invited the Israeli rabbi to come see him at his home later that evening.

At nine o'clock that night, Rav Grossman stood outside a palatial mansion in Miami Beach situated right by the ocean. The rabbi rang the bell, but nobody answered. He rang the bell a few more times, and finally, the door glided open, but there was nobody on the other side waiting to welcome him in.

Following the sounds of footsteps hastily walking toward the living room, Rav Grossman walked through the gigantic house until he found the host sitting back down on a wraparound couch, staring at something that was showing on the incredibly large television screen mounted opposite him on the wall. He was so absolutely hypnotized by what he was watching that he didn't even realize that the rabbi had followed him into the room.

Rav Grossman couldn't help but notice that the man was watching a boxing match on the big screen. Boxing as a sport was something the rabbi had never seen before in his entire life, and the sight of it made his blood run cold. Two young, powerful, muscled men were pummeling each other with all their strength, to the delight and enthusiasm of the spectators standing around the ring, who were jumping up and down and screaming themselves hoarse. The host himself, who still didn't realize that his guest was standing behind him, was up on his feet and yelling at the screen, "Hit him with a right hook! No, don't use your left hand — use your right hand! Hit him! Hit him hard!"

Clearly the man had made a bet on one of the boxers and was heavily invested in the outcome of the match.

Rav Grossman stared at the man as if he had lost his mind. Suddenly the match was interrupted by a commercial break, at which point the master of the house turned away from the screen and caught sight of the rabbi standing there.

"Rabbi Grossman," he said apologetically, "please forgive me for not greeting you at the door. I was just so involved in the boxing match that I couldn't pull myself away from the screen."

"Not only do I forgive you," Rav Grossman replied, "I thank you."

The man was taken aback by the rabbi's response. "Why are you thanking me?"

"Because I just learned a very important lesson in *avodas Hashem*, the service of G-d."

"What do you mean?"

"A lot of my work involves *baalei teshuvah*. One of the most common questions they ask me is, if Hashem wants us to live our lives as tzaddikim, why did He give us the *yetzer hara*? Why give us an evil inclination? If He would just give us the *yetzer tov* that constantly pushes us to do good, we would worship Him all the time without interruption.

"Tonight, I received an answer to that question."

"How?" the boxing enthusiast asked.

"I'll tell you how. Where is the game that you're watching taking place?"

"In Chicago."

"How many people are watching the game right now in Chicago?"

"Thousands."

"And in the country?"

"Millions."

"So tell me this. What would happen if only one of those fighters would enter the ring and begin boxing without a partner, punching the air and doing his moves. Would anyone care? Would anyone be interested?"

"No."

"Of course not. They'd send him to a hospital for the mentally ill. What makes the game interesting? That there are two people fighting each other. You want this fighter to win, and someone else wants the other fighter to win. You scream at your screen here, and a million other people scream at the screens in their homes, each rooting for their man. That's the fun and the challenge and the reason that millions are completely engrossed in the match.

"It's the same thing with the Master of the World. If a person just had a *yetzer tov*, he would have no interest in doing any *aveiros*. He would not even think about sinning. There would be no fight and nothing interesting about the person's service of G-d. Hashem has billions of angels who serve Him all the time with unconditional love and perfect behavior. So why does He need us?

"His pleasure stems from the fact that we have both a *yetzer tov* and a *yetzer hara* — two equally powerful inclinations within our hearts — and that we battle it out and fight the *yetzer hara* to do His will. And just as you stood up before and shouted at the screen, 'Give it to him! Give it to him!' so does Hashem watch us, calling out to the *yetzer tov*, 'Give it to him!' — encouraging our *yetzer tov* to beat the *yetzer hara* and deal him a knockout punch.

"So you see, I just learned a major lesson about serving the Creator of the world, and that's why I have to thank you."

All in all, it ended up being quite an interesting night. And while he had learned and taught a phenomenal lesson that night, Rav Grossman knew that it would be quite all right if he never saw another boxing match for the rest of his life.

CHAPTER THIRTY-EIGHT

Arik Sharon's Farewell Call

Prime Minister Ariel "Arik" Sharon spent his entire life moving up from one position to the next. This was the situation in the army, where he rapidly rose through the ranks, and the same was true later on, when he served in numerous ministerial positions before finally being elected prime minister of Israel.

During the eighties, Rav Yitzchak Dovid continued expanding Migdal Ohr, constructing building after building and establishing more and more institutions, each one addressing yet another vital social need for children from underprivileged homes. In addition to buildings for the boys and girls schools of Migdal Ohr, there were day care centers, kindergartens, an orphanage, and after-school programs.

Hundreds, and eventually thousands, of children were sent to Rav Grossman by social workers from various communities. At one point, Rav Grossman envisioned an entire community where families living in apartments owned by Migdal Ohr would foster young children from dysfunctional backgrounds who needed to be raised in a warm, loving atmosphere. But in order to provide for the children being sent his way from around the country, and even abroad, another major construction project was called for.

This new need would lead him to the office of a good friend, former general Ariel Sharon.

Rav Grossman first met Ariel Sharon in an interesting turn of events. Part of his responsibilities as rav of Migdal HaEmek was to oversee the kashrus at many of the factories that manufactured food in and around the city. One of the bigger concerns was a slaughterhouse that *shechted* (slaughtered) thousands of Cornish game hens on a daily basis. Once slaughtered, the hens were separated into different parts of the complex depending on whether or not they were kosher. One day the *mashgiach* (kashrus supervisor) came to Rav Grossman and reported that a number of crates filled with non-kosher hens that had been earmarked for disposal had gone missing from the warehouse.

"When I left last night," the *mashgiach* said, "there were many crates in the room, and when I returned in the morning, they had somehow disappeared."

An investigation into what happened showed that the owner of the factory had arrived the night before, and upon realizing that so many crates of chickens would not be offered for sale because they weren't kosher, he'd asked the cleaner to move half the non-kosher crates into the kosher area. When Rav Grossman figured out what happened, he contacted Tnuva, the factory's primary purchaser, and informed them that he had removed his supervision from the chickens slaughtered at this factory and they should no longer purchase the hens.

It didn't take long for the situation to become complicated. The moment Tnuva ceased purchasing the hens, the factory was in danger of closing down. The owner then went to Ariel Sharon, who was then serving as minister of industry and trade, and complained that Rav Yitzchak Dovid Grossman was shutting him down and the factory was going to go out of business very quickly unless the minister got involved and convinced the rabbi to reinstate his *hechsher* (kashrus certification.)

The next thing he knew, Arik Sharon was on the phone.

"Rav Grossman," he said, "'*Ha'ish echad yecheta v'al kol ha'eidah tiktzof* — If one man sins, will you be angry at the whole congregation?' The boss makes a mistake, so now all the workers have to lose their jobs?"

Sharon was quoting Scripture here. Suddenly he was a Torah scholar when it suited him.

"This is not the kind of conversation one has on the telephone," Rav Grossman said. "If you want to discuss this properly, it must be done face-to-face."

The first part of the meeting was spent with Rav Grossman giving Sharon a short crash course in what kashrus was all about. The next part of the meeting was spent with Rav Grossman giving Sharon a short crash course in what taking responsibility for something that's important was all about.

"For many years, you were one of the highest-ranking officers in the army," he said to Sharon. "What would you have done in a situation where one of your officers was given clear instructions and then went and did the exact opposite of what he had been ordered to do, endangering an entire mission? Would you have kept silent in the face of such insolent and irresponsible behavior?"

Sharon was silent, listening intently.

"I, too, am an officer in the army," Rav Grossman said, "and people are relying on me to keep them safe and to make sure that when I give my *hechsher* to something, they can rely on it. Here you have the owner of a factory that slaughters thousands of hens every day and makes millions in profits, and instead of focusing on the big picture, he interfered in a matter that involved only a few crates of hens, which were completely inconsequential in the long run. If one looks at this situation in the context of the size of the factory compared to the loss of a few crates of chickens, how he was willing to endanger his entire company for no good reason — well, to me this type of behavior is a sign of mental instability. And if that's the case and he really isn't stable, then I can't rely on him to follow the rules, and I can't provide a *hechsher* for such an enterprise. The only way this factory will be able to remain under my kashrus supervision is if the owner sells out to someone else. I won't deal with the factory as long as he is the boss!"

Ariel Sharon promptly informed the owner of the factory that he had to sell the company to someone else. It took some time, but in the end the former owner left, and Rav Grossman agreed to reinstate his *hechsher*.

After that initial meeting, Rav Yitzchak Dovid Grossman and Ariel Sharon became friends, and Rav Grossman invited the politician to come and visit him at Migdal Ohr so he could see for himself the miracles that were happening there every day. Sharon came and became a chassid of Migdal Ohr.

Now Rav Grossman wanted to build a Migdal Ohr community where families could live and foster young children. A meeting was arranged in Sharon's office, and Rav Yitzchak Dovid spent a few minutes catching up with his friend before showing him the plans for the new neighborhood.

Sharon didn't say a word. Instead, he went into action.

He picked up the phone on his desk and dialed the number of one of the most successful contractors in the country, a man by the name of Uri Dory.

"Uri," Sharon said when the other man answered the phone, "you have twenty minutes to get to my office."

When the contractor arrived a short while later, Sharon said without preamble, "Uri, Rav Grossman wants to go into competition with you."

"What?"

"Rav Grossman wants to build an entire neighborhood. If you won't do it, he'll find someone who will."

Sharon then offered Dory several financial incentives to take on the project. Within the year, construction on two hundred and twenty buildings was complete. Migdal Ohr's new foster village was up and ready.

In the years that followed, Rav Grossman maintained contact with Arik Sharon as he advanced from position to position. Their relationship was such that when Arik's wife, Lily, was sick, the only person Sharon allowed to come to his Negev ranch to speak with her and give her *chizuk* was Rav Grossman. Later, after her passing, Rav Grossman arranged with Ira Rennert, one of his major donors and a close friend of Sharon's, to dedicate a building on the girls Migdal Ohr campus in the memory of Lily Sharon. The building was called Beit Lily, and when Ariel Sharon arrived at the dedication ceremony and saw the building emblazoned with his dear wife's name, the tough general couldn't help himself, and he broke down and cried.

Rav Grossman would never forget the phone call from Prime Minister Ariel Sharon asking him to come see him at his office in Yerushalayim. Curious as to what his old friend wanted, Rav Grossman arrived at the designated time and was shown into the oversized office, where he took a seat across the desk from the prime minister.

"I wanted to tell you," Sharon began, "that I have recently learned something extremely frightening."

"What's that?"

"I discovered just how many Jewish children are currently living in government-run orphanages in the Ukraine."

The next sentence he uttered shook Rav Grossman.

"They're living in the orphanages so neglected, the mice are eating them alive!"

"What can I do?"

"I want you to bring these children to Israel, and I want you to raise them at Migdal Ohr."

"The Ukrainian government will agree to this?"

"We'll make a deal with them. But I want them to live with you once they arrive in Israel. That's crucial."

At the time, Shaul Amur, who had served as mayor of Migdal HaEmek, was the Israeli ambassador to Belgium (he would later return to the position of mayor of Migdal HaEmek), and Rav Grossman reached out to him. Shaul was more than happy to hear from his dear friend, and it was decided that Rav Grossman would travel to Brussels, where an agreement would be signed between himself and the Ukrainian representative with regard to the children in question. The initiative was dubbed "Gesher Perach" — Bridge of Flowers.

Because the children were so young — most of them around three years old — Rebbetzin Grossman took charge of the project, arranging for a brand-new building that was specially designed to become their future home and traveling to the airport to pick them up when they landed. She also arranged a special welcome: on every bed lay a towel with the child's name on it and a large package of candies and treats.

At one point before becoming prime minister, Ariel Sharon decided that he wanted to move into a house in the Arab Quarter of the Old City. This caused a major uproar, which Sharon disdainfully ignored. When the future prime minister moved into his new home, the King David Hotel in Jerusalem sent him a gigantic complimentary cake, which was the center of attraction at the housewarming party.

"Nobody touches that cake," Sharon told the crowd. "I have plans for it."

Of course, everyone wanted to know who was going to have the honor of eating the special cake.

"This cake is going to be sent to Migdal HaEmek, and it will be eaten by the children of Migdal Ohr," Sharon declared. Then he added, "I believe that the reason we're able to exist here in Eretz Yisrael is in their incredible merit!"

Prime Minister Arik Sharon hosting Migdal Ohr children
at a Chanukah party in his office

That wasn't the only time Sharon showed his feelings for the children of Migdal Ohr. One Chanukah Sharon invited the children of Migdal Ohr to come and celebrate with him in the prime minister's office in Yerushalayim. All the furniture was removed from one of the largest rooms in the building, so that as many children as possible were able to enter it at the same time. Sharon spoke (it was all recorded) and stated emotionally that Migdal Ohr was completely unique and that there wasn't another place comparable to it in the entire world.

One night in 2006, Rav Grossman was at home with his brother Rav Zalman, who'd dropped by for a visit. At around eight o'clock in the evening the phone rang.

"Rav Grossman," came the voice of the prime minister's secretary, "I have Prime Minister Sharon on the line."

"Please put him through."

Moments later, the prime minister was on the line.

"*Shalom, HaRav Grossman! Mah shlomcha?* How are you doing?"

"*Baruch Hashem*, thank G-d. How are you?"

Rav Grossman and Arik Sharon, in his office on Purim.
The rav gave him a *Megillas Esther*.

"I miss you, Rav Yitzchak Dovid, and I miss the children."

Rav Grossman was extremely touched that the prime minister of Israel had called him up to tell him that he missed the children of Migdal Ohr.

"Tell me, Rav Grossman, are the children still playing the violin?"

When he had come to visit Migdal Ohr, Sharon had watched children playing musical instruments, and clearly the sight had left a lasting impression on him.

After a few additional questions about the music programs at Migdal Ohr, Sharon bade his friend a good evening and said goodbye. Replacing the phone in its cradle, Rav Grossman wondered what had just occurred. Since when did the prime minister have so much free time that he picked up the phone and called the head of an institution just to ask if the children were still playing the violin? The whole thing was bizarre. Then he shrugged it off and returned to his previous conversation with his brother.

Half an hour later, Rav Grossman found out that Ariel Sharon had suffered a massive stroke and was on the way to the hospital. It was almost as if the prime minister had had a premonition that he was on his way out of the world and wanted to say goodbye to a dear friend before trading this world for the next.

CHAPTER THIRTY-NINE

The Neshamah Computer Chip

As time passed and Migdal Ohr expanded, taking more and more children and their families under its widespread wings, the city began to change — change that was accomplished without throwing stones, without protests, without rallies. Rather, it all happened through gentle love, acceptance, and positive education.

Of course, as the people became more religious, the crime level fell drastically. Migdal HaEmek changed from being a place where people didn't want to live to being a sought-after location. Not only did many more people choose to make Migdal HaEmek their home, but over one hundred high-tech companies set up shop within the city limits, so that some began referring to Migdal HaEmek as "Israel's Silicon Valley."

In 1993, a new company, Tower Semiconductor, was founded with the acquisition of the National Semiconductor water purification facility in Migdal HaEmek and the goal of producing computer circuits. Eventually it would operate seven manufacturing facilities worldwide, two situated in Migdal HaEmek.

With the arrival of this major player on the high-tech scene in his city, it didn't come as a surprise to Rav Grossman that Ezer Weizmann, then president of Israel, would be coming to Migdal HaEmek for a guided tour of the state-of-the-art facility. As chief rabbi of the city, Rav Grossman was invited to accompany the president and join the tour, and so he found himself standing beside Weizmann on the appointed day in the company's brand-new atrium just prior to the onset of the tour.

Before they entered the part of the facility where the computer chips were actually manufactured, the manager provided his guests with a little background.

"On the first floor of the site, the company manufactures chips for regular computers. One floor below," he continued, "is where we manufacture computer chips for the Israel Air Force."

As one of the first pilots to serve in Israel and a founding father of the IAF, Ezer Weizmann was naturally intrigued and wanted to see it all for himself.

"The only way to do that, sir," the manager replied, "is if you're willing to get into that suit." He pointed to something that looked like the kind of flight suit an astronaut might wear in orbit.

With no choice, Weizmann and Rav Grossman each donned a suit, looking for all the world like two astronauts about to board a spaceship for a round of intergalactic travel.

After the tour, Rav Grossman was asked to say a few words in honor of the occasion.

"I would like to begin my speech," he said, "by thanking the President of Israel because it's in his merit that I learned an amazing lesson in *avodas Hashem*, the service of G-d."

This opening caught the listeners by surprise. What was the rabbi talking about? And what did *avodas Hashem* have to do with computer circuits?

With President Ezer Weizmann

Seeing the puzzled looks on the faces in the crowd, Rav Grossman said, "Don't worry. I'll explain exactly what I mean."

"As you know, President Weizmann and I have just been taken on a tour of this facility, and while we were being shown around, a thought occurred to me.

"The fact is, on both the first floor and the lower level, computer chips are being manufactured. Not only that, but if you were to see the computers that are being used for the manufacturing process, you would assume that they're all pretty much the same on both floors — at least on the surface. So if they're using the same computers to manufacture the same product on both floors, why is it that a visitor is allowed to walk around in his regular clothing on this floor, but must get into an 'astronaut suit' if he wants to walk around on the level below it? What's so special about the process happening one floor beneath us?"

Rav Grossman paused for a few seconds, allowing his words to linger in the air before he went on.

"The answer, my friends, is this. On the lower level, the computer chips are being manufactured for the air force. For that reason, they're treated with extra sensitive care, and no foreign substances are allowed to come in contact with them. If I were to walk into the area dressed as I normally am, there's a fear that maybe a speck of dust will find its way into a chip that's designated for a jet, and then, instead, of sending a missile where it needs to go, the trajectory of that missile will be compromised and it may strike the wrong target! Obviously, there are safeguards upon safeguards in place to ensure that such a scenario doesn't occur, but we still need to wear a full-length body suit to keep those chips completely pristine and free of contamination.

"On this floor, the computer chips are being designed and produced for businesses, so even if something happens and a speck of dust manages to infiltrate production, the danger is not that great, and the precautions taken are nowhere near those taken for the air force computer chips. It's all a question of the level of safety needed due to the sensitivity of the chip being produced."

Everyone in the atrium was listening with interest, wondering where the rabbi was headed with his speech.

"Many times, fresh *baalei teshuvah* come see me," Rav Grossman continued. '*Kevod HaRav*,' these returnees to Judaism say, 'Hashem created the entire world, both Jews and non-Jews. If you look at a non-Jew and you look at a Jew, you'll see that we all look the same. On the surface, there's no difference between us. We both have eyes, ears, and mouths. We all smile and frown, speak and laugh, sing and yell. To all appearances, we're the same.

" 'But if that's the case, why is it that Jews must wear a special suit — a protective layer over their eyes so as not to see forbidden sights, a protective layer over their ears so as not to hear things that shouldn't be heard, a protective layer over their mouths so as not to ingest prohibited foods. Non-Jews can do whatever they want — they can say what they want, eat what they want, listen to anything they want. Why is this the case? Weren't we all created in the same company and produced by the same manufacturer?'

"Today I finally understood the reason for the different treatment toward Jew and non-Jew. The answer is simple and rings with truth. The reason we are treated differently is because we have different missions. We, the Jewish people, have been tasked with the job of bringing the *shefa* — the spiritual bounty — down from the heavens and into this world. And in order to accomplish this very special mission, Hashem enclosed within us a very special and unique computer chip called a *neshamah,* a soul, regarding which we say in our davening, '*Elokai neshamah shenasata bi tehorah hi* — My G-d, the soul that You have put in me is pure.'

"This *neshamah* comes from a very high place up in heaven, and it is through the *neshamah* that we are able to channel the *shefa* from on high to this world below. And because of the unique mission that we have been given, we need to wear special protective devices on our eyes, ears, and mouth to make sure that no spiritual dust enters the system and keeps us from carrying out our special task."

That was the speech he gave that day.

When it was over, no one spoke as the message resonated and they absorbed it. Even Weizmann and all the attendees were quiet, pondering the rav's message.

That wasn't the only time Rav Grossman used the differences between Jew and non-Jew to make a point.

During one visit to the United States, he boarded a flight from New York to Miami, and once the plane was in the air, he settled back in his seat beside the window, closed his eyes, and began softly singing the song of the Skulener Rebbe made famous by chazzan Dovid Werdyger: *"Zeidim helitzuni ad me'od miTorascha lo natisi..."*

His singing was laced with the trepidation he was feeling about his upcoming trip and the knowledge that he was going to have to raise a significant sum of money for Migdal Ohr. He was in a different world, and apparently the sight of his holy face lost in a trance and immersed in his own world made an impression on one of the stewardesses, because she turned to Rabbi Paysach Krohn, who had accompanied Rav Grossman on the trip, and asked, "Excuse me, do you happen to know who that rabbi is?"

"Sure," Rabbi Krohn answered with his trademark smile. "He's a very famous rabbi from Israel. He's known as the Disco Rabbi and devotes his life to the rehabilitation of children who are growing up in disadvantaged homes."

"Can I ask the rabbi a question?"

"Go right ahead. I'm sure the rabbi won't mind."

Moments later, the stewardess was introducing herself to Rav Grossman.

"My name is Miriam," she began. "I was born into a Jewish home, but I know nothing at all about Judaism. Could you tell me if there is anything I can do to actually feel like a Jew?"

"Do you see how the two of us ordered special kosher meals?" Rav Grossman answered, pointing to himself and Rabbi Krohn. "If you want to feel like a Jew, then I suggest you begin ordering special kosher meals for yourself, and then you'll start feeling like a Jew."

"You mean to tell me that the special meals that people sometimes order have to do with being Jewish?"

"Exactly."

"That's so interesting. I always thought it was because they have a restricted diet or they're vegetarians."

She was quiet for a few moments, then said, "Okay, I'll try to start ordering special kosher meals, but would you mind explaining to me what the word *kosher* means?"

For a moment, Rav Grossman was at a loss how to explain so complex a concept as kashrus in a very short amount of time to a person who had never heard of it before. But then suddenly he had an idea.

"I'm sure you're familiar with the Ford Company, correct?"

"Of course."

"Did you know that Ford manufactures both trucks and regular cars?"

"Yes, Rabbi."

"Now I want to tell you something that you might not know. The trucks made by Ford use a type of fuel called diesel, while the cars and sedans fill up on regular gasoline. The diesel fuel happens to be cheaper than the gasoline that fuels cars.

"Now imagine for a moment that someone driving a car made by Ford pulls into a gas station where he sees a truck driver filling up his tank with diesel. He might think to himself, *He's driving a truck made by Ford, and I'm driving a car made by Ford. If diesel works for him, then it will also work for me.*

"But if the driver fills up his car with diesel, he'll only damage his car. Why? Because the engines in cars and the engines in trucks are built differently, and where the larger and more powerful engine thrives on diesel, the smaller and more delicate engine will be ruined by the unrefined diesel fuel.

"It's the same thing with people. G-d in Heaven created the entire world. It's His company. His firm. He created two different types of people — Jews and non-Jews — each of whom were gifted with different missions. The mission of the non-Jews is to develop the physical world, to build it and take care of it.

"Jews have a different purpose. Theirs is not a physical mission but rather one of a spiritual and more sensitive nature. We have been put in this world to serve as the ambassadors of G-d down on earth. We accomplish this through studying the lessons written in the holy Torah. And just as He commanded us how to live our lives, He also told us which type of gasoline to use to fuel our respective engines.

"The non-Jews are allowed to use almost any type of gasoline they want. They can eat and drink almost anything they wish, and their engines will work and run just fine. The engine that was built for the Jewish body, on the other hand, is more fine-tuned and sensitive, and the gasoline that a Jew puts into his body has to be more delicate and tailored to his special soul. In a nutshell, that is the purpose of kosher food, and that's why G-d gave us rules to determine what is deemed kosher and fit for our consumption."

The young woman loved the explanation, and after thinking about it for a while, she said, "I live in Florida, and I'd really like to learn more about what it means to be Jewish. Where and how can I do that?"

"I have a cousin who lives in Florida," Rav Grossman said. "His name is Rabbi Groner, and I'll be staying in his home while I'm there. I'll give you his phone number. If you're serious about learning more about what it means to be a Jew, then give him a call and he'll help you."

Rabbi Avrohom Yeshaya Groner

The young woman did end up calling Rabbi Groner, and she began learning about *Yiddishkeit*. Eventually the stewardess turned her entire life around and became a Torah Jew. And once again Rav Grossman couldn't help marveling over the power of one conversation, one powerful idea. In this case, the road to her becoming religious passed through the concept of kashrus and kosher food. But there's no question that it can happen through any mitzvah. At the end of the day, every Yid has to regard himself as an ambassador for G-d above and do his best to spread His message. The rest is up to Him.

A day after he landed in Florida, Rav Grossman found himself sitting and learning in one of the local shuls as he waited to daven Minchah and Maariv, when he overheard the following conversation between two of the shul members.

"Say, Katz, who is that young rabbi sitting over there?"

"That's the rabbi who's looking for the checks…"

There was no question in his mind that the two men had no inkling that the Israeli rabbi actually understood English and knew what they were saying about him. He remained in his seat and continued learning, paying no attention to their exchange.

A few minutes later, the rabbi of the shul entered the room and spied Rav Grossman, who was promptly invited to address the congregation between Minchah and Maariv.

Standing at the *bimah*, Rav Grossman looked around the room, levelly meeting the gaze of every person sitting there.

"I want to tell you all a story about a young rabbi from Eretz Yisrael," he said. "This individual was raised in the Meah Shearim home of a learned tzaddik and *talmid chacham*. But there came a time in his life when he felt he could no longer remain in his comfortable life in Yerushalayim, and he relocated to a crime-ridden city in the Galil where he knew there was much work to be done to bring Jews back to their Creator. The rabbi from Meah Shearim sacrificed much to build his new home, working day and night to establish a host of Torah institutions and save the lives of countless children.

"In a fascinating turn of events," Rav Grossman continued, "this rabbi found himself sitting here, in this very shul, when he overheard the following conversation between two of the members."

And he proceeded to repeat the exchange he had heard earlier.

"*Rabbosai*," Rav Grossman said to his audience, "I want to tell you something. I'm not looking for the checks. I'm looking for *neshamos*..."

His speech that night was surprisingly brief. But it sure made an impression.

After Maariv, Rav Grossman went to thank the rav for giving him the opportunity to address his congregation.

"Rav Grossman?" the rav said.

"Yes?"

"I've been thinking..."

"Yes?"

"I've been thinking that Miami is not the kind of place where a Yerushalmi Yid like yourself should have to wander. How much money did you think you were going to raise during your time here?"

Overcome by the rav's sensitivity, Rav Grossman replied, "I have no idea."

"Well, how much money can someone like yourself who is here for the first time hope to raise? I would imagine that it would be in the region of four thousand dollars. [This was a long time ago — life was cheaper!] Here's what I want to do. I'm going to write you a check for the full amount, and then I want you to cut your trip short and continue collecting the funds you need in New York."

With that, the rabbi of the shul wrote out a check for the astounded Rav Grossman, who didn't disagree with the statement that Miami wasn't a place for a person like him.

The next day Rav Grossman was at the airport boarding a flight for New York. Hashem had helped him finish up his business in Miami faster than he had planned, and who was he to argue...

CHAPTER FORTY
The Captive

It was seven o'clock in the morning when Rav Grossman heard a pounding on the front door. While there was always something happening at the Grossman home, it was somewhat unusual to hear such a loud and persistent knocking at such an early hour, and Rav Grossman came to the quick conclusion that someone was in trouble and needed help. He opened the door and found himself face-to-face with a man he had never seen before. Yet the look of terrible anxiety that he saw in the stranger's eyes was a look that he'd seen way too many times in the past. Clearly something was very wrong.

He never could have anticipated the words that came out of the stranger's mouth.

"Rav Grossman, I've been kidnaped!"

This was the first time someone had told Rav Grossman he was kidnaped while standing in the doorway of his home.

"I don't understand. Aren't you standing in my doorway talking to me right now? How could you have been kidnaped?!"

The man opened his mouth to explain but no words came out. He got all choked up and started to cry.

Rav Grossman looked at him kindly. "Come inside and tell me what's going on."

Once they were seated at the dining room table, the man explained that he lived in Cholon where he worked as the manager of a thriving gas station at the edge of the city.

"So what brought you here?"

"I got mixed up with the Israeli mafia. I borrowed money and couldn't pay it back. Of course, the thugs weren't interested in my excuses, and they began turning up at the gas station, threatening me and making my life miserable. When that didn't work, they decided to teach me a real lesson. Last night they broke into my house, tied me up, and threatened to kill me. Then they picked me up, threw me into their car, and drove to the beach in Yaffo. There they placed me in the water and held me down under the waves.

"It was the most frightening thing that ever happened to me in my life! Realizing that they meant business and were prepared to go all the way, I told them the only thing I could think of to say."

"What was that?"

"I told them that if they took me to Rav Yitzchak Dovid Grossman, he would pay them what I owed."

He delivered the line with miserable shame, shaking and crying. But Rav Grossman would later find out that he left out a crucial detail that he'd told the mafia. To convince his kidnapers that Rav Grossman would assist him, he'd told them that the rav was a relative of his. When he told Rav Grossman the story, he neglected to mention that these Mafia criminals believed they were family.

"Where are these people right now?"

"Outside, waiting in their car."

Leaving the captive from Cholon in his house, Rav Grossman went outside to meet the members of the Mafia who were relying on him to repay the gas station manager's loans.

It was not yet seven-thirty in the morning.

Rav Grossman found the two men sitting in their car in front of his home. One look at them and it was clear that he was dealing with authentic criminals. Theirs were faces that radiated evil — faces that instilled fear in all those they encountered.

"Come into my house," he told them. "I'll serve coffee, and together we'll figure this out."

They followed the rabbi up the stairs and into his home, taking seats across the table from the gas station manager, who looked at them and cried in silence, his shoulders heaving as he tried to suppress his fear and anxiety. The newcomers were unmoved, and after accepting the cups of coffee that the rabbi prepared for them, they turned the discussion to the topic at hand: the money they were owed.

Rav Grossman turned to the two thugs. "I understand that this man owes you a substantial amount of money."

They nodded.

"And while I have never met this man before today, every member of Klal Yisrael feels responsible for the other, and I want to help him."

The rabbi got no further because the moment the two men understood that their prisoner hadn't told them the truth, and that Rav Grossman was not related to him, one of the heavily built goons leaped up from his chair, rounded the table, and slapped the gas station manager across the face hard enough to make his entire body spin.

"How dare you lie to us!" he bellowed. "How dare you tell us that Rav Grossman is your relative!"

The captors hadn't counted on their host, who jumped to his feet and threw himself in front of the prisoner while raising his voice to its fullest capacity and yelling at the two kidnapers, "You will not raise your hand against another person in my house! Don't you dare raise your hand in here! There will be no violence in this house!"

Seeing that the rabbi meant business, the thugs calmed down, and the one who had slapped the gas station manager returned to his seat.

"Now we will talk," Rav Grossman said.

"This man owes us money. A lot of money. And we've been asking him to pay what he owes for a year already. But instead of paying his debts, he plays games and constantly finds ways to evade us. Now we think that he has no intention of repaying what he owes. We had to teach him a lesson to show him that we're serious. That's why we broke into his house last night."

"If you want the money," Rav Grossman said, "I'll have to go to the bank and get it for you."

"We'll be here when you return," they replied. "But don't even think of going to the police. We are dangerous people and the police are afraid of us, too. Go to the bank, bring us back the money, and we'll be on our way with no complications."

While he had put on a brave exterior when dealing with the two thugs drinking coffee at his dining room table, Rav Grossman couldn't help but feel slightly worried. It wasn't every day that he dealt with members of Israel's mafia, and the situation was apt to turn ugly at any time.

Now, what to do? The truth is, he didn't really have the kind of money they were demanding. As he walked down the street in the direction of the bank, his mind raced, trying to come up with a solution, and a silly tidbit of Jewish humor popped into his mind.

"Your chassidim are a bunch of low-life *shkotzim* (thugs)," said one Rebbe to the other.

"What did you think?" the other Rebbe responded. "That if I need a low life *sheigitz* (thug) I'd come to you? If I need a *sheigitz*, I'll turn to my own..."

What are you so worried about? Rav Grossman asked himself. *You have plenty of "shkotzim" of your own!*

So many of the "tzaddikim" that Rav Grossman encountered when he first arrived in town lived the same kind of lives as that of the two criminals sitting in his house. They, too, had occasionally been sent by the bigshot criminals living in the high-rise towers of Tel Aviv to do the dirty work that they didn't want to do themselves.

The tzaddikim will know how to talk to the two mafia thugs sitting at my dining room table. They'll know exactly how to put them in their place until we can arrive at some sort of agreement.

He was talking about the youths he had found in the discos, whom he called his tzaddikim. Many of them were now fine, upstanding *bnei Torah* who learned in the local kollel, but they were still familiar with the view on the flip side of the coin.

Having made a decision, Rav Grossman turned on his heels, and instead of going to the bank, he paid a visit to a few of his tzaddikim. They quickly assembled a group of like-minded individuals to present themselves at the Grossman home where the criminals were waiting.

When the tzaddikim came pouring through the Grossmans' front door and into the living room, the two mafia representatives almost had a heart attack.

"If you speak with respect," the spokesman for the tzaddikim told them, "we can put all this behind us with a positive ending. If you try to play tough with us, you'll find yourselves tied up in a sack and dropped off in one of the local Arab villages. Your choice. What's it going to be?"

It only took the goons seconds to grasp that they were in the company of people who were not intimidated by them and were intimately familiar with their methods. What ensued was a civil discussion that focused on finding a way for the gas station owner to repay his debt.

Of course, the tzaddikim ended up telling the two men how they had gone from being like them to growing beards and *peyos* and spending the majority of their days learning Torah. The two men were obviously very moved by what they heard.

It took time, but an agreement was finally reached. The gas station manager would sign over ownership of his expensive car to his creditors, and the debt would be considered paid in full.

And so the negotiations ended. The gas station manager thanked Rav Grossman profusely for saving his life, the mafia people thanked Rav Grossman for putting together the negotiating team, and the tzaddikim went back to kollel.

The next night, Rav Grossman's brother made a wedding in Bnei Brak for one of his children. In the middle of the spirited dancing, Rav Grossman spied two familiar faces standing at the side of the hall — faces of people he had no interest in ever seeing again.

The two mafia boys from the day before had somehow managed to track him down at the wedding! Seeing them there, obviously waiting for him, got the rabbi good and nervous. Maybe the mafia wasn't satisfied with the deal that had been negotiated? Maybe they had been sent to teach him a lesson?

Not one to beat around the bush, Rav Grossman approached them and asked to what he owed the honor of seeing them again so soon after their first visit.

"Could we take a little walk?" one of the men asked.

Quite nervous now, Rav Grossman didn't see that he had much of a choice and agreed. The three of them left the hall and walked down the quiet Bnei Brak street until the sounds of the music grew faint.

"What can I do for you?" Rav Grossman asked at last.

"Rav Grossman," one of them replied, "the fact is, we are small fish in the world of organized crime. We have no say in anything, we have no power. We are dispatched to carry out the demands of the bosses living in their fancy mansions and the penthouses of luxury hotels. They live large while we do all the grunt work. We are prisoners just as much as the man we brought to your house yesterday. One wrong move on our parts and we would be dead, no questions asked, no second chances. But we never dreamed there was anything we could do about it.

"Until yesterday."

Rav Grossman stared at the men standing before him, and he could see that they genuinely wanted to change.

"What happened yesterday that made you realize that it doesn't have to be this way?"

"Yesterday we were introduced to a group of men who were just like us once. But they aren't anymore. They were saved. And we also want to be saved, and we need your help to do the same!"

"No problem," Rav Grossman said. "You can come and join me in Migdal HaEmek anytime you want. The door is always open!"

The two men made the move a few days later, when they presented themselves at Migdal Ohr. They were warmly welcomed and given a place to live and people to learn with. In an interesting Ruth and Orpah kind of situation, one of them was unable to make the transition and he left not long after he arrived, probably returning to the world he knew best. But the other returnee entered the tents of Torah and never left.

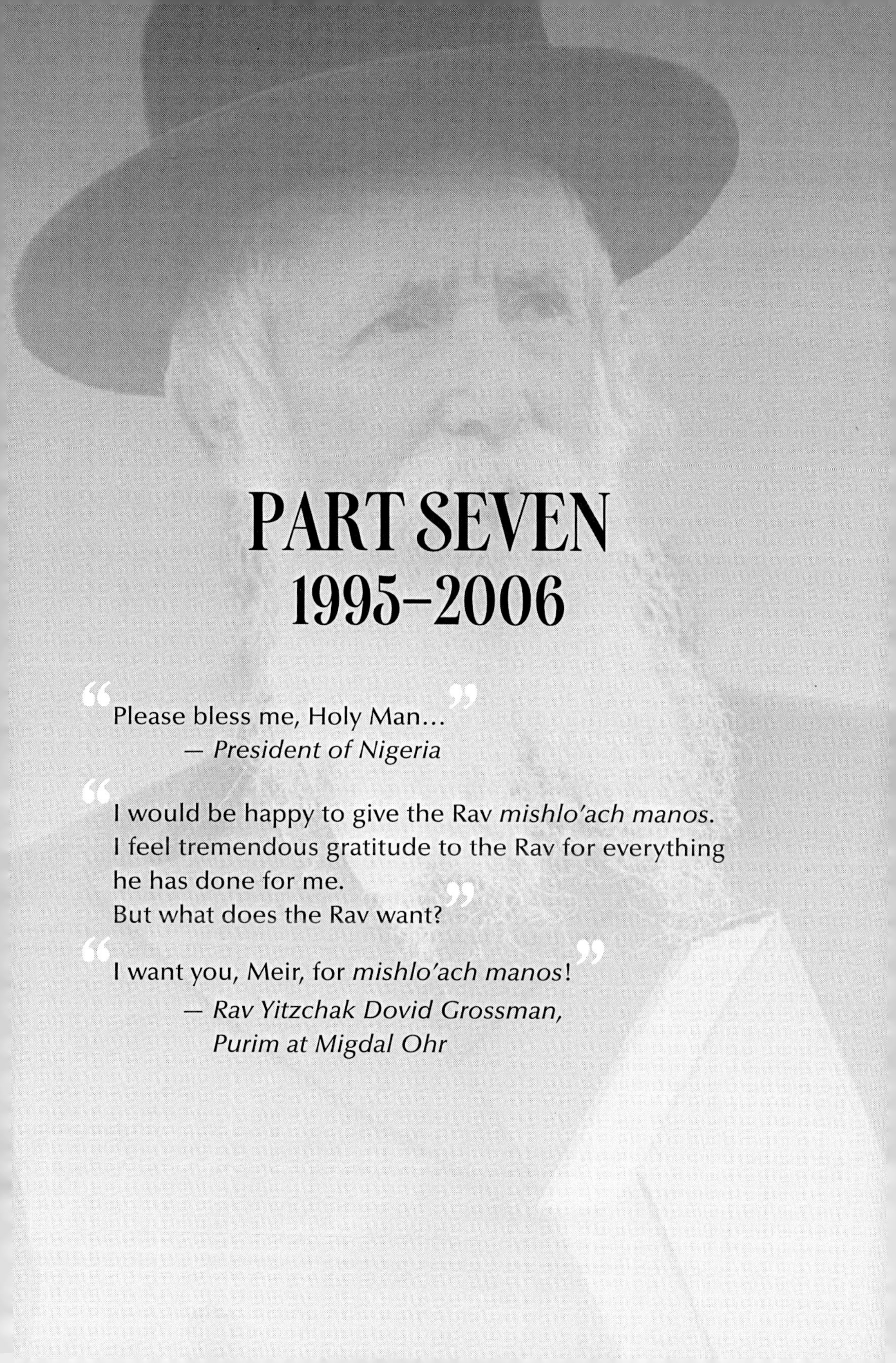

PART SEVEN
1995–2006

"Please bless me, Holy Man…"
— *President of Nigeria*

"I would be happy to give the Rav *mishlo'ach manos*. I feel tremendous gratitude to the Rav for everything he has done for me. But what does the Rav want?"

"I want you, Meir, for *mishlo'ach manos*!"
— *Rav Yitzchak Dovid Grossman, Purim at Migdal Ohr*

CHAPTER FORTY-ONE

Erev Yom Kippur at a Monastery

As the years went by, Rav Yitzchak Dovid Grossman earned a reputation as a man who could accomplish the impossible. And because of that reputation, more and more people beat a path to his front door, each with his or her own personal challenge, each with a request for the tzaddik of Migdal HaEmek.

And he did his best to help them.

Time and again.

An elderly chassid from Yerushalayim knocked on Rav Grossman's door two days before Yom Kippur. He could barely talk, he was crying so hard. Rav Grossman brought him into his home and calmed him down. When the man had caught his breath, Rav Grossman asked him what had brought him to his home.

"One of my sons moved to Germany for business. The trouble started with his son, my grandson. He returned to Eretz Yisrael to study at Bar Ilan University and ended up sharing an apartment in Ramat Gan with a young man who turned out to be a missionary with a golden tongue, who was able to convince my grandson to abandon his religion and heritage. He left Bar Ilan and is now living in an Arab village up north not far from Tzefas called Deir Chanah."

Yisrael Kenig

"What's he doing in Deir Chanah?"

"He's not living in the village itself. Deir Chanah sits at the foot of a very tall mountain. And at the very top of the mountain is a Christian monastery. That's where he is."

The man was quiet for a few seconds while tears rolled down his cheeks. "Rav Grossman," he said at last, "how is it possible that one of my grandsons will be spending Yom Kippur in a monastery? I have no desire to live — not when my own flesh and blood is spending his life in such a place. Rabbi, promise that you will do your best to help save my grandson!"

The man's anguish cut to the core, and Rav Grossman's heart went out to the distraught grandfather. His pain was palpable and couldn't be ignored, not that Rav Grossman could ever ignore anyone…

On the spot, Rav Grossman reached out to his old friend Yisrael Kenig, an influential politician who was head of the entire northern region of Israel, and asked him to call the *muchtar* of Deir Chanah — the village head — on his behalf.

"Please inform him that I plan on visiting his village today and that he should help me if I need any sort of assistance."

After receiving Kenig's assurance that he would call the village leader, Rav Grossman set off on his mission, with Kobi in the driver's seat.

When they arrived at the Arab village, their first stop was the home of the *muchtar*, who gave Rav Grossman a gracious welcome and inquired as to the purpose of his visit.

"There is a Christian monastery at the top of the mountain just behind the village," he replied, "and I need to go there for a visit. Can you help me get to the summit?"

"We are Muslims," the *muchtar* replied, "and they are Christians. We have nothing to do with them or they with us. The only contact we have between us is that they purchase their food from the local store, which we then deliver to the top of the mountain."

"Who makes the deliveries?"

"My son. The road is difficult for a car, so he drives up there on his tractor at least twice a day with everything they need."

"Please ask your son to give me a ride to the top of the mountain."

"Right now?"

"Yes, right now."

"But it's almost dark!"

"Yes, and I don't have much time. I need to get there as soon as possible. Now would be perfect." Tomorrow, after all, was Erev Yom Kippur. "Oh, and do you by any chance have an empty room that I could use?"

"Certainly," the *muchtar* said to his esteemed guest.

The village leader led the way out of the living room and into one of the bedrooms, leaving Rav Grossman alone. Once the door had been shut behind him, Rav Grossman changed into a blue T-shirt and a pair of jeans and slipped one of his rebbetzin's short *sheitel*s (wigs) on his head, making sure that his *peyos* were well hidden beneath it. Then he emerged from the room and boarded the tractor along with Kobi for the ride to the monastery at the top of the mountain.

The ride took more than twenty minutes. As they drove along the trail, which curled around the base of the mountain and carried them higher and higher, Rav Grossman couldn't help but reflect on all the different and fascinating directions his life had taken him. Here he was, crowded in the cabin of a tractor in the company of an Arab driver and an ex–gangster leader who had turned his life around, and they were on their way up a steep and narrow mountain path so that he would have the opportunity to convince a young man to have a little sympathy for his *zeide* (grandfather).

It was almost Erev Yom Kippur and Rav Yitzchak Dovid Grossman, scion of a long line of distinguished roshei yeshivah and tzaddikim, was wearing a pair of jeans and a *sheitel* on his head while attempting to infiltrate a monastery and save yet another life. Hashem was clearly on his side, right here, right now, since he had very quickly found a ride to a building standing on a peak in the middle of nowhere. Had they had to walk the trail by foot, it would have taken him hours to get there. Now all he had to do was sit back and enjoy the ride.

As they made their way up the mountain, with the sun setting above the trees, the view was astounding, and he drank it in, delighting in the beauty of Hashem's world.

Their arrival didn't go unnoticed, and someone quickly came out to meet them as they pulled into a square in front of a one-story building that was surrounded by numerous outbuildings.

Upon seeing the jeans-clad Rav Grossman and Kobi stepping out of the tractor, the man asked, "Who are you? What do you want?"

"I'm a friend of Justin* (the grandson)," Rav Grossman introduced himself. "I've come to visit him. Is there anywhere we can talk in private?"

"You can talk in his room. Please come with me."

Rav Grossman followed the man to one of the nearby caravans, and the manager knocked on the door and informed Justin that he had company.

"Hello, Justin," Rav Grossman said. "Do you mind asking your roommate to wait outside for a little bit?"

The roommate left, and Rav Grossman was left alone with Justin in the caravan.

"Look, Justin," the rabbi began as the young man stared curiously at his unexpected visitor. "The truth is that I'm not what I appear to be. My name is Rav Yitzchak Dovid Grossman, and I am the rav of Migdal HaEmek. I don't normally wear jeans, and I have long *peyos* under this wig. So why am I here? I'm here because your grandfather came to visit me a few hours ago. He's at my house right now, sitting in my dining room and crying. After a conversation with him, I decided to come here and see you."

"Why? What do you want?"

"I've come here to talk to your heart. I don't want to debate with you on the topic of Christianity versus Judaism. I want just one thing from you."

"What is that?"

"I want you to have mercy on your grandfather and come and spend Yom Kippur in my house. That will calm him down, and you will be doing a big favor for your *zeide*."

"I don't plan on fasting," Justin warned.

"So what's the problem? There's a fridge in my house and plenty of food. You can eat as much as you want. The main thing is that you will be at my house. The thing is, I'm afraid for your grandfather's health. Do you understand what I'm telling you?"

Justin nodded.

"Justin, you have to understand something here. Your grandfather went through the Holocaust. His entire family was murdered. The fact that he survived is a miracle. The fact that he managed to build a family after the war is another miracle. But now he is being forced to watch one of his descendants throwing away everything he worked so hard to sustain. Can you understand why that would upset a man like your grandfather?"

This prompted Justin to tell the rabbi about the anger he felt toward various members of his family. Rav Grossman listened until he finished talking.

"I get it," he told the boy. "I really do. You're angry. But no matter how angry you are, you still don't want to kill your grandfather, am I right?"

Justin nodded again, tears welling in his eyes.

"I want you to come with me right now," he told Justin.

"I can't."

"Why not?"

"If I leave with you, I have a feeling they will do everything in their power to try and stop me. Better that I downplay this and don't act in a hasty fashion. But I promise that I'll come to your house tomorrow, before the start of Yom Kippur. You can tell my *zeide* that I promised to be there and that I will keep my word!"

The way down the mountain took longer than the drive up, since it was already quite dark by then and the tractor's driver had to take the turns with careful precision. When they returned to the village, Rav Grossman thanked the *muchtar* for all of his help, and then Kobi drove him back to Migdal HaEmek, where Justin's grandfather was waiting in his house, waiting to hear word of his grandson, waiting to learn if the miracle worker had been able to find a common language with the boy.

When the grandfather heard what had occurred, he couldn't contain his rage and frustration. "You were sitting with him!" he yelled at Rav Grossman. "You had him in your hand! How could you have allowed him to escape? How could you have left him in the monastery?"

"*B'ezras Hashem*, please G-d, he will be here in time for Yom Kippur," he reassured the *zeide*, inwardly praying that the boy wouldn't turn those words into a lie.

The grandfather left his home a few minutes later, leaving Rav Grossman deep in thought.

It took him a very long time to fall asleep that night.

Erev Yom Kippur. As the rav of the city, Rav Grossman had to leave for shul with sufficient time to address his people with the traditional Kol Nidrei *derashah*. But he felt that he couldn't leave the house until Justin had walked through his door. As the hour grew later and later, his eyes kept switching between the door and the window, hoping that he would see the boy walking up to his house in time for the holiest day of the year. But there was no sign of Justin.

There was nothing he could do about it, and time was running out, so he left the house and went off to shul. It wasn't a very relaxing Yom Kippur because Rav Grossman knew that it was going to be followed by a phone call from a certain grandfather who would want to know if his grandson had shown up as promised.

When the phone rang after the fast, Rav Grossman didn't want to answer it, but he had no choice, so he lifted the receiver and said hello.

"Rav Grossman."

It was Justin's *zeide*, as he had expected. "Yes?" Rav Grossman replied with trepidation.

"I want to thank you."

This was a shock. "Thank me?"

"Yes. From the bottom of my heart."

"What are you thanking me for?"

"My grandson showed up at my house in Bnei Brak and spent Yom Kippur with me."

The relief that flooded him couldn't be described. Justin had kept his word as promised — only better.

"Rav Grossman?"

"Yes?"

"We're coming over to see you right now."

"Both of you?"

"Yes, both of us. Together."

They arrived later that night, and Rav Grossman spent a long time in deep conversation with the young man, the two of them connecting in a very real and meaningful way, culminating with the rabbi asking Justin to remain with him in Migdal HaEmek. Justin agreed and spent some time learning Torah at Migdal Ohr. At some point he left, and Rav Grossman lost touch with the young boy he had rescued from the monastery at the top of the mountain.

Many years later, he was visiting Monsey and went to daven in one of the local shuls where someone approached him.

"Do you remember me?" he asked the rav.

It was none other than Justin, who had since married and was raising a *Torahdik* family of *kinderlach* (children) who were following in the way of their ancestors. Then and there, Rav Grossman recalled the grandfather's visit and his visit to the *muchtar*, the tractor trip up the mountain and the conversation in the caravan, and the endless wait on an Erev Yom Kippur for someone who had gone to Bnei Brak. And he reflected on how happy he was with the ending of this particular story.

He shook Justin's hand for a long, long time.

CHAPTER FORTY-TWO
The Adopted Daughter

One afternoon a girl wearing an army uniform showed up at the Grossman house. He quickly realized that she wasn't an Israeli and asked her where she was born.

"I'm from South America."

"What brought you to Eretz Yisrael?"

She explained that in the twelfth grade, her class had been given an assignment in school to write a comprehensive paper on a serious topic, and she chose to write about the Holocaust.

"Are your parents Jewish?"

She shook her head. "I never really understood why I chose that particular topic, but that was my decision, and I devoted a lot of time to researching my paper. The more I read and understood, the more troubled I became. How was it possible that a nation like Germany could do such a thing? I read about Hitler and his dream of making the world *Judenrein* — free of Jews — and I asked myself, *What can I do to combat the evil that Adolph Hitler introduced into the world?*

"I asked myself this question over and over, and after much thought I concluded that the best and most effective revenge against Hitler for the terrible atrocities that he perpetrated was for me to convert and become a member of the very nation that he tried so hard to destroy. In addition, in the course of my reading I had also become familiar with writings on the Torah and mitzvos, and I realized that they were true."

"That must have come as a surprise to your parents."

"You can't imagine. When I went home and I told my mother and father about my plans, they refused to allow it under any circumstances."

"So what did you do?"

"I said goodbye to them and moved out of the house. It took some time, but eventually I found a *beis din* (religious court) willing to guide me in my quest, and I succeeded in having an Orthodox conversion. After my conversion, I presented myself at the local Jewish Agency office, where I told my story and explained that as a Jew, I wanted to make aliyah and move to Israel.

"They agreed that I was a perfect candidate for aliyah and helped me make the move, even assisting me when it came to finding an apartment near Haifa. I was also informed that since I was the right age, I would be drafted into the army."

Here the girl paused, drawing a breath before she went on to tell the rest of her story.

"Then I heard that my mother was very sick, and even though we hadn't been in touch for so long, I knew that I had to return home to be with her before the end. There was one problem: I didn't have enough money to pay for the ticket. I asked the army to loan me the money — the ticket cost twelve hundred dollars — but I was told that the army doesn't lend money to its soldiers. I went to the Agency and asked them for a loan, and they turned me down as well. With no choice, I asked one of my neighbors in Haifa if he would be willing to lend me the sum I needed to pay for the ticket. I promised I would repay him as soon as I returned.

"He agreed, gave me the money, and I flew home."

"How did the trip turn out?"

"It was awful. My family barely paid any attention to me, and I was hardly allowed to see my mother in the hospital. Aside from that, no one offered to help me cover the cost of my ticket. This meant I had no way to pay back my neighbor. When I returned to Haifa, my neighbor wanted his money back, and, of course, I didn't have it.

"It became very uncomfortable for me to be home, knowing that he could come banging on the door at any minute demanding that I repay him. I asked my commanding officer for help yet again, and as before, I was informed that the army didn't get involved in such things, and there was nothing they could do for me. I went back to the Agency as well and received the same answer."

"So what did you do?"

"I didn't know what to do. I was becoming more and more desperate when I saw an ad in the newspaper that seemed to promise salvation and hope."

"It was a pretty simple advertisement. It stated that a company in Herzliya was looking for people who were fluent in Spanish. I applied and got the job. Offer in hand, I returned to my commanding officer and told her that since the army wasn't prepared to assist me financially, I had found a job and I needed them to adjust my schedule accordingly to allow me to repay my debt. The army considered my request and responded with a favorable reply — they do that sometimes, in special cases like mine. I would be allowed to take off enough time from my army service to pay back my debt. Things were finally working out. I had a job and a plan to pay back my debt.

"Obviously things didn't end up working out as planned," Rav Grossman guessed.

"Unfortunately, you couldn't be more right. Last night I returned to my apartment to pack for my trip to Herzliya. My neighbor realized I was leaving, and although I tried explaining to him that the only reason I was leaving was to earn money in order to pay him back, he didn't believe me and gave me a severe beating!"

Her breath hitched as she tried to control her emotions. It was obvious that she was trying not to cry.

"When I finally managed to get away from him, I ran outside to the street, where I stood crying bitterly from the pain and from the shame of having received a physical beating. Someone passed by and saw me crying. He came over and asked me what happened and tried to calm me down.

"I told him the entire story. He wanted me to go to the police, but I refused.

"'If you don't want to go to the police,' he said, 'I have another idea. Why don't you go to Rav Grossman in Migdal HaEmek? I'm sure that he will be able to help you.' And so, here I am."

Her narrative concluded, she looked at the rabbi, her expression hopeful.

"First of all," Rav Grossman told the girl, "you obviously can't return to your apartment right now. Tonight you'll eat supper at my house, and you will stay in our guest room. Tomorrow morning we'll figure out what to do to resolve your situation once and for all."

In the morning, Rav Grossman called one of the officers he knew at the Ramat David army base near Migdal HaEmek, where the girl was stationed, and asked her to check into the girl's story and verify that it was accurate.

The officer asked for the soldier's name, and as soon as she heard the name, she gave a shout of excitement and cried, "Hashem runs the world!"

"Obviously Hashem runs the world," Rav Grossman replied, "but why did you come to that realization now?"

"I know this girl," the officer told Rav Grossman. "She's very special and has been through a lot. When she told me about the job offer in Herzliya, I had someone investigate the company that wanted to hire her. Just yesterday I learned the truth about the place."

"Which is?"

"It's a cult, Rabbi, and there is no way I could possibly allow this girl to get sucked into such a place. She has sacrificed so much to convert to Judaism and move to Israel. I cannot send her off to stay in such a place, unprotected and vulnerable!

"So now I had a problem. I knew the truth about the place where my soldier was going but didn't have a way to reach her and stop her from going there. (This was prior to the days of everyone having a cell phone.) From the moment I learned the truth about her future workplace, I've been trying to track her down but with no success.

"There I was, sitting by the phone and trying to figure out who to call next, when it rang and it's Rav Yitzchak Dovid Grossman calling to let me know that the girl I'm desperately searching for is currently staying in his home, safe and sound!"

Once it became clear that the girl's story was true down to every detail, Rav Grossman told her commanding officer that he was sending the money she owed over to the base so that the officer could repay the neighbor. But he didn't stop there. He got in touch with the appropriate parties in the army and set up a meeting, where he explained that the soldier who had somehow managed to show up at his house was all alone in the country, and even though she had gone out of her way to convert to Judaism upon her arrival in Eretz Yisrael, she had never been taken to visit any of the important sites, such as the Kosel, Kever Rachel, or Me'aras HaMachpeilah.

"The fact is, the moment she landed in Israel," he told the army officers, "she was given a place to live near Haifa and was then drafted into the army."

"So what does the rabbi have in mind?"

"I'll tell you. The army gave her a few months off so that she could work and pay back the money she owed her neighbor, correct?"

"Yes."

"Well, even though the debt is paid, I am respectfully requesting that you allow her to still take off time."

"For what?"

"To be part of the Grossman family. We'll treat her as one of our own, and we'll take her around and show her the sites that are important for every Jew to visit. Until now, she was alone, with no friends and no one to look after her. I plan to change that."

The powers that be decided that Rav Grossman's suggestion had merit, and the convert from South America went to stay at the Grossman home for a few weeks.

"Those few weeks ended up stretching into a year," Rav Grossman says with a smile. "She managed to get a discharge from the army and transfer into a seminary for *baalei teshuvah*. Of course, any time she wanted to leave school for Shabbos and return 'home,' she knew that her room was waiting for her and that she would be welcomed with open arms."

One Friday afternoon Rav Grossman heard knocking on his door. Shabbos was rapidly approaching, and he wondered who it could be and what they could possibly want or need. He answered the door and found a redheaded young man standing there.

"Can I help you?"

"Are you Rav Grossman?"

"Yes, I am."

"I've come to stay here for Shabbos."

The young man exuded a positive energy, and it was obvious he had an optimistic mindset. Rav Grossman invited the newly arrived Shabbos guest into his living room, where he spent a few minutes getting to know him.

"Where are you from?" he asked.

"Spain."

It turned out that the unexpected visitor hadn't grown up in a Jewish home and had traveled to Israel to volunteer on a kibbutz.

"But everything changed for me when I met some Chabad guys."

"How did you meet Chabad *chevrah* on the kibbutz?" Rav Grossman asked curiously.

"They came to the kibbutz on Purim to read the Megillah and give *mishlo'ach manos* (gifts of food traditionally given out on Purim). One thing led to another, and I decided to become a Jew. Today I'm a student at a yeshivah in Kfar Chabad."

"So how did you end up here?"

"My rebbi at the yeshivah told me that the Rav would be a good person to talk to about a certain problem I have. I took his advice and decided to travel to Migdal HaEmek for Shabbos, hoping that I would have the opportunity to not only meet the Rav but to even spend Shabbos at his house."

That Friday night Rav Grossman looked around his dining room table, and his gaze was caught by the two special *geirim*, two converts, sitting there — a girl from South America and a boy from Spain, both religious and both having arrived at their current places in life through two separate and fascinating journeys. It wasn't long before he advised them to go out with each other, and then he watched with satisfaction when they decided to get engaged. The wedding was held at a hall in Petach Tikva, and Rav Grossman married them off as if they were his very own children — which in a sense they were.

CHAPTER FORTY-THREE

Double Bar Mitzvah at Migdal Ohr

Every child who found his or her way to Migdal Ohr was sent there by the Master of the World, Who choreographs every single movement in a person's life, from the biggest events down to the tiniest happenings.

One afternoon Rav Grossman had a meeting with Dror Fogel, the mayor of the nearby town of Ramat Yishai. The reason they were meeting was because there were children from Ramat Yishai who were being raised at Migdal Ohr, and Rav Grossman wanted the mayor to contribute toward their education and general needs.

As Rav Grossman walked into the mayor's office, he saw a boy and girl waiting in the hallway. He didn't pay them much attention and went inside for the meeting. After they had taken care of business, Fogel said to Rav Grossman, "Tell me, did you happen to notice those two children sitting outside my office?"

"Yes, what about them?"

"Their father threw them out of the house in the middle of the night."

Rav Grossman felt an instant tugging at his sensitive heartstrings.

"How is that possible?" he exclaimed. "How can a father throw his children out of his house, and in the middle of the night yet?"

"There's a very simple answer to your question," the mayor replied. "He's not normal."

"If that's the case," Rav Grossman replied, "I'm going over to see him right now."

Taking the boy (we'll call him Eli*) with him to show Rav Grossman the way to the house, the rabbi and the child walked through the streets of the town, until they arrived at the one-story home from which Eli had been ejected just a short while before.

Rav Grossman gazed at the house. The windows were shuttered, and there was every impression that the doors were locked, an unusual circumstance in a quiet Israeli town. Eli went around to the back of the house, climbed through the window, and opened the door from the inside to enable the rabbi to enter.

Upon entering the small house, Rav Grossman walked into the living room and immediately noticed a scrap of cardboard laying face up in the middle of the table. On it there was a message written in big block lettering:

"I don't want to suffer any longer, and I have decided to end my life."

Hoping that he hadn't arrived too late to save the man's life, Rav Grossman ran into the bedroom and found the father lying face down. From the empty medicine bottles on the floor, the rabbi was able to deduce that the man had swallowed a huge number of pills. He immediately called the police and emergency services, and it wasn't long before the man was being carried out of the house and into an ambulance, which delivered him to the hospital in Afula. There the medical staff managed to save his life.

Rav Grossman went to visit him in the hospital a short while later. "What happened to you," he asked the man, "to make you want to kill yourself?"

He told the rabbi that his wife had passed away a few years earlier. He himself was already in his fifties and he was not a healthy man, and the kids were driving him out of his mind.

"What did they do?" Rav Grossman asked.

"They wander the streets at night," the father replied. "I warned them to make sure they got home at a normal hour, but they disobeyed me and walked into the house at three in the morning. I was out of my mind with worry and anger, and I told them to leave and not to come back. Then, feeling like the worst father in the world, I decided that I didn't want to live anymore."

Rav Grossman spent a lot of time with the man, encouraging him and reassuring him that his children were going to be okay.

"I can't raise them by myself," he said.

"That's all right," Rav Grossman said. "They're going to move into Migdal Ohr, and that's where they'll live and go to school. Everything will be okay."

That wasn't all. When he was released from the hospital, Rav Grossman gave the man a job at Migdal Ohr, and he was able to see his children on a frequent basis.

The children grew up at Migdal Ohr and today have kids of their own.

Like many others, Meir Levy came to Migdal Ohr from a complicated family situation.

Rav Grossman first met Meir at his bar mitzvah (the family had invited the city's rabbi) and it wasn't long before Meir was enrolled at Migdal Ohr, where he remained from the age of thirteen until graduation. After leaving Migdal Ohr, Meir unfortunately drifted back to his former friends and former life, and gradually his religious leanings fell by the wayside.

Purim at Migdal Ohr is always a unique and special experience. There's dancing, singing, and games throughout the night and all day, the music playing nonstop. For those who were raised at Migdal Ohr and have since moved on, Purim is a day when they try their utmost to return to that magical corner of the globe in order to spend Purim at "home." So it was that Meir Levy made it his business to put in an appearance at Migdal Ohr on the happiest day of the year.

Meir (right) in Migdal Ohr

Rav Grossman was dancing in the middle of the circle in Migdal Ohr's big dining room when he noticed that Meir had arrived. Immediately, Rav Grossman danced over to him and extended his hands. Meir accepted the invitation with a big smile on his face, and the two of them began to dance together in the middle of the gigantic circle. The more they danced, the more Rav Grossman felt that this was the moment to try to bring him back.

Meir and Rav Grossman

The dance over, Rav Grossman went up onto the stage, and when all the students had quieted down, he addressed Meir directly from where he stood.

"Meir!"

Meir looked at the rabbi expectantly, waiting to see where this was going.

"I see that you've decided to join us this Purim!"

Meir nodded.

"Meir, you know that on Purim everyone gives one another *mishloach manos*, right?"

"Yes, *kevod HaRav*."

"Well, Meir, did you think about what you're going to give me for *mishloach manos*?"

"I would be happy to give the Rav *mishloach manos*," Meir replied. "After all, I feel immense gratitude to the Rav for everything he has done for me. But what does the Rav want?"

"I want you, Meir. That's what I want for *mishloach manos*!"

It took Meir a few seconds to grasp what Rav Grossman was saying.

"I want you, Meir," Rav Grossman repeated. "I want you to return to the way you used to be. If you agree to do that for me, it would be the most amazing *mishloach manos* you could give!"

Meir was overcome with emotion. With tears streaming down his face, Meir made a declaration.

"I promise to return to the Meir that I used to be, and that will be my *mishloach manos* to Rav Yitzchak Dovid Grossman!"

That Purim was the catalyst for a dramatic change that impacted the rest of Meir's life. Then and there he became a different person and eventually ended up joining the staff at Migdal Ohr, where he has worked for years, teaching and inspiring the boys who have the good fortune to be part of his life. His *mesirus nefesh* for his students is legendary, and his results are astounding.

And it all began on a Purim night at Migdal Ohr.

The dining room at Migdal Ohr has been the scene of so many incredible moments in Rav Grossman's life. The Motza'ei Shabbos that the Grossman family was celebrating the bar mitzvah of their own grandson was no different.

The music was loud and fast, calling people to dance, and the guests were doing their best to bring joy to the bar mitzvah boy. No one paid any attention to a few strangers standing off to the side, their eyes devouring the sight of everyone dancing with so much fervor and excitement.

Then Rav Grossman spied the little group and realized that he didn't know the couple and their son. He left the circle and went over to get acquainted.

"Before you say anything," he said to them, "please come and dance."

They agreed with shy smiles. The father and his son joined the circle on the men's side, and the wife joined the festivities in the women's section. When the dance came to an end, Rav Grossman introduced himself and asked the newcomers to tell him their names and where they were from.

"We're *baalei teshuvah* from Germany," they informed him.

"How did you become religious?"

"We did it on our own. We discovered *Yiddishkeit* and pursued it until we succeeded in finding our way. But we've lived without a supportive community for many years, clinging to the mitzvos that we have learned about despite the lack of religious services. Even kosher food we've had to order online for the past several years."

"What about Chabad? Surely they would provide you with all the support you need."

"There's no Chabad House in our area. We've really been on our own."

Rav Grossman was impressed. It's rare to find people with that level of dedication.

"So what brings you here to Eretz Yisrael?" Rav Grossman asked.

"The reason we came to Israel was in honor of our son's bar mitzvah. We booked rooms at a hotel in Nazareth, but when we arrived, we were extremely disappointed to discover that there was no shul in the vicinity. With no choice, we walked a very long distance until we finally found a shul, where someone" — they pointed at a man standing nearby — "invited us to spend the rest of Shabbos at his home.

"We had an incredible Shabbos, spending the entire day discussing Judaism and our heritage. When Shabbos came to an end, our host suggested that we visit Migdal HaEmek, which is how we happened to have found ourselves at your grandson's bar mitzvah."

It was an amazing story, and Rav Grossman decided to share it with all the boys at the bar mitzvah. Gathering everyone together, he sat them down and told them the story of the family from Germany and the self-sacrifice with which they lived their lives.

"This is no longer just a regular bar mitzvah," Rav Grossman said to the assembled. "We are now taking part in a double bar mitzvah celebration."

Minutes later Rav Grossman invited the bar mitzvah boy from Germany to take a seat beside his grandson at the head table. Then he asked his young guest to say a few words in honor of the festivities.

The bar mitzvah boy hesitated for a moment. Then he closed his eyes and recited the Shema with concentration: "Hear, O Israel, Hashem is our G-d, Hashem is One."

His proud parents wiped their eyes (as did many of the other people watching the scene), and the celebration continued. Rav Grossman also gave the new bar mitzvah boy a gift: a pair of tefillin. The boy kissed them reverently and, looking at the rabbi, said, "I promise to wear these every single day!"

Then, turning to the parents, Rav Grossman said, "Now there's something that I want from you."

"What is it, Rabbi Grossman?"

"I want you to please, please, send your son to learn here at Migdal Ohr!"

"I couldn't help myself," Rav Grossman says. "This was such a special boy and such a special night."

And they promised they would.

CHAPTER FORTY-FOUR

Abdallah

Not far from Migdal HaEmek is a Bedouin town called Zarzir, and one afternoon Rav Grossman found himself visiting the town, since he had a meeting with a local contractor whom he was interviewing for a job at Migdal Ohr. The rabbi was on his way back to his car after the meeting when he was approached by a young Bedouin man.

"I need to speak with you," the man told Rav Grossman, his voice urgent. He introduced himself as Abdallah.

"What can I do for you, Abdallah?"

"I need your help."

This was a surprise. While Rav Grossman was used to people asking for his help day and night, both from within Israel and abroad, it was usually a Jew who did the asking. This was the first time he'd been approached by a Bedouin seeking his assistance.

"I've got to leave now, but if you need my help, come and see me in Migdal HaEmek, and I'll be more than happy to listen to your story." He gave the man the number to his office, and they parted ways.

When Rav Grossman left the village, he didn't know whether Abdallah was actually going to follow up on his request, but sure enough the Bedouin called the office the next day and made an appointment to meet with the rabbi. Clearly, there was something troubling him, and for some reason, he imagined that Rav Yitzchak Dovid Grossman was the proper address to help him handle it.

When they were finally seated across from each other, Rav Grossman encouraged his visitor to open up and explain why he was there.

"The reason I need the rabbi's help," he said, "is because I am certain that I am a Jew!"

Startled, Rav Grossman asked, "What do you mean?"

"I mean that I'm almost one hundred percent positive that the people who raised me are not my parents and that I was kidnaped as a young child. I want you to help me find my real parents."

Shocked, Rav Grossman stared at the man who appeared, for all intents and purposes, to be a full-fledged Bedouin. How was he to know whether the man was telling the truth?

Abdallah obviously realized that the rabbi wasn't sure whether to believe him, and he burst into tears.

"Calm down," Rav Grossman told him. "Calm down and tell me why you think you are a Jew. You must have proof. Otherwise, you wouldn't be making such a claim. Please share your proof with me."

"I was looking at my mother's *teudat zehut* (Israeli ID card) and I noticed the year she was born. It took me a second, but I realized that there is no way she could possibly have become a mother when she did. She was too young! I am twenty-seven years old, and twenty-seven years ago, the woman claiming to be my birth mother was all of twelve years old. Even among Bedouin, who marry young, it's not possible for her to have given birth to a child at that age."

When the rabbi still didn't respond, Abdallah said, "It's not just me who suspects that my origins are Jewish."

"What do you mean?"

"This goes back to when I was still in school."

"Go on."

"I was on my way out of the building one afternoon when the janitor passed me in the hallway. He met my gaze and said, 'I want to tell you something. A secret.'

"I was surprised. It wasn't like we were close or anything. What he said next was shocking: 'You are a Jew. You were kidnaped when you were a small child and brought here to live.'"

With that, Abdallah started crying again. Rav Grossman studied the man and felt sympathy for him. Regardless of whether or not he had really been kidnaped, just thinking he had been kidnaped was sufficient to mess with a person's mind.

"Listen," he told Abdallah, "it's almost Succos. I'll be returning to

Zarzir in a few days to buy my *schach* (the branches used to cover the succah) for the festival. Meet me then, and we'll see what can be done."

Abdallah agreed.

But when the time came, Rav Grossman was busy with Succos preparations, and he didn't have time for a lengthy conversation. Instead, he asked that the man come and see him a few days later, on Chol HaMo'ed, during the days between the first and last part of the holiday.

Abdallah was nothing if not committed to the idea of his being a Jew. He showed up during Chol HaMo'ed and presented himself to Rav Grossman, who was sitting in his succah when Abdallah arrived.

Many people come to visit Rav Grossman during Chol HaMo'ed every year, and when Abdallah walked in, it so happened that one of the other visitors who was present was a senior journalist from *Yediot Acharonot*, Israel's national daily newspaper. His name was Immanuel Elmikabeh.

Elmikabeh quickly realized that he had a story on his hands. Here was a Bedouin claiming to have been kidnaped from his Jewish family as a child. The reporter acted fast and wasted no time interviewing Abdallah. That same day, he sat down and wrote a full-length article about the Bedouin Jew he had met in the succah of Rav Yitzchak Dovid Grossman. The story ran the next morning on the front page, alongside a large photograph of Abdallah.

The story was read by millions of Israelis and made waves in many homes. Since Abdallah had given the paper permission to write his story, and even went public with his picture, he was no longer safe in Zarzir, and Rav Grossman invited him to stay in his own home until they could work out what to do with him long term.

First page of a long article about the kidnaped boy

It was five o'clock in the morning, the day after the article was published, when someone came knocking on Rav Grossman's succah door.

Actually, it was more like a pounding on the door, and Rav Grossman couldn't ignore it. He wondered who could be coming to see him at such an hour, but whatever he'd imagined when he went to open the door, it was definitely not the sight that greeted him. There, standing in his threshold, was an entire extended family — grandparents, parents, children, aunts, and uncles.

He ushered them into the succah, and they took seats around the table as he offered drinks and refreshments, before asking them the reason for their sudden and unexpected arrival.

"We live in Tirosh," the family spokesman explained, "a moshav that is not far from Beit Shemesh. Last night we read the story in *Yediot Acharonot*, and we knew that we had to come and see you. It was too late for us to drive to you, but we left early this morning to discuss it. You see, one of our children was kidnaped many years ago, and when we saw the picture in the paper, we knew that we were looking at our son, now all grown up and living as a Bedouin!"

"How can you be sure?" Rav Grossman asked. "The last time you saw your child he was a little boy. Do you have any way to prove that he is, in fact, your son?"

"Yes, we do. When our son was a small boy, he fell and we had to take him to the hospital for an operation. The operation was successful, but he was left with a noticeable scar on his back."

"A scar like that should settle the question one way or another," Rav Grossman agreed. "Well, it happens to be that Abdallah is staying with me for a while. Make yourself comfortable, and we'll find out the answer to your question as soon as Abdallah wakes up."

It was around eight o'clock in the morning when Abdallah finally woke up and walked into the succah, surprised to see that it was full of people. What happened next was absolutely incredible.

"Abdallah," Rav Grossman said, "I want you to tell me something."

"Yes?"

"I want you to look at all these people, and I want you to tell me if any of them is your father."

Abdallah took a good, long look at all the people standing and sitting in the succah and then pointed directly at one of the men. "That's my father!"

He said the words without hesitation, with utter finality, his voice ringing with confidence and sincerity, as if there was no question in the world that the man standing there was his father.

The man rose from where he'd been sitting at the table and walked over to where Abdallah stood. Without saying a word, he reached over and lifted up Abdallah's shirt, exposing his back. There, as clear as daylight, was a scar — the scar from the operation that had been performed over two decades earlier.

The next few minutes are indescribable as the entire family was reunited with the son who had been taken from them — the son they had been longing for, the son they had never given up hope of seeing again. There was laughter and tears and shouts of wonder and blessings and sobbing. It was surreal. At the same time, there was no question that it was happening. Who can describe the sense of wonder that exists between parents and child reunited?

The story was reported on the front page of every newspaper, and the country buzzed from the news. What a story it was! A Bedouin man who turned out to be Jewish had been recognized by a picture in the paper and was identified by the scar on his back! Everyone was happy, everyone rejoiced.

Although that's not entirely true, because there were some people who were not doing any rejoicing. Rav Grossman learned about this development when he received a phone call from the chief of police of the northern district of Israel, who called him up and asked for a meeting. When they were sitting together, the police chief explained that the town of Zarzir was up in arms because of the story, and they were out for blood.

"I'm afraid that the Rav is in danger," the police chief warned. "The Bedouins may decide to take revenge against the rabbi for what happened."

"So what do you want me to do?"

"The police department has decided to assign a squad of officers to guard the rabbi for as long as we deem necessary. We'll reevaluate when the situation starts to calm down."

So it went for a few days, until Rav Grossman picked up the phone and dialed the number of his friend Yisrael Kenig.

"Reb Yisrael," Rav Grossman said when he got him on the phone, "I need your help."

"What can I do for the Rav?"

Rav Grossman explained the situation. "Here's what I would like you to do," he said. "Please invite the chief of Zarzir and his top people to a meeting. Much of their budget comes through your office, so he won't be able to refuse."

"What should I tell them at the meeting?"

"Please explain that I didn't seek out Abdallah in any way. He came to me. He was the one who initiated the entire sequence of events. There's no reason to blame me for what happened."

The meeting took place in Yisrael Kenig's office with all relevant parties in attendance. Kenig relayed Rav Grossman's arguments to the leaders of Zarzir, who eventually agreed to make "*sulcha*" (a peace agreement) with the rav of Migdal HaEmek and let bygones be bygones.

The *sulcha* celebration was held a few days later at Migdal Ohr. The children couldn't believe their eyes when a delegation of distinguished-looking Bedouins walked into the dining room. A lamb was served (of course), having been *shechted* by a local *shochet* and prepared for the festive meal that followed the official peacemaking ceremony.

As for Abdallah, he returned with his family to the moshav of Tirosh, where he began making up for all the lost years.

CHAPTER FORTY-FIVE

"Holy Man From the Holy Land"

One of Migdal Ohr's supporters had a son-in-law named Uri Baron* who ran a shipping business out of Nigeria. The Nigerian government owed him a vast amount of money and wasn't getting around to paying him for his services. He would have considered complaining to the Nigerian president, but the man had a reputation for dealing harshly with people he didn't like. (Many of them ended up losing their lives.) Since Mr. Baron wanted to carry on living, he hesitated to say anything that would create a formidable enemy. On the other hand, he was standing on the brink of bankruptcy.

It was a few days before Rosh Hashanah when Rav Grossman met Uri Baron at an event somewhere in Israel.

"Rav Grossman, I need a blessing from you!"

"What's the matter?"

Uri explained the situation involving the president of Nigeria and asked Rav Grossman to daven for things to work out.

"They owe me millions of dollars, but I'm afraid to pressure them for the money. Yet I'll lose everything if I don't make a move."

"Tell me, Uri, do you know the president of Nigeria personally?"

"We've never met, but I do have a relationship with his chief of staff."

"Here's what I want you to do," Rav Grossman said. "Tell the president's chief of staff that you know a 'holy man' who lives in the 'Holy Land.' Tell him that the holy man wants to come and give a blessing to the president."

Uri Baron looked at Rav Grossman dubiously. Here he had asked the rabbi for a blessing, and he was going on about a holy man in the Holy Land. It was incredibly bizarre, and Uri didn't know what to make of it.

"When you ask someone for a *berachah,* you need to follow his instructions," Rav Grossman told Uri. "This is the idea that Hashem put into my head in order to assist you, and this is what you need to do."

Shortly after Rosh Hashanah, Uri Baron called to let Rav Grossman know that he had received a message from the president of Nigeria saying that he was very interested in meeting the "holy man from the Holy Land."

"We have to leave for Nigeria right away," Uri told Rav Grossman.

"In the middle of the *Aseres Yemei Teshuvah* (the ten days of repentance between Rosh Hashanah and Yom Kippur)?"

"Yes. Now it's a matter of *pikuach nefesh,* of life and death!"

"How so?"

"I offered to bring the holy man to Nigeria so he can give the president a blessing, and he accepted the offer. If I don't keep my word, it will be a slight to the president's honor, and I don't even want to think about what will happen if he thinks that his honor has been slighted!"

"In that case," Rav Grossman replied, "we're going to Nigeria."

The next thing he knew, Rav Grossman was seated in a private plane with Uri Baron and they were taking off from Ben Gurion Airport. Destination: Nigeria with a brief stop at Entebbe, Uganda, to refuel. When the plane landed in Nigeria, Rav Grossman looked out the window and saw fifteen military officers standing at attention, their uniforms splendidly pressed and rows of medals adorning their chests. They waited with their faces downcast, giving the impression that they were frightened at the prospect of meeting the "holy man from the Holy Land."

The door opened, and Rav Grossman emerged into the sunshine of Nigeria. He paused at the top of the steps, his white beard and distinguished visage drawing the attention of everyone there. A long black stretch limousine glided to a halt at the bottom of the stairs. Rav Grossman and Uri got inside, and they left the airport with a police escort leading the way and another following behind them. Every intersection through which they passed was closed to traffic, and it wasn't long before they had entered the palace compound, where they followed the roads to the palace itself.

There, standing outside in full ceremonial garb, was what seemed like half the cabinet ministers of Nigeria, all of them waiting to receive a blessing from the holy man. Rav Grossman entered the palace with Uri, and they were shown into a sumptuously decorated room, where the rabbi would be able to hold court.

The wife of one of the ministers had just given birth to a son, and the baby was presented to Rav Grossman for inspection and a blessing. So it went for the next hour and a half, as the ministers and members of government passed before him, one by one.

And then Rav Grossman was escorted from the room and taken down corridors and hallways, each exquisite in its own right, until they came to a room the likes of which he had never seen in his life. Marble pillars that seemed to soar off into the distance supported a high ceiling. Tapestries depicting hunting scenes filled with muscled men and wild beasts covered the walls.

Rav Grossman was led to a seat beside the president, and a fascinating conversation ensued, with Rav Grossman telling the president all about his work at Migdal Ohr and the children they raised and the lives they saved. He showed the president an album full of pictures — of smiling children playing together, school performances, and graduation ceremonies. And here and there were pictures of Rav Grossman with people the president recognized, famous figures such as Moshe Dayan and Yitzchak Rabin. The president took his time leafing through the album, enjoying the pictures and the happiness that permeated the pages, cutting through time and space.

When they had grown comfortable with each other, Rav Grossman told the president of Nigeria that he wanted to tell him a story.

"By all means," the president agreed, nodding his permission.

Settling back in his chair, Rav Grossman told the tale of a friendship between a Roman emperor and the *nasi*, the prince, of Klal Yisrael.

> Rabbi Yehudah HaNasi was the leader of the Jewish people in the days of the Romans. Kind of like a president. Rabbi Yehudah had a wonderful relationship with the Roman emperor, a man by the name of Antoninus. To show his friend how much he valued their friendship, Antoninus sent Rabbi Yehudah HaNasi a crate filled with precious jewels and diamonds whose value was astronomical.
>
> Rabbi Yehudah sent a present back to his friend. Something called a mezuzah. An object that Jews place on the doorposts of

> their homes for protection. This present was worth about fifty dollars. A holy object to be sure, but not priceless. At least in terms of money.
>
> Antoninus was more than a little upset at the exchange of gifts. "I've given you a gift worth millions," he told his friend, "and you've given me a gift worth fifty dollars?"
>
> "You presented me with a present that will need a contingent of guards to watch over it," he told Antoninus. "I, on the other hand, have given you a present that will guard over you!"

With that, Rav Grossman removed a beautiful mezuzah from inside his pocket and handed it to the president of Nigeria.

"In the spirit of Rabbi Yehudah HaNasi," he said, "I've also brought you a mezuzah — and may this gift watch over you."

The president was so touched by the rabbi's thoughtful gift that he rose from his throne-like chair and sat down on the floor before his visitor, folding his legs beneath him and laying his head on Rav Grossman's knees. "Please bless me, Holy Man," he said.

Placing his hands on the president's head, Rav Grossman murmured a blessing that befit the president and his position as leader of Nigeria. After receiving the blessing he had sought, the president rose and sat back down in his chair. Meeting the president's gaze, Rav Grossman decided the time was ripe to help Uri Baron, which was, after all, the reason they had flown to Nigeria in the first place.

"Sir," he began, "the man I came here with, Mr. Uri Baron, helps me considerably with the holy work I do back in Israel. I've heard that he is dealing with some sort of challenge here in Nigeria. I am therefore requesting that if there is anything that you, Mr. President, can do to help him, please do so."

"I will do everything in my power," the president replied.

The meeting came to an end a few minutes later. The holy man from the Holy Land took leave of the president of Nigeria with good wishes and warm smiles all around. An hour later they were back on the plane, and shortly after that, they took off from Nigeria and were flying back to Eretz Yisrael.

Two weeks later, Uri Baron received the full sum he was owed by the Nigerian government. So ended the story of the "holy man from the Holy Land."

CHAPTER FORTY-SIX

Payback in Netanya

Murray Appelbaum is another long-time friend and supporter of Migdal Ohr. One day he called Rav Grossman and told him that his mother's first *yahrtzeit* (anniversary of death) was to take place on the coming Friday.

"Where is she buried?" Rav Grossman asked.

"In the cemetery in Netanya."

"May her *neshamah* have an *aliyah*. (May her soul be elevated.)"

"Amen! Thank you, Rabbi. But I do have a request to make of you."

"What's that?"

"As you know, lately there have been many terrorist attacks in Israel, and people are even afraid to walk the streets."

"True."

"Unfortunately, the city of Netanya has seen more than its share of terrorist attacks, including the brutal massacre at the Park Hotel on Seder night. And because of everything that's been happening there lately, my wife doesn't want me to visit my mother's grave until the situation has calmed down."

"What can I do to help?"

"I would be incredibly grateful if the rabbi would arrange for a minyan to gather at the grave on the day of the *yahrtzeit* for a little learning, davening, and saying Kaddish."

"Murray, don't worry about a thing," Rav Grossman told him. "I'll take care of it."

Taking into account that it was the deceased's first *yahrtzeit*, Rav Grossman decided that in order to ensure that there would be a minyan at the grave on the designated day, he himself would travel to Netanya that Friday, where he would join the minyan from start to finish.

Along with two students from Migdal Ohr, Rav Grossman traveled to the Netanya cemetery that Erev Shabbos. They arrived at around eleven in the morning to a very empty cemetery. In his mind, he'd imagined that there would be plenty of people around to ask to join the minyan, but as he looked around the cemetery, he realized that this might be a little more complicated than he'd first thought.

Rav Grossman is nothing if not optimistic, and now, too, he began putting the puzzle together piece by piece, asking any and all passersby to join him in the mitzvah (commandment) of saying Kaddish for a departed soul. It took a while, but eventually there were nine people, and all they needed was one more.

Suddenly he spied movement in the distance among the graves. Figuring that it was probably a person, Rav Grossman headed over in that direction and found that it was indeed a person. He was quite short, which is why Rav Grossman hadn't seen him clearly, but he was a bonafide tenth man and Rav Grossman asked him to join the minyan, explaining that it was the deceased's first *yahrtzeit*.

The man answered in French, gesturing with his hands to show that he didn't understand what the rabbi wanted from him. Rav Grossman responded in kind, also using his hands. He broke it up for him, saying individual words like *minyan*, Kaddish, and mitzvah, hoping the man would get the message.

This time he grasped the idea and agreed to accompany Rav Grossman back to the *kever*. There the gathering learned some *Mishnayos* in the departed soul's memory and recited Kaddish. When they were finished, the French Jew made it clear that he had something to say. This would have been a bit of a problem, but one of the other members of the minyan understood French and was more than happy to serve as the translator.

So it was that the minyan stood around the *kever* and listened to an impromptu speech delivered by their tenth man.

"Today is the *yahrtzeit* of my father," he began. "I have traveled to Netanya from France to be here today, knowing that I am but one person, and hoping that somehow I would be able to put together a minyan at the *kever* while I was there. *Baruch Hashem*, the rabbi saw me and asked me if I would be willing to join you — and now I want to ask all of you to come with me back to my father's *kever* so that I can recite the Kaddish for him with a minyan."

Now Rav Grossman turned to the group and spoke.

"*Rabbosai*, here we see the concept of *mitzvah goreres mitzvah* at play — how one mitzvah leads to another. You agreed to join me so that we could recite Kaddish on the first *yahrtzeit* of one *neshamah*, and now Hashem has sent you the opportunity to do another mitzvah and help someone who has come all the way here from France to honor his father."

Two minutes later, the entire group was standing at the *kever* of the French Jew's father. When he was standing before the *kever*, Rav Grossman received a shock. On the grave there was a little sign made from copper, upon which was written a short message.

It turned out that the man buried there had worked for the Tunisian *chevrah kaddisha* (burial society) for forty years and had put tremendous effort into organizing minyanim for people who didn't have family of their own to come and pray at their graves.

"Look how things work up in Heaven," Rav Grossman told the assembled. "Here lies a man who went out of his way time after time to organize minyanim for every Jew — no matter who he was. So what does Hashem do for this man? He sends me to the cemetery here in Netanya, where I find myself in need of a minyan, which is completed by the son of a man who spent his entire life doing the exact same thing for other people! And look at how Hashem orchestrated the events of our lives so that this man would have a minyan at his *kever* on the day of his *yahrtzeit*!

"'You worried about other people's minyanim,' said Hashem. 'Now I will worry about a minyan for you.'"

CHAPTER FORTY-SEVEN

The Nazi's Request

Due to the sensitive relationship Israel shares with Germany and the long history between the two nations, Israeli politicians ironically find themselves visiting that country on a fairly regular basis. A number of years ago, a man by the name of Moti Dotan was invited to Germany to attend a ceremony in the city of Hanover. Dotan was the head of the Lower Galilee Regional Council, and he had flown in for a celebration of the twenty-five-year anniversary of the twin cities pact between the Galilee Region and the Hanover district.

After Dotan's speech was over, one of the German politicians approached him and asked if they could meet in one of the side rooms.

"I have a private matter that I want to discuss with you. Would you mind?"

Moti Dotan didn't mind, and they found a place to talk.

"My father passed away two weeks ago," the German said. "Before he died, we had a conversation that has shaken me to the core."

A pause as the German considered what he wanted to say.

"I always knew that my father had served in the Luftwaffe, the German air force, during World War II. What I didn't know was that in addition to everything else he did during the war, one of my father's tasks was to bomb any synagogue he spotted as he flew overhead. One day my father said to himself, *You're spending so much time bombing the Jewish prayer houses. Why don't you land the plane near one of them, and see what it is you keep destroying day after day?*

"My father landed his plane outside a village. He got out of the plane and walked into the village to find the bombed-out synagogue. It had been almost completely obliterated by the Nazi bombs, but the ark at the front of the room was still intact."

"The *aron kodesh*," Moti Dotan clarified.

"Yes. The *aron kodesh*," the German repeated. "My father opened the ark and found a Torah scroll inside. Removing the scroll, he laid it out on one of the tables, and when it lay exposed before him, he felt the thick parchment with his fingers.

"*This would be very good to use for my flight documents*, he told himself. You see, every pilot had a little booklet, a "soldbuch," from the air force in which they documented every single flight — every bombing run, every trip, every time the plane was used.

"We Germans are very meticulous and the pilot's 'soldbuch' needed to be updated scrupulously. My father decided that the parchment lying in front of him would make a good protection for his documents, like a leather case or wallet. Removing the little book from his pocket, he laid it down on top of the Torah scroll and proceeded to cut out a piece of parchment, which he fashioned into a wallet for his documents. He kept this with him until the end of the war.

"After he was released from the air force, my father returned home to Germany and settled back into civilian life, but he never got rid of his flight documents or the piece of parchment that he'd cut on the day when he landed his plane and went to see what exactly it was that he'd been bombing. For sixty years, the parchment cut from the Torah scroll sat in a drawer in his desk. We, his children, had no idea that it was even there. We never saw it and he never told us about it.

"I don't know why he finally made the decision to show it to me," the

The pilot's "soldbuch" and the piece of a *Sefer Torah* it was wrapped in.

German continued. "Maybe it was the fact that he was on his deathbed and he knew that he was about to leave this world. Whatever the case may be, he finally admitted to us that while he had served as a pilot during the war, his particular service had been less than honorable, because it had entailed bombing Jewish prayer houses in addition to enemy installments. And he told us the story of how he had landed the plane one day, entered a synagogue, and cut out a piece of parchment to use as a wallet for his flight documents.

"My father could barely talk by this point, but he forced himself to speak. It was clear that he wanted the truth to be on record.

"'I cut this piece of parchment from a scroll that is holy to the Jewish people,' he said, 'and I'm asking you to return it to the first Jew you meet. Please ask the Jew not to keep it himself, but to make sure that it goes it to a holy Jew in Israel. It is important to me that you do this, since I see that there are many people around the world who want to deny what happened during the war. This will serve as proof that the Jews are telling the truth about the atrocities that happened in the concentration camps and all over Europe.'"

With that, the German lawmaker handed the Israeli mayor the piece of *klaf* (parchment) that his pilot father had cut from a Sefer Torah so many years earlier.

"Please take this with you back to Israel," he said, "and give it to a holy man. This was my father's last request."

In an astounding turn of events, this mission wouldn't prove very difficult for Moti Dotan since he happened to live but a few short miles from the home of none other than Rav Yitzchak Dovid Grossman, the rav of Migdal HaEmek. A short while after his arrival back home, Dotan came to see Rav Grossman, told him the entire story, and handed him the piece of parchment that had spent over half a century lying in the desk drawer of a German pilot.

Rav Grossman was understandably overcome by the story and was filled with emotion at having in his possession the piece of parchment from a defiled Torah scroll. But before anything else, he needed to know which part of the Sefer Torah the piece of parchment had been taken from.

Rav Grossman held up the *klaf*, which was all of five by seven inches, and read the words written on it — words that were still clear and

Moti Dotan hands the precious parchment and the "soldbuch" to Rabbi Grossman

legible even after so many years.

The Nazi could have cut out any part of the Torah. The *pesukim* (verses) could have been taken from the passages of Pesach or Succos, from that of the *korbanos* (offerings) in *Vayikra,* from the story of Adam and Chavah or that of Korach. It could have been from any of those places in the Torah.

But they were from none of those places.

The seven lines that the German pilot had cut out from a Sefer Torah in a bombed-out shul in war-ravaged Poland came from the *tochachah* in *Parashas Ki Savo* — from the curses promised to the Jewish people should they not keep the Torah and obey its laws:

"... your enemy will distress you in your own cities...then Hashem will make extraordinary your blows and the blows of your offspring — great and faithful blows and evil and faithful illnesses. Even any illness and any blow that is not written in the book of this Torah, Hashem will bring upon you until you are destroyed. You will be left few in number, whereas you were as the stars of the heavens in abundance..." (*Devarim* 28:57–62).

The parchment also contained another verse from the end of the *parashah,* the one that states, "*Vanikach es artzam...* — We took their land and gave it as an inheritance..."

The German had somehow gone unerringly to the exact place where Hashem details what will happen to His people should they choose to ignore His laws and commandments. And yet, at the same time, he had also cut into another place where the Torah states that Klal Yisrael will receive the land of their enemies as an inheritance....

The piece of parchment could have easily been given to any number of holy Yidden living in Eretz Yisrael. But the Master of the World wanted this piece of *klaf* to become famous and for the message and meaning of the story to spread all over the world. And so He sent it directly to the hands of Rav Grossman, who after recovering from the emotional shock of what he had just seen, went out of his way to spread the incredible story of the parchment's return on Israeli media, where it was promptly picked up by media around the world.

There is no way to know how many lives were changed by the story, but many later testified that they made real life changes after hearing Rav Grossman tell the story of the *klaf*, the parchment that was cut from a Torah scroll by a German pilot — and the way it finally returned home after so many years.

Rav Grossman has received many offers for that piece of *klaf* — one from Yad Vashem among others. But Rav Grossman turned them all down. That holy piece of parchment stays with him, and he takes it with him wherever he goes.

Some things are just not for sale.

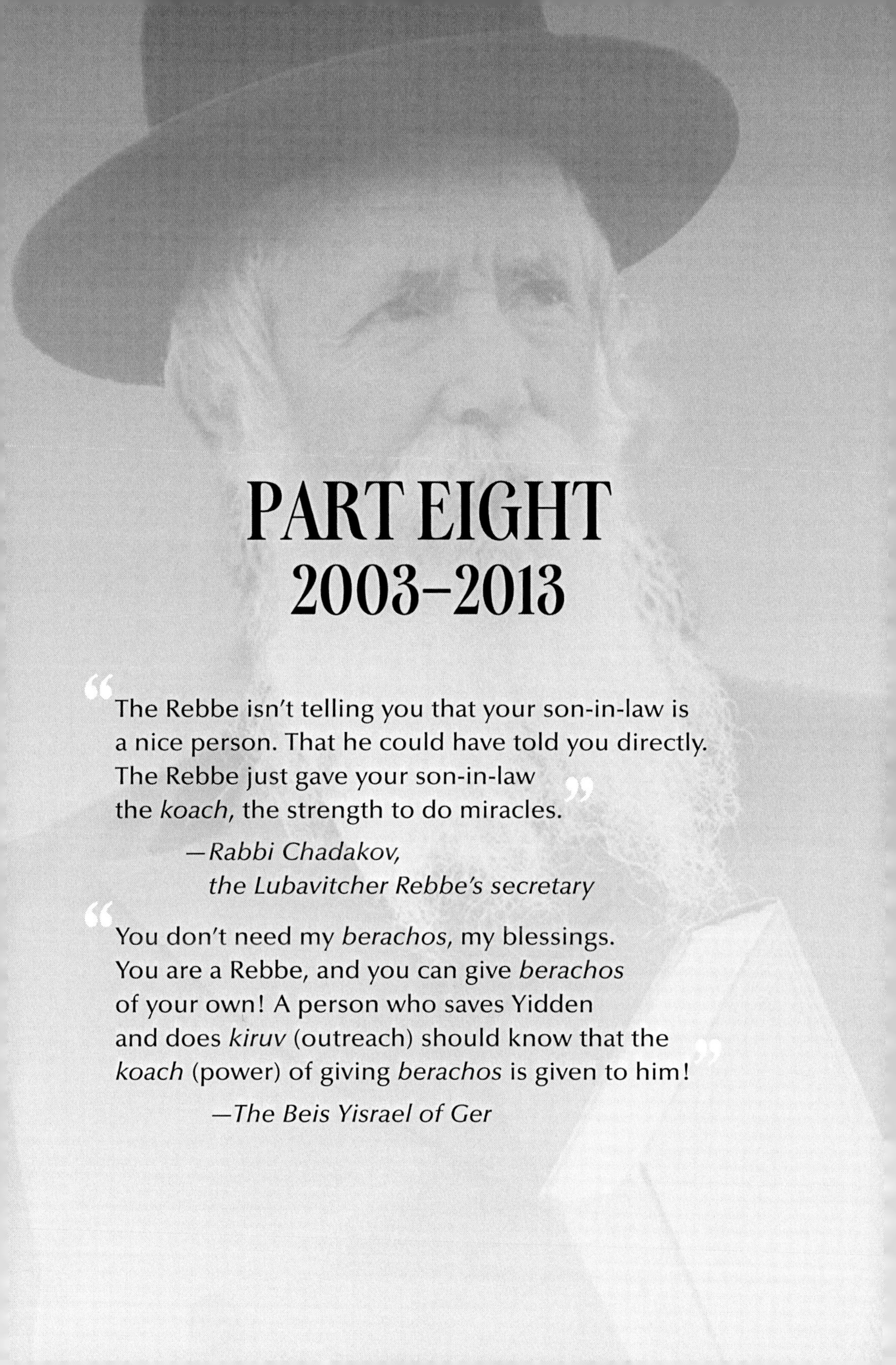

PART EIGHT
2003–2013

"The Rebbe isn't telling you that your son-in-law is a nice person. That he could have told you directly. The Rebbe just gave your son-in-law the *koach*, the strength to do miracles."

—*Rabbi Chadakov,*
the Lubavitcher Rebbe's secretary

"You don't need my *berachos*, my blessings. You are a Rebbe, and you can give *berachos* of your own! A person who saves Yidden and does *kiruv* (outreach) should know that the *koach* (power) of giving *berachos* is given to him!"

—*The Beis Yisrael of Ger*

CHAPTER FORTY-EIGHT

A Father Knows

Rav Grossman never stopped looking at his role models for advice and guidance. Even once he was running a complex of institutions with a multi-million-dollar operational budget, he still turned to those he trusted, those to whom he would always remain "Itche Duvid." This characteristic came to the fore when Rav Grossman had to make one of the most momentous decisions of his life.

It started the day that Rav Ovadia Yosef, the Sefardic chief rabbi of Israel, called Rav Grossman and asked him to come and see him in

Rav Grossman with Rav Ovadia Yosef

Yerushalayim. Once Rav Grossman was seated, Rav Ovadia looked at his guest and said, "I want you to accept the candidacy for the next Ashkenazic chief rabbi of Israel."

Rav Grossman was hesitant. "The job entails a great deal of responsibility," he said.

"I will be with you at every step," Rav Ovadia reassured him.

The position of chief rabbi of Israel is an elected position. It was 2003, and the post would soon be up for election. Since the position is for a term of ten years, the candidacy has actually been offered twice to Rav Grossman in two decades. The first time, no less than three great personages were extremely insistent that he take the job: Rav Yosef Shalom Elyashiv, Rav Mordechai Eliyahu, and Rav Ovadia Yosef. So sure was Rav Ovadia that Rav Grossman was the right man for the job that when he presented Rav Grossman with a copy of his *sefer Yabia Omer*, he wrote in the inscription, "To the chief rabbi of Israel, Rav Yitzchak Dovid Grossman."

Rav Ovadia felt that there was nobody more suitable for the position because Rav Grossman had a good relationship with every faction of the Israeli public — Litvish, Chassidish, Mizrachi, those who were religious and those who were not. Above and beyond that, he was also close to many politicians, and they, too, wanted him for the job. There are one hundred and twenty people who are eligible to vote for a chief rabbi. This group includes the mayors of large cities, prominent rabbanim, MKs, and ministers of the government. Taking everything into consideration, Rav Ovadia felt that his dear friend would have a relatively easy time getting elected to the office of chief rabbi.

It wasn't only about politics. The *gedolim* (great Torah leaders) wanted someone in the chief rabbi's office who would insist on maintaining Torah standards when it came to important national matters such as the observance of *shemittah* (the sabbatical year), the appointment of worthy *dayanim* (judges) and rabbanim, and the supervision of kashrus in restaurants and factories across Eretz Yisrael. Rav Grossman would also work to strengthen the bond between Ashkenazim and Sefardim.

There was one problem. Rav Grossman consulted with his father and informed him of the intense pressure he was under to accept the position of chief rabbi of Israel, but Rav Yisrael Grossman was in total opposition to the idea. He forbade his son to submit his name as a candidate in the election.

In the aftermath of the campaign, when it became clear to one and all that Rav Yitzchak Dovid Grossman, the rav of Migdal HaEmek, had turned down the position because his father forbade him from running, the Israeli media came banging on his door, clamoring for interviews.

"Can you please explain to our listeners why your father doesn't want you to run for the position of chief rabbi?" one television reporter asked. "Some people are claiming the reason for his refusal has to do with his involvement with the Eidah HaChareidis, the body that governs the most Orthodox segment of the Jewish nation."

It was true that Rav Yisrael was very involved with the Badatz (the Beis Din Tzedek of the Eidah HaChareidis). Rav Yisrael Grossman was one of the chief *poskim* (halachic decisors) for the community that followed the Eidah HaChareidis. That was one school of thought. Others claimed that Rav Yisrael's vehement opposition to the job was due to the fact that he saw his son succeeding so well in his chosen field and didn't want him spending time on anything that would detract from that.

With so many rumors flying around, it made sense for the interviewer to try to get to the bottom of it all, which is why he pressed Rav Yitzchak Dovid for the real reason for his father's unequivocal no.

Rav Yitzchak Dovid's answer shocked the TV journalist who was running the interview.

"I was raised in a home where a child was taught not to demand an explanation for a parent's decision. I don't know why my father said no."

"You didn't ask him?"

"No, I didn't. It was enough that he said no."

Not only did Rav Grossman's answer make a deep impression on the interviewer, it also resonated with thousands of parents around the country, many of whom went out of their way to actually call Rav Grossman and thank him for clarifying what parenthood is truly all about, how it's the parent's job to make decisions and not the reverse.

Rav Grossman wasn't a twenty-two-year-old kid when all this took place. He was already a middle-aged man with a long greying beard. Someone who had accomplished many things in his life. He had built an educational empire and was now under pressure to put his hat in the ring for one of the most important posts in the country. Yet with all that, he had still looked the interviewer in the eyes and informed him that his father had spoken, and that was that.

Rav Ovadia Yosef wasn't ready to give up. He promptly wrote a letter to Rav Yisrael Grossman.

"The *gedolei Yisrael* (Torah leadership) have laid their eyes on your son for the position of chief rabbi of Eretz Yisrael," he wrote. "We are sure that if he is elected to the position, it will bring honor to the Torah and strength to Judaism. Therefore, your honor (Rav Yisrael) has no permission to get involved in this matter. You have no permission to get involved because this has been decided in Heaven!"

Rav Ovadia went even further:

"According to the *Shulchan Aruch*" — here he cited the relevant sources to which he was referring — "your son has no halachic obligation to obey your command in this matter."

It was an extremely powerful letter, written with the full confidence of one of the greatest Torah leaders of the generation, and was delivered to the home of Rav Yisrael Grossman by Rabbi Aryeh Deri.

Rav Yisrael opened the letter and read it while Reb Aryeh waited patiently for his response. When he finished reading the letter, Rav Yisrael turned to Reb Aryeh Deri and said, "*Af al pi chein*. Even so, even so. Please tell the Rav that even so, I do not agree."

It wasn't over yet. Rav Elyashiv sent word to Rav Yisrael Grossman that he wanted to visit him at his home to discuss the matter. Rav Yisrael responded by entreating Rav Elyashiv to please not come and went so far as to sit down and pen a letter that he sent to the *gadol hador* with Rav Elyashiv's right-hand man, Rav Yosef Efrati, to be read by Rav Elyashiv and no one else. Rav Grossman never found out what was written in the letter, but it didn't matter because the father didn't change his mind, and in consequence, neither did the son.

In the end, someone else was elected to the position, and the situation reverted to normal. The pressure was off for the time being.

Ten years passed, and once again it was time to discuss the question of who would be voted into the office of chief rabbi of Israel. Rav Yisrael Grossman had passed away and was no longer there to voice his opposition, and Rav Ovadia began a new campaign to put Rav Yitzchak Dovid Grossman into office. Clearly the Sefardic *gadol hador* felt that it was imperative for Rav Grossman to do the job because once again he began exerting tremendous pressure on the younger rabbi to accept the idea and agree to run in the election.

"You are my son," he said to Rav Grossman, "and Yitzchak is my son" (referring to the son who would go on to be elected Sefardic chief rabbi in that election), "and I want both of my sons serving as chief rabbis."

There was no question that the pressure was off the charts.

"But my father, *zecher tzaddik livrachah* (may a tzaddik's memory be blessed) said no," Rav Grossman protested.

"Nishmato Eden," Rav Ovadia replied. A Sefardic saying, roughly translated as "His soul is in Gan Eden."

Rav Grossman wasn't sure how to defuse the situation so he said nothing. Yet it was clear to him that he was going to have to make a major decision one way or another. And soon.

After leaving the home of Rav Ovadia, Rav Grossman's phone rang. He answered and was soon speaking to the grandson of Rav Aharon Leib Shteinman, the *gadol hador* and successor to Rav Elyashiv, who had passed on since the previous election.

"My grandfather wants to speak with you."

Rav Grossman promptly made his way to Rav Aharon Leib's austere and simple apartment on Chazon Ish Street in the heart of Bnei Brak. When he was sitting with Rav Shteinman, Rav Grossman was told in no uncertain terms that his hour had come and that it was his destiny to serve in the position of chief rabbi.

"But my father forbade me from being elected," he protested. "How can I disobey him when he stated his feelings so clearly?"

"It's very possible that since his arrival in the *Olam HaEmes*, the World of Truth," Rav Shteinman replied, "your father has changed his mind."

Facing unprecedented pressure from *gedolim*, yet instinctively knowing that he wouldn't be able to live with himself if he disobeyed his

A moment of laughter with Rav Aharon Leib Shteinman.
The rav's brother, Rav Zalman Grossman, is in the middle.

father's direct command (especially since a person must honor his parent even after the parent is no longer alive), Rav Grossman said, "I must ask the Rav to forgive me, but I would like to pose this as a halachic query to Rav Shmuel HaLevi Wosner."

Rav Aharon Leib agreed to wait until they had asked the world-renowned halachic authority for his ruling. And so their meeting ended, with Rav Grossman having been granted a temporary reprieve.

A quick phone call ascertained that the Shevet HaLevi (Rav Wosner was known by the name of his very famous *sefer*) was not in the country at the time. He was in Vienna.

"Please tell Rav Wosner that Rav Yitzchak Dovid Grossman is taking the next flight to Austria to meet with him."

The response was immediate and to the point.

"There is no reason for Rav Grossman to trouble himself to such a degree. He can speak with the Rav on the telephone."

The conversation lasted longer than half an hour. In the end, Rav Wosner told Rav Grossman, "*Chas v'shalom*, don't accept the position! It will bring you nothing but *tzaros* and hardships! You are taking care of Klal Yisrael's children, saving lives on a daily basis. There is no question

Rav Wosner, at a visit to Migdal Ohr

that your father saw everything you do and knew that there is nobody else who could step in and take over. Someone else can serve as chief rabbi, but who will look after the children if you leave Migdal HaEmek?

"I know that you have wondered for years why he was so opposed to your taking the position of chief rabbi. In my opinion, this is the reason your father was so adamant in his refusal."

Rav Grossman returned to the home of Rav Aharon Leib.

"I came here to tell the Rav that Rav Wosner rules against my taking the post."

Rav Aharon Leib accepted the ruling without argument.

Rav Grossman then called Rav Ovadia and said, "Please have mercy on me and don't force me to do something that I don't want to do. I can't and won't go against my father's wishes in this matter."

Seeing how distressed Rav Grossman was at the idea of disobeying his father, Rav Ovadia gave him a reprieve.

In an interesting turn of events, after Rav Ovadia passed away, someone played Rav Grossman a piece from one of Rav Ovadia's Motza'ei Shabbos *shiurim* (Torah classes), which were watched by thousands around the country every single week. In one of the *shiurim*, Rav Ovadia told his audience that Rav Grossman saved six thousand children from the former Soviet Union alone, turning them into *talmidei chachamim*.

"I went and saw this with my own eyes," he said. "It was a wondrous thing to see!"

He went on to say, "I wanted him to become the chief rabbi of Israel, but he didn't want the job. Instead, he chose to remain where he is and to save the lives of more and more children. He chose to forego honor and money for the sake of his children!"

CHAPTER FORTY-NINE

Traveling First Class

With a philosophy based on the idea that every child is an entire world and needs to be treated as such, the assorted institutions of Migdal Ohr grew beyond anything anyone had ever imagined. Today there are tens of thousands of alumni who have graduated from the schools and gone on to live productive lives as rabbanim, *dayanim*, doctors, lawyers, and engineers, along with numerous other professions.

One evening, Rav Grossman was visited by two police officers who came by his home to ask for help.

"Here's the story," they began. "There's a family that moved here recently from France. The mother passed away not long after the move and the father doesn't seem to be mentally stable. One of the daughters was thrown out of the house and she showed up at the police station asking us for a place to sleep for the night. We want to help this girl, but we are a police station, not a youth hostel. We aren't equipped for her. We don't have pillows and blankets. In the morning we will talk to social services and get the ball rolling, but the question is whether you can put her up for the night?"

She ended up living at the Grossman home for the next three years.

"I can't describe the challenges that we experienced with this girl," Rav Grossman said to me. "I am not blaming her — she was never given a decent *chinuch* (education) — and she was without question the wronged party in the story. Many times we ended up running to the

The girls of Migdal Ohr

emergency room with her, since she would start to shake in the middle of the night and nothing we did could calm her down. Eventually she stabilized and we were able to move her into the dorm, where she attended high school like everyone else. After graduation, she was introduced to a local boy and the two of them married and have built a beautiful family together."

This story was just another example of the reason Rav Yitzchak Dovid felt that he needed to establish a school for girls. It's not that he had any free time. If anything, the opposite was true. He was already busy 24/7 with the boys in Migdal Ohr. But he had no choice.

The girls school was established with twenty students. Should you happen to be in the area today and decide to pay a visit to Migdal HaEmek and the world that Rav Yitzchak Dovid had the *siyata d'Shmaya* to create, you will find yourself staring at many large, beautiful, modern buildings, filled with state-of-the-art furniture and equipment for the thousands of girls who are enrolled at Migdal Ohr.

Of course, there is a story of how this came about.

Rav Yitzchak Dovid took genuine enjoyment in the fact that the boys of Migdal Ohr were so well taken care of in the sprawling campus that they called home. At the same time, he felt that his work was just beginning, because he wanted to build a number of dormitory buildings that would be just as special for the girls in his institution. And while the cost for such a project was prohibitive, the rabbi had come to learn that his job was to think of things that needed to be done — and then to begin the process, leaving the rest in the very capable hands of the One Above. Time and again he'd found that Hashem somehow relieved him of his financial burdens and came through for the institution just when the help was most needed. All this can explain how Rav Yitzchak Dovid signed a contract in the year 2004 for the construction of a gigantic campus for the girls division of Migdal Ohr.

The price for the first few buildings was a whopping seven million dollars, and Rav Yitzchak Dovid had only managed to put aside half a million dollars for the project. At the time of the signing, the rabbi was filmed writing his name on the contract. After he signed, he looked up to the heavens and said, "Ribbono shel Olam, I am signing and You will pay."

The year 2004 was special for another reason. The rabbi had just been awarded the "Israel Prize" — one of the most prestigious awards in the country — for his life's work and unique contribution to Israeli society. The prize was given to him and a handful of other awardees at

On the way to receiving the Israel Prize:
The rav's mother, his wife, and Rav Yitzchak Dovid

Politicians from every sector respect Rav Grossman for his achievements for all Klal Yisrael

With President Ruby Rivlin and Prime Minister Binyamin ("Bibi") Netanyahu

With Prime Minister Ehud Barak

Prime Minister Yitzchak Rabin at a visit to Migdal HaEmek

With U.S. President Bill Clinton in Migdal Ohr

With Prime Minister Ariel ("Arik") Sharon

With Natan Sharansky

With Prime Minister Yitzchak Shamir

With Prime Minister
Menachem Begin

Prime Minister
Shimon Peres with
Migdal Ohr children

Receiving the Israel Prize (l to r): President Ruby Rivlin,
Supreme Court Judge Aharon Barak, Jerusalem Mayor Uri Lupolianski

a ceremony that took place at the Israel Museum on Independence Day.

As millions of viewers watched, the rabbi with the shining face, long *peyos,* and beard stepped up to receive the prize. It was obvious to anyone watching the proceedings that every one of the politicians on the stage, from the prime minister down, had profound respect for the unapologetically religious Jew whom they were welcoming with handshakes and warm smiles. They respected the fact that he had never compromised on who he was. And they loved him for his care and concern for every member of Klal Yisrael, no matter who they were, how religious they were, or where they placed themselves politically.

To the rabbi from Migdal HaEmek, every Jew was worthy of unconditional love, and the country loved him right back.

Two weeks after the ceremony, Rav Grossman was driven to the airport, in an attempt to raise the funds he needed for the new buildings for which he had signed a contract. As someone who travels abroad on a frequent basis, Rav Yitzchak Dovid was a familiar face at the El Al counter and lounge, and he was immediately recognized by the staff. They greeted him warmly, congratulating him on having been chosen as the winner of the Israel Prize for that year.

"On behalf of El Al," one of the staffers said, "we would like to thank you for all the hard work you do for the children of Israel, and to express our appreciation by offering you a free upgrade to first class for your flight to America."

Until that point Rav Yitzchak Dovid had rarely flown first class, reasoning that since his journey to the States was in order to raise funds, it would be wrong for him to use the money to sit in the first-class section of the plane. In addition to not wanting to use *tzedakah* (charity) money for personal benefit, Rav Grossman was also uncomfortable with people judging him for having the temerity to sit in first class while fundraising. He therefore made a point of staying out of first class even if people who had paid for him to attend their *simchahs* offered him a first-class ticket. But here it was El Al that was offering him a free upgrade, and he decided to make an exception to his long-standing policy.

He didn't really understand why he was choosing to do this — after all, he had turned down so many first-class trips. But something intangible pushed him to accept, and he thanked the staff and took them up on their gracious offer.

So it was that Rav Yitzchak Dovid Grossman boarded the plane to the United States, taking his seat in the almost empty first-class section.

There were six seats in first class. Rav Grossman was seated in one of the seats on the side of the cabin. At first it seemed that he was going to have the entire section to himself for the flight, but a few minutes before takeoff a couple entered the cabin and took the center seats. The plane was cleared for takeoff not long after.

At first the rabbi kept to himself, but after the "fasten seatbelt" light was turned off, he had an idea, which he considered quite inspired. Since they were going to be together for the duration of the flight, and since the man and his wife had nowhere to go, Rav Yitzchak Dovid decided that now would be the perfect time to show the couple the brand-new DVD clip that his staff at Migdal Ohr had put together for him to show prospective donors in the States.

Carrying the portable DVD player in his hand, he approached the couple. Sticking out his hand to the man, he said in his accented, yet completely understandable and even somewhat charming English, "Hello, my name is Rabbi Grossman. They used to call me the 'Disco Rabbi,' since I have done a lot of work with many young people in the discos and jails."

"What type of work do you do, Rabbi?"

"I work with children from broken homes — many of whom are orphans. Perhaps I can interest you in watching a short video presentation about my organization. This will give you a better idea of what we are all about."

With hours of flight time ahead of them and nothing that important to fill the time with, the couple agreed to watch the DVD. They were also unquestionably intrigued by the fascinating rabbi whom "fate" had chosen as their travel partner for the next eleven hours.

Rav Yitzchak Dovid handed them a pair of earphones to use and pressed the play button. He then returned to his seat as the husband and wife grew immersed in the magical world of Migdal Ohr. Having seen the clip numerous times, Rav Yitzchak Dovid waited until he recognized the final scene heralding the conclusion of the short film. When it was over he rose from his seat and returned to the couple, figuring that he would take back the DVD player and hear their impressions.

The next twenty seconds, however, did not play out in any way that he could ever have imagined.

Without much experience in first-class travel, what the rabbi didn't know was that there was a button in the armrest of the first-class seat which, when pressed, transformed it from a seat into a bed in a matter of seconds. As he stood over the man, Rav Yitzchak Dovid reached over and took hold of the DVD player with his right hand, not realizing that he had unwittingly placed his left hand on the seat-shifting button. The button immediately responded to his pressure and laid the seat down full length, sending the unsuspecting passenger into a supine position with no warning whatsoever! As Rav Yitzchak Dovid watched in stupefied horror, the man who had just graciously consented to watch his DVD went from sitting up to lying down, shocked beyond all words by the sudden shift, not grasping why he was suddenly horizontal. And it was all the rabbi's fault!

Standing beside his fellow passenger and mortified beyond all measure by what had just occurred, Rav Yitzchak Dovid tried to figure out what he could do to fix the situation he'd created. Without thinking too deeply into his next action, only trying to make amends, Rav Yitzchak Dovid leaned down over the man and gave him a kiss on his forehead — as if to apologize for the uncomfortable situation he had put him in, saying, "Excuse me, excuse me — please forgive me!"

He didn't know what had come over him. He felt completely discombobulated and unsure of himself, as if he were operating in the middle of a fog. Taking the time to lift the seat back into an upright position, the rabbi hastened back to his own chair, where he sat down and immediately began castigating himself. Not only had he sent the unsuspecting stranger into this embarrassing position, but then he'd kissed him on the forehead, no doubt adding insult to injury!

"Itche Duvid," he said to himself, "how could you have done such a thing?! Who does this? Who acts this way? Why couldn't you have just stayed in your seat and left those people alone? You're on a plane — you didn't have to show them the DVD. You could have spent your time doing the things you need to do and left them alone to spend their time as they pleased! Instead, look what you did! You shamed your fellow passenger, and then instead of apologizing and returning to your seat, you went and kissed him on his forehead. He probably thinks you're a crazy person!"

So it went, with Rav Grossman castigating himself, asking himself over and over why he had felt the need to act in such an outlandish fashion...

A few minutes later the couple rose from their seats and made their way over to their cabin-mate, who was still smarting from the shame of what had just transpired.

"Rabbi," the man began, "I want to tell you something."

Rav Yitzchak Dovid sat straight up in his chair, prepared for the worst.

"My wife and I came to Israel with a very large sum of charity funds which we earmarked for dispersion," the man continued. "Although there are many worthy organizations in the country, we have always been interested in helping out children from dysfunctional families or who are orphans, and we were hoping to be introduced to such an organization, with the intent of making a serious contribution. I am a good friend of Bibi Netanyahu and Ze'ev Bielsky, the head of the Jewish Agency, and the two of them told me about many different organizations who deal with this type of cause. For some reason, though, none of them spoke to me. All of them seemed to be worthy causes, yet I didn't connect with any of them — and I didn't end up making a contribution.

This meant that we found ourselves leaving the country with all the charity funds with which we arrived. Seeing that I hadn't succeeded in accomplishing what I had planned on doing, I had a conversation with G-d."

Here Rav Yitzchak Dovid leaned forward, very interested and, to be honest, relieved that he wasn't getting a tongue-lashing.

"This is what I said to G-d: If a person will introduce himself to me — a person who works with these kinds of children — and he will give me a kiss on the forehead, this will be a sign that this is the person to whom I need to give the charity money. I don't have to tell you, Rabbi, that you fit all the criteria. You run Migdal Ohr, which I see changes countless lives every year for the better, and you gave me a kiss on the forehead!"

Rav Yitzchak Dovid was blown away by what the man was telling him. Hashem had made it happen, using the most incredible turn of events to bring him to kiss a complete stranger — who had been specifically waiting for that exact thing to happen! The whole chain of events boggled the imagination. El Al offering him a free upgrade, his decision to show his fellow passengers the DVD, making a mistake and "helping" the man lie down — all leading up to the kiss and the outcome of the most extraordinary deal he had ever heard of.

Over the next two years, the couple that he met on the plane donated over four million dollars to the Migdal Ohr institutions.

CHAPTER FIFTY

May These Letters Be a Shield

Rav Grossman made waves around the country when he initiated a bi-yearly charity drive that he dubbed "Chag Savea — An Abundant and Satisfying Holiday," in which packages of food items were distributed before Rosh Hashanah and before Pesach to needy families around the country.

The idea was a simple one. Some of the largest supermarket chains in Israel — Supersol, for example — have around three hundred and fifty branches around the country. Before Rosh Hashanah and Pesach, gigantic signs would go up in every branch. Shoppers would see an image of a smiling Rav Yitzchak Dovid and other well-known Israeli personalities, inviting them to take part in the campaign and donate food items to those in need. Shoppers were asked to "Buy one for you, and one for someone else. Buy a bag of sugar for you and a bag of sugar for someone in need. Buy a bottle of grape juice for you, and a bottle of grape juice for someone in need."

Large cartons were set up in every branch for the items that were donated. The food was collected from the supermarkets by Rav Grossman's youth movement "Ohr Yisraeli," a movement that was established in 2003. With one hundred and sixty branches around the country, it was geared toward non-religious youth. Every branch featured a game room outfitted with ping-pong and pool tables, a dining room, and a room where the kids learned about different, interesting topics. It took time for the movement to gain momentum, but after a few years, Ohr Yisraeli had six thousand members.

Thousands of Ohr Yisraeli boys join together at the Kosel for Selichos

With branches throughout Israel, the members of Ohr Yisraeli were uniquely positioned to go from supermarket to supermarket, where they collected the items that had been deposited in the cartons. They delivered all the goods to one location and made sure everything was loaded onto trucks. One of the country's major trucking companies, Movilei Dror, volunteered its services for the mitzvah. The trucks delivered the food donations to the Sirkin Army Base in Petach Tikva, which was the designated headquarters for "Operation Chag Savea."

There at the Sirkin base, volunteers, in addition to one hundred soldiers who were sent by the army, gathered to assemble the boxes. Major companies and organizations participated in the campaign by sending their employees to help make packages. Some days Bank Leumi would send volunteers. Other days it would be Bank Hapoalim, Israel Discount Bank, Osem, or Bnei Akiva. The program was completely apolitical and became beloved and appreciated by one and all, irrespective of party affiliation, creed, or background.

At Sirkin the packages were picked up by other volunteers, who delivered them to addresses, from way up north to all the way down south. The lists of recipients were compiled by the welfare services, who were positioned to choose the families who most needed the assistance. People would be sitting in their homes, dealing with health, financial, or a million different kinds of issues, when they would hear an unexpected

Saying *Shema Yisrael* together at Selichos

knock on the door. When they opened up, they would find themselves staring at a smiling volunteer bearing a large package.

"This is for you," they'd be told, "compliments of Chag Savea."

It was sure to brighten anyone's day.

The range of volunteers was eclectic and varied, with no common denominator other than the desire to help someone else. One of the vans that pulled up at Sirkin was driven by a man who had lost both legs but was offering to drive the boxes and two volunteers, who would carry them out of the van and into people's homes.

"I may have lost my legs," he said, "but I still have a heart."

It didn't take long for "Operation Chag Savea" to become so successful that movie stars and musicians all wanted to take part in the campaign. Serving as the voice or face of the campaign meant that a celebrity had truly arrived.

But for Rav Grossman it still wasn't enough. Traveling to the Beit Hanasi in Rechavia to see his old friend Shimon Peres, who was then eighty years old and president of Israel, the rabbi suggested that it would be a good idea for Peres to come in person to Sirkin, where he could join in assembling the boxes.

"If the citizens of Israel see that even the president of the country has arrived to help in the campaign, what an example this will be for the youth and everyone else!"

President Shimon Peres presents Rav Yitzchak Dovid
with the President's Medal of Honor

Some of the president's advisors who were there at the time did not think much of Rav Grossman's idea, and tried to convince Peres to stay away, claiming that such activities were not befitting the exalted office of the president. Shimon Peres brushed them off, saying, "If the Rav is asking me to help, how can I refuse? Besides, he is right for asking me. Don't I need to do mitzvos just like everyone else?!"

Shimon Peres presented himself at the Sirkin Army Base the

Chag Savea volunteers meet President Shimon Peres and Rav Grossman following morning, where he stayed for a while, helping to put together quite a number of boxes. The fact that the president of Israel had come in person to participate created a major buzz, and for a while the whole country was talking about "Operation Chag Savea" and the need to do *chesed* for someone else.

Why was Sirkin the place chosen to serve as their headquarters?

As with everything else that happens in Rav Yitzchak Dovid's life, there was a story here as well.

It all started when a man named Yossi Paluch, a friend of Rav Yitzchak Dovid, called Rav Grossman to tell the rav about something he'd seen. The country was engaged in the Second Lebanese War. Yossi had a son who was a reservist in the paratroops, and he had gone to visit him.

"My son is at Sirkin," he told the rav, "along with another seven hundred soldiers, all part of the army reserves. I don't know what's going on at army headquarters, but the soldiers who were supposed to stay at Sirkin for one day before boarding buses bound for Lebanon ended up staying there for ten days and living in a tank hangar unfit for human habitation. There are no tables to eat at and no showers to use for washing. And while soldiers are capable of roughing it for a day or two, forcing reservists to stay in such a place for ten consecutive days is completely unacceptable!"

When Yossi Paluch came to visit his son and saw the situation, he was shocked beyond all measure. That was when he picked up the phone and called Rav Grossman.

"You cannot imagine what I saw when I arrived at Sirkin," he told the rav. "Seven hundred soldiers lying around in a hangar, every last drop of motivation to fight gone!"

"The first priority is to get the soldiers out of Sirkin," Rav Grossman told the concerned father, "and I will get in touch with the army to extend an invitation for all seven hundred soldiers to leave Sirkin and to be immediately transferred to the dormitory at Migdal Ohr, where they will be comfortable and looked after."

Rav Yitzchak Dovid was true to his word, and immediately got on the phone to track down the unit's commanding officer. Six hours later the army decided to accept his offer and to move the soldiers from Sirkin to Migdal Ohr. When the soldiers learned that they were being moved from the hangar to a dorm, most were happy. Some, notably those with left-wing leanings, were somewhat suspicious of the rabbi offering to host them. This is the personal account of one such soldier.

I'm a regular kind of guy. But the whole story was anything but regular. They called us up for the Second Lebanon War and we came with the goodwill to fight, but it was so dangerous and we weren't even provided with the equipment that we needed. There were so many things we were missing from our basic kit. Toothbrushes for example. Backpack water canteens, that was another thing and believe me, when you're going to be hiking through the Lebanese mountains with who knows how many pounds on your back, you need a canteen for water. But we didn't have one. The country, simply put, hadn't been prepared for war. And the fact that they weren't ready for war translated into people, friends being killed, because an army that's unprepared, is an army that's going to lose.

What can I tell you, morale was low in our platoon… And then we received the news. All 700 of us were being transferred from where we were to a dorm at an institution up north, headed by Rav Yitzchak Dovid Grossman, who had extended an invitation for all of us to come and spend the night and day as his guests before going into Lebanon!

"That's incredible! What a man!"

That's what the guys around me were saying, but I had a few other thoughts in mind.

"I don't know about you boys, but it seems pretty clear why the rabbi invited all of us out to his ranch," I said. "I'm thinking that the second our buses hit his campus, he'll be all over us with tefillin and stuff! I'm not so sure that this is such a great idea. I mean he's getting us when our morale is low. It's going to be pretty hard to fight him off!"

"You are so wrong," said someone else. "Rabbi Grossman is the ultimate righteous man. All he cares about is doing *chesed*. You'll see. There are no hidden agendas here. If you end up putting on tefillin, it will only be because you decided that you want to."

When we rolled up to Migdal Ohr, we were greeted with a Gan

Rav Grossman and some of the 700 soldiers

Eden such as we hadn't even imagined in our wildest dreams. The buses entered the lush campus and this old-time rabbi with a lovely white beard and luminous eyes came forward to greet us.

"Boys," he said to us, and when he said boys, we felt as if we were his boys, "jump into the pool and go for a swim. When you come out, there will be refreshments waiting for you. There will be entertainment and music and an evening that you will remember for the rest of your lives!"

We couldn't believe our ears. We rubbed our eyes! How wonderful, how incredible! We were away from the battlefield and going for a swim! That swim was absolutely amazing! So rejuvenating and relaxing for those who had felt nothing but the stress and the grit of army life for the past few weeks. And when we emerged from that pool there was a table piled high with 700 pairs of brand-new undergarments. Do you have any idea what it's like to don a brand-new, clean garment in place of the mud- and sweat-encrusted clothing that we had been wearing for so long? Gan Eden, that's what it was like.

Wearing brand-new garments and feeling outstandingly relaxed after our swim, we moved on to the dining area where we found a band playing soft music and tables piled high with delicious foods of all kinds. Soft drinks and dips, vegetables and fresh rolls, cheeses, cold watermelon and a splendid assortment of fresh cakes. We had never encountered a man like Rabbi Grossman before. Like Avraham Avinu of old, all he wanted was that we be as comfortable as possible, that we should be happy and well fed and feel as if someone cared for us. I was not the slightest bit religious, but even I could tell that this man was a genuine tzaddik. There was such *simchah* in his eyes, such complete immersion in his mitzvah — we were blown away by his selflessness.

Before we retired for the night the rabbi said to us, "Boys, I heard that you are missing quite a bit of equipment. Please write down the items you need on these pieces of paper and leave it on the table."

We had an evening of entertainment arranged for us by Rabbi Grossman: music, dancing (we danced out all our stress from the ten days at Sirkin), and a fantastic BBQ. But listen to what happened next.

In the middle of the dancing, one of the officers received a phone call from his uncle who lived in France. Knowing that his nephew was supposed to be up in Lebanon, the French Jew probably thought that the call would go straight to voice mail — or if the call was answered, that he'd hear the sound of gunfire. But instead of hearing the sound of shooting, the uncle heard the sound of loud music and singing.

"Is that a band playing?" he asked his nephew in disbelief. "I don't understand. Since when does the IDF send their troops out to war accompanied by an orchestra?!"

"No, it's a long story, but basically Rav Grossman invited our unit — all 700 of us — up to Migdal Ohr, and right now we're in the middle of a BBQ that he threw for us. That's the music that you're hearing."

The uncle was extremely excited and emotional by what his nephew was telling him.

"Please give the phone to Rav Grossman," he told him. "I want to speak with the rabbi."

"Rav Grossman?"

"Shalom aleichem."

"*Aleichem shalom.* Rav Grossman, I want to tell you something. Recently I ordered a Sefer Torah from a scribe in Yerushalayim for my community here in France. I paid a lot of money for the Sefer Torah. I am so overwhelmed by what my nephew tells me that you're doing for the soldiers, that instead of bringing the Sefer Torah to France, I want to donate it to the Migdal Ohr Institutions, as a thank you for everything that you're doing for seven hundred soldiers!"

Grabbing the microphone, Rav Grossman called out, "*Chevrah,* listen to the incredible gift we have just been granted in your *zechus*!"

His announcement caused the hundreds of soldiers in the square to start dancing as if this were a Simchat Torah celebration. The joy was immense, the emotions palpable.

On the spot, Rav Grossman called the *sofer* (scribe) in Yerushalayim and asked him to please come with the Sefer Torah to Migdal Ohr the next day.

"What time should I be there?"

"Seven o'clock in the morning."

"How much do you have left to write?" Rav Grossman wanted to know.

"A nice amount."

That night we slept on fresh linen in air-conditioned rooms. It was a sleep like we hadn't had in months! When we got up in the morning, we found a mountain of brand-new gear that Rabbi Grossman had purchased for us while we slept. He had gone out of his way to find out what we were missing and made sure we got it!

Rabbi Grossman, the miracle man, had spent over $80,000 for the equipment that had been purchased. Helmets, canteens, knee pads, toothbrushes, water canteens, ceramic bulletproof vests, night vision goggles, socks, and much more! He left a note beside the gear, "To my dear soldiers from all my heart!"

We were astounded. We were touched!

And then we were escorted into the dining room where the *sofer* was waiting for us.

"*Chevrah,*" Rav Grossman cried out, "the present that we received in your merit is here! Whoever wants to have the *zechus* to write a letter in the Sefer Torah should come over here and the scribe will help them. *Rabbosai,*" he continued, "I want to share a thought with you in honor of this momentous occasion. The word 'Yisrael' stands for '*Yesh Shishim Rebo Osios L'Torah* — There are sixty multitudes of letters in the Torah.' This idea is alluding to the concept that every Jew has his own spiritual letter in the Torah. I want you to remember that every single one of you has a letter in the Torah — which is yours…

"Now whoever wants to write a letter come on up."

We stared at Rabbi Grossman in wonder, not being able to comprehend that we were going to have the chance to participate in something so, so holy. We didn't consider ourselves to be holy people, and we knew that such an opportunity arrived only once in a lifetime.

Before we began the actual writing, Rabbi Grossman spoke to us in loving tones.

"Boys," he said, "I want you all to know that filling in the ink on the final letters of a Sefer Torah is an extraordinary *zechus*, an outstanding merit! When each of you is called up to fill in the ink, I want you to daven to Hashem that the merit of what you are doing, that the completion of these letters, should serve as a shield for you when you return to battle. Pray to Hashem that these letters, the letters that you are filling in, should protect you from harm."

We obeyed him, the tears streaming down our faces as we were guided in our holy task. If you could have seen us in the midst of this. How silent we all were! How we filled in those letters with the cherubic innocence of newborn babies. How uplifted we were. How we felt reborn!

I called my mother and I cried to her on the phone, explaining to her how incredible I felt that a person such as me, a man so completely removed from his heritage, had had the chance to take part in something so holy.

"Ima," I said to her, "you know me. No Shabbos, no kashrus, no nothing. A totally secular man. But this was the most amazing experience that ever happened to me. To be able to write a letter in Hashem's holy Torah! To have the chance to wrap myself inside its protective grasp! Ima, I can't believe this!"

And I cried and I cried, and all 700 of us cried together as we were touched like never before in our entire lives. This had become our Sefer Torah. We felt as if we had a part in it, that it would protect us, that it would watch over us with its love. That we were children and it was a benevolent parent, ensuring that all would be fine with its young ones.

You should have seen the line. Seven hundred paratroopers lined up in front of the *sofer*. It didn't matter if they were kibbutznikim or leftists or whatever — every single soldier wanted to have a part in the *zechus* of finishing the Sefer Torah that morning."

Later that day, Rav Yitzchak Dovid gave the children of Migdal Ohr a job. He asked them to put seven hundred individual shekel coins into seven hundred individual plastic bags. When all seven hundred bags had been prepared, Rav Grossman told the soldiers that there was a concept in Jewish thought that stated that a "*shaliach mitzvah eino nizak* — an emissary on his way to do a mitzvah will not be harmed."

"I want each one of you to take a bag. In the bag there is a shekel. When you take the bag, I want you to tell yourself that you plan on giving this shekel to charity upon your safe return from the battlefield. This will turn you into a *shaliach mitzvah* and ensure your safe return."

Every soldier became a *"shaliach mitzvah"*

Every single soldier eagerly accepted the little plastic bag containing that mitzvah shekel. They then searched for the ideal place to keep it safe during the battles that were facing them. One placed it in an inner pocket, the next stuck it deep into his ponytail where it wouldn't fall out.

The soldiers were about to leave. Gone were the smiles and the feeling of ease and serenity. They were all serious now. The buses had already arrived to transport them to the battlefield. At that moment Rav Grossman stepped over to the group, right before they boarded those buses, and he uttered words that would go down in history — that's how incredible they were.

"Boys," he said, "my sweetest boys. I want to tell you something. You have such merit now! Every one of you put on tefillin, every one of you wrote a letter in the Torah scroll.

"In the merit of all these mitzvos, I promise you that each and every one of you, all 700 of you, will return to us here in Migdal HaEmek safe and sound, in body and in spirit. You are sheluchei mitzvah and you will be safe. I promise you that every single one of you is going to return from the battlefield healthy and whole! Nobody will be wounded and nobody will be killed.

"But I also want something from you."

They looked at him curiously, wondering what the Rav could possibly want from them.

"I want you to promise me that when the battle is over and you are on the way home, healthy and whole, alive and unwounded — I ask you all to return here to me first thing; after leaving that army base, you drive those buses over here and we will thank Hashem together for your deliverance. And only then, will you all go home!"

The commander of the brigade accepted the condition on behalf of all 700. They would be coming back as soon as the war was over. And if all went according to Rabbi Grossman's promise, ***they would all be coming back***!

If you were to ask Rav Yitzchak Dovid Grossman how he was able to make such an incredible promise to 700 people — his only explanation is that it was only because of the great feelings of emotion and *emunah* (faith) that were coursing through him at the moment that he made that fantastic promise.

While many people will read this story and think to themselves, "Wow, look at that, look at what a tzaddik like Rav Grossman can promise," you need to understand that when he returned to earth after the soldiers had pulled out of Migdal Ohr, Rav Yitzchak Dovid was beside himself with worry for the soldiers, and not at all sure his words would be fulfilled. In fact, he asked himself many times, how on earth had he given such a promise to seven hundred people?

From that time until the soldiers' return, Rav Grossman traveled to numerous graves of the holiest tzaddikim to daven for their safety. He drove to Meron and poured out his heart at the *kever* of Rabbi Shimon bar Yochai. He traveled to Tiveria and davened at the *kevarim* of the many tzaddikim there.

> I rose early in the morning to learn and daven in their *zechus*. Basically, I did every single *segulah* (protective kabbalistic charm) that I could think of for the merit of those soldiers. But my heart pounded away anxiously the entire time they were away. I was so worried about them that I even traveled to Lebanon in the middle of the war to visit them and to see how they were doing for myself. I wasn't allowed to go all the way into the battlefield, but I went as far as the army permitted. When one of the officers asked me what I was looking for, I told him that I had come to visit my children.
>
> Immediately the officer gave me a report, even taking out maps

Visiting his "children" in Lebanon

to show me where the platoon was and what they were up to.

"But I need them to know that I was here and that I made the trip to Lebanon especially to see them and to encourage them that my *berachah* will come true…" I told him.

The officer promised to make sure that the soldiers got the message. Then I turned around and returned home.

Two weeks later Rabbi Grossman received a phone call at midnight. Yoni, the commander of the brigade, was on the other end of the line.

"Rabbi Grossman," he said, and his voice was filled with such emotion that it fairly sizzled and crackled through the phone lines, "your promise came true, one hundred percent. We are all safe, every one of us! Nobody died on the battlefield, nobody was injured. We are about to leave from Moshav Shtula near the Lebanese border, and we will be on our way to Migdal Ohr shortly."

"How soon do you think you will arrive?"

"About two-thirty in the morning."

Rabbi Grossman swung into action. He called the kitchen staff and instructed them to prepare a memorable meal for the occasion. Then he began calling around for a band. People were shocked that the rabbi

Back home, safe and well

needed a band at two in the morning. Finally, he reached a wedding band in Afula and asked them if they could be at Migdal Ohr at two-thirty.

"Who plans on dancing at two-thirty in the morning," the band leader wanted to know, "is Mashiach here and I didn't know about it?!"

"Just be here on time."

"Don't worry, Rav Grossman, we will. You can count on us."

The buses rolled up to the campus. The soldiers alighted from the buses. Their faces were still black, still covered with camouflage from the battlefield. The tables were set for them. The band was waiting. One by one the soldiers got off the bus carrying their gear. Instead of heading in the direction of the dormitory and the showers, they made their way over to Rabbi Grossman, who was waiting for them — the expression on his face betraying the depth of his feelings at seeing all "his boys" returning home alive and well.

The soldiers were very emotional. Each one received a warm hug and a loving smile and was treated like a long-lost son. They hugged and kissed him and he hugged and kissed them in return. Fourteen hundred hugs and kisses. The greeting ceremony took hours above and beyond the embraces, because each one of the 700 soldiers wanted to tell Rabbi Grossman about the miracles that had happened to him, the *nissim* (miracles) they had personally witnessed in the course of the war.

Rabbi Grossman was overcome by emotion and joy. It was clear that he was in an extremely uplifted place. Almost every soldier had experienced a personal miracle! The Hand of Hashem was clearly visible among these boys. One of the soldiers, a lawyer, a man who lived on a kibbutz who had had nothing to do with religion until this time, told the rabbi the incredible story of his deliverance, just one of the many miracles that had occurred.

"A bunch of us were hiding in an abandoned house in a small Lebanese village," he began. "We sat in this old Arab house and had to keep still and not do anything to alert the enemy terrorists to the fact that we were close by. We were meant to remain in complete darkness the entire time we were in the house, but one of the boys made a terrible mistake, a life-threatening error that could have destroyed every single one of us inside."

"What did he do?" Rabbi Grossman asked.

"The soldier lit a cigarette," answered the lawyer. "It was one of the stupidest things he could have done, because the slightest flash of light, the most minute smidgen of flame is sufficient to give away your position when everything around you is smothered in complete darkness. The moment the guy lit up, the darkness was broken. The next thing we know, we can hear the sounds of the enemy launching an anti-tank missile straight at our hiding place. One flicker of the lighter was all it took, and an extremely powerful missile is heading straight toward us! There wasn't even time for us to run out of the house! Missiles move much quicker than humans. We heard the missile heading our way. We knew that it was all over. Only seconds remained before the missile would come blasting into our shelter, destroying the house and all of us in a fiery inferno! All this took place so very quickly. We barely had time to register that our lives were almost certainly over.

"And then," the lawyer continued, his voice low and steady, "they came."

"Who came?"

"Horses. Out of the blue, out of nowhere, here come horses galloping into the missile's line of fire. Literally milliseconds before the missile would have blown up the house and all the soldiers inside, those horses jumped in front of the missiles and took the full brunt of the attack on themselves! The horses were blown to smithereens by the missile, while the soldiers were totally fine. Not a scratch, nothing! Saved by the Hand of Hashem! It was clearly something straight from Heaven. No other way to look at it!"

The men had a beautiful meal, an emotional experience for everyone there. When they finished they recited the *Nishmas* prayer together, and all 700 soldiers *bentched Hagomel*, the traditional blessing said upon being saved from a dangerous situation. And then they sang and they danced for hours and hours, only concluding the festivities as the sun rose above the horizon and a new day emerged in Migdal Ohr — the tower of light.

Before they left the campus, Rav Grossman told them about the numerous trips that he'd made to *kivrei tzaddikim* on their behalf, pouring out his heart and davening to Hashem to keep them safe.

"After everything that happened between us," he told them, "we are family, and I expect you to invite me to join you when you make a *simchah* (joyous life event) — be it a bris, bar mitzvah, or wedding." For their part, the paratroopers gave the Rav a present of their own — a phone book with the phone numbers and addresses of every one of the group that they'd carefully prepared for him during the small amount of leisure time they'd had. This present enabled Rabbi Grossman to stay in touch with every single one of them until this very day.

Nowadays a *hachnassas Sefer Torah* is usually accompanied by a musical van leading the way, and so it was here as well. Because Rav Grossman had let every one of "his boys" know that they were expected back at Migdal Ohr three weeks later, for the gala inauguration of the brand new Sefer Torah — every soldier with his wife and children.

A van lit up with festive colors played loud music as it drove slowly in front of them, with the Torah beneath its *chuppah* following behind. All seven hundred soldiers danced with "their" Torah, escorting it, swirling, dancing, looking with love and tears at the beautifully bedecked Torah scroll being held with such tenderness under the silky canopy. They followed it with their eyes as they danced and cavorted, every one of them sharing the sheer joy of survival, and the joy of this, their Sefer Torah.

Rav Grossman writes an "*os*" in the *Sefer Torah*

Years later the army offered Rav Grossman the use of parts of the Sirkin Army base, including the hangar where this story began, for use in his Chag Savea program. The army had heard that he was looking for a big place, and they told him that they wanted to repay him for what he'd done for the soldiers by giving him a large area in the army base. They also sent 100 soldiers each day to assist with the program. Their offer was accepted and thousands of people have donated their time and energy on a yearly basis to help put together the packages of joy that are delivered all across the country.

CHAPTER FIFTY-ONE
Berachos

During his formative years, Rav Grossman developed close relationships with numerous *gedolim*. One of those was Rav Chaim Kreiswirth. Rav Chaim's feelings for the young rabbi were made clear to him during a gathering of rabbanim in Yerushalayim. When Rav Yitzchak Dovid entered the *beis midrash* where the assembly was taking place, Rav Kreiswirth descended from the dais, walked directly to the newcomer, and told him that he wanted to discuss something with him. Needless to say, none of those in the vicinity of the conversation could understand what would make a legendary Torah scholar like Rav Kreiswirth act in such a fashion, seeking the counsel of a person so much younger than himself.

Rav Kreiswirth ignored all the perplexed looks, and asked Rav Grossman to accompany him outside the room so that they would be able to speak privately. Once outside, he explained that a relative of his was very ill and he was requesting that Rav Yitzchak Dovid give him a *berachah*.

"Are you making *leitzanus* (a mockery) of me?" Rav Grossman asked the eminent Rav Kreiswirth incredulously. "You are the *gadol hador,* who am I?"

"Ich veist nisht fun kuntzen — I don't play games," Rav Chaim replied. "The Gemara writes that if someone saves the most precious item in the world — referring to another person's *neshamah* — from a terrible place, Hashem says about such a person, *'k'fi tiheyeh,'* that such a person's mouth should be like Mine. This means that what such a person says, and the *berachos* that he gives, will come true!

Rav Kreiswirth and Rav Grossman in Migdal Ohr

"It is true that I am a greater *talmid chacham* (Torah scholar) than you are," Rav Kreiswirth continued, "but I am not a person who is constantly busy saving the most precious objects in the world from the worst and most degrading places — and you are. The Gemara doesn't say that a *talmid chacham's* mouth is akin to the mouth of Hashem, but the Gemara does say that about someone like you! And that is why I am requesting that you give me your *berachah*."

That encounter made a profound impression on Rav Yitzchak Dovid, for it helped him comprehend the importance of his chosen path in life. If a tzaddik and *gaon* (genius) like Rav Chaim Kreiswirth could speak to him in such a way, surely it was a sign from Heaven that his decision to move to a place like Migdal HaEmek had been correct.

"That interaction with Rav Chaim Kreiswirth," said Reb Nuchum Donner, Rav Grossman's right-hand man for over forty years, "taught the young rabbi of Migdal HaEmek who he was and what he was capable of doing.

"However," continued Rabbi Donner, "that wasn't the only time that a great tzaddik commented on Rav Yitzchak Dovid's unique abilities. When Rav Grossman was a young man, Rav Yitzchak Dovid's father-in-law, Rav Berish Rosenberg, went in to the Lubavitcher Rebbe for a *yechidus* (a special meeting with the Rebbe), handing the Rebbe a paper with the names of every member of his family: sons, sons-in-law, daughters and daughters-in-law. Near the top of the page was the name Yitzchak Dovid ben Guta Perel.

"After examining the list of names," Reb Nuchum continued, "the Rebbe did something which to the best of my knowledge was never done before or after. Picking up a pencil, he wrote two words beside Rav Grossman's name: '*oseh niflaos* — he performs wonders.'

"After the *yechidus*, Rav Yitzchak Dovid's father-in-law left the room. Seeing the Lubavitcher Rebbe's secretary, Rabbi Chadakov, he asked him what the Rebbe was telling him with the addition of those two words.

"'The Rebbe isn't telling you that your son-in-law is a fine person,' he answered. 'That he could have told you directly. The Rebbe just gave your son-in-law the *koach*, the ability, to perform miracles.'"

On one occasion, Rav Yitzchak Dovid needed to go see the Beis Yisrael, the Rebbe of Ger. Rav Yitzchak Dovid was slightly apprehensive about the visit, since he had recently been featured in a documentary on Israeli TV, and he was afraid that the Rebbe was going to rebuke him for having participated in such a thing. He therefore asked his father to accompany him.

When they entered the Rebbe's room, Rav Yisrael told the Rebbe, "This is my son, the Rav of Migdal HaEmek."

The Beis Yisrael turned toward Rav Yitzchak Dovid and said, "*Rabban shel Klal Yisrael* — the rabbi of the entire nation!"

Seeing that the Beis Yisrael was not upset with him, Rav Yitzchak Dovid had a conversation with the Rebbe. Before he left, he asked the Beis Yisrael for a *berachah*.

"You don't need my *berachos*," the Beis Yisrael replied. "You are a Rebbe, and you can give *berachos* of your own! A person who saves Yidden and does *kiruv* should know that the *koach* of giving *berachos* is given to him!"

Indeed, Rav Yitzchak Dovid's *berachos* seem to have a special power, which he often ascribes to the *zechus* of "his" tens of thousands of children. Wherever it comes from, the power is there — as you'll see in the following incidents.

Another day, another phone call. This one was from a woman in Kfar Chassidim.

"Rav Grossman?"

"Yes?"

"I am calling on behalf of a neighbor of mine."

"What's the problem?"

"She has been married for over twenty years and hasn't yet been blessed with a child. There were many misses along the way and many disappointments."

"Go on," he said.

"After twenty years, the Ribbono shel Olam saw fit to bestow the greatest gift in the world on this couple, and they were blessed with a baby girl. However, after one day, while still in the hospital, the baby contracted a virus and passed away!"

Rav Yitzchak Dovid listened with empathy, his heart going out to the parents who had just had the dream of their lifetime snatched away from them.

The woman continued the sad tale. "This brand new mother is made from incredibly powerful stuff and she didn't break. Instead, she approached the nurses and made a request.

"'Before you take my daughter away for burial,' she told them, 'I would like to hold her in my arms and feel her one last time.'

"The nurses agreed and the mother stood in the hospital ward holding her baby daughter in her arms. She then began to talk to Hashem.

"'Ribbono shel Olam,' she said, 'Only You know the agony of what we went through during the last twenty years. You know how many doctors' appointments I had. You know the disappointment and the shame. And now after twenty years, You gave me a daughter. Yet at the same time, You have decided in Your infinite wisdom to take her away from me. Before I send her away, I want to give my baby a name. I want to call my daughter Emunah. This way, whenever I recall that I had a daughter, I will also have the opportunity to focus on my *emunah* (faith) at the same time, and to remember that I trust that every single thing that Hashem does is for the best.'

"It was an absolutely incredible speech — unlike anything the hospital staff had ever heard from a bereaved parent.

"The reason I am calling you," she concluded, "is I wanted to ask the rav whether he'd be willing to call Emunah's mother and strengthen her in her great moment of trial."

Of course, he agreed.

Rav Grossman had barely finished introducing himself when the bereaved mother began to sob. At the same time, she couldn't stop thanking him for taking the time to call her.

"Can I ask the rav a question?"

"Please do," he encouraged her.

"Can the Rav please explain to me the idea of *gilgul neshamos* (reincarnation)? If Hashem gave me a baby and then took her back, it seems like she must have been a *gilgul*. Would the Rav be able to clarify this for me?"

"I am not the person to explain *gilgulim* to you," he said, "but there is something else that I can tell you."

"What's that?"

"At the time that you were holding your baby and you said those awe-inspiring words to the Ribbono shel Olam — naming your baby Emunah after twenty years of such monumental pain and agony — I have no doubt that your words resounded across all the heavenly worlds, and that even the *malachim* and *serafim* (angels) were shocked and shaken! I am sure that the words you said caused a furor up in heaven, and that all were astonished over the fact that a mere woman of flesh and blood could possibly speak this way!

"And since I am sure that this was the case, I want to give you a *berachah*, that in the merit of what you have done, you should merit to have a healthy son in the year to come!"

The conversation came to an end shortly after that. Rav Grossman had given her a blessing — which he felt was the least that he could do — and now it was up to the Master of the World to decide where He wanted to go with this.

Time passed. It was Chol HaMo'ed Succos and Rav Yitzchak Dovid was sitting in his succah, which he tries not to leave throughout the festival. Suddenly a couple entered the succah. The woman was holding a small boy in her arms. The moment she caught sight of Rav Grossman, she burst into tears.

"Kevod HaRav," she said, *"El hana'ar hazeh hispalalti*! This is the child that you blessed us with! A healthy boy!"

Rav Yitzchak Dovid with the little boy whose mother had *emunah*

She then related the story to the guests sitting in the succah. Of course, Rav Yitzchak Dovid had to pose for pictures with the child in his arms. It was an incredibly emotional moment in a place used to emotional moments.

Rav Grossman was in his living room meeting with two lawyers, when he heard knocking on his front door. The lawyers had come to consult with the rav about the halachic and Torah angle of a particular case, and they were deep in conversation when the interruption came. Standing in the doorway was a young couple, and it was obvious to the rabbi from the looks on their faces and the tears in their eyes that something tragic had occurred — something that they weren't equipped to handle.

"I am in the middle of a meeting," he told them, "but since I see that you are dealing with some sort of crisis, I will tell the people that we need to take a break and then you can tell me what happened."

When they were seated together, the wife opened her mouth to speak and immediately burst into tears. When she had calmed down a little she explained that she was expecting a baby, and that they had learned that it was very sick.

"We are not religious people," she told the rav, "and I do not see myself being able to raise such a child! We already have three children, and I do not have the energy to care for such a medically challenged child!"

"What are you saying?" he asked her.

"I am saying that I do not feel capable of raising such a baby and I want to terminate the pregnancy."

"And?"

"And my husband doesn't agree. At all. We have an appointment tomorrow to go to the hospital for the procedure, but my husband is completely against this, and begged me to come and see you before we do anything. I gave in and that is why we are here."

"You are already in a later month," Rav Grossman said to the mother. "At this stage, the baby is unquestionably alive and a real person according to every school of thought. How then can you even consider murdering a living human being?"

"So what should we do?"

"I will tell you. My youngest daughter runs an institution for children with the exact diagnosis as your baby — and I promise you that when your baby is born, if it really has the condition the doctor thinks it does, I will take it myself to my daughter's institution and you won't have to deal with it at all!"

"I am not okay with your idea," the mother protested. "I refuse to bring a child into the world whom I am not prepared to raise. I will not bring a child into this world only for him to spend his life in some home for sick people!"

She was adamant.

Rav Grossman looked at the distraught mother and realized that all of the things that he normally told people in her situation to calm them down were not going to work in this case. Suddenly he felt a certain indefinable sense of spiritual understanding flood his very being. Taking the mother over to the side of the dining room, he showed her the *aron kodesh* that he kept there

"Do you see this *aron kodesh*?" he asked her.

"Yes."

"What does it contain?"

"Sifrei Torah."

Looking the couple in the eye, Rav Yitzchak Dovid Grossman said, "If you both promise me that you will begin to keep the laws of family purity, and that you will dedicate your lives to helping other Jewish people, I promise you that you will have a completely healthy baby."

Amazingly, unexpectedly, the couple accepted the deal.

There was a platter of cake on the dining room table. Rav Yitzchak Dovid took two pieces of cake and wrapped them in a napkin. Handing the napkin to the father of the child, Rav Grossman said, "I want you to give this cake back to me when I am serving as the *sandek* (godfather) at his bris!"

After they left, with thanks and new hope in their hearts, Rav Grossman returned to his original meeting. "Rav Yitzchak Dovid," one of the lawyers said to him, "forgive me, but sitting here we were able to hear your conversation and the promise that you made to that couple. How could you have made such a promise? How could you have possibly taken such a responsibility on your shoulders?"

"I don't know how to answer you," he replied. "All I can say is that my promise came from a place of deep feeling and emotion. My entire being was aroused and I couldn't ignore the situation. Basically, I had no choice. Besides, I believe that Hashem will hear my prayer in the *zechus* of all the children who are being helped in Migdal Ohr — children who have become mine, in every sense of the word."

There was nothing left to say.

The call came a few months later.

"Rav Grossman?"

"Yes?"

"Our son was born a few minutes ago. He is completely healthy, just as you promised us!"

Of course, Rav Grossman was called up to serve as *sandek* at the bris. Afterward, surrounded by a crowd asking for his *berachah*, Rav Yitzchak Dovid suddenly felt the father of the baby grab his hand. He handed the Rav a napkin.

"You said to me that I needed to give this to the Rav, when the Rav serves as the *sandek*. Here it is."

He handed Rav Yitzchak Dovid Grossman the very same pieces of cake that he had given them on the fateful night when their baby's life had been saved. They were a little stale — and without question, some of the best cake anyone ever ate.

אינדקס
העמק והגליל
מי שלא רצה אותו כראש עיר
יקבל אותו כחבר כנסת.
עמוד: 28
הבאבא
גרוסמן
רבה הראשי של מגדל העמק הרב
תושבת העיר אשר כל הרופאים קבעו
כי בנה יוולד עם תסמונת דאון, לא
להפילו. השבוע הוזמן הרב גרוסמן
לשמש כסנדקו של התינוק הבריא.
זל טוב.
עמוד: 22

A local Migdal HaEmek newspaper shares the news: The "Baba Grossman" convinced her to have the baby — and the baby was born completely healthy!

Reb Nuchum Donner has seen so many examples of the power of Rav Grossman's *berachos*. Here is one such story:

We were on a fundraising trip to Mexico and went into an office building to meet with one of the businessmen. There we came upon a secretary sitting at a desk. She had obviously been crying. Of course, Rav Grossman couldn't stop himself and asked her what was wrong.

"My ex-husband gave me a *get* (divorce) today."

Rav Yitzchak Dovid didn't miss a beat.

"Don't cry," he replied. "I promise you that you are going to become a *kallah* (bride) to the best *chassan* (groom) in the world. And I will officiate at the wedding as your *mesader kiddushin*."

"This year?"

"This year. Before the next Rosh Hashanah."

Rosh Hashanah was about eight months away at the time.

I had seen this a million times and it never ceased to amaze me. Rav Grossman was able to meet a person and become their best friend — and promise them a miracle — all without worrying how he was going to be able to keep his part of the deal!

The months flew by. Although I live in Boro Park, I had come to Eretz Yisrael a week before Rosh Hashanah to produce a film for Migdal Ohr. One afternoon I was filming in the Golan, and when we were done for the day I got in the car and began driving back to Yerushalayim. I was passing near Migdal HaEmek on the highway, about two kilometers away from Rav Grossman's house, when my phone rang.

I answered. It was Rav Yitzchak Dovid.

"Nuchum?"

"Yes?"

"*Vi bist du?* — Where are you?"

"I am on my way back from the Golan. Right now I am stopped at a red light just outside Migdal HaEmek."

"Pull over to the side of the highway," he said, "and wait for me. I'm going to meet you in five minutes."

A few minutes later his driver deposited him by my car, and he got inside and handed me directions to a wedding hall.

"Nuchum, I need you to step on it. We have to get to this wedding as soon as possible."

As we drove, Rav Grossman said, "Do you remember the secretary that we met in Mexico about eight months ago?"

"Of course."

"She found a *shidduch*, really a truly incredible match, and the wedding is taking place as we speak."

"Who is the *chassan*?"

"A successful lawyer here in Eretz Yisrael, from a fine family."

"So your promise to her came true."

"*Baruch Hashem.* The problem was — she called the office and asked the secretary to remind me that I had not only promised her that she would get engaged to the best *chassan* in the world before Rosh Hashanah, but that I would also serve as the *mesader kiddushin* at the wedding. The secretary asked me if I was available on the night of the wedding, but I checked my calendar and saw that I was going to be at an important event in Los Angeles. Meanwhile the *kallah* was in touch with my staff, telling them that her father had suffered a heart attack and was unable to attend her wedding, and she feels like she is going to her wedding without any close family.

"*Baruch Hashem,* at the last second something happened and I didn't have to go to LA, freeing me up to be able to surprise the *kallah* at her wedding here — which is tonight. Right now, she is at her wedding, thinking that I am in LA — while I am here and about to bring a gigantic smile to her face when I surprise her!"

I saw tremendous *siyata d'Shmaya* (Divine assistance) on the roads that evening. I was able to reach Yerushalayim from Migdal HaEmek in record time. Once in the city I had no idea where to go. Every time we hit a light I asked the rabbi, "Right, left, or straight?"

His eyes were closed and he wasn't looking at the road. Despite that, he answered me every time, telling me how to drive.

"Right."

Then, "Left."

He wasn't even looking where we were going, yet somehow, his directions took me straight to the hall! I had never seen anything like this. He was like a spiritual GPS!

Eventually I reached a sloping road lined with candles, which I understood would lead us to the actual hall. I drove up the road, and arrived at the gravel parking lot, which was filled with what looked like five hundred luxury cars. I hadn't even parked, and Rav Yitzchak Dovid told me to let him out. Then he was off and running in his typical fashion toward the *chuppah*.

When Rav Yitzchak Dovid arrived at the *chuppah*, he found another rabbi holding the cup of wine in his hand, serving in the role of *mesader kiddushin*, ready to begin reciting the *berachos*. When the rabbi caught sight of Rav Yitzchak Dovid entering the hall, he put down the cup and said, "*Kevod HaRav*, we would be honored if you would read the *kesubah* (marriage contract)."

Obviously Rav Yitzchak Dovid agreed (he wasn't about to start arguing in the middle of the *chuppah*) and he went to stand near the edge of the *chuppah*.

The *mesader kiddushin* lifted the cup of wine in his hand and prepared to begin reciting the *berachos*. Amazingly, though his mouth was open and he was trying to speak, no sound emerged!

Somehow comprehending that the roles at this particular *chuppah* needed to be reversed, the rabbi handed the glass of wine to Rav Grossman and said, "Please take over and serve as the *mesader kiddushin*."

And Rav Yitzchak Dovid acquiesced, thereby fulfilling the second promise that he'd made to the secretary months earlier in Mexico.

"You cannot imagine the glow on the face of that *kallah*," Reb Nuchum ends the story. "It was not to be believed. Throughout the wedding, she went from person to person telling them of Rav Yitzchak Dovid's promises to her. 'Both of his promises came true,' she repeated over and over.

"It was yet another reminder that when Rav Yitzchak Dovid makes a promise, it's something to take seriously."

It was Erev Rosh Hashanah (the day before Rosh Hashanah), and this author called Rav Grossman to wish him a good year. During the course of our conversation, he shared still another "miracle" story with me, one that had occurred not long before.

> This past Tuesday we were in the middle of a crisis in one of our programs. My entire living and dining room were filled with the program's staff, and we were trying to figure out how to address the situation we were dealing with. It was one of the most complicated situations I could remember, and we were sitting in my house trying to work things out when the doorbell rang. It was an American couple who had last been in my home fourteen years earlier.
>
> I took them into a side room to speak with them and give them a *berachah*. We spoke for a few minutes, and at one point they told me that one of their sons is a commercial pilot. I don't know what came over me. I said, "A pilot! That's such a dangerous occupation! I need to give your son a *berachah* that he should be safe!"
>
> Closing my eyes, I said, "*Esah einai el heharim* — I lift my eyes up to the heavens — Ribbono shel Olam, please look after this young man! May he be healthy and well, and may he be successful in everything that he does!"
>
> The couple was clearly a little taken aback at my reaction to their son's way of earning a livelihood, and when we emerged from the room, they asked one of the people there if everything was okay and if I was all right. They left my home soon afterward.
>
> As I heard from the couple the day after their visit, two hours after they'd left, their son, the pilot, tried to come in for a landing, when he realized that the landing gear was not responding to his repeated commands and wouldn't open! He tried everything he could think of to get the craft to land safely, but in the end he was forced to land without the gear — ON THE BELLY OF THE PLANE — which skidded along the runway.
>
> The entire plane was wrecked beyond repair, but the pilot himself miraculously walked away from the scene of the accident, completely healthy and well!

"Rav Yitzchak Dovid," I said to him, after I heard the tale. "You know that there have been many times during the course of your life when you have given *berachos* to people and they have been fulfilled. Why do you think that is? To what can you attribute your unique ability to give *berachos* that actually work?"

He was quiet, listening to what I was telling him.

Without landing gear — the plane was wrecked, but the pilot came out without a scratch.

I then said, "I will tell you what I think the reason is. I think the reason Hashem gives you such a *zechus* is because you have sacrificed so much for the children of Klal Yisrael your entire life. You have traveled the world to make sure thousands of children have what they need. Your every thought from morning till night is 'What can I do for my children?'

"I think that Hashem really appreciates what you do for His children, and rewards you with the special and unique power that you have as a way of showing you that He is happy with you and that He wants you to carry on."

"I was so exhausted from all the stress before you called," Rav Grossman told me when I finished speaking, "but now I am feeling revived. As if you have given me an ice-cold glass of water when I was walking through the middle of the desert."

We spoke for a few minutes more and then we wished each other a *gut gebensht yuhr*, a blessed new year. After all, it was Erev Rosh Hashanah and there was still much to do…

CHAPTER FIFTY-TWO

In the Footsteps of Reb Elimelech

In the month of Adar of 2008, Rav Yitzchak Dovid went to spend a Shabbos in Lizhensk just prior to the *yahrtzeit* of the *heilige* (holy) Rebbe Reb Elimelech. He was not alone. Thousands of people had traveled to Lizhensk from all over the world, and the atmosphere at the *kever* was one of uplifting excitement.

The *chazzan* had just begun chanting *"Lechu Neranenah,"* the opening words of *Kabbalas Shabbos*, when Rav Grossman suddenly felt an inexplicable urge to immediately leave the premises. This was easier said than done, since the shul was packed and there was no clear path to exit the building. Had he chosen a place not too far from the door he might have found it difficult but still manageable to leave, but Rav Grossman had arrived early enough to find a spot all the way up front, which meant that it was virtually impossible to get out. But Rav Yitzchak Dovid had long learned to trust his instincts and they were telling him to go outside now!

Somehow, he managed to do so.

Once outside, he looked around him and tried to comprehend what instinct had propelled him to come out into the crisp night air. Moments later he understood. Driving toward him were three buses — all about to pull over and allow their passengers to disembark outside the *kever* of the Rebbe Reb Elimelech on a Friday night!

"Who could possibly be driving to the *kever* now, just as Shabbos begins?" Rav Grossman asked himself.

The answer was not long in coming. The buses were inching down the road and he could see dozens of Israeli students inside. A few seconds later he realized that they were part of a program organized by the Israeli Ministry of Education, which brought students from Israel to Poland, taking them to heartrending places like Auschwitz and Majdanek, but also to happy and uplifting places like the *kever* of the Rebbe Reb Elimelech.

Rav Grossman was of the opinion that every Jewish student should be encouraged to visit places like Lizhensk. But driving into such a place on a Friday night was not the most intelligent of moves — and it wasn't long before some of the chassidim from one of the many minyanim in the area were emerging to see what was going on. It also didn't take long for the initial shouts of "Shabbos! Shabbos," to be heard. You didn't have to be the world's smartest person to figure out what was about to happen here — at the grave of the Yid who had been one of the greatest defenders of the Jewish people's actions that Klal Yisrael had ever known, the one who could find something positive in every single Jew.

Rav Grossman could already picture the screaming and the yelling, and he knew that this could easily lead to fist fights — and if that occurred, they were looking at the headlines in tomorrow's Israeli papers. Running across the street to where the group of yellers was standing, Rav Yitzchak Dovid placed himself directly in front of them, and sternly ordered them inside the shul in a voice that brooked no refusal.

"I will take care of this," he told them, while simultaneously motioning to the Polish bus drivers not to park adjacent to the *kever*. The drivers obeyed the long-bearded rabbi and parked the buses further along, where they opened the doors and allowed the students to disembark.

A few minutes later Rav Grossman addressed the group of students and their counselors. "I don't have any complaints against you. You are not at fault for what is happening here. But I do have a serious complaint against the people who organized your program. Right now, all of you are here in Poland on what is called a Tiyul Shorashim, a trip to discover your roots. How can people be sent on a trip to discover their roots, while trampling and uprooting the very roots they are meant to discover?

"While you are not at fault here, it still wouldn't be okay for you to enter the *tziyun* right now, when it is obvious that you have arrived on Shabbos. We will find you a place to stay while your guides talk to you."

Rav Grossman was very upset at the Israeli Education Ministry, and he resolved to make a major issue about it when he returned to Israel. In the meantime, this seemed the best way to handle the situation.

However, he hadn't counted on the kids themselves.

With tears in many of their eyes, they approached him and said, "*Kevod HaRav*, we prepared notes with our prayers and our requests for blessings, and we were looking forward to leaving them at the grave of the *tzaddik*!"

They spoke with *temimus* — a pure naiveté that found favor in the rabbi's eyes.

"You know what," he said to them, "give me the notes and I will place them near the *tzaddik*."

The students stood in a circle and Rav Grossman walked from teenager to teenager, his hands cupped and open to receive their notes. Suddenly a student named Doron burst into tears and refused to place his note in Rav Yitzchak Dovid's outstretched hands.

"I have been preparing for a long time to go into the *tzaddik* and I want to be the one to bring my note to his *kever*!"

"When I saw Doron's tears," Rav Grossman remembers, "and how seriously the others were taking their visit to the *tziyun* of Reb Elimelech, I said to them, '*Chevrah*, follow me! I will bring you inside!' "

I don't know what's going to happen now, he thought to himself, *but with the kind of pure emunah that these kids are showing, there is no way I can refuse them entrance to the Rebbe Reb Elimelech. The people inside are going to have to understand!*

"Let them in and bring them close," Rav Yitzchak Dovid cried out to the chassidim standing inside the shul, who moved aside as much as they were able to allow as many students inside as possible. The boys went to one side, the girls to the other.

"Most of the chassidim inside were Vizhnitzers. Vizhnitz is a Chassidus that is built on *ahavas Yisrael*, on love for the Jewish people,"

Rav Grossman said, when remembering that night, "and as the students entered the shul, they were made to feel welcome. The minyan was already in the middle of davening and the people inside the room were singing and dancing. The newcomers joined without hesitation, joining hands with the chassidim and dancing with enthusiasm, as if they had been doing this their entire lives! This continued for the entire time that they remained inside the *tziyun* — which wasn't very long — because soon their counselors appeared and told them that it was time to leave. Minutes later they were gone."

When the davening was over and the Shabbos meal had begun, an argument broke out among the people whether Rav Grossman's approach had been the correct one, or whether the buses should have been greeted with shouts of "Shabbos!" and the students chased away. It wasn't long before there were two camps debating the argument. Eventually it reached the point where Rav Yitzchak Dovid decided to give a little speech explaining why he had chosen to welcome the students instead of using the opposite approach.

Rising to his feet, he began his speech with a story from the Gemara.

> The Gemara in *Sanhedrin* tells us about a group of ruffians who lived in the neighborhood of Rav Zeira, who instead of pushing them away, did his best to be *mekareiv* them and draw them close, despite the fact that many of the other sages were unhappy with his decision. The Gemara relates how after Rav Zeira passed away, the ruffians said to themselves, "Until now, Rav Zeira used to take care of us and daven for us. Who will daven for us now that he is gone?"
>
> In response to their new situation, they decided to do *teshuvah* and repent so that they would be able to daven for themselves.
>
> This means that the fact that Rav Zeira drew them close caused all those people to end up doing *teshuvah*.
>
> I want to tell you something else. I grew up watching the master of *chesed* Rav Aryeh Levin, who was a legendary figure of kindness in Yerushalayim. One time, Rav Aryeh met a Jew in the street who was smoking on Shabbos. When he realized that Rav Aryeh had seen his cigarette, the man tried to hide it behind his back. Rav Aryeh, for his part, acted as if he hadn't noticed anything. Instead of commenting about the cigarette, he shook the man's hand and

gave him a warm "Good Shabbos." The man immediately threw his cigarette onto the ground and accepted upon himself to keep Shabbos in the future in the way it was meant to be kept. Do you know why he decided to begin keeping Shabbos? It was because of Rav Aryeh's warm greeting and his smile and the fact that he treated him with respect and love.

Rav Yitzchak Dovid could see that the people were listening and he decided to share one more story along the same theme.

> I used to pass a neighbor of mine mowing his lawn every single Shabbos morning when I left my house to walk to shul. Every time I saw him, I did the same thing, wishing him a warm "Shabbat Shalom." I did this, week in and week out. One Shabbos morning, I left the house and realized that he wasn't out mowing the lawn like every week. I soon discovered the reason for his absence from a different neighbor.
>
> He told me that I had walked by the week before and wished this neighbor a "Shabbat Shalom," like I always did. But because the lawn mower was so noisy the neighbor didn't hear me. So I repeated myself and called out even louder, "Reuven, you didn't hear me, I wished you a 'Shabbat Shalom!'"
>
> Reuven then said to his neighbor, "If the Rav can wish me 'Shabbat Shalom' twice, while ignoring the fact that I am mowing my lawn, I no longer want to do this on Shabbat."

"Do you understand what I am telling you?" Rav Grossman said to the others. "If you want to get through to people, the only way that really works is with patience and love. And definitely not by yelling and screaming. Love, warmth, and kindness are what will bring our people back."

Not long after he arrived home, Rav Yitzchak Dovid received letters from several of the students who had been on the trip to the *tziyun* of Reb Elimelech. This was one of them.

> *Dear Rav Grossman,*
>
> *I just wanted to thank you for treating our group with such love and respect and for going out of your way to protect us and to help bring us inside the kever (when so many of the other people there were upset with us for arriving when we did). I know that I will*

never forget the way you acted for the rest of my life, and I want you to know that I decided to begin keeping Shabbat.

The other letters contained similar messages.

Love, warmth, and kindness had won again.

CHAPTER FIFTY-THREE

Halftime Show at MSG

The average Israeli takes great pride whenever one of their national teams does well in a sports competition against another country. On the evening of the game, gigantic screens are erected all over the country and thousands gather to watch the match, cheering when their side scores a point and groaning loudly when the home team loses.

Rav Yitzchak Dovid was not raised in a home where sports was a topic for discussion, and it was only after he had grown up and was exposed to people who had been raised differently than he, that he came to understand that such a pull existed. But the whole idea of sports competition was really brought home to him on the night when Maccabi Tel Aviv played their Russian equivalent, CSKA Moscow, in an exciting game of basketball that must have been watched by half the country.

The rabbi hadn't even known about the European championship, which was why he was taken aback when his "tzaddikim" came knocking on his door after he'd already taken off his shoes for the night. In response to the heavy banging, Rav Yitzchak Dovid opened up the door to see a huge gathering of the *chevrah*. They were smiling from ear to ear and in a buoyant mood, ebulliently singing at the top of their lungs. Still not grasping what had occurred to have made everyone quite this happy, the rabbi was surrounded by his tzaddikim as they chanted, "*Yesh Elokim, Yesh Elokim* (there is a G-d)."

Whisking the rabbi away from his home, they gently placed Rav Yitzchak Dovid on the roof of a nearby car which began to drive slowly, while about fifty young men surrounded the car still yelling *"Yesh Elokim"* at full volume.

Maybe there was a terrorist attack that was prevented in time, he thought to himself. *Better yet, maybe Mashiach (the Messiah) just arrived! What could have happened to have put the boys in such a mood?!*

It wasn't long before the truth emerged and the rabbi discovered that Maccabi Tel Aviv had just played the Russian team. This was a major event due to the fact that the two countries were not the greatest of friends at that time. The year was 1977 — the Cold War was still extremely frigid — and the European Championship was played in full view of the entire world, with Israel taking home the win.

"Rabbi, do you want to know how it went?" they asked him.

"Why not."

"Well, the game was tight, the action fast, both teams neck and neck. Then Tal Brody scored the winning basket."

Tal Brody was Israel's star player at the time. Ironically, he was an American. He became hugely famous all over the country with a line he delivered in his unmistakably thick American accent, *"Anachnu al hamapah, v'anachnu nisharim al hamapah* — We are on the map and we are staying on the map!" Brody's words would go down in Israeli sports history, quoted by many and relished and enjoyed due to the deeper meaning of what they represented. Here was a victory on the part of the underdog — a classic example of the weak against the mighty. Statistically speaking, the Israeli team hadn't had a chance, yet they'd pulled it off — and the boys of Migdal HaEmek were ecstatic.

"You should have heard the announcer," they said enthusiastically.

"Was he good?"

"He was fantastic. He was so quick with the play-by-play, getting every listener into the game, sucking them in by virtue of his contagious excitement. And then when Tal Brody went up for the final shot of the game and Israel won, the announcer gave a mighty scream that resounded from one corner of the country to the other, bellowing out the words, *'Yesh Elokim,* there is a G-d' — a chant and cry that was echoed by one and all."

In Tel Aviv, people threw themselves into the pools of water near the city's municipality building, shrieking with joy at having successfully defeated their rivals. The *chevrah* in Migdal HaEmek, also wanting to join the national festivities, gave vent to their feelings by putting their rabbi on top of a car and dancing around him, all the while telling the world that there is a G-d. It was a wild night and Rav Yitzchak Dovid was only delivered back home hours later.

In the days to come, Rav Grossman grew increasingly intrigued by Tal Brody, and he decided to reach out to him. Catching the ball player on the phone, the rabbi introduced himself and told Mr. Brody that he wanted to meet with him. The meeting led to Rav Yitzchak Dovid inviting Brody to come and visit Migdal Ohr, an invitation he accepted, visiting Migdal Ohr along with his wife. It wasn't long before the rabbi and the basketball star had formed a very close relationship.

Over the years, Rav Yitzchak Dovid became a familiar face around the world, and he was inevitably stopped whenever Israelis caught sight of him, wherever they might be. This happened very often in the United States, where so many Israelis made new lives for themselves after finishing their army service. And every time he exchanged a few words with yet another not-yet-religious Israeli, Rav Grossman told himself yet again that he really should be doing something — reaching out as it were — to the many Yidden who were living lives completely devoid of any connection to *Yiddishkeit* (Jewish observance).

The big question was what to do and where to do it. Rav Yitzchak Dovid lived in Eretz Yisrael and was usually busy with his thousands of children. He didn't have time to run around the United States giving unlimited classes. And the US is one big country. No. The connection would have to be made with as many Israelis as possible in one location.

And then an idea came to him. An idea which, while possessing merit, would be incredibly challenging to pull off. Yet if by some chance he could make it happen, he would be given the chance to speak to tens of thousands of Israelis at the same time — live.

The idea?

To bring Maccabi Tel Aviv, Israel's premier basketball team, to New York and have them play the New York Knicks at Madison Square Garden in an exhibition game that no self-respecting Israeli would want to miss.

Once the idea had entered the world, Rav Yitzchak Dovid's next move was to figure out how to move it from the realm of theory and into the realm of reality. He considered the matter for a while, and in the end decided this was not that different from anything else in life. If the issue on the table had been one of politics, Rav Yitzchak Dovid would

The Rav and Tal Brody

have turned to one of the many top-ranking politicians he was friends with. Here too, he decided to go straight to the top — to Tal Brody, the man who had won the European championship for Israel against Moscow — the man who had uttered the famous line about Israel being on the map to stay.

"I had a good idea," he told Brody.

"What kind of an idea?"

"Maccabi Tel Aviv has never visited America."

"That's correct."

"Imagine for a second that they flew into the States and played a game of basketball against the New York Knicks. Do you think Israelis would be interested in seeing such a game?"

"Sure."

"Okay, that's part one of my idea."

"What's the second part?" Brody asked.

"The second part is this. After the game in New York, I want Maccabi Tel Aviv to get on a plane and fly out to LA, where they will play the Los Angeles Clippers. This way I will be able to speak with thousands of Israelis in New York and thousands of Israelis in California."

Knicks vs. Maccabi TA:
A poster advertising the basketball game

Tal Brody loved the idea and promised to reach out to his contacts at the Knicks and Clippers, especially after Migdal Ohr's New York office undertook to be involved in advertising the games and in selling the tickets for both sporting events.

Which is how Rav Yitzchak Dovid Grossman came to deliver a rousing speech during half-time while standing in the center of MSG's gleaming hardwood floor.

Instead of people leaving the arena in the middle of the game to replenish their popcorn and soda supply, everyone was asked to remain in their seats and to get ready for a wonderful surprise. Meanwhile the house lights were dimmed in anticipation of whatever exciting event was about to begin. The next thing the spectators knew, Rav Yitzchak Dovid had entered the arena, cordless mike in hand, and he was singing a song that everyone sitting there knew: "*Od avinu chai, od avinu chai, Am Yisrael, Am Yisrael, Am Yisrael chai!*"

Seconds later twenty thousand people had joined in, belting out the words to the famous song. And when they saw who it was who was singing with them, the entire arena began to smile, because their favorite rabbi had come all the way from Eretz Yisrael to sing and spend time with them.

Rav Grossman didn't speak at length that night. It wasn't the time or place. Instead, he gave a short yet powerful speech, exhorting the Israelis in the audience to reconnect with the Ribbono shel Olam, giving them an *emunah* jolt and reminding the crowd of the timeless message of *Shema Yisrael*. The Garden was filled with the enduring words of Klal Yisrael's credo, as sung by many people who hadn't davened in a very long time, but who were suddenly filled with a very real inspiration and desire to be connected to their roots.

The sound of twenty thousand voices singing full strength made the very walls and floor shake. And they weren't only singing, since the majority of the huge crowd was up, standing on their feet, some even dancing in their places. As for the basketball players watching from the sidelines — many of them were sure that the rabbi with the long white beard and piercing eyes was an angel himself! It was a phenomenal night — a night that anyone who had the good fortune to have been part of, knew they would never forget.

This being *Olam Hazeh*, there had to be a wrinkle somewhere along the way, and a story developed in the middle of the game that was not only talked about by everyone back in Israel, but by pretty much anyone interested in sports.

It all began with Pini Gershon. Gershon was the coach of Maccabi Tel Aviv and was in the arena giving directions to his team as he always did.

And I quote…

> A slew of calls had been going against Maccabi when New York's Al Harrington was whistled for an offensive foul with 5:05 remaining in the third quarter, right in front of the Maccabi bench, for pushing off with his elbow. Perhaps not realizing the call was being made in favor of his team, Gershon started screaming at replacement referee Ben Taylor, who immediately whistled Gershon for his second technical foul and gave him the heave-ho signal.
>
> But Gershon immediately made it clear that he was not leaving, standing upright in front of his bench and shaking his head "no" — even after security officials from the NBA and Madison Square Garden tried to coax him off the floor.
>
> As Taylor stayed away, referees Victor Montgomery and Williams Mensah also tried unsuccessfully to convince Gershon to leave, and an elderly rabbi from an Israeli charity that sponsored the game came onto the court and pleaded with the NBA referees to reverse their call.
>
> "He's not leaving," said Maccabi forward Yaniv Green, a former Pistons summer league player who was clearly amused by the turn of events.
>
> — *Chris Sheridan writing for ESPN*

Rav Yitzchak Dovid watched in horror as Pini Gershon was ordered out of the arena and stubbornly refused to obey the NBA referees,

Rav Grossman and Pini Gershon

knowing that he wasn't from America and that there was not much they could do to him.

That, however, was not the point.

Rav Grossman had worked tirelessly to arrange the event for the purpose of making a *kiddush Hashem* and for the purpose of drawing the audience closer to their Father in Heaven. There was no question that should Gershon not leave, it would put a major damper on the proceedings. Many people came forward begging Pini to leave the arena and not to cause a huge rift, but he refused, ignoring one and all.

With the entire arena watching, Rav Yitzchak Dovid approached Pini Gershon. Putting his hand on the coach's shoulder like a good friend, the rabbi said, "Pini'le, we can't afford to embarrass ourselves here. For the sake of Hashem and for Migdal Ohr, please listen to the refs and do as they ask so that this event goes down as a *kiddush Hashem* and not the opposite."

Rav Yitzchak Dovid breathed a sigh of relief when Pini finally agreed to obey the referees and leave the arena. It had been a close call.

Back home, the media was abuzz with talk about the game and Gershon's argument with the American refs. But Rav Yitzchak Dovid didn't care about any of that. The main thing was the fact that the game was a success and the Israelis in the audience were walking away with an infusion of a Torah message.

And then it was time to drive to the airport and to board another flight — this one headed to LAX — for the big Maccabi Tel Aviv versus L.A. Clippers game. Here too, it was a very similar night. An action-packed game and a half-time speech by the esteemed visitor. Songs, *divrei Torah,* and a powerful message. The major difference in L.A. was that Pini Gershon got along with the referees and nothing untoward happened.

The incident that took place on the MSG court was widely reported in the media, with nobody failing to notice the white-bearded and charismatic rabbi who hadn't shied away from saving the day — in the nick of time.

As quoted in the Associated Press:

> NEW YORK — The president of Maccabi Tel Aviv has apologized to the NBA and the Knicks for its coach's behavior during an exhibition game at Madison Square Garden.
>
> Pini Gershon, the coach, also said he was sorry in letters that were sent Monday to league Commissioner David Stern and Knicks president Donnie Walsh, and seen by The Associated Press.
>
> "Having had time to reflect on my actions while our team was in New York, I would like to apologize to the New York Knicks franchise, the NBA and basketball fans not only at Madison Square Garden but throughout the country," Gershon wrote.
>
> "Our trip to the U.S. was for a wonderful cause — the children of Migdal Ohr — and hopefully a few minutes of bad behavior on my behalf won't detract from all the good that was accomplished by our spirited competition with the Knicks and the Clippers..."

For years afterward and even today, Rav Yitzchak Dovid runs into people who were at those games and they tell him about the inspiration they felt while sitting in the audience. Some of them tell him how being there at his half-time speech led them to begin taking on long-forgotten mitzvos. Some began putting on tefillin after a hiatus of many years. Others began attending services at their shuls. Many of the children who were there walked out of the arenas both in New York and in L.A. feeling pride in being Jewish.

It was a fine culmination of Maccabi's win against Moscow years earlier, on the night when Rav Yitzchak Dovid had been lifted up by the "tzaddikim" who danced him through the streets, singing *"Yesh Elokim."*

That two-word slogan seemed to be the general consensus as well during Rav Yitzchak Dovid's two basketball games in the States. And the ramifications still continue to ripple until this very day. That, you see, is the way it works. You do your part, and let Hashem worry about the rest.

Since the plan had worked out so well and with such *siyata d'Shmaya,* and since the NY Knicks had been so welcoming to Maccabi Tel Aviv, Rav Yitzchak Dovid decided he'd like to welcome a top NBA team to

The NBA superstars meet the Migdal Ohr boys

Migdal Ohr's home turf. He wasted no time in extending the invitation — which is how a group of NBA stars on a goodwill tour to Israel made a stop at Migdal HaEmek an important part of their itinerary.

The "NBA Legends" played on Maccabi's court. After a spirited game, which NBA stars won, the American team traveled up north to the city of Migdal HaEmek, where they played a convivial game of ball against the local basketball team (the NBA superstars won that one too) at the sports center on the Migdal Ohr campus. The gym was packed — people had come from all over to watch these legendary NBA players' visit to a yeshivah campus.

After the game was over, the players spent time playing games and teaching moves to some of the students from Migdal Ohr. It was beautiful and heartwarming to watch. At one point, one of the team — a famous player by the name of Dr. J — told Rav Yitzchak Dovid that he wanted the rabbi to take a shot on the court.

Rav Yitzchak Dovid had never thrown a basketball before in his life, but being Rav Grossman that didn't stop him. He decided that there was a time for everything in life (as Shlomo HaMelech — King Solomon — writes) and that this was the time to throw a ball.

"Okay, Rabbi," Dr. J said, "bend your knees and hold the ball like this," and he began giving Rav Grossman a lesson in how to shoot.

Rav Yitzchak Dovid told the player that he wanted to do it all by

Perfect shot

himself. Then, focusing on the basket, the rabbi of Migdal HaEmek, the rabbi with the long white beard, the rabbi who had never held a basketball in his life, lifted the ball and threw it at the basket. It arced high up in the air and as the entire audience held its collective breath, descended over the basket and swooshed through the net without even touching the rim!

It was the first and probably will be the last time Rav Yitzchak Dovid threw a ball. For the basketball players from the States, and for the rest of the people in the gym, it was a moment they would never forget.

Many watching, though, were not surprised. After all, Rav Yitzchak Dovid was a tzaddik and tzaddikim make the shot! How could it be otherwise, when Hashem was so clearly on his side?

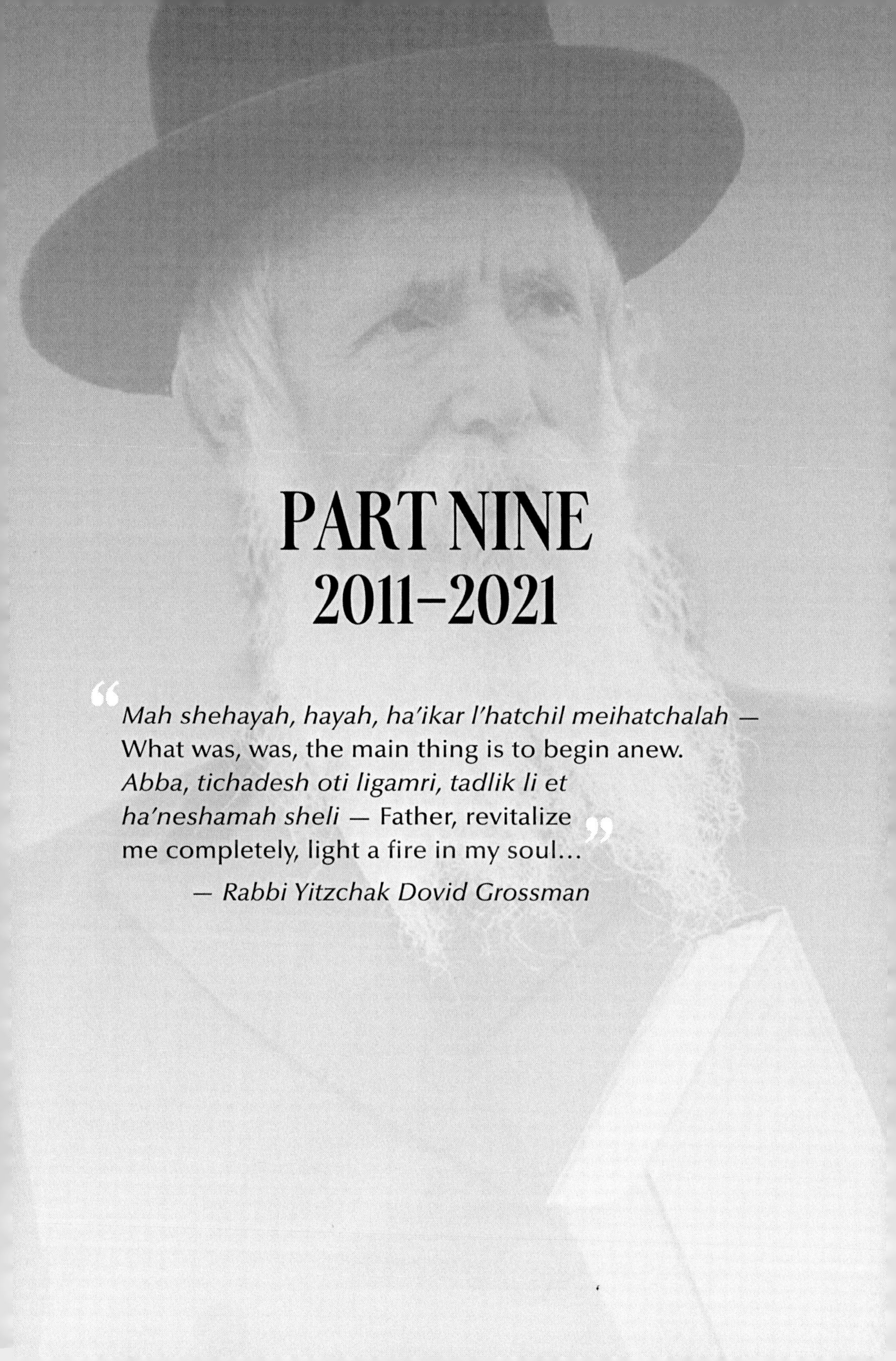

PART NINE
2011–2021

“*Mah shehayah, hayah, ha'ikar l'hatchil meihatchalah* — What was, was, the main thing is to begin anew. *Abba, tichadesh oti ligamri, tadlik li et ha'neshamah sheli* — Father, revitalize me completely, light a fire in my soul...”

— *Rabbi Yitzchak Dovid Grossman*

CHAPTER FIFTY-FOUR

When Gilad Came to Migdal Ohr

Although the telephone seemingly never stops ringing in the Grossman home and office, it is not that common for the rav to hear the voice of a child on the other end. That was why he was surprised when he answered the phone one day and heard the voice of a twelve-year-old boy. A few questions from the rav to the child, and he learned that the young man really wanted the opportunity to meet him. More than that. He *needed* to talk to Rav Grossman.

"What is your name?"

"Gilad."

"Gilad," Rav Grossman said, "why is it so important that you meet with me?"

"I am going to be bar mitzvah soon," he replied, "and I want a *berachah* from the Rav."

"By all means," the rav told the twelve-year-old. "Come to my house and I will give you a *berachah*."

The boy's father brought him to Migdal HaEmek a short while after their initial conversation, at which point it became clear to the rav why he had specifically chosen Rav Grossman as the person he wanted to give him a *berachah* prior to his bar mitzvah. The boy was a sweet-looking child with kind eyes and a ready smile.

A very special boy:
Rav Grossman with Gilad and his father

"Now that I am about to become bar mitzvah," he told the rav, "I decided that I wanted to take on a specific mitzvah in honor of the occasion and to put a lot of work into that mitzvah."

"What mitzvah did you have in mind?"

"The mitzvah of *ahavas Yisrael,* of loving my fellow Jews. I have heard a lot about the Rav and how he epitomizes that mitzvah. I therefore decided to come and ask the expert how to develop this *middah* (character trait) in myself."

"So you don't just want a *berachah*, you want to actually learn what *ahavas Yisrael* is all about?"

"That's right."

He was very eager. Clearly this was a very special boy and Rav Yitzchak Dovid was very impressed.

"Come with me," he told the father and son.

"Where are we going?"

A hug for Gilad

"On a tour."

Rav Grossman gave the two of them an in-depth tour of the world of Migdal Ohr and what it was all about. He showed them around the many schools and campuses, he introduced them to the children, older, younger, and very young. He explained that so many of the children he was seeing didn't have parents, or didn't have parents that were able to take care of them — and were desperate for love.

"We need to be their fathers and mothers," Rav Grossman explained to him.

The tour took a few hours, and when it was over, the Rav gave the boy a very warm *berachah*, and they parted ways.

A few years passed.

On the 12th of June 2014, three students were making their way home from yeshivah to their respective communities. They didn't return home, and their friends and families began to fear that something had happened to them. The fear turned out to be all too true, and soon Klal Yisrael would learn the bitter news — Gilad Shaer, Naftali Fraenkel, and Eyal Yifrach had been kidnaped by terrorists they had assumed were Jewish. They had put up a fight, but were presumed dead. A nation prayed, and then a nation cried.

When it was finally confirmed that the worst was true and that the boys were no longer alive, thousands of people streamed to the homes of the three friends, to pay their final respects to their grieving family members.

Rav Yitzchak Dovid left his Migdal HaEmek home during the week of shivah and joined the thousands of people coming to comfort the mourners in their respective homes. And while his heart was filled with sadness over the terrible tragedy, he never dreamed that one of the teenagers who had been murdered was the twelve-year-old boy who had come to ask his advice in the matter of *ahavas Yisrael.*

The first house he visited was the Yifrach family, where he delivered an emotional *hesped* (eulogy) for Eyal, and sat and spoke with the family for quite some time. Eventually he rose, recited the traditional words one says when taking leave of mourners, and continued on his way

— this time, to the home of the Shaer family. Entering the shivah house, Rav Grossman found it packed with numerous visitors. As he walked into the room, he saw Gilad's father showing the assembled an enlarged picture of his son meeting with — himself! Gilad's father was sharing the story of how that picture came to be taken, and what kind of a son he'd been fortunate to have — a boy who had begged to meet with Rav Yitzchak Dovid Grossman so as to receive a tutorial in the mitzvah of *ahavas Yisrael.*

As the father spoke, memories of Gilad's visit to Migdal HaEmek began to float through the rav's mind. He remembered the hours they'd spent together, and how he had given Gilad the grand tour. The fact that he'd entered the house at the exact moment when Gilad's father was telling the story was a true example of Divine Providence, and everyone in the room was overcome. Of course, Rav Grossman stood up to speak, telling the assembled of Gilad's phone call to him, and his request for a *berachah.* He told them how he'd invited the boy to Migdal HaEmek and how impressed he had been once they'd met and he'd had the opportunity to get to know him.

Rav Yitzchak Dovid is still in touch with Gilad's family. And if you ask him to tell you about Gilad, he will describe a young man with a unique focus and strengths — a young man who truly cared about the people around him and did his best to take care of them, to make them happy and to love them. As a bar mitzvah boy, Gilad Shaer hoped to develop his *ahavas Yisrael;* clearly, he had done so in the few years he was granted.

CHAPTER FIFTY-FIVE

A Thank You for the Judge

Dov Levine was a judge on the Israeli Supreme Court for years and, interestingly enough, a descendant of the Vilna Gaon. He was also a person who had heard enough about Migdal Ohr to know that he wanted to come there for a visit. Even for Migdal Ohr, which has seen more than its fair share of visitors, it is not every day that a Supreme Court Justice asks for a tour, and Rav Grossman was happy to accommodate. As the two of them discussed the concept of eternal Torah justice as opposed to the justice of man, Rav Yitzchak Dovid told the judge that he wanted to give him an example that would showcase how different the two approaches were.

"The Torah tells us," Rav Yitzchak Dovid began, "that if a person steals from someone and doesn't have a way to repay what he stole, he is sold as a slave. At the same time, the Gemara in *Kiddushin* tells us that anyone who purchases a Jewish slave is in reality buying a master for himself. The master is not allowed to eat bread baked from fine flour while feeding his slave bread baked from coarse flour. *Tosafos* adds that if the master has one pillow, he must give it to his slave! What's the takeaway from all this? The lesson is simple. The Torah is teaching us that we are supposed to take a person who stole and treat him with respect and care — to the point where your one pillow will go to him!

"And yet, despite the fact that the Torah provides us with clear guidance on how best to rehabilitate prisoners," the rav continued, "I have visited prisons on many occasions and I am constantly struck by the terrible contempt shown to the prisoners by the guards and by the system.

"In my opinion, the Torah is also showing us how people turn into thieves in the first place. How is it even possible for a Jew to become a thief? It must be that he grew up in a poverty-stricken home. Probably the parents weren't around to give him the *chinuch* that he needed and to take care of him. Comes the Torah and instructs us to draw this person close and to treat him with kindness and respect. And while you may have to sell him as a slave so he can pay back his debts, you still have to treat him with honest and authentic respect. You need to feed him before you eat and give him the same quality food that you eat. Give him your pillow. Make him feel that he has the potential to become a worthwhile member of society. And through this approach, you will find that the thief will turn a new leaf and become a different and better person!"

At one point in the conversation, Rav Yitzchak Dovid decided to tell the judge a story — a story that had happened to his parents, and which had had a lasting influence on his life.

> My mother was once out shopping for Shabbos in the Meah Shearim *shuk*. She was on the way home, shlepping the heavy packages toward our apartment, when a young man suddenly approached her and asked if she needed help with her bags.
>
> My mother gratefully accepted his offer of assistance and the young man helped her carry the packages into the apartment. The following Thursday afternoon, my mother was once again making her rounds of all the stores in the *shuk*, when the same young man appeared with the same offer. This time the two of them shared a little conversation as they walked, and my mother found out where he was learning.
>
> As she was putting away the groceries a few minutes later, my mother opened her purse, and she quickly realized that she was missing money. It didn't take her long to figure out who the culprit was.
>
> Once she figured it all out, she told my father that she intended to go and speak with the boy's rosh yeshivah and tell him the truth about what he was up to. But my father didn't agree. Instead, he told his wife to let the young man know that he wanted to talk to him.
>
> When he was seated in our house, my father asked him about his life. It wasn't long before the boy broke down and began to

With Judge Dov Levine

cry, explaining that he had been raised in one of the development towns and had grown up in a broken family.

"I managed to escape from the town," he told my father, "but even here in Yerushalayim I find myself in a situation where I never have enough to eat or anyone who cares whether I go to bed hungry."

Immediately, my father invited the boy to become a *ben bayis* (almost like a family member) in our home. He told him that he could come and eat by us whenever he was hungry, that there would always be a bed waiting for him, and that he was welcome to stay with us for Shabbos any time he desired.

But my father didn't stop there. After years of looking after the boy and making sure that he had what he needed, he then found him a *shidduch* and married him off.

That was the story that Rav Yitzchak Dovid told Judge Dov Levine.

Judge Levine was moved by everything that he'd heard, and had many questions for his host as they passed through the different institutions of Migdal Ohr. When they walked into the Migdal Ohr kollel, something very interesting occurred. Many of the members of the kollel were people who had spent time in prison, where they were rehabilitated and where they altered the course and trajectory of their lives from crime to Torah. There in prison they'd become *talmidei chachamim,* learning under the guidance of Rav Chaim Golombeck, who had spent the majority of every week living in prison with his *talmidim,* learning Torah with them from morning till night.

As they entered the room, one of the kollel members was delivering a *chaburah* (a high-level Torah lecture) to the rest of the group. The moment he caught sight of the judge, he stopped virtually mid-sentence and said, "Your Honor, I need to give you a sincere thank you!"

The judge was taken aback, not at all sure what the man was talking about.

Seeing the judge's confusion, the *avreich* (married Talmud student) said, "Your Honor, I am really serious. I owe you a major debt of gratitude!"

"What for?"

"For sending me to prison!"

"What are you talking about?"

"I am talking about the fact that being sent to prison was the cause of my being able to take part in Rav Grossman's rehabilitation program, which in turn introduced me to the world of Torah and mitzvos. Your decision to send me to prison helped introduce me to my future teacher, Rav Chaim Golombeck, who lived with us and taught us Torah for the next five years! Today I am the happiest person in the world, and I want to thank you for the part that you played in turning my life around!"

Judge Dov Levine looked the *yungerman* in the eye and replied, "This is the first time in my life that someone is actually thanking me for sending them to prison!"

All in all, it was quite a day.

During a 2015 gathering to discuss the question of how to best rehabilitate prisoners, a professor rose and addressed this question to Rav Grossman.

"*Kevod HaRav,* the prison system spends millions of shekels every year trying to rehabilitate the prisoners in our jails. Many of the brightest people have worked long and hard trying to figure out a way that works, but have been forced to concede defeat time and again, when prisoners who were released wind up back in the very same prison cell that they vacated just a short while before for committing the same crimes.

"Here's my question. How is it that you send young Talmud students into the prisons, people without a degree in criminology or psychology or any of those things, and yet such a person will enter the prison and begin learning Gemara with the prisoner — and within a short while the prisoner changes completely! How is this possible? What is it about the things they are learning together that brings about such change, when none of our criminal experts or social workers are able to accomplish anything?"

"In order to understand the answer to the question you are asking," Rav Yitzchak Dovid replied, "you need to come and learn Torah for a year. Then you'll understand perfectly."

"I can't grasp it now?"

"No."

"Why not?"

"Because Torah learning is a spiritual matter and a matter of providing the Jewish soul with the proper nourishment that it needs to feel happy and satisfied. Without that learning, the Jewish *neshamah* will always feel empty and no amount of psychology, sociology, or criminology will make any difference at all. But a couple of pages of Gemara will change everything — and that's a fact of life!"

Rav Yitzchak Dovid then told the assembled the following story.

One of the prisoners in our program in Afula, let's call him Doron, succeeded in completely reinventing himself until he was unrecognizable from the person he had previously been.

One day, while driving through Migdal HaEmek, I caught sight of a taxi driving in front of me. The entire car, including the roof rack, was filled from top to bottom with shoe boxes. It appeared to be a shoe store on wheels. When we stopped at the next red light, I was able to see into the car, and recognized this tzaddik, Doron, sitting next to the driver.

I became very nervous, worried that he had returned to his previous occupation and that the shoes had been stolen from somewhere. Wanting and needing to know what he was up to, I turned to my driver and told him to follow the taxi.

"But don't get too close to the car, I don't want Doron to see me."

The taxi was driving in the direction of Afula, and we followed, a few car lengths behind them. Once in Afula, the taxi continued until it reached a building that belongs to Migdal Ohr. There, Doron jumped out of the taxi and proceeded to unload all the boxes of shoes from the roof, trunk, and back seat. When they were all piled up outside the door of the Migdal Ohr branch in Afula, he got back into the taxi and drove away.

I told my driver to catch up to the taxi and to start beeping the horn so that he would understand that someone wanted to talk to him.

My driver followed my instructions and soon enough we were face to face, both cars pulled up at the side of the road.

"Rav Grossman," Doron said, a big smile lighting up his face, "it's so good to see you!"

"It's good to see you too," I replied, "but what's going on over here? I saw everything that you did with all those shoes and I want an explanation."

He was silent for a while, but eventually he began to speak.

"The Rav knows that I have stolen many things that do not belong to me in my life. *Baruch Hashem* I have come to a place where I would like to do *teshuvah* and to make amends for all the evil I have done, but I do not know where to start or who to return the stolen objects to. I stole from so many people. I don't even know if they are still alive or if they have passed on. So I asked a *shailah* (a question of Jewish law, asked to a rabbi) what to do. The rav advised me to use my money to purchase items that will be used by many people, and that this action will serve as my *tikkun* (rectification).

"I learn in kollel during the day, and I drive a truck for the night shift. After a year, I was able to put aside a significant amount of money."

"What did you do then?"

"I went to the institution in Afula and I asked them for the shoe sizes of the kids living in the orphanage. I then took the money, bought enough pairs of shoes for every kid in the building, and left them outside the front door. This way I was finally able to do *teshuvah* for some of the evil I was responsible for in my younger years."

"My dear friends," Rav Yitzchak Dovid said to the group of rehabilitation experts sitting in the audience, "can you think of any prisoner who wasn't introduced to the beauty of Torah who would even consider doing such a thing? It would never happen. Such behavior can only come about through Torah, fear of Heaven, and *emunah*. No other way."

In 2020 there was a gathering of the heads of the police force, prison service, and justice system. The gathering was dedicated to the topic of prisoner rehabilitation. During the meeting a comment was made by one of the officers in the prison authority who stated that the most successful rehabilitation program in the country was the one established by Rav Grossman when he was a young rabbi in the early 70s, and which is still in operation today. Many of those prisoners have gone on to learn in Migdal Ohr's kollel and their children and grandchildren would never dream that the patriarch of the family had once spent time in the Israeli correctional system.

Of course, when he first started the program, Rav Grossman had no idea that it would go that far or accomplish so much. That was never important to him. In his mind, all he needed to do was plant a seed and leave the rest up to Hashem.

Rav Yitzchak Dovid would end up calling his prison rehabilitation program "Shaked," an acronym for "Shikum Dati," or "Rehabilitation through Religion," which has reduced the recidivism rate of its participants down to twenty percent. Participants also have one-third of their sentences reduced due to good behavior.

Today (in 2021) there are more than one thousand prisoners actively involved and engaged with this program at various prisons around Israel: a program that has proven to be the most successful rehabilitation program in the country, a program that is run under the auspices of a genuine yeshivah in every prison, where prisoners sit and learn Torah with true *hasmadah* (diligence) for many hours every day, changing themselves completely in the process. The wardens of every prison testify that seventy percent of the prisoners who join "Shaked" manage to stay out of prison upon their release — an incredible accomplishment.

CHAPTER FIFTY-SIX

Emunah Dishes

Another day, another story. And once again, it began with a knock at the door.

It was Motza'ei Shabbos. Rav Yitzchak Dovid went to answer. Standing at the door was a man the rabbi knew very well. He was a *talmid chacham,* a man who had a busy life learning and teaching Torah. If he had come to see him, Rav Grossman was sure there was a good reason for the visit. He invited him into the house, and the two of them sat down. Rav Yitzchak Dovid waited to hear what was on his mind.

"It's my sister," the visitor said. "She was married, but it didn't last long. Unfortunately, the other side hid some very crucial information from us, and my sister understood very quickly that it wasn't going to work. The marriage ended shortly afterward, and since then she hasn't been successful in finding another *shidduch.* It happens to be that she was just visiting my house from Europe and of course the conversation turned to her situation."

"Please continue," Rav Grossman prodded.

"I asked her if she would be willing to come with me to see the Rav and receive a *berachah* from him. She agreed that it would be a good idea. She's waiting outside to see if she can speak with the Rav."

"Please bring her in," the rav said.

When the two of them were seated before him, Rav Yitzchak Dovid blessed the woman with a long list of *berachos,* delivered with his trademark warmth and sincerity. That was all to be expected. But then Rav Grossman took the conversation in an interesting direction.

"I don't know if you are familiar with what I'm about to say," he told the woman, "but in the world of chassidim, there is a tradition, a *minhag*, to relate a story from the Baal Shem Tov on Motza'ei Shabbos. Since it happens to be Motza'ei Shabbos right now, and since you are here, I would like to share a story from the holy Baal Shem Tov."

She was, of course, very interested in hearing which particular story he had in mind.

"A woman came to see the Baal Shem Tov," Rav Grossman began the story. "This woman was unable to have children and so she traveled to the Baal Shem Tov hoping for a *berachah* that would lead to salvation. The Baal Shem Tov, however, knew that she was unable to have children, and he was reluctant to give her a blessing since that would entail changing the course of nature — something which he tried not to do. But the woman did not give up and returned to the Baal Shem Tov's home, where she threw herself down on the threshold just before he had to leave to daven Minchah.

"If the Rebbe wants to leave the house," she said, "he must step on me, for I will not move from this spot! Or, the Rebbe can just give me a *berachah*, and I will get up at once."

What was the Baal Shem Tov supposed to do in such a situation? With no choice he blessed the woman that she should merit to hold a child in her arms. Overjoyed, the woman thanked the Baal Shem Tov over and over, before taking leave of the holy tzaddik.

A year passed and the couple invited the Baal Shem Tov to serve as the *sandek* at the bris of their newborn son.

Knowing that his *berachah* had caused nature to change on their behalf and that this was a very serious thing, the Baal Shem Tov asked his *gabbai* to find out what the woman had done after receiving his blessing, and whether she had done any special mitzvah that had caused Heaven to agree to alter what had already been decreed.

"I didn't do anything out of the ordinary," she replied in response to the question. "After the Rebbe blessed me with a child, I went home, where I immediately began preparing the room for the baby. I put up new curtains, and purchased a crib. Then I made sure we had a beautiful new baby carriage and whatever else we might possibly need for the arrival of our baby — who I knew was going to be here soon."

When the Baal Shem Tov heard her answer, he said, "Now I am calm.

It wasn't me who made this miracle happen. It was the woman herself who convinced the Ribbono shel Olam to give her a child — by her actions and her *emunah*!"

This was the story Rav Grossman shared with his visitors that Motza'ei Shabbos. After he finished sharing the story with them, they thanked him for his time and blessings, and they left the house.

The next afternoon the man arranged a time to meet his sister so that they could visit some of the *kivrei tzaddikim* located in the north of the country. When he arrived at the agreed-upon spot, however, he didn't see her waiting for him. He dialed her number.

"Where are you?"

"I'm in the supermarket."

"What are you doing in the supermarket?"

"I had a few things to pick up."

"Okay, wait outside and I'll be there in five minutes."

When he pulled up in front of the store a few minutes later, he saw his sister emerge with a wagon full of bags.

"What's going on," he asked her, "what's with all the shopping?"

"Look," she replied, "yesterday, we were sitting with Rav Grossman and he told us the story of the Baal Shem Tov and how the woman in the story went out and bought everything she needed for her baby because she had been on the receiving end of a *berachah* and "knew" that it was going to come true. I too received a *berachah* yesterday from Rav Grossman and I decided to follow the example of the woman in the story. I went to the supermarket and purchased everything we might possibly need for my *vort* (engagement party). I bought the nicest paper goods and plastic ware — I really splurged — but look, you don't get engaged every day, right?!"

All this happened on Sunday.

On Monday, a *shadchan* (matchmaker) from Yerushalayim called the woman's mother in Europe and told her that she had heard that her daughter was currently visiting Israel, and that she had an idea for a *shidduch* for her.

"I would like to meet her," the *shadchan* said. "Is that possible?"

"Stay on the line," the mother replied, "and I will call her on my other phone right now."

"Where are you right now?" she asked her daughter when she got on the line.

"I'm in Yerushalayim."

The mother relayed the information to the *shadchan*.

"Great," she said, "I'm also in Yerushalayim. Where is she right now?"

"Where are you right now?" the mother asked her daughter.

"I'm in Geulah."

"Geulah."

"I'm there too."

They made up to meet five minutes later.

The meeting went well, and the *shadchan* suggested a *shidduch* for the woman with her nephew, who was learning in Lakewood.

When something is supposed to happen, it happens. Though a *shidduch* can be derailed for a thousand reasons, that didn't happen in this case. Here, everything went smoothly, and less than a month later they were celebrating the couple's engagement at her home in Europe — and the table was covered with every single fancy dish, plate, and cup she had purchased at the supermarket in Migdal HaEmek. The joy at that engagement party was so intense that the roof of the house could barely be convinced not to take off from sheer happiness. Every dish was used, every bag of expensive cutlery opened. It had all been purchased for the special occasion and fell in the category of "Emunah Dishes."

Five months later everyone gathered in the city of Yerushalayim for the wedding itself, which was celebrated at a beautiful hall in the center of the city. Of course, Rav Yitzchak Dovid was invited to the wedding and he made sure to attend. After all, it's not every day that one is able to partake in a modern-day Baal Shem Tov story, and such a celebration should not be missed.

CHAPTER FIFTY-SEVEN

A Chinese Shalom Zachor

One of the Grossman grandchildren, a devoted chassid of Chabad like his maternal great-grandfather, is today serving as a Chabad *shaliach* (representative) in the Chinese city of Chengdu. His name is Rav Dov Berish Henig and he consistently makes his *zeide* proud through the *kiruv* work that he does in the capital of southwestern China's Sichuan province.

If you ever have the opportunity to visit Chengdu, you will want to drop into Rabbi Henig's Beit Chabad, where together with his rebbetzin, he draws Jewish visitors back to *Yiddishkeit* — with a special focus on the many Israeli visitors who somehow manage to find their way to China and to his beautiful edifice in the middle of the Torah wilderness. Of course, Rabbi Henig shares the stories that happen to him (and there are many) with his grandfather, who derives exceptional *nachas* from seeing his grandson continuing on the path he has long trod.

Rav Grossman and Rav Dov Berish Henig

When the Henigs had a baby boy, Reb Dov Berish invited his *zeide* to fly to the bris, honoring him as the *sandek*. This meant a flight to China, but there was no way Rav Yitzchak Dovid was going to let something inconsequential like that get in the way of participating in his great-grandson's bris. So off he went to China.

Rav Grossman landed in the Chengdu airport on a Friday morning, one rabbi in a throng of businessmen coming and going to and from the hub of commerce and tourism that drew people from all over the globe. Never one to allow an opportunity to go to waste, Rabbi Henig did a lot of advertising about the fact that his grandfather, the famous Rav Yitzchak Dovid Grossman, was going to be spending Shabbos in the community, and that everyone was invited to join them for Shabbos. A gala Shabbos was planned with beautiful *tefillos*, communal meals, and an uplifting *tisch* with singing, stories, and words of Torah for all.

More than one hundred and thirty people gathered in the Beit Chabad that Friday night to celebrate the *shalom zachor* (celebration of the birth of a boy). The atmosphere was warm and festive, with all the guests sharing in the rabbi's *simchah* and the fact that his *zeide* had flown in to join all the way from Israel to be with them. Suddenly the door of the room opened and a young Israeli entered. He walked inside and looked around, catching sight of Rav Yitzchak Dovid sitting at the head of the table. But when he saw the rabbi, his reaction was bizarre, for the young man began to shake and cry! It was almost as if he had seen a ghost and didn't know how to react!

Everyone in the room turned to stare at the newcomer, trying to figure out why he seemed to be in such a state of shock. Within seconds, Rabbi Henig was at the man's side, welcoming him into the shul and making him comfortable. Once the newcomer had settled down and seemed calmer, Reb Dov Berish began to skillfully draw him out, asking him how he had ended up coming to be with them that night.

This is the story he related.

> Like many Israelis who have finished their army service, I have been hitchhiking around the Far East for the past year and a half. This morning, when I got up, I decided that I wanted to make a trip to a city that was located three hundred kilometers from where I was. Driving three hundred kilometers in your own car takes a while, but I knew that my journey would take a lot longer

than that because I was hitching rides and I didn't know if anyone was going to stop for me and even if they did, how far they would be willing to take me toward my destination. I went to stand in a nearby hitchhiking spot, and it wasn't long before a truck stopped and offered me a ride, which I accepted.

We had been on the road for a good two hundred kilometers, when we suddenly encountered a construction zone. It seems like the Chinese were in the middle of a major urban construction project and the truck was unable to continue on that stretch of highway. The truck driver informed me that he was going to have to turn around and find an alternative route, but I had no interest in retracing the path we had taken and asked him to let me off right where we were.

The driver was agreeable and I alighted from the cab in the middle of nowhere, while the truck roared off into the horizon. I began to walk, entering a wheat field that stretched on for all eternity... I had no idea where I was or in what direction to walk.

All I could see was wheat.

After I had been walking for what seemed like a very long time, I reached a road. I couldn't walk anymore. I was too tired. Then to make matters worse, the skies overhead opened up and it began to rain. It was a thunderstorm of epic proportions and I didn't even have a raincoat for protection. There was nothing to do and I didn't even bother trying to protect myself from the elements. Instead, I slipped my pack off my back and withdrew a bottle of whiskey from inside. As I sat on the ground making a *l'chaim* with myself, I suddenly recalled an incident that I experienced ten years earlier.

Ten years before, I was a student at a Jerusalem school. It was an upper class school — a school that took the students on trips on a fairly regular basis. One of the trips they took us on was to Migdal HaEmek, where we were introduced to Rav Grossman. The rabbi was a very unusual individual and instead of talking to us like one might have expected, he chose to teach us a song instead. The song he taught us went like this.

"Mah shehayah, hayah, ha'ikar l'hatchil meihatchalah — What

was, was, the main thing is to begin anew. *Abba, tichadesh oti ligamri, tadlik li et ha'neshamah sheli* — Father, revitalize me completely, light a fire in my soul…"

(Author's note: This is a song that Rav Yitzchak Dovid has sung to many, many audiences all over the world.)

The second the memory of the rabbi teaching us the song flashed through my mind, I began to sing it to myself, right there in the middle of a Chinese wheat field. I had no idea where I was, I had no idea when or how I would be able to reach civilization, but I was completely immersed in the song I had heard from Rav Grossman ten years earlier, and I sang it over and over. As I sang, I clapped my hands and raised my face to the sky in sheer ecstasy.

Suddenly I noticed a truck approaching on the road. The Chinese driver looked out the window and saw me clapping my hands and singing, but he stopped for me anyway, pulling the truck to a halt, and asking me, "What are you doing here?"

The driver knew a little bit of English and we were able to communicate.

"I'm an Israeli Jew and I'm lost. Someone gave me a ride, but there was construction and I got off in the middle of nowhere thinking that I would be able to find my way. Instead, I got hopelessly lost."

"If you're a Jew," the driver said, "I will take you to a place where you'll be able to find other Jews."

No sooner said than done. I got into the cab and he drove me all the way to this spot, dropping me off right outside the Beit Chabad of Chengdu!

Showing him the menorah on the building, the driver said, "You will find other Jews here."

I thanked the driver and alighted from the truck. Seconds later I was opening the door to the building and walking inside. And then as I entered the room where all of you are sitting, I glanced over at the head table, and who do I see — none other than Rav Grossman himself! There I was just a short while ago, sitting in the middle of a storm in a wheat field in China, remembering the rabbi and singing the song that he taught me, and now, I was meeting the man himself in the middle of China! You can imagine my utter shock at seeing him here!

Meeting Rav Yitzchak Dovid's eyes, the young man broke down and began to cry once again, seeing their unexpected reunion as a sign from above. It shouldn't come as a surprise that the young Israeli became extremely connected to Judaism and within a short time had started keeping Shabbos.

So ended the story (or really so began the story) of the Israeli hitchhiker who got lost and comforted himself by singing Rav Grossman's song over and over.

You know what they say. Truth is stranger than fiction. And there's no question that that line is true. Especially when you're talking about Rav Yitzchak Dovid Grossman.

CHAPTER FIFTY-EIGHT

A Personal Mussar Schmooze

Rav Yitzchak Dovid has been visiting jails, prisons, and courthouses on behalf of different members of Klal Yisrael for many years now. Many times he comes to give assistance to prisoners in his prison program, but there are numerous other times, when people who know him ask him to appear in court on their behalf for a wide array of reasons.

One afternoon the phone rang and an old acquaintance was on the other end. He explained that he had been arrested due to a complaint that had been filed against him (which he claimed was untrue) and that he needed Rav Yitzchak Dovid to come and help him in court.

"What exactly do you need from me?"

"The prosecutor is demanding that I remain incarcerated and behind bars until the trial. Obviously, I am against this and feel that it's unfair. If the judge rules I am guilty, I will go to jail and complete my sentence. I know that I am innocent and I do not think that I will end up being sent to jail. However, if that's what happens, I accept it. On the other hand, I do have a problem with sitting in jail before I have been proven guilty. So I am asking if you can come to court for me, and ask the judge to release me into your prison program, where I will stay until my case begins and the matter of my innocence or guilt is decided — one way or another."

Rav Yitzchak Dovid had provided this service for many people over the years. The judges knew they could trust him to keep the rules, and they also felt that in many cases it was better for people to remain out of prison whenever possible, especially since Rav Grossman had special lodgings set aside for exactly these kinds of situations.

Feeling bad for the man, and also having the feeling that he was innocent (you develop a kind of sixth sense about these things when you deal with people in the prison system as long as he has), Rav Grossman told the man that he would make sure to present himself at the courthouse on the day in question.

As it happened, the Moetzes Rabbanut Yisrael (the organization of rabbis in Israel) was planning to hold a very large event in Yerushalayim, to which all the Rabbinate rabbis in the country were going to be invited. Featured speakers were Israel's president, prime minister, and both chief rabbis. The organizers of the event wanted to have at least one additional speaker, who should be a member of the "Moetzet Rabbanut Rashit," roughly translated as the Rabbanut's governing forum. The council is composed of ten rabbis — five Ashkenazi and five Sefardi. It is this council of ten that basically decides the Rabbanut's policy on a host of issues. Rav Yitzchak Dovid was voted onto the council in 1980 and in every single election since.

The obvious question was: Who should be asked, a Sefardic rabbi or an Ashkenazic rabbi? In the end, it was decided to choose Rav Grossman, since, in the words of the person who raised the motion, "He is both a Sefardi and an Ashkenazi." The fact is, everyone loved and loves Rav Grossman and he was a person who would be acceptable to one and all, no matter their background or their style and tradition of davening.

So it was that Rav Grossman received a call from a Rabbanut representative, informing him that he had been chosen to address the audience at the big event. Rav Grossman agreed to speak, but it didn't take him long to realize that he now faced a conflict, because he had already agreed to give a speech somewhere else. This speech was to be given before a very small audience in a courtroom in the north of the country — a far cry from the major event in Yerushalayim that he had been invited to.

What to do?

It was a hard decision to make, even for a man who has devoted his life to the art of giving to others. To be chosen out of thousands of distinguished people to share the stage with the prime minister is not a simple thing, and would, without question, prove beneficial for Migdal Ohr. On the other hand, he had already promised to try and keep a man out of prison, which was a modern-day example of the mitzvah of *pidyon shevuyim*, of redeeming people from captivity.

In the end, Rav Yitzchak Dovid met with two lawyers whom he knew well and trusted and asked them to represent him and to speak in his name at the courthouse, requesting that the judge release the prisoner to his care.

But he didn't feel good about his decision.

Throughout the journey from Migdal HaEmek to the center of the country, Rav Yitzchak Dovid tried to ignore the little voice straining to be heard. Finally, when they reached Ramle and were already not far away from their destination, he sat up straight and began talking to himself.

> Itche Duvid, all of your *derashos* (speeches) have to do with the idea of "*V'ahavtah lirei'acha kamocha,*" that a person must love his fellow Jew as he loves himself. This is the foundation of everything you speak about, and it is the foundation of your entire life!
>
> You speak and you speak and you speak — giving over the message of *ahavas Yisrael*, love of the Jewish people. Now Hashem has sent you a *nisayon*, a test. They asked you to speak at a venue where you will receive a lot of honor and the prime minister of Israel will shake your hand and all the rabbanim will stand up for you. At the same time, a Yid is sitting and waiting in a courtroom to learn whether he will be incarcerated even before his guilt has been proven! And while you did send two very competent and professional lawyers to help him out, you know that they will not have the same kind of rapport with the judge — whom you have no doubt met on numerous occasions!

At that moment Rav Yitzchak Dovid made the decision to turn around and to drive to the courthouse in Nazareth as quickly as possible, hoping that he wasn't already too late. As the car took the next exit, Rav Grossman called his contact at the Rabbanut and let him know that he was not going to be able to make it to the big event.

The hearing was scheduled for 11:00 in the morning, and the moment his car pulled up outside the courthouse, Rav Yitzchak Dovid jumped out and raced into the building, taking the stairs three at a time. As he reached the courtroom, he saw the attorneys filing in and realized to his relief that he had made it back in time. As he stood in the hallway catching his breath, the district attorney for the entire northern section of the country suddenly appeared, having arrived to argue for the prosecution. Seeing the rabbi, a man she had come up against in court on a few occasions, the attorney put a smile on her face and said, "Rav Grossman — and what are you doing here today?"

"I am here for Greenberg's case."

The moment she heard his words, the smile on her lips was instantly replaced with a chilling look of something akin to rage.

"THIS TIME YOU WILL NOT SUCCEED," she said. *"Hapaam zeh lo yaazor lecha!"*

Rav Yitzchak Dovid didn't answer her. There was no point. What would be, would be.

They entered the courtroom a few minutes later and the judge entered shortly after everyone was seated and waiting. He was an Arab judge named Zuabi, someone Rav Yitzchak Dovid knew fairly well. Catching sight of Rav Grossman, the judge commented, "I see we have a distinguished guest in the courtroom. Rav Grossman, what brings you here today?"

"Your Honor," Rav Yitzchak Dovid replied, "I have come here today on behalf of Yaakov Greenberg, a man I know well and for many years. I am not going into the question of whether or not Reb Yaakov is innocent. That will be decided in due course by the court. I am here for a different reason."

"Please continue," the judge said.

"As Your Honor knows, there are many times when it takes months and even a year for a case to come before the court. And since that is the case, I have come here to request that during the time before the case is heard, Reb Yaakov Greenberg should be remanded to my custody and be allowed to live under my supervision instead of having to be locked up in a jail cell before being proven guilty! I am prepared to sign a document stating that I am taking full responsibility that he will not try to flee."

He had barely finished pleading the case when the prosecutor rose

— about to erupt — but before she had a chance to get one word out, the judge called out to her, "*Hapaam zeh lo yaazor lach* — this time you will not succeed!" — using the very words she herself had used just a few minutes earlier!

"We are going to honor Rav Grossman's request and remand Mr. Greenberg into his supervision."

The decision was duly recorded and the two of them left the courthouse shortly afterward.

To Rav Yitzchak Dovid the message was clear. In his mind, the judge's verdict had come directly from Hashem to show him that he had made the right decision while on the journey to Yerushalayim earlier that morning. His willingness to forgo what would have been a fantastic experience for the sake of another Yid was the catalyst for the miracle that Hashem had done for them that day in a Nazareth courtroom, a miracle made clear when the prosecutor and judge used the exact same words.

CHAPTER FIFTY-NINE

Two Weddings and an Engagement

In the winter of 2020, Rav Yitzchak Dovid served as the *mesader kiddushin* at two weddings that took place one day apart — one in the city of Yerushalayim on a Sunday night, the other in Tiveria on Monday evening. While every wedding is a cause for joy, these particular weddings were particularly moving. In order for you to understand why this was so, we have to provide the backstory of each of these events.

A number of years ago, the Israeli media was abuzz with the story of a sixteen-year-old boy from the city of Tiveria. The teen had been diagnosed with cancer and was in Rambam Hospital in Haifa, where the oncology staff was anxiously waiting to begin treating him. The problem was that the boy refused to allow them to begin administering treatment. For its part, the hospital wanted to force the boy to allow them to give treatment, and they turned to the courts, asking the judge assigned to the case to give them the legal ability to administer treatment — even against his will. When the boy understood where his situation was headed, he made up his mind to escape from the hospital — which he did twice. When he was returned to the hospital, he let it be known that if he was forced to accept treatment, he would find a way to jump into the nearby ocean. Needless to say, the story caused an uproar, with everyone having something to say about it.

Rav Yitzchak Dovid was also following the saga as it developed, and when he saw that matters were not calming down — on the contrary, they were escalating — he decided that he could no longer sit down on the sidelines. Leaving Migdal HaEmek, he traveled to Rambam Hospital in Haifa where he would be able to speak with the patient face to face, and find out the underlying cause of all the issues. Haifa is not very far from Migdal HaEmek, and in a short time he was walking into the hospital and asking the receptionist for the number of the patient's room.

Sitting with the patient, Rav Grossman talked to the boy for about two hours, explaining that allowing the hospital to administer treatment was a matter of *pikuach nefesh* (life and death) and that he had to keep the halachah of *"U'shmartem meod l'nafshoseichem"* (guard your health and life) like every other mitzvah that he kept. The rav spoke and spoke and spoke, but no matter what he said, he could see that he wasn't really getting through to the boy. Suddenly the patient burst into tears.

"What's the matter?" Rav Grossman asked him. "Tell me."

"I want to take the treatments," the boy said, "but I am not allowed."

"Who doesn't allow you to get healed?"

"My parents have forbidden me from having them."

"I will go and see them immediately," he told the boy. "Don't worry, everything is going to be okay."

Then Rav Yitzchak Dovid left Rambam Hospital and told his driver that they were headed to Tiveria with no time to waste.

The scenic flatlands leading into Tiveria gave way to the sloping hills that border the city situated on the edge of the jewel-like Kinneret. Evening was fast approaching as Rav Grossman's driver parked outside the apartment building the patient called home. After knocking on the door and being welcomed into the simple home, the rav took a seat across the table from the boy's parents. This was followed by the most cursory of salutations before Rav Grossman grabbed the bull by the horns and asked the parents in the most direct fashion imaginable why they had forbidden their son from seeking treatment for his dangerous illness.

"How is it possible that parents would deny their child the opportunity to live?"

In the beginning the parents didn't want to tell him their reason, but Rav Grossman doesn't let simple opposition get in his way, and he spoke and spoke and spoke (mainly about the importance of each and every life) and in the end, the parents had to tell him the truth.

"We are followers of a particular rabbi," they told Rav Grossman, "and he has ruled against the treatment."

"So you are refusing your son's treatment because of your rabbi?"

"Yes."

"And if your rabbi tells you to go ahead with it, then you will?"

"Yes."

"Well then," Rav Grossman said, "I will just have to go and see your rabbi."

It was nine in the evening when Rav Yitzchak Dovid was shown into the room where the rabbi was sitting and learning. After exchanging a few words of greeting with each other, the two of them got down to the business at hand.

"Why is the rav refusing to allow the patient to be treated?"

"I do not believe in the hospital's treatments," he replied. "In my opinion, they are the cause of many people dying and not the other way around! And not only do they kill patients, they cause them to suffer miserably along the way!"

Rav Yitzchak Dovid tried reasoning with him, quoting the words, "*v'rapo yirapei,*" the Torah's permission for doctors to do their utmost to heal patients, but it didn't take him long to realize that there was no way he was going to change this man's mind. So he decided to take another approach.

"If Rav Chaim Kanievsky rules that this boy must be given treatment for his illness, will you give the parents permission to follow his ruling?"

"Yes."

"Then I will go and speak with Rav Chaim and let you know what he says."

And with that, Rav Grossman left the home of the rabbi and instructed his driver to head for Highway Six and the city of Bnei Brak. It was an emergency and there was no time to waste.

Rav Grossman reached Rechov Rashbam around 11:30 that night. When he arrived at the world-famous address, he learned that the *gadol hador* (Torah leader of the generation) wasn't home. He was attending an event and would be back shortly.

"I need to see Rav Chaim as soon as he returns," he told the *gabbai.*

The *gabbai* (assistant), who knew Rav Grossman (who doesn't?), replied, "Can't it wait until tomorrow?"

"No. It's a matter of life and death and needs to be dealt with immediately."

The *gabbai* had nothing more to say and allowed Rav Yitzchak Dovid to wait inside the house until Rav Chaim returned. When the venerable *gadol* finally arrived, Rav Grossman told Rav Chaim the entire story, and asked him what he should tell the family's rav.

"He absolutely must take the treatment," Rav Chaim said. *"Al pi Torah,* according to the Torah, he must take the treatment. Tell the rav that I said so!"

Thanking Rav Chaim for his time, Rav Yitzchak Dovid left the house and got back into his car.

"Where to?" his driver asked.

"Back to the house of the rav we just came from."

(Author's note: At this point in the story I asked Rav Yitzchak Dovid if they'd had to stop to fill up the car with gas, or whether it had been miraculously taken care of for them... He thought that was funny.)

It was a little after two in the morning when Rav Grossman reentered the study in which he had argued the patient's case just a few hours earlier. The rabbi was up and learning, as he did every night.

"I just returned from Rav Chaim," he told the rabbi.

"What did he say?"

"That the patient must accept the treatment *al pi Torah*!"

The rabbi immediately took a piece of paper and wrote a note for the parents.

"Kol mah she'haRav Grossman omer lachem, atem tzrichim laasot — You need to do whatever Rav Grossman tells you to do."

Rav Yitzchak Dovid left the house a few minutes later, precious note in hand. It was now close to three in the morning. He would have returned to the boy's parents already then, but there was no difference if he spoke with them at three or waited until seven; the hospital would not start the treatment at this hour. Therefore, he returned home to Migdal HaEmek, caught a few hours of sleep, and was back in Tiveria at seven o'clock sharp the next day.

After reading the note from their rabbi, the parents agreed to follow all of Rav Grossman's instructions regarding their son.

"I want you to come with me to Rambam Hospital right now."

There was no resistance, and they set out for Haifa a few minutes later. The first stop upon arrival was in the patient's room, where the parents informed their son that he was now free to be treated due to their rabbi's acceptance of Rav Chaim's *psak* (ruling). They then met with the professor in charge of the oncology department, where the parents let her know that the hospital was free to try and heal their son using any means at their disposal. The doctor couldn't believe what was happening in her office and was overjoyed at being given the opportunity to try and save their son. The patient's treatment regimen was initiated shortly afterward.

"In a miraculous turn of events," Rav Grossman said, "it wasn't long before the doctors began seeing fantastic results as he turned the corner and started to get better. Looking at the boy, one would have been hard-pressed to believe that only a short while before, he had been lying in bed with no hope of survival. And yet, with eight car rides to different parts of the country and a halachic ruling from Rav Chaim Kanievsky, everything turned out differently."

Migdal Ohr provides a very unique service to needy *kallahs*, assisting them with all their wedding needs at their bridal salon. Located in what was the first building used by the institution, the rooms are now filled with exquisite bridal gowns, shelves of shiny white shoes, glass counters showcasing an array of jewelry, makeup, and hair stations — basically everything a *kallah* needs to look her best on her big day.

"They leave from the salon directly to their weddings," Rav Grossman explains. "The salon was created by my rebbetzin, who built it in memory of her sister Nechama, who was killed in a car accident just two weeks before her wedding. With the help of Fabia Preminger, who puts her heart and soul into the salon, every *kallah* leaves the salon looking and feeling like a princess."

It is not uncommon for alumni of Migdal Ohr to come back "home" to prepare for their weddings. (The same thing is true for *kallahs* who have never stepped foot into Migdal Ohr in their lives. Rebbetzin Grossman is more than happy to help everyone in need.)

Shortly after Succos 2020, one such student arrived at the salon and gave the rebbetzin the date of her wedding, booking the salon for the afternoon prior to Rosh Chodesh Kislev.

"Where is the wedding?"

"In Tiveria."

"And who is the *chassan*?" Rebbetzin Grossman asked her.

It was none other than the patient from Rambam Hospital, the patient for whom Rav Yitzchak Dovid had made eight different trips in his car for the purpose of saving his life. He was now marrying a student of Migdal Ohr — and of course Rav Yitzchak Dovid was invited to serve as the *mesader kiddushin* at the wedding. And while he seldom attended weddings during the months of the Covid-19 virus, here he felt he must, since it was the wedding of a boy whose life he'd had the *zechus* to save.

The second wedding? Let's have Rav Grossman tell the story:

> I served as the *mesader kiddushin* at a wedding on Sunday and Monday. Monday was the boy from the hospital. And Sunday — well, Sunday brings me back half a century, to when I first arrived in Migdal HaEmek. We didn't have a school of our own yet, and I used to bring students to other institutions in Bnei Brak or Yerushalayim. Sometimes those trips took me a few days since I had to go everywhere by bus. It wasn't easy, but I was determined to try and save as many lives as possible.
>
> There was one specific girl whom I worked very hard to save from the streets. I cannot tell you how much time I spent convincing her to leave Migdal HaEmek for a religious institution in the center of the country. Finally she agreed, and I took her to Bnei Brak. I cannot accurately describe the happiness I felt when she

was learning in Ohr HaChaim. I knew that a few years in that environment would give her a new lease on life.

And as gratified and optimistic as he'd felt when she was safely ensconced in Bnei Brak, that's how sad and worried he became when he saw her back in Migdal HaEmek not long afterward.

To my immense sadness, the girl had a breakdown and ran away from the school. I knew that if I didn't convince her to return within the next few days, she would be lost forever. Already she was a different person from the girl I knew, and she'd only been back in Migdal HaEmek for a short while.

You cannot imagine how hard I worked to convince her. She didn't want to go. It was too difficult and there were too many rules and she didn't have any friends and the staff was too demanding. I don't know how I did it, but somehow, miraculously, she agreed to return to Bnei Brak. And this time she stayed.

She ended up marrying one of our *talmidim* — a genuine *talmid chacham* — and the couple was blessed with thirteen children!

Every one of those children is a diamond. They are the cream of the Torah world and are married to the best families of the Torah world. And this girl — now a mother, grandmother, and great-grandmother — was marrying off her youngest child on the night before the wedding of the boy from Rambam Hospital. And yes, I agreed to serve as the *mesader kiddushin* at that wedding as well — how could I not?

As I looked around the hall at the couple's children and grandchildren and great-grandchildren, the matriarch of the family — the girl that I rescued from the streets of Migdal HaEmek — came over to me.

"Rav Grossman."

She was radiant — glowing with the kind of joy that comes from the deepest, most powerful part of a human being.

"Yes?"

She waved her arm, encompassing the entire room and everyone in it — all the children and grandchildren, all the *doros* of *ehrliche Yiddishe neshamos*, the generations of pious Jewish souls, and said, "They are all yours, Rav Yitzchak Dovid. All yours."

It was a kind of closing of a circle that began when a young man from Meah Shearim got off a bus and walked into a crime-ridden city, where there were no yeshivos or shuls. A city where he became the "Disco Rabbi" and, over the years, a living legend.

Because that was the role Hashem sent him to play, in order to save His people.

CHAPTER SIXTY
"Zoharim"

During the course of the interviews that I conducted for this book, Rav Yitzchak Dovid invited me to visit a place called Zoharim. Zoharim is a tiny village that he founded as a home/school for boys from *chareidi* homes who fell out of the system and couldn't find their way back. Zoharim boasts a high school for these boys and is set in an incredibly beautiful, peaceful, and pastoral environment not far from Beit Shemesh.

An abandoned shack on the site where the boys would build Zoharim

Aerial view of Zoharim today

The history of Zoharim goes back in time to a man named Charlie Biton who formed a political party called the "Black Panthers," which succeeded in garnering four Knesset seats (out of 120) in the 1977 elections.

One of the Black Panthers' requests was that they wanted the government to give them one hundred dunams of land, which they would then turn into a village for drug rehabilitation. The drug rehabilitation program continued for a while, but the village was eventually closed down by the government for a variety of reasons. When that occurred, the village was abandoned and remained unused for many years. Real estate developers wanted to purchase the land from Charlie Biton to build housing projects, but none of those plans came to fruition because the land could not legally be used for profit or business, but only for the type of institutions that help people.

And then Rav Yitzchak Dovid heard about the hundred dunams of land in one of the most beautiful areas of Israel — land that had just been sitting there, deserted and forlorn.

"I went to meet with Charlie Biton. We got to know each other and it wasn't long before we had become friends. I explained to him that I had the perfect use for his property — not for residential purposes, not for real estate development, not to make money.

"I need your one hundred dunams for rehabilitation purposes — for the exact reason that you established the village in the first place."

They ended up making a deal, and Rav Yitzchak Dovid purchased the property from Biton. It cost millions, but was worth every shekel. Standing in the middle of one hundred dunams of prime real estate,

Rav Yitzchak Dovid looked around him and envisioned a youth village that would save lives and bring peace to many who had suffered.

Then he set out to form the nucleus of the pioneers.

"For the first time in years," Rav Yitzchak Dovid remembers, "I returned to the days of my youth, removing my hat and jacket and sitting down with the kids in the parks, talking to them and getting to know them. It took time, but eventually they learned to trust me. These were boys who had been through the system and fallen through the cracks. I ended up selecting thirty teenagers and gathering them together. I shared my vision for Zoharim and offered them the opportunity to be the founding fathers (as it were) for what could possibly become a genuine game changer for boys like them."

He then shocked them by explaining that the land was empty right now, and that they, the first group of boys to move in, would be building the village with their hands, from the ground up.

"Boys, you are going to build your own homes. We have the land. Now you need to come and build."

Within a short time, the first thirty boys were living in caravans and the real work began.

For the next nine months, the boys worked at a feverish pace to build themselves a village. They succeeded in putting together a picturesque paradise — something akin to the kind of thing you might see while driving in the middle of the mountains somewhere in Europe.

Today there are one hundred and twenty students at Zoharim. A number of families live there too — families who "adopt" the students during the boys' stay at Zoharim. Here the students undergo therapy and work with animals on the ranch. They get in touch with the land, and are taught carpentry and agriculture and how to become productive members of society. The most amazing thing about it is the fact that it was all built by the students themselves, who helped create an incredible little world where lives are altered forever in a positive way.

"Sounds like an amazing place," I told Rav Grossman.

"It is an amazing place. And the reason that I'm telling you about it now is because I'm going there tonight, and I want to know if you and your wife would care to join me."

Rav Grossman was going to Zoharim that evening to attend the 12th grade graduation ceremony. This was the first time that he left his home after the first wave of Covid-19, and we met him there. My wife and I walked through Zoharim, past wooden structures and homes, past a giant stable housing the horses, and down a flight of stairs, onto the grassy playing field. There we spent the next few hours being introduced, singing, and speaking. We watched a play they staged and heard Rav Grossman speak. We left Zoharim thankful for having been given the opportunity to witness miracles in operation.

In the days leading up to Rosh Hashanah 5781 (2020), Rav Grossman was extremely busy with the thousands of details that come with running numerous programs for thousands of students of all ages and backgrounds. With the second wave of Covid-19 a persistent threat to schools, he was swamped from morning till night, dealing with the constant decisions that needed to be made. At the same time, he was also extremely busy with something else — another magnificent program that had long been on his "to-do" list.

Another Zoharim. This one for girls.

Many people had asked him why he had only established a place like Zoharim for boys, when there were so many girls, also from *chareidi* homes, who were in dire need of such a place. It had taken him time, but they were finally ready to open the program — Zoharot — on the 7th of September 2020.

On the morning of the grand opening, Rav Grossman's phone rang — as it does dozens of times a day. It was the prime minister of Israel on the line. As old friends, they speak to one another on a regular basis, and Rav Yitzchak Dovid waited to hear why Bibi was calling him.

The prime minister explained that he was calling to invite Rav Yitzchak Dovid over to his office for a meeting with a few key members of the *chareidi* world, with whom he wanted to discuss the best way to handle Covid-19 within the religious communities.

"I am very sorry to have to do this to you," Rav Grossman told his

Rabbi Grossman and "Bibi"

old friend, "but I won't be able to join you. Today is the grand opening of a new program for girls — something along the lines of Zoharim — and I wouldn't miss it for the world. You understand why I won't be able to make it," he told the prime minister of Israel. "It's just that my children have to come first."

CHAPTER SIXTY-ONE

A Final Chapter From the Author

About an hour after I got off the phone from one of my lengthy interviews with Rav Yitzchak Dovid, my phone rang. I answered. It was an old friend of mine whom I hadn't spoken with in years.

"I don't know if you can help me," he said, "but I am in desperate need of help and I thought of you."

"What happened?"

"You know my son," he said.

"Yes, a wonderful boy."

"He was the top student in his yeshivah until a few months ago. Then he had a breakdown and everything fell apart. From the top of the mountain to the bottom in a very short time. I don't know if there is anything you can do for me, but for some reason I decided to call you. Do you have any ideas?"

I thought for a second. And suddenly I knew that this boy just had to meet Rav Yitzchak Dovid Grossman. I thought of the stories he'd just told me, of how he drove to Haifa and to Tiveria and to Bnei Brak and here and there and back to Haifa — to save a boy's life. And I thought about how he had taken a young girl to Bnei Brak and fought to save her life and fought again when she wanted to give up — and how she had just celebrated the wedding of her thirteenth child.

Having heard all of this just an hour before, I knew beyond a shadow of a doubt that Rav Yitzchak Dovid would want to save my friend's son's life as well.

I told my friend about Rav Yitzchak Dovid and how he was one of the most famous rabbanim in Eretz Yisrael.

"It's very difficult to get an appointment to meet with him," I said, "but if your son wants me to, I will try and set up a time for him to meet with Rav Grossman. So call me back and let me know if he wants me to try."

He called me back twenty minutes later.

"He would like to meet Rav Grossman."

"I will do my best to set up a meeting and get back to you."

I picked up my phone. I wasn't kidding when I said that getting through to this man is no simple job. I dialed his number. Guess what? He answered right away!

I told him why I was calling. I described the boy and the breakdown. I asked if he would be willing to meet with him.

He agreed right away.

They met a few days later. The father called me afterward to tell me how it went, describing the way Rav Grossman spoke to his son, and the stories that he told him, and the spell that he cast, and the ideas that he provided, and how he promised that he would remain at the boy's side and help him find his way back.

Yes, my friends, this is the way it is with Rav Yitzchak Dovid — a tzaddik equally comfortable giving a speech at the Knesset, meeting the most important people in the world — or spending as much time as is needed with a young yeshivah *bachur* who is lost and needs to find his way back home.

This is who he is.

The real thing.

Because he cares.

Afterword

And so we arrive at the end of the book — although by the time you'll be reading this, no doubt another hundred stories will have happened to Rav Yitzchak Dovid Grossman.

Yet even without everything that is surely to come, his is without a doubt an incredible life story.

How was it possible that a young boy from the streets of Meah Shearim found his way to the urban jungle and knew the right words to use with each and every person that he met on his amazing journey?

From that initial foray into the disco of Migdal HaEmek and the three-hour meeting where he enchanted the city's youth, Rav Yitzchak Dovid experienced miracles. But they were miracles that he helped make happen.

The miracle of taming the local crime chief by selling his own apartment in Yerushalayim to buy the man a truck.

The miracle of using Rav Aryeh Levine's life lessons to convince the businesses in Migdal HaEmek to close down on Shabbos.

The miracle of a Rosh Hashanah drama where he saved lives and averted a possible lynching — and didn't eat for two days straight.

There are so many memories.

Memories of meeting men like Reb Zev Wolfson and Rabbi Leizer Rosner. Rabbi Kugel and Tzvi Eldorati. Yisrael Kenig and Yaakov (Jack) and Belle Rosenbaum. Memories of the time spent in the home of Rabbi Paysach Krohn in Queens, New York. Memories of the numerous *gedolim* whom he knew and with whom he was close. Memories of Rav Ovadia Yosef and Rav Elyashiv who so wanted him to become chief rabbi of Israel.

So many memories of the donors who gave support, the politicians who helped him build, the staff who were the heart of his many institutions. Beloved friends like Reb Nuchum Donner, who has stood by his side for close to half a century.

And, of course, memories of all the tens of thousands of children that passed through the doors of Migdal Ohr. The beautiful, shining faces of so many precious children who were given the opportunity to become something great — all because they were part of his circle.

More memories.

The Kaliver Rebbe and a boat ride across the Kinneret.

The Ribnitzer Rebbe and the pile of hair that he purchased from a boy.

The jeans and *sheitel* that he wore to a monastery on the top of the mountain in an Arab village called Deir Chanah.

The poignant letter from an unhappy prisoner who'd never been hugged.

An encounter in a first-class cabin, a kiss on the forehead of a man he had never met before — a meeting that sparked a contribution of millions to Migdal Ohr.

Memories of his visit to China and the young backpacker that he met on a Friday night and the song that the man sang.

There were also songs sung on the hardwood floor of Madison Square Garden and the time Rav Yitzchak Dovid took a shot and watched as the ball sailed through the net. A trip to the Abir Yaakov where a mysterious hand grabbed his shoulder, saving him from death. A trip to Nigeria to meet the president of the country.

Purim and Chanukah parties and an endless array of Shabbos meals, speeches and fundraising and staff meetings and encouragement, and building more buildings and then more buildings and then an entire neighborhood. Foster families and hundreds of little children and even babies, a state-of-the-art gym and a pool, and the hosting of seven hundred soldiers on their way to Lebanon, when they needed it most, combined with a promise and the writing of *osios* (letters) in a brand-new Sefer Torah.

Dinners, and new programs, and Zoharim and Zoharot and meetings with Bibi Netanyahu and with Shimon Peres and with Arik Sharon — and really with who not? — up to and including a young Bedouin man who was really a Jew. There were trips to Russia and concerts with MBD and Mona, and a replay of that once-in-a-lifetime journey on a Bnei Brak stage decades later.

There was an epic adventure at the foot of Mount Hermon on the eve of an historic battle, and encouragement to countless soldiers, and *Sedarim* for Russian immigrants, and programs for Ethiopian Jews and for Yemenite Jews and for all Jews — for love is the type of miracle that never runs out and replenishes itself on a daily basis.

And it all began in a little apartment where Rav Yisrael Grossman and his wife taught their talented son how to think outside himself and what it meant to be *moser nefesh* for Klal Yisrael. It was a home where words were important, and actions even more. Where a father might travel to the United States for months at a time because the Jews of Eretz Yisrael needed him to help build Chinuch Atzmai, and the kind of home where a father would relocate to Migdal HaEmek because a group of *bachurim* needed a rosh yeshivah.

Most of all, one cannot forget the *mesirus nefesh* of the rebbetzin, who heard the call just as her husband had. She would not only join her husband for the epic journey of a lifetime, but would be a full partner at all times — a mother to countless children — as her husband was their father.

It was never just Rav Yitzchak Dovid — they were there as a team

A heritage of *mesirus nefesh* for the *Klal*:
Rabbi Yisrael and Rabbi Yitzchak Dovid Grossman

— and the results of what they built are a testimony to the willpower of man and the meaning of the words *siyata d'Shmaya*.

And, of course, one cannot forget the Lelover Rebbe, Rav Moshe Mordechai Biderman, who, when asked where his *talmid* should go, replied with a line that would change the course of history: ***"Efsher vest arupgein a kik-tun vos mir ken eppes oiftun in Migdal HaEmek?*** **Maybe go down, look around, and see if there is anything for you to accomplish in Migdal HaEmek?"**

So are worlds created and pages of history written.

This book tells the story of a tzaddik who does his best to fulfill the *ratzon Hashem*, Hashem's will, and how the Ribbono shel Olam rewards him with the kind of results that the vast majority of humanity can only dream of.

Because Rav Yitzchak Dovid Grossman has never stopped dreaming and will never stop dreaming. Not as long as there are children who need him.

You see, Rav Yitzchak Dovid is their father, and a father never forgets his children.

Timeline — Achievements of Rav Yitzchak Dovid Grossman

1966 — Worked in disadvantaged neighborhoods in Yerushalayim and established an educational institution for underprivileged children.

1967 — Received *semichah* (Rabbinical ordination) from *gedolei Yisrael.*

1968 — Moved to Migdal HaEmek where he began a lifetime of extensive educational work.

1969 — Began to work with the youth he found in the local discos and clubs and instilled hope in their hearts. He became known as "The Disco Rabbi."

1970 — Appointed Chief Rabbi of Migdal HaEmek.

1972 — The Migdal Ohr School opened its doors in Migdal HaEmek with eighteen students, rapidly expanding into a nationwide educational network.

1975 — Laid the cornerstone for a building for homeless children.

1980 — Was awarded the "Rabbi Aryeh Levin Father of Prisoners" award.

1983 — Was awarded the "Love of Israel" award by the President of the State of Israel, Chaim Herzog, and by Prime Minister Menachem Begin.

1987 — Established a children's day care center and began construction for a village for foster families.

1988 — Was awarded a certificate of merit by the Paratroopers Unit Liberators of Jerusalem Foundation.

1990 — Established educational centers for young girls, the Talmud Torah School, and opened the gates of the "Machshavah" grade school.

1991 — Was awarded the "Shield of Tolerance" by the Speaker of the Knesset. In the same year, a program was initiated to absorb Ethiopian immigrants from Operation Solomon into the Migdal Ohr educational campus.

1992 — Established branches of Migdal Ohr in Moscow and Saint Petersburg and began absorbing immigrants from the former Soviet Union at the Migdal Ohr educational campus.

1993 — Took part in the operation to bring Yemenite immigrants to Eretz Yisrael and absorbed many of them into Migdal Ohr.

1994 — Was awarded an honorary doctorate by Yeshiva University in New York.

1995 — Began working with French youth, and brought many of them over to be educated in Israel.

1997 — Completed construction of the Maor Israel high school building.

2000 — Established a private medical center for the students on the Migdal Ohr campus.

2001 — Opened a sports center for the main boys campus.

2003 — Established the "Ohr Yisraeli" youth movement that has a national membership of some 8000 youth in 160 branches. In the same year, Rav Grossman instituted another program called "Chag Savea for the Children," in which food parcels are distributed for needy families throughout Israel before Rosh Hashanah and Pesach.

2004 — Was awarded the "Israel Prize" for his life's work — and for his special contribution to the country and society.

2006 — Was awarded an honorary doctorate by Bar Ilan University. In the same year he provided a warm and welcoming place for 700 soldiers to recharge during the second Lebanon War.

2008 — Was awarded a Medal of Distinction and Merit by Youth Aliyah — and was honored with lighting one of 12 beacons at the Memorial Day for the Fallen Soldiers of Israel and Victims of Terrorism ceremony on Mount Herzl in Yerushalayim.

2009 — Was awarded the prestigious "Caring Award" by the Caring Institute of America.

2012 — Established an educational therapy youth village called "Zoharim" — offering youngsters a warm and accepting home and a new direction in life.

2014 — Awarded the Presidential Medal of Honor by the President of the State of Israel, Shimon Peres.